THE BLACK FAIRY

MARCUS BLAKE

THE BLACK FAIRY

A Mavericknes Media / Truesource Publishing book

Published by arrangement with the author
Copyright © 2019 by Mavericknes Media and Truesource Publishing with Marcus Blake. Printed through Mavericknes Media. Cover design by Mavericknes Media - All rights reserved. This book, or parts thereof, may not be reproduced in any form without permission. The book cover and author photo of Marcus Blake is by Deborah Frances.

The Black Fairy is edited by
Carol Felder and J M Almgreen

The story is fictional and any resemblance to actual people, places, and certain facts associated with the characters created by Marcus Blake is purely coincidence.

Mavericknes Media : Dallas Texas

Truesource Publishing : Dallas Texas

www.truesourcepublishing.com

ISBN : 978-1-932996-72-2

Printed in the United States of America
Published in Dallas, Texas

For more information on Marcus Blake go to....

www.marcusblake.net
www.facebook.com/themarcusblake
www.twitter.com/marcusblake
www.instagram.com/marcusblakeauthor
www.thatnerdshow.com

About the Author

Marcus Blake is an author, editor, producer, musician, film, tv, and gaming critic, He was born in Chicago, Illinois in 1977. He grew up in Chicago and East Texas. His education is in History, Literature, Psychology, Religion & Philosophy. Marcus Blake has studied at many universities, but his Alma Mater is Stephen F. Austin State University, which is also where he wrote his first novel. Marcus Blake has written 15 books as of 2022. His books are The Music of Life, My Reflections, Returning Home, Sex Game. The Lonely Girl, Stories From Wrigley, The 30 Minutes Series, The Ring of Warrior Series, The Black Fairy, and the Annmar Chronicles. He created the collaborative fantasy world, the Annmar Chronicles (**www.annmarchronicles.com**) in 2019 and serves as the Publisher and one of the main authors. Marcus Blake served in the Army. With a background in Journalism, Marcus Blake created *That Nerd Show (www.thatnerdshow.com)* in 2012, a "nerd" entertainment news outlet that covers movies, tv shows, games, comics, and pop culture. Marcus Blake is the editor and producer as well as a senior film critic of That Nerd Show. In 2021 he became the Editor and Publisher of *That Nerd Show Monthly*, the digital and print magazine for That Nerd Show, which centers on featured articles and editorials about nerd-related subjects in the entertainment industry. He is also the host of the Saturday Morning Nerd Show Podcast and a senior interviewer of celebrities and filmmakers for That Nerd Show. Marcus Blake currently makes his home in Dallas, Texas.

Other Books by Marcus Blake…

The Music of Life

My Reflections

Returning Home

Sex Game

The Lonely Girl

Stories From Wrigley

30 Minutes: Trust and Lies

30 Minutes: Guilty Until Proven Innocent

30 Minutes: A Soldier's Song

30 Minutes: A Badge of Honor

Windows

Ring of Warriors: Making a Fighter.

Rangers of Liberus: The One With Magic (Book 1) An Annmar Chronicles Book

For Blue

*She has a knack for giving me
good ideas when it comes to stories!*

    The face of the Devil is seldom scary, it will feel familiar. For that is how the Devil will seduce you, tempt you, and make you believe that their cause is righteous, thus becoming your true nightmare.

1

It was late when she finally arrived home, later than usual. It was almost time to go to bed. During the week she always went to bed early so she could be well rested when she got up at the start of dawn. And while she was not the type of person who showered right before bed, this particular night, she needed one more than ever. Her gloves were so filthy that she didn't even bother cleaning them…she turned them inside out as she pulled them off her hands and threw them away.

The hot water from the shower felt amazing. Her apartment had great water pressure, that's what she loved most about her apartment. For ten minutes, she stood still underneath the water and let it naturally wash everything away. She was filthy and the filth seemed to burrow beneath her skin. It was an irritating feeling. But it washed away easily, and she felt reborn from the warm relaxing shower. She felt as if she had been baptized over and over until nothing of her old life remained. That was the point, right? The last thing she did before she went to bed was hold her rosary tight, kneel beside her bed, and say a prayer. She prayed the same thing almost every night.

"Dear Lord, grant me the strength to be your servant. Give me the courage to see your work through until the end. To give hope where there is none. To give justice to those who cannot get it elsewhere. Let me be an instrument of righteousness. In nomine patris, et filii, et Spiritus Sancti. Amen." Then she did the catholic cross to complete the prayer.

Finally, she lit a candle; it was her St. Philomena Candle. She was a patron saint of impossible causes and known as the Daughter of Light. She could certainly sympathize with the saint. In many ways, they were kindred spirits if you believe in that sort of thing. Perhaps, that was why St. Philomena was her favorite Saint. She needed it that way.

Lightning filled the sky as he was racing up Highway 35. A storm was coming. And in Texas, it could rush upon you suddenly and then disappear in the blink of an eye. Weather never had a set timetable in Texas. Detective Jim Summers could already tell that he was going to have a shitty time in Dallas and the weather would be the least of his worries. As an SIS officer, if he was called to another city, then it was really bad. He never went to Dallas for anything good.

It normally took about three hours to get from Austin, where he was stationed, to Dallas. He was going to make it in two and a half hours. Getting to the crime scene was imperative. Regular cops always seem to contaminate his crime scenes before he got there. And if this turned out to be what he thought it was then finding any kind of physical evidence was important to catching a killer that had eluded him for years. If it was the same killer.

The rain was already coming down when he reached the city limit. He hated the rain about as much as he hated religious fanatics. Some things just can't be tolerated and always inconvenience you. But on the bright side…at least this crime happened indoors. The weather couldn't destroy it…only the incompetence of city cops who were too narrow-minded to think outside the box when it came to solving a crime.

He arrived at a house on the West side of Plano. Whoever owned the house had money. That much was clear as he walked into a crowd of black and blue. There was too much space and too many nice things bought only to impress visitors. He showed his badge to the first cop, he saw and asked for the cop in charge. There was a police lieutenant, who seemed out of his depth with this kind of crime. It was a gruesome crime and he had never seen anything like this before. Detective Summers couldn't fault him for that.

Detective Summers walked up to him. "Hi…I'm the SIS officer you requested."

The Lieutenant responded. "What…we requested a State CID officer."

"I know, I'm the same thing, but I work in Special Investigation Services. We handle violent crimes and because of the nature of the crime, we're the ones that get sent out."

The Lieutenant looked confused. "I wasn't aware that we gave out the details…only that we requested a CID officer."

Jim smiled. "Well, you didn't, but when you call CID, it's usually bad and then I made a few more inquiries once I heard about it. Your medical examiner is quite chatty. Sounds like it's a serious crime."

The Lieutenant never wanted to admit that the crime wasn't anything that he and his department couldn't handle especially to the boys in Austin. He was starting to get mad but bit his tongue. He simply said. "That may be true, but I don't think this is any more violent of a crime than some of the murder scenes we walk upon."

"When there can be a potential serial killer, we need to be called out, and according to the ME, this fits the bill, but why don't you show me, and we will find out for sure." The Lieutenant gave him a dirty look, but led him down the hall of the big house to the kitchen where the victim was crouched over, dead at the kitchen table. The scene was shocking even for Jim who had seen some pretty shocking murders. He had been investigating violent crimes for a long time, now, and this shocked him enough that he got that sick feeling in his stomach like he was going to vomit. One of the cops taking pictures actually started to get sick. The

Lieutenant stopped him and said. "Son, go take a break...we don't need you contaminating the crime scene." Then he turned to Detective Summers. "As you can see, we have one hell of a gruesome scene here. No one around here has seen something like this before...have you?"

Jim started to walk around the body to get a closer look. He replied. "I have never seen anything exactly like this... not staged in the same way, but something similar. "

"Well, this is new for us...we don't get satanic ritual murders in Plano, Texas."

"This isn't Satanic. The murder is staged, yes, maybe a little ritualistic, but not Satanic. I admit there might be some religious overtones here, but this is something else entirely... not Satanism."

Jim walked around a few times and bent down to really get a good look. The body was bent over the glass table in the dining room. He was naked except for his underwear pulled down around his ankles. His legs were chained to the legs of the table...one on each side. The hands were gripping his fully erect penis and glued to it with what seemed like some kind of industrial strength glue or pipe cement. The hands were definitely not coming off unless the outer layer of skin of his penis was torn off. One of his eyes was cut out and put on the table facing the victim. But the most gruesome part of the scene was a police baton shoved up his rectum. It was so far in that it must have ruptured the rectal wall. They couldn't tell what actually killed Don Bennett until a full autopsy could be performed.

One of the other cops standing next to the lieutenant responded. "Is this some sort of gay thing...maybe some disgruntled homosexuals raped him or something?"

Everybody standing seemed to roll their eyes in unison at the narrow-minded notion. Jim tried to not laugh at the patrol cop's stupidity, but it was hard not to. Before anybody else could say anything, he replied. "Just because something is shoved up a guy's ass doesn't mean it's a gay thing and I seriously doubt he was raped, but I can tell you this for certain. This man was being punished. The killer staged this in a way so he could see that he was being punished."

"Punished for what," the patrol cop asked.

"I don't know yet, but that's what I'm here to find out. Do we have a positive ID yet?"

The lieutenant rolled his eyes. "You're kidding; right…you don't know who this is?"

Jim gave him a dirty look. It looks like former State Senator, Don Bennett, who got kicked out of office for ethics violations, but we still need a positive ID."

"I don't know what for; we all know it's him."

"It's protocol."

"Maybe, but I'm not going to call his daughter or ex-wife down here to do it and see him like this."

"How about you see if you can get his fingerprints or check dental records, first? I don't want his family to have to see this either. It's going to be hard enough keeping this out of the press to begin with…certainly don't need them seeing the crime scene and telling the news about the way he was killed."

The lieutenant motioned for the Crime Scene techs to come over and try to get fingerprints. He commented. "Maybe, we should tell the press about what we found so we can get people to help us find the depraved psycho who did this… you know set up a tip line."

Jim rolled his eyes out of view of the other cops. "Sir, that's the last thing we want to do. We don't have enough details yet and a tip line will only flood your office with unnecessary phone calls that we will be forced to check out and just end up wasting everybody's time."

"Then what do we do, hot shot, since you seem to know everything."

Jim laughed at the snarky remark. "I never claimed to know everything, but I know a lot more than you. As far as what we do next…does anybody have a large black light." One of the crime scene technicians brought one over. It had to be big, so it could shine enough light on the victim's entire back. The rest of the cops standing around gave Detective Summers a strange look. But those looks turned to shock once they saw what was found beneath the black light sketched out in some kind of invisible ink on the victim's back. They were wings.

The lieutenant responded. "Holy shit...he's been marked by the angel of death...how did you know?"

Jim still shocked at what he was seeing, replied. "I had a hunch...I've seen this before."

"Are you sure it's not a satanic ritual?"

"Positive...this is a killer who loves to torture and is sending us a message." He looked at the Lieutenant. "You have a serial killer on your hands. I need to see your chief of police ASAP!"

2

Her hand moved ferociously as she cut up onions and green peppers for her omelet. She was fast with a knife just like a professional chef. Then again, she had always been good with a knife. Gina McCarthy was a woman of routine. Every morning except on Sunday, she would get up, make a pot of coffee, workout, and then make breakfast before she went to work. She worked Saturdays, editing films. Most mornings consisted of three to four cups of coffee and a southwestern-style omelet. The routine kept her focused…it kept her grounded considering that when she was young, she was all over the place with her thoughts and desires. She was wild back then, but it also made her bohemian lifestyle seem romantic at the time. Now, she was perfectly content with a simple routine and a little boredom

As she was making breakfast, she was watching the local news to see if anybody important had been reported dead. She only really cared about one news story, but it never came. Maybe it was too soon for it to be reported. Although, the day was still early. She lived in a fairly nice apartment complex just south of Highway 635 on the second floor. Most of the apartments on that level were two bedrooms and still not too expensive to rent. But the best part, she was only fifteen to twenty minutes from downtown Dallas, where she worked at the main criminal courts building. She lived in the kind of apartment complex where you didn't really have trouble with the neighbors. Everybody was nice and kept to themselves. Occasionally you would run into some angry boyfriend pounding on his ex-girlfriend's door because he just couldn't accept that it was over. But rarely made the situation escalate to violence, especially after the cops were called.

  The only thing Gina ever had to deal with was her bitchy neighbor across the way who had gone through a nasty divorce a year before and was living off alimony while in the middle of a custody battle. She had two kids, Audra and Josh. Both were good kids, polite and well behaved despite their mother always being in a foul mood and drunk off cheap martinis she made herself throughout the day. The mother could easily put away a liter or two of Vodka every day. The only thing she seemed to be good at was drinking and insulting her ex-husband about every five minutes. When Audra was twelve and starting to become a woman. Her mother wasn't much help when she got her first period about nine months ago. Audra knocked on Gina's door asking for help with a tampon when her mother was passed out drunk. That's when they met for the first time. Josh was eight and quiet. He mostly stuck to himself and tried to ignore what was going on around him by playing games on his iPad, a gift from his father in order to buy his love.

  Gina could hear the mother screaming in her apartment before she ever opened the front door to leave for work. As she walked outside, she found Audra and Josh sitting outside at the little patio table next to their front door waiting for their mother to finally be done screaming at their father on the phone. Gina sighed. She looked at Audra. "Hey kid…your mother forget to take you to school?"

  Audra with a sad look, replied. "She knows we have school and she'll drive us there soon." Josh looked up at Gina and tried to smile, then he went back to playing his game.

  Gina shook her head. "How long will *soon* be because at this rate you'll miss the first hour of school. " Audra shrugged at the comment. There was no telling with her mother, how long it would be before she realized her kids were late for school. Gina responded. "Looks, like you're ready to go, why don't I take you." Audra smiled as Gina continued saying. "We'll just leave a note for your mother, so she doesn't worry." She had taken the kids to school before, so she knew where she was going, and the schools were on the way. Sometimes their mother would be nice and ask her to do it. Sometimes, like today, she would just do it when the mother was too hung over to be a proper parent and forget that her children had school. But the mother never seemed to mind a virtual stranger taking her kids to school, which was even more concerning.

Gina got Audra and Josh to school. It made her just a few minutes late to work. Her best friend, Lori, who worked in the county clerk's office was not far behind her as they made their way through the security check and the metal detector in the courts building. Lori was usually a few minutes late. As a local actress, she was not a morning person, but artists rarely are. She was surprised to see Gina, running late, but she knew the reason why and it certainly wasn't because a man kept her up late.

Lori commented. "Wow, you're getting here late...let me guess, you had to take your neighbor's kids to school, again."

Gina gave her a sarcastic smile. "Yep...their mother is a real piece of work."

"What was the reason this time...was she drunk or stoned?"

"Probably both as she got into another fight with her ex-husband on the phone. Could hear the yelling all the way from my bedroom."

"Poor kids...it's sad when children would be better off without their mother."

Gina sighed. "True...I'm just waiting for the day when the police show up and I have to give a statement. I'd bet anything that it's coming soon!"

They got through security and headed to the clerk's office on the second floor. Lori asked while they got on the elevator. "I got an audition for a movie being shot in Dallas, want to help me run lines tonight... I stocked my wine cabinet."

Gina smiled. "Glad to but depends on the case I'm assigned. If I can't get out of here early and do my errands this afternoon, then I have to do them tonight and won't have time."

"You know, I can help with the case you're assigned and make sure you get an easy one."

"I know, but I don't mind doing the big cases even it if takes more time. Somebody has to."

"I never understood why you take so many of the big cases…that's too much work when you can be out drinking with friends and fucking around…besides, it's not like you've gotten laid in a while."

Gina laughed. "Don't remind me…one of my errands is getting new batteries for my little helper."

Lori smiled. "If it's another long day, then we can at least still work out together and maybe run lines later."

"Deal and I need the workout, anyway… so do you."

Lori gave Gina a dirty look. "I know you like the MMA workouts, but can we leave my joints in place this time…I'm not actually training for a real fight, and I don't know why you would be either."

Gina politely smiled at her friend. In her mind, you always train for something real because someday it might be real. Unfortunately, she knew that to be true all too well.

It was a busy morning at the Plano Police Station, more chaotic than usual. The murder of a state senator was no small thing even if he was thrown out of office for corruption. You just didn't go around murdering politicians no matter how much you might want to. Those were the rules or so the police thought. Detective Jim Summers was waiting to talk to the chief of police as he sat at a desk outside his office looking at the crime scene photos taken earlier that morning. He was studying them like he was about to walk into a college final examine. But he needed to know what he was talking about if he was going to convince the chief of how serious this was. The chief was running late, and he was about to find out why.

The chief of police finally came bustling down the hallway and he wasn't alone. With him came the Sheriff of Colin County, the Sheriff of Dallas County, and the Dallas Chief of police. A potential serial killer got everybody's attention and the fact that the Texas SIS division was investigating added to its importance. Jim was happy that they were taking him somewhat seriously… at least for now. Plano Police Chief David Abbott looked at Jim sitting at the small desk. "So, you're the big shot from Austin…well, it's your show…tell us what you know."

Everybody scurried into the Chief's huge office. Jim looked around and said. "Thanks for seeing me. I didn't expect a full crowd, but glad you're here."

Chief Abbot replied. "When we hear there might be a serial killer in the Metroplex, you get to talk to all of us. We share information between the counties when the crime is this horrific."

Jim nodded in agreement. "You've seen photos of the crime scene. I take it."

"Yes, sir, nearly threw up my coffee and donuts and that's a cruel thing to do to any cop. Why do you think this is a serial killer?"

"Has everybody seen the photos?" The rest of the men all said "yes."

Jim pulled out some other case files and told the men in the room that they would probably have to share. "First of all, we have seen something like this before. I have two other murders similar in the sense that they were staged. Both were gruesome, both, the victims were probably tortured before they died. "The other men in the room looked at the photos from the case files. The crime scenes were just as horrific as the one from last night. Jim continued. "We don't know for sure how many murders there have been, but these two we know fit the same MO. Local police tried to solve them and then they got kicked to us. We never had any viable suspects and there's no physical evidence linking any suspect to the crime. They're ongoing investigations, but to be honest, we don't have any serious leads and they're on their way to being cold cases."

The Sheriff of Dallas responded. "I don't understand, besides being staged as you say. What do these murders have in common?"

"Both victims were accused of sex crimes against women and were never prosecuted…at least to the full extent of the law.

Both of them had lawsuits brought against them by the alleged victims, but the suits were dropped. Essentially, both men got away with it. That's the only connection we could come up with. How they were chosen …we don't know."

The Dallas Chief of Police replied. "Can you elaborate since none of us have read the case files?"

Jim nodded. "Sure." He pulled out a photo of Hugo Blackmon and showed the men in the room. "This was the Hollywood producer that ran a studio in downtown Austin who was murdered four years ago. He was quite well known and brought a lot of film work to Texas. We believe this is the first victim. When the maid found him, he was sitting on his new black leather couch, naked, with his assistant bent over his knee. She was also naked and had a plastic bag wrapped around her head. She suffocated to death while he was spanking her with a meat cleaver."

The Dallas Police Chief replied. "Holy shit, what a sick fuck."

Jim chuckled. "That's not even the worst part. His penis was cut off and put in the glass of bourbon he was drinking at the time. The glass was in his other hand. And on top of that, his wrists were slit, which made him bleed out…slowly. The bourbon he was drinking was his own brand…he was part owner of a Bourbon distillery here in Texas." All four men in the room were shocked, especially at the mutilation and that was before they had a full look at the crime scene photos. Each of them was thinking the same thing…this was one of the most brutal things you can do to a man.

The Plano Police Chief responded. "This Hollywood producer, I thought the news said it was some kind of suicide pact with his assistant. Could have sworn that's what I read."

"That was the statement released by his publicist and business manager. We never gave the details of his death to the press since this is still an ongoing investigation, so the press based their facts on the statement and now it's become Hollywood folklore. There was no evidence to suggest that it was a suicide pact. It was murder."

"What about the other case?"

Jim showed them more photos from that crime scene. "This was the Texas Oil Barron. His name was Jack Perry... a third-generation oilman and his family owns like a third of West Texas. When his wife found him, he was naked and tied to the arms and legs of a chair in his office at home. His assistant and best friend were also murdered, In fact, he was dressed as a transgendered woman with a dildo belt wrapped around his waist, but instead of a dildo, it was a hunting knife. Jack Perry was placed in a position where he was giving his friend who was sitting on the desk, a blow job... the knife was stuck in his mouth and pierced the back of his head...that's what killed him. The friend was poisoned. And no, he did not die of natural causes as the family reported."

The four men in the room all had a sickened look on their faces. A couple of them looked as if they were about to throw up. The Sheriff of Colon County responded. "So, all these crimes are sexual in nature...that's what you're trying to tell us?"

"The staging of these murders is sexual and sadistic in nature. There were tortured before they were killed, but they weren't violated or raped in any way?"

"Do you know how they were targeted?"

"No, we don't...these case files are sealed."

"But you know why they were targeted."

"Our working theory is because they got away with a sex crime against women."

The Plano Police Chief responded. "Can you please elaborate?"

Jim nodded again at the men in the room. "Hugo Blackmon had been accused by at least a dozen women of sexual assault or harassment. Allegedly, he forced some actresses that acted in films produced by his studio to give him fellatio. One actress even filed charges against him down in Austin, he was indicted, but the case quickly got dropped after a couple of days because the witness died. She was killed in a car accident under mysterious circumstances, according to the police report. Three of the women filed lawsuits, but they were all dropped, and I could never find any record of payouts for them. Pretty much all who accused him, never did anything else in the film industry. They essentially got blackballed. One of them did a couple of porn films, but then was never heard from again in any aspect of the film industry."

The Dallas County Sheriff spoke up. "Are any of these women suspects?"

"They were in the beginning, but they all had solid alibis and were ruled out quickly...so were the husbands. I even thought some of them might have hired a contract killer, but after looking into their finances... none of them had enough money to hire someone with the kind of skill-set to brutally murder and stage the crime scene."

"What about the oil man...what's the motive for killing him?"

"He was accused of rape along with some of his employees. A few years before, his lawyers were able to argue eminent domain in order to buy the land of a low-income housing project so he could put up another oil well. But before they won that decision, I guess he had some of his employees terrorize the women in the area, hoping they would get so scared that they would move on their own. The story goes that one night, about six Hispanic women were abducted and brought to some warehouse where there was a sex party. They were forced to dance and perform sex acts for the men who were there. All of them were raped. Two of them said that Jack Perry was in the warehouse and took turns along with some of his employees, raping them.

The Dallas Police Chief replied. "For Christ's sake, any of it true?"

"There were six women who were raped, we found the hospital reports, but no concrete evidence that Jack Perry was there. There wasn't any physical evidence that puts him at the crime scene. One of his employees was tried and convicted, but he claimed that Perry wasn't there. No formal charges were filed against him. There was a lawsuit brought against him, but the judge dismissed it right after opening statements."

"What makes you think this murder is linked to the two you just described, other than the staging of the crime scene...I'm mean, anybody can could have done that...maybe it's a copycat killer. I've heard of them, they're out there, right?"

"Yes, sir, they're out there, but there's a connection with the Don Bennett's murder to Jack Perry's murder… a calling card of sorts." He showed the men in the room another photo of the two victims. "This was the symbol found beneath a black light on both victims. Some kind of wings! The killer sketched this out on their backs, and I don't think this is a copycat killer."

The Plano Police Chief commented. "Looks like angel wings…I guess the killer is supposed to be the Angel of Death!"

"That's a theory, but the killer now has a calling card and that's where we start in catching them."

"What do you need from us?"

"Manpower… I am going to be setting up a task force and I would like detectives from each major city…the ones you have or can spare. Good ones if I can get them. And we will need a workspace to accommodate at least ten people….we will be going back through old cold cases revolving saround ex crimes and seeing if anything can be linked to this killer."

"What makes you think the killer is still here in DFW…the other murders were done in other cities, which suggests that the killer moves around."

Jim shrugged. "Because this is where the latest murder happened. And I don't think they're done yet…could be, they just set up shop here in Dallas/Ft. Worth.

"You're saying this is only the beginning."

Jim laughed to himself. "Call it a hunch, but yes, this is only the beginning."

3

Gina did get assigned a big case. She knew right off the bat that it was going to be a lot of work and the trial could take months. The really bad criminals don't have short trials unless they end in acquittal. The trial finally had a break for lunch. Every day, Gina had lunch with her friend Lori. It was part of her comfortable routine. In many ways, it kept her sane.

They always had lunch in the cafeteria, usually a table all to themselves, like they were the unpopular kids in school. But mostly, they were trying to avoid the unwanted advances from some of the more smug lawyers who worked in the building because they were under the poor assumption that they could get any woman they wanted. A couple of judges were on that list too. Lori was the first one to speak.

"I heard you got assigned the scumbag case?"

Gina gave her a surprised look. "What do you mean the scumbag case?"

"Oh, that's what some of the women in the clerk's office are calling it... but I thought it was fitting."

Gina laughed. "You're right, it is fitting. I guess it's one of the nicer things you can call the guy who's on trial."

"I'm sure he will be called worse before it's all over. And I hope he gets what he deserves."

Gina nodded in agreement. "By the way, did you hear anything on the news about a murder in DFW the last few days?"

Lori gave her friend a strange look. "What kind of murder?"

"Somebody important."

"No…I think there were some gang bangers in Ft. Worth that were killed last night…that's all I heard about. Why do you ask?"

"Just curious."

"Well, speaking of news, I have a date tomorrow."

Gina got excited. "Oh…you finally broke up with Dave."

"Yes, and for good this time. If he can't make a commitment, then I'm going to start dating again."

"Well, you go girl…how did you meet this guy?"

"It's just a tinder date."

Gina was a little shocked. "Tinder… the app where men just want to get laid."

"I'm sure that's with any dating app…after all, they're men."

"True, but you don't think you're actually going to find love on Tinder, do you?"

Lori gave Gina a snarky look. "Who says I'm not using the app just to get laid."

"I don't think, you need an app for that…you have tits and an ass…they work in any bar if you want to get laid."

"Yeah, but I also like a little conversation before sex. I can get that on tinder too."

"But is it good conversation?"

"it's conversation…good conversation might be asking for too much."

Gina didn't say anything. She just laughed at her friend's comment. No matter what, Lori could always make her laugh. One of the main reasons they were friends, they had the same sarcastic sense of humor and when it's mixed with witty conversation then you definitely have a good match.

While the new task force office was being prepared and case files were being driven up from Austin, Detective Summers went straight to work. No more delays, they were already too far behind in catching this serial killer…especially now that they knew there was one and these weren't isolated incidents. He stopped by the Medical Examiner's office, now that the body had been brought there.

He knocked on the door as he walked in so he didn't just startle anyone who might be usual a scalpel. Using an instrument like that could be tricky and one little screw-up could be very, very bad. There was only one doctor in the office, Dr. Vanessa O'Connor. She looked up and already had a sense of who it was because she had never seen him in the building before. Jim started to say something, but before the words came out of his mouth, she responded. "Hi…you must be the man from Austin."

He gave her a funny look. "How did you know?"

"I've never seen you before and I figured you would be coming to see me today."

"Good intuition."

"Thank You. I'm also the one you spoke with on the phone."

"Ah, Dr. O'Connor…nice to finally meet you."

"And you, Detective Summers."

"If you don't mind me saying…you don't look like an O'Connor unless you're married, and I don't see a ring."

Vanessa smiled. "I get that a lot. My Father was from Ireland and my mother is Hispanic. Strange mix, I know, but how many can actually say they speak Spanish and Gaelic? "

Jim laughed. "You're the first I've met. Although, I don't see many opportunities to use Gaelic around here."

"You'd be surprised. There's a couple of good Irish Pubs around here where some of the patrons and musicians speak Gaelic."

Jim shook his head, not quite believing what he was hearing. It seemed unlikely that, that was true, but he had seen stranger things in Texas. After all, there were a few close-knit German communities where English was rarely spoken. And they usually had the best beer in Texas. After enough small talk, Jim got right down to business.

"Dr. O'Connor…"

"Vanessa is fine…I'm not hung up on titles…I already know that I'm smarter than the men around here and don't need a title to prove it."

Jim laughed, "Alright … Vanessa… do you have a cause of death yet on Don Bennett and are we absolutely sure, that it's him?"

"Yes, dental records and fingerprints gave us a positive match. As for the cause of death… he bled out… that's what killed him."

That seemed strange to Jim. There was hardly any blood at the crime scene. He replied. "Really…there should have been a lot of blood. The only blood I saw was from where the killer cut his eye out."

"I don't know what to tell you, but the Celiac Trunk and the small intestines were ruptured, causing the victim to bleed out." She asked Jim to look at the left side of the body. "If you look right here, you can see where it was pierced by a large, sharp object… probably a long hunting knife or even sa mall sword." Jim hadn't noticed that before."

"You say that whatever pierced his side had to be a long knife or even a sword?"

"It would have to be long enough to get through the intestinal wall and all the way through the Celiac Trunk because every artery was cut."

Jim paused for a moment, trying to fully comprehend what she was saying. "Okay, just so I understand, the stick shoved up his rectum, wouldn't have killed him."

"No…not even rupturing the rectum wall…it just causes a lot of pain. He might have passed out from the pain, but that's it."

"And cutting his eye would not have killed him?"

"Not unless he had a weak heart and extreme pain caused it to stop. But from what I can tell, that's not the case and his medical records didn't indicate that he had a weak heart."

"Then the eye, the stick up his rectum, and his hands glued to his penis, had nothing to do with his death. It was simply torture."

Vanessa nodded "yes." And like a perfect example of Occam's Razor, it was the simplest explanation. "Now, Detective Summers, I can tell you this. The killer cut him first and let him slowly bleed out before doing anything else. He was still alive when the eye was cut out and the stick was inserted in his rectum, and his hands were glued to his penis. Yeah, I'd say he was tortured"

"Okay then….when will you have a full report"

"You'll have my full report tomorrow."

Jim was starting to walk out when he remembered the wings on the victim's back. He turned back around. "Oh, one more thing," as he pulled out a picture of the wings outlined on the victim's back, "what do you make of this?"

Vanessa looked at the picture closely. "You mean, the fairy wings?"

Jim was stunned by her comment. "Fairy wings…what do you mean? The look like angel wings to me."

Vanessa smiled. "No, I don't think so. They look more like fairy wings. Angel wings are longer and look more like bird wings, long and curved like half an oval with feathers." She made Jim take a closer look at the picture. "These wings are curved more like in the shape of butterfly wings…a top wing and a bottom wing. The design comes from Old English folklore. This is how they were drawn and which our image of fairies is based on."

Jim gave her a surprised look. "Wow, you mean fairies like Tinkerbelle from Peter Pan?"

"Well, that's one version, but yes, the wings are similar. Plus, fairy wings sparkle. The killer used some kind of phosphorescent invisible ink, which under a black light makes the wings look as if they are sparkling."

Jim was astounded. He never would have figured that out. "How do you know all of this?"

"I've loved other cultures since I was a kid, so I have an anthropology degree along with my medical degree."

"Sounds like you should be investigating crimes."

"True, I do in my own way, but I have a fascination with dead bodies…it's weird. Although, my investigative nature makes me really good at my job."

Jim laughed. "I would say so, but why fairy wings…that's an odd thing to outline on your victim, especially as a calling card."

Vanessa smiled at the snarky comment. "To some, maybe, but if you really think about it…not really. In Celtic Christian Mythology, fairies are considered fallen angels, pushed out of heaven along with Lucifer. They live in between heaven and hell. Some fairies are good, influencing humans when it comes to love or finding happiness. Some are bad and steal the joy from human beings. But there are dark fairies who are more violent… some believe that they brought justice to humans who could not find any. They bring balance to good and evil. Dark Fairies are like a different version of the Archangel Michael. This is steeped with Celtic Mythology, going all the way back to the pagans before the Roman Empire conquered Britannia."

"You learned all this in your anthropology studies."

Vanessa laughed. "No…from my father. I had a very strict Catholic upbringing and part of my education was learning Celtic Mythology. My father wanted me to know where I came from on his side of the family and where the Irish belief system originated from even before the Catholic Church took hold in that part of the world." She got a little flirtatious as Jim continued to look surprised by her knowledge. Vanessa smiled as she responded. "You find me pretty amazing, now, don't you? More than just a pretty face!"

Jim laughed. "I do actually, but I shouldn't say anything else, you know with the whole 'MeToo' movement and all. We men have to watch what we say now."

"That's okay, let's just say you agree with me and gave me one hell of a compliment. "

Jim smiled. "Deal."

"In all seriousness, if this is a calling card, the killer is being very specific with the meaning. The angel of death motif is too common, especially with the torture aspect." Vanessa grabbed a book offer her desk. It was a book on Symbols, Signs, and Dream

Interpretations. "You should do some serious research about fairies within Celtic Mythology. You can start with this book."

"Thank You. I may have more questions for you when it comes to this stuff."

Vanessa smiled. "Well, my catholic education should be good for something. "Jim couldn't help but laugh, he liked that she could be witty. The medical examiners he usually dealt with didn't have a sense of humor and it could be very annoying at times to say the least.

4

Gina moved like she was possessed. She was a completely different person when she was in the gym or on the training mat. Most people who trained in mixed martial arts did it for the exercise. That's why Lori did it, plus she loved working out with her best friend. Lori seemed to be holding her own against Gina. That's all she really could do because Gina was clearly better at mixed martial arts than she was. Lori was trying to keep her distance and look for an opening at the same time. She just needed one to land that one really good shot. In her mind, if she could do that then it was a victory.

She saw an opening, but just as she was lunging forward, Gina used her legs to go up high and flip Lori forward. Gina completed the move by pinning her to the mat while holding her arm in a position to where Lori couldn't move it. The competitive side of Gina came out as she said. "Tap out bitch, it's over. Do it…tap out."

Lori was shocked and a little angry. "Alright, for fuck's sake… you win." She quickly tapped out." The trainer who had been monitoring the fight, rushed over to help Lori up and to make sure she wasn't hurt. Fortunately, she wasn't except for having the wind knocked out of her as she was flipped forward. Then he congratulated Gina for her flawless move. He was truly impressed because he had never seen her do that before. He had only seen professional fighters be able to do that.

Lori was shaking her head in disbelief as she got their towels and walked over to Gina. She said. "Holy fuck, what was that? You've never done that move before."

Gina smiled. "Did you like that..."

Lori cut her off. "No…you could have actually broken one of my bones."

"Sorry about that…didn't mean to lose control."

Lori smiled. "On the other hand…that was pretty damn impressive. You did a move that only the pros can do."

"Thanks…I've been working on it for a little while along with some others."

"What are you actually training for? It can't be about losing weight because you're already thin and gorgeous…which I hate." Gina laughed at the last comment. No matter how good of friends, they might be, women would always be jealous of each other in some way or another.

Gina answered her question. "I'm not training for anything, just want to perfect my skills…you know I'm a perfectionist. "

"True, but you act like you're training to take on Rhonda Rousey."

"Or I'm learning how to defend myself in case I start dating again and meet some guy who thinks he can take advantage of me."

Lori smiled. "God, help any man who tries to do that."

"You still up for running lines?"

"Actually, no, I'm going home to take a nice hot bath and drink some really good wine to help dull the pain you caused."

"Really…I'm sorry for being so rough."

Lori smiled. "It's okay, but as good as you're getting then we might have to find you another sparring partner. Then again, great job on the move."

Lori gathered her things and walked out of the gym with a slight limp. She was going to need a hot bath and ice packs tonight. Gina went and worked on one of the heavy bags for another ten minutes. When she was done, she headed home. It was getting late, close to being past her bedtime, but she did have one more stop to make. It was part of her routine. She stopped by St. Joseph's Catholic Church. Sometimes she did confession, but most nights during the week if she couldn't attend one of their weekly masses, she simply lit a candle and prayed in one of the pews. And she usually prayed the same thing every night.

Gina got home late. It was already dark outside. As she came up the stairs to her second-floor apartment, Audra was sitting outside at the little patio table, reading a book. It was the same spot she found Audra in when she was leaving this morning. It was almost becoming routine. Gina smiled when she saw the kid. "Hey kid, what are you doing out here."

Audra tried to crack a smile of her own. "I didn't want to smell the weed anymore."

"Ah, your mother getting high again."

"Among other things."

"Was your mother mad that I took you to school?"

"A little. She said something about filing kidnapping charges against you."

Gina laughed at the comment. "Next time she says something like that, ask her if she knows the penalty for child endangerment."

Audra looked a little confused but could tell that the comment was meant as an insult. Gina unlocked her door and was about to walk inside when Audra replied. "Thanks for looking out for us."

"Anytime, kid. If the smell gets too unbearable, come over and you can crash on the couch. I'll put some blankets out. You know where the spare key is…right?"

Audra smiled. "It's under the plant."

"Good girl." Her look towards Audra lingered. She thought to herself, this kid has gone through too much at twelve. No girl should have to go through the shitty parts of life at such a young age. There should be some absolute rule against it. But life doesn't work that way. Something Audra and Josh were learning the hard way.

The Plano Police Station was too small for a task force between different police departments to be working out of, so it was moved. The main Dallas Police Station seemed like the only logical choice. It had more than one conference room, which meant one of them could be spared for the "Dream Team of cops in Dallas/ Ft. Worth. Jim got there early. He wanted to be there when everybody showed up, kind of like the teacher being there on the first day of school and welcoming their students. The files hadn't arrived from Austin yet, so they just had the few case files he brought along with the new one on Don Bennett, the latest victim. Jim made copies for everybody. He was getting two detectives from Dallas, two detectives from Ft. Worth, one from Plano, and one from the city of Arlington.

Around 8am, the first of them rolled in. It was a man and a woman. The man was the first to say something. "Is this where we report for the DFW task force?"

Jim looked up from the file he was reading. "Yes, and you are?"

"Detective Ron Jackson, from Ft. Worth." He was tall, well built, and looked like he had been captain of his football team in high school. But college never panned out so he stayed home and become a cop. It was his way of still being a local hero."

Jim replied. "This is the place. I'm Jim Summers from SIS in the State Criminal Investigation Department." The two shook hands. Jim looked at the woman. "How about you?"

"Detective Maisie Green. I'm from Dallas and I have a tone of questions so you might be annoyed with me by the end of the day." Jim had to smile; her comment was humorous. At least she was honest. She seemed like the class know- it-all and always had her hand raised in class. Detective Green may not have looked as sure of herself compared to the other guy, but he could already tell she was probably smarter. She took the time to ask questions instead of fooling herself that she already knew the answer.

Jim replied to her. "That's okay, I'm sure that I won't...asking too many questions is a good thing when it comes to this kind of case."

"Good, then we'll get along just fine."

The other detectives strolled into the conference room a few minutes later. One of them was even nice enough to bring coffee. They didn't look like much. The other detective from Dallas looked as if retirement was right around the corner and this was one last shitty assignment before he could be fishing every day in some god-awful place like Florida. He was at least nice and didn't come off as some cranky curmudgeon. The task force consisted of five men and one woman, typical for Texas law enforcement. As soon as everybody did their little meet and greet, Ron was the one who spoke up first, taking the lead as if he commanded a huddle right before a winning drive down the field. "Now, that we are all acquainted, Detective Summers, why don't you tell us what this is all about."

Jim nodded and looked down the conference table at the other investigators sitting down. "As I'm sure you have already heard, yes, we have a serial killer that may still be in Dallas. Confirmed by the murder a few days ago and the calling card that the killer left behind." Jim showed them the picture of the Fairy Wings on both victims' backs.

Detective Brian Carter from Arlington commented. "Angel wings…the killer draws angel wings on them like they're the angel of death?"

"Actually, no, that's what we thought at first too. Turns out, they're fairy wings." Everybody else in the room pretty much had the same strange look on their face. Another one of the detectives, Steve Costa, from Plano, responded. "Is it some kind of sexual thing? Were the victims gay?"

"There's no evidence to suggest that. While it is a symbol for something, I think it has more to do with Celtic Mythology and the original meaning behind fairies."

Maisie Replied. "Did you come up with that?"

"Sadly, no, the medical examiner in Plano suggested it to me. Honestly, I don't know what it means, but it's something we will be researching."

Ron asked. "How many murders do you think the killer has committed?"

"Three that we know of. If you take a look at the bottom case file, this is the first murder we think the killer did. It was staged in a similar fashion, but there wasn't a calling card like with the last two. However, personally, I think there's been more and we haven't found them yet."

"Why, maybe the killer has just done three. Maybe they took their time in picking who they were going to murder so no one would think it's a serial."

Jim nodded. "It's a good theory, but I disagree because when killers get a taste for killing, they have to keep doing it. I don't think this killer could wait this long between murders. 99% of the time, it will become an obsession to where they want to keep doing it…like a fetish or even an addiction."

Maisie responded. "Have you found any more cases that fit the MO?"

"I found one from a few years ago. Two hunters were killed by their deer stand. They were shot with arrows. Gutted with a knife so they bled out like an animal, and then tied up like they were game. The crime scene was staged, it may not have been as elaborate, but because it was staged and the use of a knife to where they bled out…I think it might have been the same killer….that is just my theory.

Detective James Cross, the other Detective from Dallas, asked the question that was on everybody's mind. He was the oldest and near retirement but had more experience than anybody in the room. He had been on the force for over thirty years, most of them as a homicide detective. James asked. "While all these questions are good, we will have plenty of time to pour over the details of the crimes and figure out if there are more murders, but what I would like to know as I'm sure everybody does…what's the motive here, other than they like to kill?" Everybody turned around since he was sitting at the back of the conference table and looked at him with the same curiosity, they would for a stranger who seemed out of place in a crowded room. He responded to his question. "I'm sure you have some kind of theory and is it just your theory or is everybody on the same page down in Austin?"

Jim paused for a moment. He couldn't tell yet if Detective was going to be more trouble than he was worth, but he also knew how valuable experience could be. He replied. "I can tell, you don't beat around the bush…you ask the direct questions."

James sarcastically smiled. "I'm too old to waste time with my questions. That's for younger cops."

Jim laughed. "In answer to your question, yes. I think these men were killed because they got away with a sex crime…at least the first two did…we are still looking into Don Bennett's murder for a possible motive."

"So, it's a revenge killing?"

"Possibly."

"And you completely ruled out the women who accused these men of sex crimes?"

"Yes, except for Bennett's murder, which we will, but we will be going through the cases to see if the boys in Austin missed anything."

Ron spoke up. "Where do we start and If I may make a suggestion…"

Jim cut him off before he could finish the statement. He knew what kind of cop Ron Jackson was and if he had his choice, then he would not have him on his team. He didn't mind cops that were "gung-ho" in their jobs, once a football captain, always a football captain and they never worked well with others unless they were running the show. Jim knew that he would have to assert his authority, or it would be a case of the nuts running the hospital with Detective Ron Jackson. He didn't have time for that. Jim responded. "Before you finish that statement, let me make this very clear. This is an SIS investigation, and I am running the show with this task force. All strategy will be run through me and when I assign you tasks, I expect them to be done in a timely manner…no questions asked. I value your input and want your expertise since you were chosen for a reason, but this isn't a place where you get to do your own thing unless it's cleared through me. Is that understood?"

Everybody in the room nodded "yes," but Ron did it with a dirty look. He tried to hide it, but Jim felt it from across the room. He knew that he and Detective Jackson weren't going to get along. There would always be tension. Before anybody could say anything else, Jim continued with his instructions. "This is what we are going to do. I'm having boxes of cold cases being driven up from Austin. We will be going through all of them and seeing if any of them fit the MO of our killer or even close to it. We want to see if we can link anymore murders to our serial killer. I will be getting court files on Don Bennett regarding the lawsuits brought against him by women who accused him of sexual assault, and we will also look into his ethics violations with the state legislature. We will put together a list of suspects and see if any of them stick. And we'll also be going back through the first two cases I gave you and looking at all the suspects again. But most importantly, we will be looking for any connection between these cases…big or small. How were the victims targeted and why… if you have a better theory, then I am all ears! Start with the one's you have in front of you until we get the files from Austin.

5

It was lunchtime at the courts building. Not many people were working. At twelve o'clock noon, like clockwork, most employees made a mad dash out of their offices to get as much time as they could for their lunch, especially on the more hectic days with trials. In the courts building, you were lucky if you got thirty minutes. Jim didn't realize what time it was when he went to the county clerk's office to get some files. There were only two people in there. The office didn't really close for lunch, they just didn't have as many people working. Gina and one other person were in the office. Gina had only been there waiting for Lori so they could go to lunch while she ran some files upstairs.

Jim walked up to the main desk and was surprised to not see anyone there. He stood there for about a minute to see if anybody would help him. Finally, his impatience won out and he yelled for help. Gina had been sitting at one of the back desks when she got up to help him. As she walked up to the desk, she responded by saying. "You picked the wrong time to come by, everybody is out to lunch."

Jim laughed a little. "Ah, I was beginning to think budget cuts had killed the workforce around here."

"That has happened before, but this time, lunch is the culprit. However, I can help. I used to work down here and know how to find what you're looking for."

"Thank you, I really didn't want to wait an hour."

Gina smiled. "What are you looking for?"

"It might be a tall order. I need every case file related to Don Bennett, the former state senator…criminal cases, lawsuits, and even if he had to appear as a witness in a case."

Gina gave him a surprised look. "That is a lot. Some of them are sealed by court order."

Jim reached into the inside pocket of his jacket and pulled out a piece of paper. He softly handed her the paper. "I figured. This will probably help." It was a special court order to unseal the files for the State of Texas CID.

Gina looked at him closely. "Oh, I guess you are special. So you work for CID?"

"Yes Mam. I'm with SIS?"

"What's that?"

"Special Investigation Services…we work the really bad crimes."

Gina was taken back for a moment. "Did something happen to the former senator?"

"Sorry, I can't really tell you that. But there is an ongoing investigation and I need his files."

She smiled. "Got it. Give me a few minutes. If anybody comes by to see if you need help, just let them know that Gina is helping you. "

Thank You. It's nice to meet you, Gina."

"And you …"

"Detective Jim Summers."

"Nice to meet you." She scanned a copy of the court order and recorded it in the office Database as was protocol. Then she went into the back rooms to find the files. It did take her about five minutes to find everything. She brought out three file boxes. There were a lot of court transcripts. Jim was surprised by the amount.

He asked. "I thought a lot of this stuff was digitized now…"

"It is, but we still have plenty of paper transcripts in there as well. You will find a lot of flash drives with court documents.

There is also a booklet that serves as an index of sorts, so you know how to find everything. Happy Hunting!"

Jim Laughed. "I would say so…this will definitely keep me busy. Thanks for your help, Gina." He struggled to get all four file boxes, but somehow managed except for Gina helping him with the door. It was comical watching him walk with everything…she was positive he would stumble and drop everything like a Looney Tunes character, but miraculously, he made out the main doors and to his car.

Lori had only been on one other Tinder date. She didn't have a good time, then either. Lori wasn't above using a dating app or an online dating site just to get laid when she was horny. It's not like she hadn't picked up a guy in a bar before and gone home with him only to never call him again. Yeah, women did that too. And just like men, there's always a certain point in a date when we decide if we are going to see the person again, just get laid that night, or never see them again. Lori knew right off that she was not going to see him again… she was still debating the last two options.

The guy seemed nice enough, but there was something about him that just bothered her. And like a good actress, she trusted her instincts. They had two drinks each and that was it, the date was over. They were in walking distance of her place in the uptown part of Dallas. Lori never liked to go far from her neck of the woods when it was just the first date. It was a lot of easier that way when they didn't work out. She didn't have far to go when she went home early.

When Lori decided that the date was over, she excused herself and said Goodnight. The guy offered to walk her home. She didn't really want that, but she also had a hard time saying "no" and meaning it. Lori let him walk her home and when they got to her door, he leaned in and tried to kiss her. She stopped him and gave him a dirty look. He was surprised a bit because he thought all dates ended with at least a kiss. But most of the time they ended with sex at least for him. The guy responded. "What, you, like me, I like you, why not a kiss?"

Lori felt uncomfortable now. She replied. "No, that's not happening. Thank you for walking me home, but it's not going to work out."

Hearing that made him angry. He was simply an asshole who couldn't take "no" for an answer. As Lori was starting to walk into her apartment, he shoved her inside and said. "Fuck you, bitch! You think, you get to be a tease and that's it."

Lori fell to the ground when he shoved her. It wasn't a little shove by any means. She responded back. "Hey asshole, no, means no…now get the fuck out of here."

He didn't listen. He reached for her and forcibly pulled her up. He turned her around so that her back was against his chest. He held her tight and walked her over the dining room table and bent her over backward. "Look here, you fucking cunt, this date doesn't end until I'm done with it, especially after I bought you drinks." The guy had her pinned down hard and somehow got her pants unbuttoned and was able to pull them down halfway to her feet and below her legs while still keeping her pinned down. Her sexy black lacy thong wasn't hard to remove, they were easily ripped off. He started to unbutton his pants and pull them down, but Lori wasn't going to be a victim. She remembered a move that Gina has taught her during their MMA sessions on how to get out of a lock. She reached underneath and grabbed his hands, got enough leverage to raise her legs and kick him in the groin. Then she twisted out of the hold and punched him. Normally she would have stomped on his foot to get leverage, but a kick in the groin is just as effective.

The guy was hurt but wasn't enough to make him go away. He yelled, again. "Fuck you, bitch. "Then he punched her back. He knocked her to the ground, but he didn't stop there…he punched her again and again while she lay on the ground. He got three more hard licks in before a neighbor came walking by, saw the door open, and saw him hitting her. The neighbor walked in and yelled for him to stop, or they would call the police. They guy was startled. He stopped. He just ran out of there pushing the neighborhood aside and hoping they wouldn't get a look at him. Lori was hurt bad. She was bleeding and her nose was broken along with an eye that was almost swollen shut. An ambulance was called, and she was rushed to the hospital.

    There's never joy when getting a call from the hospital. Much like getting a call from the police, the first thing you feel is panic and dread while an overactive imagination plays out your worst fears. That's exactly what happened when Gina got the call from the hospital about Lori. She was an emergency contact so of course , they would call her. Gina happened to be home and working late when she got the call. She immediately rushed out of her apartment, not even stopping to say hi to Audra who was sitting outside reading at the little patio table.
    Gina wasn't that far away. It only took her fifteen minutes to get there, and it didn't take her long to find Lori in the emergency room. The doctor was working on her when she arrived. Lori looked horrible. One of her eyes was swollen shut, she was bruised on the other side, and she needed sutures to fix the cuts on her lips. Boxers didn't look as bad after a fight. Gina couldn't stop the tears flowing from her eyes as she looked at her friend. It made her sick to her stomach.
    When the doctor was done, he let Gina and Lori talk. Gina asked what happened. Lori told her the gory details. That just made Gina angry. She had a rage building up inside of her that she felt like she couldn't control. How could someone do this to her? What fucking guy thought he could just force himself on Lori and think that would be okay? Lori started to cry as she finished telling Gina what happened. They held each other, trying to protect one another as if their embrace was some kind of magical force field that even the purest of evil could not penetrate. At about that time, two police officers showed up to take Lori's

statement. The police were always called when patients came in because of a violent act. She was still pretty shook up so her statement was not as coherent as they would have liked, Lori didn't even know the guy's last name…it was a tinder date, last names weren't necessary.

While the police were finishing up with the statement, Gina was asked to go by Lori's apartment and get something for her. Lori was going to have to stay overnight. And when she went to the hospital, she didn't take anything with her. Her purse and her cell phone were still lying on the floor in her apartment from when she was pushed down by the guy. Gina had a spare key to Lori's apartment. As she walked in, she found the dining area in shambles. That sick feeling came back to her stomach when she saw the crime scene. Gina walked around and tried to clean up a bit. Lori didn't need to see the mess when she came home. As she was cleaning, she found Lori's cellphone. Luckily, the screen wasn't cracked, but she didn't really care about that… phones can easily be replaced. Gina wanted to see the fucker who did this' profile on Tinder. Lori only had two matches, so it wasn't hard to find the profile who did this.

The asshole was dumb enough to not have deleted the match yet. And the best part…he wasn't hard to find on Facebook using just a few simple pieces of information like the town he lived in, the college he graduate from, and his first name. Gina got the link to his Facebook profile and texted it to a number she kept for emergencies in her phone. The number was for a service that handled this sort of thing. Sometimes, it was also called the last resort.

Tommy was coming in late. Just like the night before, he had a date. That went a lot better. She believed his bullshit and he actually got laid. Tommy never liked being home early during the week; he got bored too easily. And it's not like he had kids to worry about. One was already out of the house. The other was seventeen and rarely at home, being away with work and school stuff. His wife was a different story. She never really asked about his extracurricular activities. Maybe she was too naïve or wanted to be naïve and spare herself the heartache. Either way, she didn't really care. Tommy was going to do what he wanted. The way he thought, men were allowed to do that because they were men.

It was about 11:30pm when he walked through the door. He knew his wife would already be asleep and his son was probably spending the night at one of his girlfriend's houses. Like father, like son! The lights were off when he walked in, which was strange because there was at least one light left on for whoever got home late. As he made his way into the kitchen, he found a light switch and tried turning on the lights. Nothing. The lights were completely dead. Even the green, fluorescent lights from the oven clock weren't blinking. Tommy quietly cursed. "Fucking hell."

The breaker box was out in the garage. He couldn't see anything except for the little bit of light coming through the windows in the living room, so he decided to walk through that room to get to the garage. Halfway through the living room, he heard a voice say. "Do you think you can hit a woman and there won't be any consequences to your actions?"

Tommy was startled. He didn't scream, but he did yell out. "What the fuck?"

The voice replied. "Did you really think you could get away with it? Just because the cops haven't shown up yet doesn't mean there aren't worse things that will make you pay for your sins."

Tommy was trying to hide that he was scared. "Who are you and what the fuck are you doing in my house?"

"I don't have a name, but why I'm here is more important. I'm here for your reckoning and there's a payment…blood for blood."

He tried not to be scared, but he knew he had done bad things. Did God send some kind of avenging angel to punish him? He remembered the stories his grandmother used to tell him after church when he was a kid. Tommy thought she was just full of old superstitions and none of it could be true. But he wasn't going down without a fight and looked around for some kind of weapon. He figured the person in his house had to be sitting in one of the chairs in the living room. He found a fireplace stoker and swung at one of the chairs. Nothing was there.

Then he heard a small voice right behind him, whisper. "Nice try." As he was about to swing around and try to hit the voice, he felt a sharp object pierce his side. It was like he had been shanked, but more deliberate. Tommy fell to his knees, his hand over the wound, trying to stop the bleeding. He didn't have the energy to swing the stoker again. The wound seemed to take his breath away. He responded. "Please, I will give you whatever you want... just stop."

The voice replied. "Even your life. Are you willing to give me your life?"

"I have money in a safe. It's yours if you want it...just stop."

"No, Tommy...we're not done. Do you think you can get away with hitting women or trying to rape them...you don't think you deserve to be punished?"

He was scared. You could tell from the sound of his voice. "How do you know about that?"

"You may be able to hide your sins from your wife, but God sees all."

"Who did that fucking bitch tell...the cops!"

The blade from the long knife slashed one side of his face. The cut was deep and long. He was cut from ear to mouth. "We always receive tips when the innocent have been hurt. Now...do you believe you deserve forgiveness?"

"I'm sorry, I know what I did was wrong."

"That's not good enough Tommy. You have to pray for forgiveness."

What...I said I was sorry."

"I don't hear you praying, Tommy."

He tried to look up at the killer. He was slashed across the other side of the face from his ear to his mouth He screamed out like a child in pain. But he knew what he had to do in order to make it stop. He started to pray. "Dear Lord, I'm sorry for what I have done. Please forgive my sins." He wasn't really a Christian.

He didn't know how to pray. He just said what he thought the killer would want to hear. Before he could say anymore, a sound from the distance startled both of them. It was the sound of a shotgun being pumped. Tommy's wife was standing behind them with a 12 Gauge shotgun that they kept in their bedroom closet. She yelled. "Get on the ground asshole or I blow your head off."

The killer slowly turned around and started towards the ground, but then in a split moment, threw the knife like a seasoned professional and caught her in the chest. She flew backwards and fired off one round as she was falling to the floor. The killer rolled out of the way of the buckshot and miraculously didn't get hit. Tommy shouted in anger. "Noooo…" He tried to swing the stoker again at the killer, but the killer blocked his arm, twisting it backwards until they could hear the break.

The killer walked over to the wife who was lying on the floor at the edge of the stairs. She was still alive, but barely. The killer said out loud. "Shit…this wasn't supposed to happen." The knife was pulled out and the killer stabbed her again in the heart. That killed her. Tommy was cursing at the killer. It sounded like gibberish because he was getting lightheaded from the loss of blood. The killer walked back over to Tommy, who was laying the floor, bleeding out. He was trying to put pressure on his side, hoping to stop the bleeding. His arm was broken, which made it extremely difficult, and he just couldn't stop it. There was too much blood.

The killer looked down. "I said your payment was blood for blood. Your wife is dead. The debt has been paid."

"Fuck you," Tommy replied. He might have been a bad man who cheated on his wife constantly. But he still loved her. He never stopped through all of his infidelity. He said. "You might as well kill me."

"You will be dead soon enough. You have lost too much blood. I'm sorry for your wife…it was supposed to be just you, but our sins always affect the one's we love the most."

Tommy was whimpering like a wounded dog. "Kill me and get it over with."

The killer took mercy on him since the debt had been paid. The killer used the same knife that had started the job. Standing behind Tommy, the killer in propping him up and in a simple swoosh, sliced his throat. As blood gushed out, he fell forward and was dead in a matter of seconds. In a way, it was mercy compared to the original plan for Tommy. Even avenging angels ordained by God were allowed to show mercy from time to time.

6

Jim Summers arrived early with a large coffee in hand. He needed it. He had been up late looking at case files, wanting to get a head start on the Don Bennett court files. Jim walked into the conference room and found it filled with boxes. Everything had arrived from Austin. The rest of the team arrived shortly after him. They had a lot of work ahead of them, hence the early start, but it already felt like they were behind. Jim said good morning to everybody and then broke them up into teams.

He looked at Ron and said. "Don Bennett used to be a cop so I am putting you on his old case files."

Ron replied. "You're thinking, it could be some guy he put away, holding a grudge?"

"Yeah…probably isn't, but we need to rule everybody out. Don Bennett used to work narcotics…back in the '90s. Look for anybody that he busted that just did a 20 to 25-year bit. Maybe even connected to a drug cartel."

"That last one sounds like a long shot."

"Might be, but it's worth a look and we have to rule everything out. Detective Cross, start looking at his ethics violations and who he was involved with when he was still a State Senator. Everybody he dealt with and see if anybody got screwed over by the guy…it's probably a long list. Detective Green, you are looking through court transcripts with me. The rest of you, start going through homicide files and seeing if there are any murders out there that fit the MO...ritualistic murders or ones that have been staged. "Jim pointed to the big Tackboard in the back. Any lead or connection, write it down on one of the note cards that are in the middle of the table and then stick it up there. Then we will start looking for connections."

It was like a study hall in the conference room, everybody quiet and everybody drinking multiple cups of coffee. Detective Jackson, the more gung-ho of the bunch kept finding so-called leads and putting them on the board. Each time he did it, he broke Jim's concentration from the long list of case files involving suits against Don Bennett.

Over the last twenty years, he had been sued a dozen times for sexual harassment or misconduct to put it lightly. Only one time did he settle the case out of court. The rest of the time, the case was either dismissed or he was found not liable. Most of them were from his time as a State Senator. But what was even more astonishing is that none of these cases made the front page of a newspaper or were even reported by a TV news station. It was as if the media was silent on the subject or he was somehow untouchable by the media. That was Jim's theory.

Maisie winced every time she read something that disgusted her in the case files. It was appalling. So many women and the only punishment he ever received was giving some small settlement to make it go away. Finally, Jim responded to her disgusted looks. "Hard to stomach, isn't it? More than just a gruesome murder!"

She gave him a sarcastic look. "How did he get away with all of this...how did not one case stick?"

"Careful Detective...just because he was accused, doesn't mean he was guilty."

Maisie shot him a dirty look. "That's a typical man's response to cases like this."

"I didn't say I think he's innocent. That many women accuse him at different times in his career; it's not an isolated innocent. His behavior has a pattern, which means he's probably guilty of at least a few of them."

"But how was he found innocent or get the suits dropped?"

"This is Texas, honey." She raised her eyebrows at Jim calling her "honey," showing a disapproving look at his comment. He knew it too, but he was trying to make a point, even if the comment was inappropriate in today's workplace. He continued. "There's always been a good ole boy system here and these kinds of indiscretions get swept away as if they're minor nuisances. Some men believe that woman should just stop complaining and just let them be men."

"That's fucking horseshit."

"I agree...just telling you how it can be. It's not right, but it's how it is."

"Sounds like you're making excuses."

"Nope. Just making you aware of the situation and it's why I understand how he could be Bill Cosby before Bill Cosby and get away with it. But you've been working how long in Law Enforcement with mostly men...you should know how it is."

Maisie still had a look of disgust on her face. "I still say it's horseshit."

Jim smiled. "I agree, but we have twelve suspects that we need to look into and these are just the suits in Dallas. I think there's more from Austin. "

"You say twelve, but the one case he settled, you think she would still kill him years later even after getting a settlement?"

"It's been my experience that revenge is worth more than money. I wouldn't rule it out. But when did he settle that suit."

Maisie looked through the file and found the date. "It was May of 1997."

"That's when he quit being a cop, right?"

Maisie looked at the case more closely. "You're right. According to the agreement, he had to retire from the force, but still got to keep his pension, and the Dallas PD insurance policy for misconduct paid out the settlement."

"So, it was the only time he settled, the rest either went to trial, where he won or the cases got dismissed. And the next year, he was elected to the State Senate."

"Sounds like he got the better deal despite settling. That would piss me off because it seems like he didn't lose anything."

Jim laughed at the notion. "No, which gives somebody a lot of motive to kill someone if they felt like the person who harmed them really got away with it because the settlement wasn't enough. And now…we check everyone who sued him, starting with the first one in 1997."

Maisie nodded in agreement, then her curiosity took over. "What did Don Bennett do to get kicked out of office…having inappropriate relationships"

Jim laughed. "You would think knowing his track record, but no. It was something else, like getting votes for using eminent domain, that helped out one of his oil friends, I think." He looked up at Ron. "Detective Jackson, since you've been going through all the files on Bennett when he was a Senator, what did he get kicked out of office for?"

Detective Jackson picked up a file and brought it over to Jim. "He was forced to resign on ethics violations for taking kickbacks. His consulting company would get what they called referral fees and since he was still a majority shareholder while he was still in office, it was a huge conflict of interest thus the ethics violations. He made like four million doing this or his company did. I should say."

Jim replied. "Oh, that's right… I forgot, he was so corrupt, it's hard to remember what they got him for."

Detective Jackson replied. "I overheard you mention eminent domain. It's actually not against the law or an ethics violation to vote on using that when it can help out a friend or someone who donated to your campaign. It may be a conflict of interest, but not against the law…something I learned when my friend's family got screwed out of their land in West Texas that went to an oil company."

Both Maisie and Jim rolled their eyes at the absurdity of that not being illegal. Maisie responded. "Of course, that would not be illegal, here in Texas because that would prevent the Good Ole Boy network from getting away with shit!." Jim didn't disagree.

Detective Jackson gave her a dirty look. "Hey, I don't make the law, I just enforce it, just like you or at least you are supposed to… detective."

She was about to say something snarky, but everybody was interrupted by Detective Cross. "Everybody, turn on the news or go to your phones. There's breaking news." Jim turned on the TV in the conference room. It was already on NBC. Even though the TV was muted, the words that scrolled at the bottom of the screen read, "Former State Senator, Don Bennett Found Murdered."

Jim cursed. The story had finally broken. He was hoping that they had at least a few more days to investigate before the media got a hold of it and said it was murder. They knew what it was, but when the news says murder; there is an unnecessary frenzy that comes with that label.

Detective Cross asked. "Now what?"

Jim responded. "Now the clock is running, and we don't have the luxury of time when it comes to finding answers. Keep working. I have to coordinate a press conference because we can't stay silent on the issue. Part of my job is talking to the media and getting them to not report false information. " Jim looked over at Maisie. "Start checking on those twelve women. I will be back later."

It had been a while since the young woman had gone to confession. She tried to go once a week, but sometimes going to mass had to be good enough. But she went to church more than the average catholic so that had to count for something or so she thought. It wasn't that busy at the church, so she didn't have to wait long. She went inside a confession booth and Father Michael entered into the other side a few moments later.

"Bless me father for I have sinned." She said.

"Tell me what sins you have committed, my child." He replied. She was hardly a child anymore, but the words always seemed to bring her comfort, like a father telling his daughter, that no matter what, it was going to be okay."

"I have had impure thoughts. Not the kind you probably think, more dangerous, though."

A naturally curious priest, Father Michael was more intrigued by her statement than with most confessions. "And what are these dangerous thoughts you're speaking of?"

"I would guess you call it revenge…"

He cut her off. He didn't mean to, it was one of his bad habits. "But you think it's something else, that's why you called these thoughts dangerous, right?"

"Yes. I prefer to think of it as justice, but if I were to harm someone that harmed me or someone close to me, isn't that just revenge?"

"I think that one word for it, yes, but there's nothing black and white about revenge. I don't know if the Bible is very clear on the subject. Take for instance, 'eye for an eye'… the Bible says that it's not a sin and yet we should turn the other cheek when someone harms us and also forgive them for their sins. The Bible says that sometimes, vengeance is okay."

"But can revenge be Justice?"

Father Michael laughed. "Justice is tricky, even when it masks itself as revenge. Do you have purity of heart or malice in your heart when you commit these acts? That's the question you have to ask yourself. I have always felt that God cares more about what is in our hearts when it comes to our actions. And saving someone from harm is always better even though vengeful acts than letting them suffer more. I guess you can call it the lesser of two evils when it comes to sin."

She tried to smile even through her own guilt. "But am I just as wrong for even having these thoughts."

"Again, it is what's in your heart that matters. You're not evil for having these kinds of thoughts, we all do, it's part of being human. Even if you slip up and commit these acts, I wouldn't say you're evil as long as you show regret and try not to do it again. Especially when saving someone from harm. We all sin. We will still sin right up to the moment of our death. But those who cannot see what they do is wrong or even care are the ones that have evil in their heart. So do you think you're an evil person for even having impure thoughts?"

The young woman sighed. "No, but that's not what worries me, Father."

"What is your biggest fear then?"

"That I have these thoughts and should know that they are wrong, but don't and it's okay to act upon them."

"Virtue is nothing without the trial of temptation, for there is no conflict without an enemy, no victory without strife according to Pope Leo, the Great. But have you acted upon these impure thoughts?"

She didn't say anything for a while. She was conflicted. In theory, she could tell the priest anything, but how much could she really say that wouldn't get her into serious trouble? Honesty is a fickle thing even when it could affect the damnation of your own soul. She gently replied. "I want to father and if I did, I don't think it would be a sin."

"My child, this is not a struggle I can bear for you as much as I wish that I could. It is yours alone to bear, but when we seek God, it is always easier. All I can say is pray, bask in the light that is the glory of God, and always help those who cannot help themselves." It sounded hokie and Father Michael knew it. It was like some Catholic Cliché that first-year priests tell people when they come to confession, but he didn't know what else to say. He was hoping the young woman, who happened to be more religious than the average parishioner, was simply embarrassed by her impure thoughts and that was it. But he could also tell that there was a deeper struggle within her soul. Something dark and perhaps she was too far gone. It stoked his own fear that he couldn't help her at all no matter how much he wanted to. So he ended the confession by saying. "For your impure thoughts, say three Hail Mary's and three Our Father's." And then they both left the booth as if it was just a routine confession in the middle of the week.

7

Sweat was dripping from her forehead. She was afraid and held her rosary tight. She held on as if it was the last good thing in her life. These bouts of fear or panic attacks, which is what a doctor would call it, were not uncommon for her. For years she had tried to control it. Therapy helped only a little. Medication never helped. But prayer, for some reason, seemed to calm her down. It brought some peace.

However, this time, it was worse, and prayer wasn't helping. Over and over, she said, Hail Mary's and Our Father's. Nothing! She was going out of her mind. Remembering that she had some St. Jude candles, she quickly found them and lit them. For a few moments, it brought peace, but it was short-lived. Finally, she did something that she has never done before. There was a business card to a suicide hotline that she had, had in her purse for ages and so she called it. When the woman on the other end of the phone answered and asked how she could help, the woman, still holding her rosary, replied. "I can't control it anymore, I have to kill. It won't let me stop. I can't stop it this time!"

The woman at the hotline was a bit confused, but she started from her script anyway, as if this was a normal case. She said. "Ma'am, let's talk about…before you do anything, let's talk about it….can we do that?"

She replied. "It won't help, but okay."

Jim hated press conferences. He had only had to do two of them before today. But both times, he was just filling in for the lead investigator. Nothing really made him flinch or sweat when it came to high-pressure situations. That's what made him a good investigator when it came to violent crimes. But talking to reporters, made him so nervous that it was like he was asking out a girl to the prom for the first time. He was trying to get his tie straight when the Dallas Police Chief came into the restroom, he walked in to see if he was ready.

Jim replied, sarcastically. "No, but it's not like I have much of a choice. It's part of the job."

The police chief smiled. "Certainly, not the fun part…right!"

"That's for damn sure. I'd rather look at dead bodies all day. It's less nauseating."

"Well, you're the big man from Austin…someone's got to do it."

Jim tried to laugh. "You would think as the big man on campus, I could delegate this sort of thing. So how many reporters do we have out there?"

"Dozen camera crews and a few print reporters."

"So, a lot then."

"For Dallas, yes. But you have reporters from Austin and Houston as well."

Jim rolled his eyes at the thought. But there was no escape, he fixed his tie and walked out with the police chief. There was a mad rush towards Jim by the reporters as he was walking down the steps to where they were having the press conference. It was set in front of the police station on purpose to symbolize the strength of Dallas PD when it came to catching the killer. They needed to make the impression that they knew what they were doing even though they didn't have answers. As soon as Jim reached the bottom of the steps, it seemed like every reporter was trying to ask the same question all at the same time.

Jim responded. "I'm Detective Jim Summers from State CID in Austin, I work in Special Investigation Services, and I am charge of this investigation. So let me tell you what we know so far and to dispense with any rumors that might be going round. Former State Senator, Don Bennett was found murdered two days ago. We can confirm that it's murder, but we don't have the full autopsy report yet. We have a task force set up and are looking into all leads…all possible suspects from lawsuits against him to guys he put in prison while he was a police offer and who might have just gotten out. That's all we know right now."

The local NBC reporter asked. "We've heard that the crime scene might have been staged."

Jim paused. "The only thing I can confirm is that it was a gruesome murder. The rest is just speculation."

"A reporter from WFAA – Channel 8 asked. "Is this a serial killing?"

Jim gave her a weird look. "Why would you ask that…is there a rumor going around?"

"SIS usually gets called to investigate serial murders or the very least the most gruesome murders in the State of Texas. Also, there has been talk…that's why I ask."

Jim couldn't just come and say it without causing some kind of a panic. There were still too many questions that needed answers. But he couldn't outright lie or it would come back and bite him in the ass so to speak. He simply answered. "We can't confirm that and there's no evidence to suggest it at this time."

The reporter replied back. "But it is a possibility, right?"

Jim wanted to say something sarcastic, but he bit his tongue. "Look, here are the facts, Don Bennett was murdered. It was gruesome. We don't have any suspects or motive as of yet, but because of the nature of the crime, SIS was called in to investigate. We have a task force set up to find the killer and get justice for the Bennett family. This is the only thing you should be reporting…everything else are just rumors."

Two other reporters were trying to ask a question at the same time, but Jim cut them off. "We don't have any more information at this time, we thank you for coming out and will report anything new in the investigation as it comes along." Every reporter tried to ask one more question and hoping to get one last answer, but Jim turned around and walked off. He wasn't going to give them the satisfaction. He loathed reporters even more than the killer these days.

Later that day, Jim decided to go by a bookstore and get some books on mythology and folklore. The medical examiner had been a good source of information, but he hardly knew anything about Celtic Mythology and Folklore. Barnes and Noble didn't really have anything. But there was a Half Price Books not too far that had a huge textbook section with many books on the subjects. He found the place and the section in the bookstore. He was a little overwhelmed after looking at it. Jim spent a good ten minutes looking through the books. There were a lot, but he picked four of them; two dealing with mythology, one about Celtic history, and one about English folklore. He was reading through one of the books when he turned the corner of the section he was just in and unfortunately bumped into a woman, knocking her down in the process.

Jim felt so embarrassed for running into the woman since he was the one not paying attention. He dropped his books, but forgot them as he quickly apologized for the incident. Strangely enough, she wasn't mad. She even admitted that she wasn't paying that much attention too, as she turned the corner. Jim helped her gather the books that she was holding at the time. "I'm so sorry, " he responded.

The woman smiled back. "It's okay. Thanks for not being a dick and helping me pick up my books."

"Well, it was my fault… it's the least I can do."

"If it's really your fault, then a cup of coffee should be the proper penance."

Jim gave her a funny look. She replied. "I'm kidding…just having a little fun with you by putting you on the spot."

Jim smiled. "Nice one." He picked up his books. "But, I would be happy to buy you a cup of coffee… it is a good way to say I'm sorry."

"I was just kidding. No need to hit on me in the process."

"That wasn't my intention."

"Oh…I'm not good enough to hit on!"

Jim was stunned again, but then realized that she was just kidding again. He replied. "You're fucking with me, aren't you?"

She smiled. "Yes, I am. I tend to be sarcastic and it causes me to mess with people when they least expect it."

"I like people that have a warped sense of humor…makes things interesting."

"Good, then we'll get along just fine."

Finally, Jim introduced himself. She replied. "I'm Gina."

Jim bought the four books he was holding, still not sure if they were going to help or not, but worth a try nonetheless. Gina didn't buy anything. She was just there looking around but couldn't find anything that she liked or that she hadn't read. They ended up getting a cup of coffee together. What started out as playful banter and perhaps a little flirting, ended up being a simple first date. There was a café connected to the used bookstore and that's where they went. The coffee was better than Starbucks and half the price.

After a few minutes of small talk, Gina asked Jim. "Do you usually pick up girls in a bookstore?"

He laughed. "I never have time to pick up girls, much less in a bookstore. Maybe the occasional dive bar."

"What do you do?"

"Would you believe it, if I told you that I was a traveling salesman?"

Gina shook her head "no," she wasn't easily fooled as she gave him a smile. "Nah…not buying it."

He laughed. "It was worth a shot. But if I tell you the truth, then you will probably like me better as a salesman."

"Probably not...any salesman I've ever known, were usually boring."

He laughed at her observation. "In that case...I'm a cop, which does tend to be more exciting than sales."

"That, I would believe."

Oh, and why's that?"

"You look like a cop."

And how do cops look...somebody who is too plain or square?"

Gina laughed. "Some do, but you on the other hand have that look...not by the way you dress or anything. But the way you study everything as if you're always trying to solve the problems given to you for a school assignment."

Jim smiled. "Never thought that about myself."

"Why would you, we rarely see ourselves as others see us unless we are deliberately trying to make others see us a certain way."

"That's true."

Gina took a sip of coffee. "Do you work in Dallas?"

"Actually, no, but I'm stationed here for a little while?"

"Why's that?"

"I work in CID down in Austin, Special Investigative Services to be exact...we work on big cases...usually the most horrific ones."

"Ah...wait a minute, there was a thing on the news about a big murder here in Dallas...that's what you're investigating, isn't it?"

Jim nodded. "You are very perceptive."

"Yeah, it was a former state senator who was murdered. Somebody said there was a serial killer who did it."

"I can't really tell you anything, but I can say, being a serial killer is a just a rumor. The local press are already spreading rumors, I see."

Gina laughed. "They tend to do that when it makes the news more exciting as if the murder of a former state senator wasn't exciting enough."

Laughing, Jim replied. "Right! You wouldn't think that was good enough for the five o'clock news without making it sound like something from Silence of the Lambs."

"Well, next week, they will say the killer is a cannibal just to add fuel to the fire." Jim busted out in laughter. She was probably right, but these days fake news was good enough. Fact checking just wasn't a priority, even at a local news station. Gina asked. "So, have you done anything fun since you've been here or just worked."

Smiling, Jim replied. "Fun isn't a word I get to use in my line of work. But if you're asking me if I have done anything that wasn't work-related, then this cup of coffee with you is pretty much it. Can't complain though…the company is fantastic!"

Gina smiled at the compliment. "Well, we shall have to remedy that. Coffee is one thing, but drinks are always better."

"It's a nice thought, but I do have to get back to work."

"Do you really think you can catch the killer tonight? Sometimes the best way to solve a problem is to take a break and not think about it for a while…that's another reason God invented alcohol."

Jim laughed. "That may be true, but…"

"But what…you can't take a break…even with a beautiful woman like me. Come on, a couple of drinks, maybe some live music…I guarantee it will do you good."

Detective Jim Summers tried to protest, but really couldn't think of anything to say to her. Didn't really have an excuse. He knew he shouldn't, but then again, he was fond of taking breaks when alcohol was involved. It did help clear his head, believe it or not. He could only come up with one response. "Okay, let's do it."

The next five hours were a blur. In fact, he couldn't remember a thing when his phone started ringing. When Jim woke up, he found himself in his hotel bed with no recollection on he got there. It was 10:30 pm. Gina was lying next to him. It looked as if they had a hell of a time over the last five hours. Jim missed the call, but before he could call the number back, his phone started ringing again. Detective Maisie Green was calling him.

He rubbed the sleep out of his eyes and answered the phone. "This is Summers…"

Maisie replied. "Hey, where are you? I've been calling the past couple of hours."

Jim looked at his phone. There was a dozen missed calls. He responded. "Sorry, I've been out…guess I didn't have my phone on."

"That's a little strange. Aren't detectives always supposed to have their phone on?"

"Yes, but sometimes I forget."

"If you're out getting laid and wanted your phone off, just say so." She was being sarcastic and just trying to bust his balls so to speak like cops often do with one another. Jim was taken back by the comment.

He replied. "That's not what happened…I don't think!"

"What, I was right," Maisie humorously said."

"No…you're not right." Jim didn't want to tell her the truth, especially if he didn't know what the truth was. "It doesn't matter anyway, why are you calling?"

"We got a break in the case."

"Really!"

"Yep…I checked out all the women that sued Don Bennett, all of them check out and have alibis except one."

"Who?"

"The first one, Amy Henderson."

Jim had a look of surprise. "You mean, the only one that got a settlement and forced him off the job."

"Yes, sir. According to her sister, Amy has been missing for almost a year. But over the last decade, she became increasingly paranoid."

"And when you say paranoid, you mean…"

"Like everybody was out to get her, especially men. And she started training."

"Training! For what?"

Maisie looked down at her list. "She started taking Ti Kwan Do. She learned how to shoot and got a concealed handgun license. In fact, according to her sister, she got some militia training with a patriot group and learned how to shoot military-grade weapons. She became a fitness freak, running, cross-fit training…stuff like that. She dropped like forty pounds and got in great shape."

"Holy shit…it's like she turned into Sarah Connor and was preparing judgment day."

Maisie was confused. "Who are you talking about?"

"You know, Sarah Conner, from the Terminator movies…nevermind, it's not important."

"Well anyway… no one has heard from her in about a year and it's not like she doesn't have the money to disappear."

"Good point. Looks like we have a prime suspect."

"She certainly has motive."

"Yeah, she does, but she only has a connection to the former senator. Right now, she is only a person of interest. We need to find her and question her so we will do a missing person's report and make it a priority with all the law enforcement agencies in Texas."

"I understand."

"Jim paused for a moment, thinking about what to do next. He responded to Maisie. "Tomorrow, we'll walk the crime scene. If she is the killer, then we need to find something that ties her to the crime scene?" Maisie agreed. She was just happy that she finally got to look at the crime scene in person. It was much better than looking through old files in a conference room with men she didn't like or at least most of them.

Gina hadn't really been asleep. She was tired and drunk but awake enough that she heard the conversation Jim had on the phone. She turned over in his bed at the hotel and said. "Sounds like you have to work late."

He laughed. "Did I wake you?"

"Not really, I'm more hungover than asleep…shots will do that to you."

"Yeah, it was work."

She sat up, not even bothering to cover her breasts with the sheet. She replied. "I guess, I should get out of here and let you get to work."

"Or you can stay…we can grab something to eat. I don't know about you, but I'm starving."

Gina gave him a strange look. "Oh, this isn't a one-time thing. I thought this was just a one-night stand?"

Surprised by the comment, Jim replied. "It can be if that's what you want, but I had fun and would like to see you again."

"Okay…it's that most men who are only visiting just want the one-night stand and honestly, I'm okay with that."

Jim laughed. "I'm not most men! And you would think that's all I wanted since I don't live here and just got divorced a few months ago. This is probably just a rebound, but no reason we can't see each other again."

"And have sex again, she replied, smiling sarcastically."

"If you want."

"When was the last time you had sex and not by yourself?"

Jim gave her a dirty look. "You're funny. I haven't since my wife."

Liking the answer, she leaned over and kissed him. "If you want to see me again, while you're here, I definitely wouldn't say "no". And I'm okay with none of this being serious in case you're wondering."

Jim smiled. He didn't really have time for serious, anyway. One should never be in a serious relationship right after a divorce, he thought…it very rarely works out as he had seen from experience. But she was nice, didn't want anything from him, she was sexy as hell, and a perfect distraction. It was the best relationship, such as it was, that he could hope for.

The house was smaller than Maisie thought. Houses in Plano always seemed bigger than they really were. It was a community portraying themselves rich enough to be in Highland Park but making the choice not to be. That kind of façade was not uncommon in the big cities of Texas, but then again, lies and myths in Texas were always larger than life, especially for those who thought themselves to be more elite than they really were.

As she and Detective Summers drove up to the house wrapped in police tape to let everyone know that it was a crime scene, it had an eerie feeling to it. Maybe it just felt that way after having seen the crime photos. Maisie was looking through those photos and the lab reports as Jim drove up and parked in the driveway. She commented. "I thought there would be more to go on here. The only physical evidence found at the scene was Bennett's DNA and blood, plus the two maids?"

Nodding at her, Jim also replied. "Yep, and they both check out."

"They have keys to the house?"

"Yeah. And from what we can tell, there are only six keys made for the house. He has two; one of them is a spare. The maids have two. His ex-wife has one, and his daughter has one. All are accounted for too?"

They walked through the door and the smell of death mixed with Lysol hit their noses hard. Somebody had to spray the place down enough that the stink wouldn't linger too much, but after a few days it wore off. Maisie covered her nose and then asked one of the most obvious questions. "Was there any forced entry?"

Jim replied. "No, which means he might have known the killer and let them in."

Maisie nodded in agreement but offered a different theory. "Or the killer is really skilled at picking locks and making it look like it wasn't a forced entry."

"That's possible, but the house has an alarm…they would have to know how to bypass it and still get inside the house undetected. One of the tech guys with the CSI team checked and according to the report, it doesn't appear to be tampered with."

"So, if we go with your theory, and Amy Henderson did this, he wouldn't have let her in… unless… was there any sign that Bennett had a Taser gun used on him?"

Jim looked back through the initial ME's report. "That's a good question and no, it doesn't look like it."

Both spent some time looking around. While they had the crime scene report inform of them, they had to see everything for themselves. They had to find the clues for themselves, go over every detail and see if anything had been missed. That is how they prove their theory or not. Finally, Jim put the pictures of the body and how it was displayed on the kitchen table. He looked at Maisie and asked. "What do you see?"

She gave him a strange look. Most cops didn't ask her that kind of question. "You want to know my theory?"

"Yes…I brought you here because you are the only one on the task force trained in Psychology and have some profiling experience."

"That doesn't mean, I have the right answers."

"Maybe not, but in solving a crime like this trying to answer why the killer did what they did, especially how they displayed the crime scene will help us catch them and you are more equipped than any of the other detectives to answer the question of why. You don't think I read all of your files before you started on this task force!"

She smiled. It was a perfect complement when it came to her profession. "Okay…this murder is more deliberate. More than your average premeditated murder. I think the killer is sending a message, but it's not like bragging about their skills…it's more like a warning."

Surprised by the answer, Jim replied. "A warning…that's interesting. Why do you say warning? Serial killers often kill because it excites them! It's almost like a fetish. Once they get a taste they can't stop. Now, the symbolism might be different in how they kill their victims, but it still comes down to, they get off on it."

Maisie nodded in agreement. "I'm not saying that this particular killer doesn't get excited when doing it, but there's a message here and I think it's a warning."

"How did you come to that conclusion?"

"It's the eyes. One of them was cut out. Why just one of the eyes… why not both. Then the killer places the eye, they cut in front of the victim."

"That is an interesting point."

Maisie got excited. She started thumbing ferociously through the crime scene report. Jim asked. "What is it?"

"I'm looking to see which eye was cut out."

"What does it matter?"

She found her answer on the report. "Holy shit, it's the left eye!"

"Why is that important?"

Maisie displayed her confident smile when she knew she was right about something. It was her way of saying that she was the smartest one in the room. "The eyes have meaning in many cultures…many religions. In eastern religion and I think in Celtic mythology, the right eye symbolizes the sun, and the left symbolizes the moon. The sun means to look forward or the future while the moon represents the past. If the killer is cutting out the left eye and places it in front of the victim then it's about the past staring back at you."

Jim got a little excited. The answer made sense. Then he added to it. "What if the victim is being forced to look at his past, like they themselves did something horrific and are being forced to relive it?"

Maisie smiled. "Right...and the warning is that our past always catches up with us... we can't escape it. I mean, if the eyes are the windows to our soul, then they also serve as a mirror especially for all of our misdeeds."

"How do you know all of this?"

"I was encouraged to take some religion courses related to symbolism as part of my Psych degree, which brings me to the other thing I see. There's a religious symbolism here. I'm not necessarily saying Christianity, but different religions."

"You think it has to do with the victims being punished. I think it's fairly obvious that they're being punished."

"I agree and I think that's part of it. I bet the killer is deeply religious or at least had a strict religious upbringing."

Jim laughed. "Sure, but it's easy to tell from the Fairy wings or Angel wings as some people think they are."

"Touché' but there are other signs. The pierced side where they bleed out like Jesus while on the cross. And it seems as if they were meant to consume something...like they were consuming the thing they used to commit their sins"

"What do you mean?"

"One thing that I noticed is all their mouths are open. Why? What are they supposed to eat or consume...maybe they were consuming the sin itself like with a sin eater."

Jim looked confused. "What do you mean a sin eater?"

Maisie chuckled. "You're clearly not Catholic. It's the opposite of a Catholic priest, that's the best way to describe them. They use a ritual where they can magically absorb the sin by eating something like bread, which we know from Christianity symbolizes the body of Christ. People who couldn't use a priest to take away their sins would use a Sin Eater. I think the first cases date back to like the 17th century. But in this case, it's the sinner who is made to absorb the sin they commit as a punishment. The killer is making the victims repent by absorbing their own sin...well, it's a theory."

Jim replied. "That's a lot of conjecture. Remember, we examine facts."

"Hey, you asked me what I saw…I see a lot of symbols…mostly religious so I am throwing out ideas. I could be way off base, but you can't deny there's a lot of symbolism here."

"You're right…now let's build a profile. You think the killer is deeply religious, right?"

"Most likely or at the very least knows a lot about religions and their symbols."

Jim popped with curiosity. "Somebody who was abused or had some kind of tragedy in their life…mixed with a religious upbringing."

Maisie started making a list of the characteristics they talked about. "Yes, but not where they feel like they have to be punished, but they have to punish others, especially the ones who get away with something."

Jim paused for a moment. "The killer is somebody that has a strong sentence of justice…they fanatically believe in right and wrong. See themselves as a servant of God, ridding the world of evil."

Maisie was impressed. "They see themselves as some kind of Archangel and not as an avenger because if they were an avenger, then it's society who gives them the right to kill in the name of justice, but the killer feels that right can only be granted by God."

Jim smiled. "So, we're looking for someone that is deeply religious, perhaps, very patriotic. Familiar with weapons. They understand cultures, different religions, and symbolism. I would go as far as to say, the killer is highly educated."

"Probably got a religious education too. Perhaps went to a Catholic School."

Jim walked around in the dining area for a moment. "It just occurred to me, the killer doesn't have to be tied to the victims directly. Perhaps they're tied directly to them because they are related to someone that was wronged in some way by the victims."

Maisie smiled. "True, but that would make one of these murders about revenge and the others would be considered Justice even though the killer doesn't see any of this as revenge. If you're right, our list of suspects just got even longer and the list for Don Bennett was already long enough."

"Then, thank God, we have a big team that can do a lot of research."

Maisie looked at the crime photos again. She was curious about something that had not been discussed yet. "The police baton that was inserted in his rectum…was it his?"

"What do you mean," Jim asked.

"Is it the one he used while he was on the job? Police officers tend to keep their old stuff as souvenirs… I'm just wondering if the killer searched his house, found his personal baton, and used it as part of the crime."

Jim contemplated the question, "That would make it more personal if it was his…maybe he used his baton to sexually assault someone."

Maisie smiled. "You know where I'm going with this. I think he might have sodomized someone with it, hence why it's inserted in his rectum. Also… the leg and handcuffs are a standard prison issue. That's deliberate. The killer wanted Bennett to know he was a prisoner…it's like they were creating a specific kind of prison for him. That's something else I see."

"And it fits within your message theory… good work." Jim continued to look around the house. "How they got in is what bothers me the most. My gut tells me that Don Bennett didn't let the killer in. They were already here." Jim saw the door to the garage. He noticed something on the floor. It was small specs of dirt on the carpet. It wasn't that strange to see something like. People track in dirt all the time, but it stuck with him. He went into the garage and found Bennett's Cadillac. Nothing out of the ordinary, but he walked around the car anyway. CSI had checked it out and didn't find anything unusual. However, as Jim walked around the car he saw the trunk wasn't closed all the way. Did CSI check something and forget to close it…it was possible, he thought, But Jim had another theory…he couldn't explain it…the idea just popped in his head.

He called out to Maisie. "Detective Green…come inside the garage for a moment."

She eagerly came in the garage and saw Jim standing by the trunk of the car. Before she could say anything, he responded. "Do you have a flashlight on you?"

"Yes...what did you find?"

"The trunk wasn't shut all the way."

"CSI could have forgotten to close it after they checked out the car."

"Yeah...but I don't think so." Maisie handed him the flashlight. He opened the trunk and commented. "You know Cadillac's have a lot of trunk space. You could fit a body in there...maybe two."

"What are you getting at?"

Jim shined the light on the inside of the trunk door behind the key mechanism and latch. There was scraped metal all around it and it looked as if somebody had tried to release the latch from the inside by trying to pick the key mechanism. It wasn't necessarily hard to do, but it would be hard not to scrape the metal and leave a mark, especially if you were doing it in the dark. You couldn't hide that no matter how skilled you were at picking locks. As the light was shining around the key and latch area, Jim showed Maisie what he was seeing. She responded. "Holy Shit...is that what I think it is?"

Jim replied. "Yeah...looks like the trunk was opened from the inside. I think that's how they got in...They hid out in the trunk and Bennett the drove the killer here."

"Smart!

"I'll say...this is a true hunter we're dealing with."

"And the other two murders...there was no forced entry into the homes, was there?"

"No."

Maisie paused and thought about it for a moment. "This is somebody who really takes the time to watch their prey...gets to know their routine...knows their calendar...gets to know every detail and stays in the shadows. This takes patience. "

"Most likely, we are looking for someone between the ages of 35 to 50....somebody older who would have more patience and wouldn't rush.

"And it's somebody who probably won't make mistakes because they're smarter than we are."

Jim smiled. "I hate to say it, but I don't think you're wrong about this killer."

Gina couldn't remember the last time that she went on more than one date with a guy. Online dates never got that far and after what happened to her friend Lori, it was a safe bet that she may never go on another one again. She had gone out with the detective three times now. He was nice. He wasn't complicated. And best of all, she liked him...a lot. Gina couldn't explain it. She just liked him. Lori was excited for Gina as she was telling her about the new guy in her life.

Lori hadn't had much of a social life since her encounter with her assailant. She was over at Gina's place trying some new wine that they had picked up at a wine festival the year before. Tonight was a good night to try it. Lori's eye was still swollen and didn't like being out in public these days. She even had to give up some acting gigs until it completely healed. As the two women were laughing at some of their bad date stories, they were startled by the commotion outside Gina's apartment door. Some guy was yelling and cursing at one of the neighbors. Gina knew immediately whose door the guy was yelling at.

Gina walked outside. The guy didn't even see her and continued to yell. "Bitch, get the fuck out here…. where's my money?"

She yelled back from behind the door. "Fuck you…I've already worked it off."

"You haven't even come close to working it off yet."

Finally, Gina responded. "Hey, asshole. Get out of here now or I will call the police."

The guy turned around and replied. "Fuck you bitch...I'll leave when I get my money."

The neighbor unlocked her door, cracking it only slightly, and threw a hundred-dollar bill at the guy. He didn't pick it up, but in a fit of anger, kicked her front door in, almost knocking her down. She was more startled when he came inside her apartment and slapped her across the face, yelling, "Give me the rest of my fucking money, now, or I fucking kill you."

Gina told Lori to call the police and then she ran toward the other apartment. She used an MMA Flying knee move to nail in the back and knock him forward. He was stunned and had his breath knocked out a little bit. Gina saw Audra and Josh crouched in a corner of the living room. Audra was trying to protect Josh, but both were equally scared. The guy had trouble getting up, but still managed to curse at Gina. "You fucking bitch...you're dead. "

Gina got in her MMA pose. "Bring it asshole."

He was finally up. "Alright...you want some bitch, here you go." He threw a punch at her. Gina saw it coming and moved out of the way while kicking him in the ribs. He went down again. She cracked one of the ribs. This time he pulled a knife and tried to slash her with it. She easily moved out of the way and did another flying knee move to his face, breaking his nose in the process. Blood went everywhere. Audra got excited and yelled, "Kick his fucking ass."

Gina smiled at her. This time the guy pulled his snub-nosed 38 revolver.. Before he could properly aim, Gina roundhoused kicked him to the side of the head. It almost knocked him out, but not quite. If it had been an MMA fight, he definitely would've been out, and she would be the winner. He slowly tried to gather himself. He saw his gun and tried to pick it up, but by that time the police had arrived. They burst through the door, almost knocking Gina over and subdued the guy. He cursed like hell when they handcuffed him, but he was down, that was the main thing. One of the cops asked what happened and Audra was the first to answer. She replied. "Gina beat the shit out of him. It was awesome."

The cop looked at the guy. "Is that true...did you get beat up by a girl? That's got to be embarrassing."

The guy yelled back. "Fuck you."

"No thank you...but where you're going, I'm sure you will be when you've made a prison wife."

The police took everybody's statement. The police never got a clear answer on the relationship between the guy and the woman he was harassing. Gina just assumed it had something to do with drugs. Her neighbor spent most of her time getting loaded. But after the statements, the cops were able to figure out that the woman had been prostituting herself for drugs, at least according to the guy they arrested. There was no evidence that it was true, so she wasn't arrested, but it didn't surprise anybody if it was for real.

The cops who showed up to the scene were impressed with Gina. One of them even asked her out for a cup of coffee. The only one who wasn't impressed or even thankful was the neighbor. She only cared about getting high again. So much so that she didn't even notice that her children spent the night at Gina's because they were too scared to be home. And Gina didn't mind, she had grown fond of the kids.

The next night, Gina went out to dinner with Jim again. The kids were already back at their own place. It was nice to have the escape. Of course, it seemed as if there was too much drama with her neighbor. Almost every night she could hear yelling. Audra and Josh got through it with the use of headphones, listening to music or playing some game on a tablet.

It had only been a day since the incident had occurred, but Gina had already become some sort of a legend with local police. She was the girl who beat up a thug almost twice her size. In Texas, cops love to talk and sometimes can be worse than women at the local salon. They're not immune to telling tall tales of their exploits taking down criminals or when something embarrassing happens to those criminals. One of them gets beat up by a girl definitely fit the bill and in what is still a somewhat misogynistic culture, they couldn't fathom something like that happening. Gina told Jim the whole story. He had already heard bits and pieces from some of the detectives talking about it earlier that morning.

Jim was impressed but wanted to hear it without embellishment. They both laughed about the incident.

He responded by saying. "You know his wounds will heal in time, but not his pride. He will never live it down and I think that's awesome. He deserves it."

Gina smiled. "I'll admit, it was gratifying hurting his manhood."

"I couldn't believe it when I heard what happened this morning. I think, my first thought was...god, I hope I don't piss her off."

"You don't seem like the type of guy that would hit me...so I think you're safe. I only fight back when people are trying to hurt me."

He laughed. "That's good to know. But I still wouldn't want to mess with you."

Gina took a sip of wine and then her phone started ringing. Normally she kept it silent when she was on a date, but she was also the emergency contact for a few people. It was Audra and she never called. Like most young girls, she texted. If she was calling, it had to be important, so Gina excused herself and answered the call.

"Audra, what is it...you never call me."

Audra was frantic. She could hardly get the words out. "My mom won't wake up. I can't feel a heartbeat. I don't know what to do." Audra was crying.

"Okay hon...just calm down. Call 911 and ask for an ambulance. I'm on my way."

Gina's joyful mood turned to panic. She could tell it was really bad from fear she heard in Audra's voice. She was a smart girl and never seemed phased by the shit her mother put her through. Yeah, this was bad...really bad. Gina looked at Jim and said. "I've got to go. I think my neighbor's mother just died. She's only thirteen."

Jim was stunned, but playing the role of the hero, he replied. "Wow, okay...let me drive I can get you there faster." He threw money down on the table to cover the tab.

One of the advantages of being a cop, he could put the sirens on and drive fast, pretty much breaking every traffic law.

They weren't that far away and arrived just before the ambulance. Audra was standing outside of the apartment waiting. Gina grabbed her and hugged her as Audra was crying uncontrollably. She told Audra that Jim was a friend and a cop. Jim rushed into the apartment and found the mother on the floor. He already knew that it was probably too late, but attempted CPR anyway, at least to make the kids feel better that somebody was trying to revive their mother.

The paramedics arrived a few minutes later and took over for Jim. They worked on her more aggressively, even shocking her heart a few times. Nothing. They concluded that she was too far gone and had arrived too late. While the paramedics worked on the mother, Gina asked Audra what happened.

Audra replied. "I don't know, she went into the bathroom and took some medicine. She was in there for a while and when she came out she stumbled around and fell to the floor."

Trying to reassure her, she replied. "It's going to be okay. Why don't you get Josh and go to my place and watch TV. Audra did just that. Jim was searching the apartment for what might have caused this. As a cop, it was instinct. He suspected drugs were involved and it wasn't hard to find the culprit. He found the mother's stash in her bedroom. Dallas PD arrived on the scene right when the paramedics called it. The mother was dead, probably had been before anybody arrived and there was no way anybody could have revived her. Gina saw them call the time of death. While she didn't necessarily like her, Gina felt sad because no one should have to die that way, she even shed a few tears.

After about thirty minutes, Jim found Gina at her place with the kids. He asked to speak with her alone. He showed her the drugs and said. "This is what killed her."

"What is it," Gina asked.

"She gave herself a hot dose, it's a mixture of cocaine and heroin."

"Holy shit...that doesn't even sound good."

"No, it isn't. It's deadly when you inject it, which is what she did. Too much coke makes the blood pressure rise and the heartbeat faster than it should while the opioids in heroine dull the pain so much that you don't feel the warning signs of a heart attack and then you'll just drop dead. Can happen in a matter of minutes and I figure that's what happened to her. I'm sure the ME's report concludes that as well."

Gina was beyond stunned. "Wow, I just can't believe it. Would've thought even she would know better not to mix the two drugs. "

"She probably didn't even know it was mixed. It looks the same on the package and she probably just thought it was just heroine. Something else you should know. I had a chance to look up the guy they arrested last night since he's in the system. He's a drug dealer and a pimp. His MO is pimping out single mothers who need the money or can't hold down a job. He also likes to string them out so they can work off their drug debt by doing small favors if you know what I mean. "Gina rolled her eyes at the disgusting notion. Jim continued. "He's been busted a few times, once for pimping out young girls. Usually, they're the young daughters of the mothers he pimps because they're so strung out and in debt that they don't care. Looks like the mother had been working for him for a while."

Gina replied. "Doesn't surprise me. Her rich bastard of a husband made sure she hardly got anything from the divorce. Even claimed that Audra and Josh weren't his kids because the mother screwed around throughout their marriage. "

"Was that true?"

"Who knows, but he had a really good lawyer and she got fucked in the divorce."

Jim rolled his eyes. He had been through that before, receiving the ass end of his own divorce settlement. "Do you know how to get in contact with their father?"

"No, last I heard, he moved to France with his new young trophy wife."

"Well, we need to get in touch with him."

Gina nodded in agreement. She replied. "Look, I understand that, but it can wait until tomorrow. I have to go tell Audra and Josh that their mother is dead. Fuck! How am I going to do that?" Gina walked away and back inside her apartment. She said. "Audra, I have an update."

Audra looked scared. Somehow, she already knew the answer, but responded. "She's dead, isn't she?" The look on Gina's face told her that it was true. Audra started crying again and this time, she couldn't stop.

10

Jim got to the office early. Yeah, it had been a long night for him and Gina. More so for her, but he cared about her. And maybe he was starting to fall for her. The best thing he could do was be there for her...be there for anything thing she might need. He could at the very least be a friend or a shoulder to cry on. Jim hadn't gotten much sleep after typing up a report for the task force. When everybody arrived, he passed it out to everyone.

As everybody looked over it, Jim said. "This is the beginning of our profile of the killer. This is what we are looking for. I'm sure, we will add more to it, but for right now this is where we begin."

Steve replied. "You make it sound like we are looking for some kind of religious nut committing vengeance on people."

Jim smirked at the comment. "Not a religious nut, but somebody deeply religious or has a religious education. Most likely, they're Catholic. This case is filled with a lot of symbolism so know that we are dealing with somebody highly educated and a religious education would give them knowledge about symbols. But we are probably looking for someone that knows how to be invisible and stalks their prey. We are also looking for someone between 35 and 48 years of age that's also in pretty good shape. They're strong and wouldn't need help moving a body. These are just some guidelines on the type of person we are looking for. Use them. "

Detective Ron Jackson walked up to Jim and said. "I think I found a connection between Don Bennett and Jack Perry. I still need to check on some things, but it looks solid."

Jim smiled. "Okay, do what you need to do and make a report. You can present it later. Detective Green and I are going to run down a lead of our own." Ron nodded in agreement. Maisie overheard what Jim had said. He hadn't said anything to her so it was only natural that she'd be curious.

Maisie walked over and asked. "What are we checking out?"

"I got a copy of that missing person's report that Amy Henderson's sister filed. We're gonna go talk to her."

"Oh, I thought I would just call her."

"No, this one we do face to face...we have to find Amy Henderson...right now and we need to know more about her."

"What if we can't find her?"

Jim smiled. "Then she becomes our number one suspect and every cop in Texas will be looking for her."

Normally the detectives might have waited until she got home from work, but she was a realtor and had flexible hours. They found out that she was showing a house in Richardson, just north of Dallas and, drove to the location. Jim and Maisie were nice enough to not disturb her while she was with her clients. But as soon theas clients were gone, they walked into the house. The sister's name was Jackie Henderson. She went back to using her maiden name after her divorce.

As the detectives walked in, Jackie said. "If you're here to look at the house, help yourself to some coffee and a Danish."

Jim replied. "We are not here to look at the house...we're detectives and wanted to talk to you about your sister Amy." Jackie got scared. Were they here to deliver bad news, news that she had been waiting for, for almost a year? She replied. "Please tell me, you found her alive."

Jim replied in a calm tone to try and reassure her. "We're not here for that...but we do want to talk about the missing person's report."

A sad look washed over her face. It was still tough to think about her sister being missing, especially since the last time talking to each other, they had a fight. She said. "What do you want to know?"

Maisie replied. "You filed the report nine months ago, but when was the last time you actually talked to her because you didn't file the report immediately, correct?"

"No, I waited a few months. We fought the last time we talked, just a little over a year ago. I wanted to give her some space, but after a couple of months, I called and when I didn't hear from her, I started looking for her."

Jim asked. "So, you looked for a month before filing the report...why?"

"I thought I could find her on my own and didn't want to make an official report. It would have embarrassed her and she would have been even angrier with me."

Jim nodded, letting her know that he understands her reasons. He asked. "What did you fight about?"

"Which time?"

"The last time you talked, but it sounds like you fought a lot."

Jackie shook her head, not wanting to believe that they fought a lot, but maybe they did. Maybe it was her fault why she disappeared, but she answered him the best she knew how. "We fought about her lifestyle and the things she was doing."

Maisie asked. "What do you mean?"

"There's something you need to understand about Amy. After she was raped by that son of a bitch, Don Bennett, for the next eight years, she was constantly fighting depression. She was in an out of Psych Clinics. It would get so bad that she wouldn't move from her bed for days, not even to eat or use the bathroom. Her husband left her and got full custody of their daughter. The settlement money didn't mean anything to her, and it wasn't even a huge payday. She couldn't handle the fact that no charges were ever brought against him. Then one day it all changed. she started doing things that most people would consider crazy..."

Jim interrupted, a habit he had never quite been able to break. "What do you mean, crazy?"

Jackie gave him a weird look. She was beginning to think, he didn't believe her and was probably exaggerating. "It started with a new workout routine. Not only did she get in shape like a pro athlete, but she started doing kickboxing, martial arts and then eventually MMA fighting. Even did some amateur MMA fights. And I know that doesn't sound that crazy, but then she started learning how to use different kinds of weapons... she learned how to shoot and got a concealed handgun license. "

Maisie replied. "That's not uncommon in Texas, even for women."

"It was for her. Our father tried to teach us how to shoot a gun; she never took to it. She pretty much hated guns, so I thought it was strange when she learned how to shoot. But what really bothered me was when she started training with one of these local militias."

Jim's curiosity piqued. "Militia...you mean like the Republic of Texas?"

Jackie chuckled. "No, it wasn't them, it was one of those what they call patriot groups ...in fact patriots was part of their name."

"Republic of Texas Patriots?"

"Yeah...you know the group."

"Unfortunately, I do...they're the most militant group in Texas." Maisie gave Jim a weird look as if she didn't know who they were. He responded. "They consider themselves the protectors of Texas values...they still think Texas should be a republic and they had quite a few standoffs with the federal government over issues like eminent domain. They like to patrol the border and arrest illegal immigrants. And they've shot a few causing a lot of controversy. You will always know their members by the Texas Flag armbands they wear and the assault rifle hanging over their shoulders. Let's just say that the ATF is always watching them. I've certainly had my run-ins with them."

Maisie replied. "Shit...are they trying to start a revolution or something?"

Jackie replied before Jim could comment. "Who knows...all I know is they're crazy and my sister got involved with them for a little while. For about a year, she trained like she was in the army and her politics changed. She was always fairly moderate to Liberal, but when she got involved with this group, she became so far to the right that it was nuts. I don't know if she believed in liberating Texas, but she would talk about liberating women from the bondage of men as she put it....she thought no woman should be married or have to take a man's name. She wanted marriage to be abolished and really championed women's rights, especially abortion. It was like she became a conservative feminist."

Jim laughed. "Is that even a thing?"

Jackie smiled. I know, right! Anyway, after her husband left her and got sole custody of their daughter, she changed. I was glad she put her life back together, but she went overboard. "

"What did you guys fight about the last time you talked?"

Jackie's eyes welled up at the thought. Of course, she loved her sister, but she could be infuriating which leads to fights. At the end of the day, she missed Amy and just wanted her back. She replied to Jim's question. "We had an incident at a family cookout...she brought her gun and was showing my kids how to use it. Didn't even take the bullets out. Said, a good parent should get their kids prepared. My kids were 7 and 8."

"Prepared for what?"

"I don't know...I guess anything. "

Maisie thought about the strange comment Amy made to her sister and then gave her two cents. "To not be a victim...you should prepare your children to not be victims like she was. I think that's why she started training the way she did... she won't be a victim anymore and wants to show others to do the same."

Jackie nodded at her. "Yeah...I can see that. Anyway, it scared the hell out of me when she did that... my kids were way too young for that. I couldn't have her around my kids anymore and I told her that she couldn't come around anymore if she had her guns on her and her knife. She also gave my six-year-old daughter a pocketknife...I mean who does that.?Amy cursed at me and said that I was a bad mother. I told her she couldn't come around anymore after that."

Jim was curious about something. "Why did she choose MMA? Most women would choose, either kickboxing, martial arts, or just plain old boxing. MMA is pretty extreme."

Jackie, agreeing with Jim, laughed a little bit at the notion. "You know, that's what I thought. Even I tried kickboxing once, after a huge breakup. I would put the guy's picture on the heavy bag so I could kick his face, but I never tried anything so extreme. To answer your question, she met someone in this therapy group she used to go to for people who had traumatic events in their lives. They became friends and she got Amy into it because she had just started doing it. It was something they could do together."

"Do you remember this person's name?"

"I think her name is Gwen…met her once, years ago, but that was it."

Maisie asked. "Dallas PD obviously hasn't found anything…looking at the file, they haven't found one lead except that her car was sold in Nebraska, did you by chance hire a Private Investigator?"

Jackie walked over to her purse and pulled a business card out it. She handed it to Maisie. "I did. Actually, this is his card. The only thing he found was a plane ticket purchased on her credit card about eight months ago then the card was quickly canceled."

"What was the destination?"

"Oregon."

Jim replied. "Sounds like she's trying to get off the grid. I wonder if she even got on the plane, maybe we are just meant to think she did." Jim looked at the cross necklace around Jackie's neck. It stood out. He asked her. "Was Amy very religious?"

Jackie replied. "She grew out of it and then went back to it after she was raped. I think she only did it as a way to cope, but after a while when it didn't seem to help, she lost interest."

"What is your religion?"

Jackie touched the cross around her neck. "We were raised Catholic. Even went to a private Catholic School from Middle School through High School."

Jim looked at Maisie, wowed by Jackie's answer. Still looking at Maisie, he replied to Jack. "Really, that's interesting."

Jackie said with a surprised tone. "Why is that?"

"No particular reason." He got one of his business cards out of his wallet and gave it to Jackie. "If you actually hear from Amy or the PI, you hired, finds something new, we would appreciate a call….its urgent that we talk to her."

The detectives walked out of the house and headed over to their car. As they were getting in, Jim looked at Maisie and asked. "So what do you think?"

She smiled. "Oh, I like this one."

"This is a good suspect…a very good suspect, in fact, but it's just one of many."

"I guess your job is to rain on my parade," she said sarcastically."

He smiled. "No, only to keep you from bending the narrative and staying objective. We still have a lot of research." And he was right. There were still too many suspects. They had only begun to scratch the service in narrowing down who could be the killer. Or if there might be more than one!

Detective Ron Jackson greeted Jim and Maisie when they got back to the task force office. He was excited. He had found something, a connection between two of the victims. Ron was like the smart kid in class who couldn't wait to show off and give the right answer. He didn't even say hi to them, just simply said. "I found something big…Don Bennett and Jack Perry knew each other."

Jim replied. "Okay, that's interesting…how did they know each other?"

As they walked into the room, Ron grabbed two files. He showed them to the detectives and replied. "Jack Perry was a campaign donor in each of Bennett's elections and not small amounts. He was behind a PAC for him."

Jim responded. "That doesn't necessarily mean they knew each other."

"True, but Perry had more than a fundraiser for the Senator down at one of his estates in West Texas, there's more than one photo of them together at these fundraisers, having a drink together. Looks like they were friends."

"Okay. You got me there."

Ron smiled. But this is where it gets interesting. That so called rape party that Jack Perry was accused of being at with his associates so they could scare the women out of their homes. One witness says a man fitting Don Bennett's description was there."

Maisie, who had been listening, rolled her eyes and replied. "What! Any other confirmed witnesses to that fact?"

Ron looked at her. "No…she didn't even make a positive ID, she said that the man looked like one of the men in Jack Perry's photos of him and the Senator. When the police were interviewing all the women who were assaulted, they were showing them photos of Perry with some of his friends or associates and trying to get Positive IDIDsThe woman said one of the men was Bennett, but she was the only one."

Jim asked. "Where is this woman now?"

"Unfortunately, dead…she died a drug overdose a few months ago. Might have been trying to kill herself because according to the police report, she had battled depression since her assault and had been on a lot of anti-depressants since it happened."

"So, a witness placed the senator at the crime scene, but now's she's dead…I see the connection between the two victims, but without her, we can't link him to that crime, which doesn't matter anyway. Still doesn't answer the question on how she was targeted and by whom."

"Maybe, I can't answer the *who*," Ron replied back. "But maybe I can the *how*. I was thinking, how did the killer get inside the houses, so I started looking at the security systems, maybe the killer knew how to bypass them? Both were state of the art and both properties were done by the same company."

Jim was taken back. "Really! What's the name of the company?"

"Highland Security Systems."

"Aren't they the largest security company in the State of Texas?"

"Yes, and it may be coincidence, but maybe that's what the killer wants us to think so I checked out the movie producer's house…his security system was upgraded by Highland a few months before he was killed. Three victims…they were killed at their homes…all three had security systems by the same company…that can't be just coincidence."

Jim looked at Maisie. She wanted to say something about the use of the trunk in getting into the houses, but Jim stopped her. He replied to Ron. "That's a hell of a connection…good work detective."

He smiled. "Thank You, I'm not done investigating, we still need to see if anybody connected to the victims works there."

"Yeah, but also check the relatives of the women who accused these men of sexual assault. Maybe we get lucky and find a husband who wanted revenge and then decided to become a serial killer. However, the key is finding a connection between an employee of Highland and one of the female victims."

Ron nodded in agreement. Maisie asked Jim. "Why didn't say anything about the trunk or let me do it."

Jim smiled. "Not yet…I want to see if he's on to something before we start sharing theories. I mean, he did find a big connection and we could be completely wrong. I just want to continue to investigate and see where both of these paths lead us."

11

Gina poured herself another glass of wine. It had been a long day. She hadn't been to work since Audra and Josh's mother had died and she had to take them in. Gina had spent the last two days cleaning her place, especially the extra bedroom, trying to make it livable for the two kids she had to take care of now. Gina stood in the doorway and just watched Audra make the bed and organize it as if it was her own. She felt like a mother watching her daughter fix up her new room after a big move. Gina had bought a bunk bed the day before so the kids could share the room for the time being. It wasn't ideal, but it would work for now.

There was a knock at her door. It was Jim and he brought dinner. A lot of her friends had helped out with food and stuff, but she was happier to see him more than them. Gina was okay with just a one-night stand, but she started to really like him. She felt a connection with Jim…something that she had not felt in a long time. Jim brought good old fashioned barbecue sausage and brisket with all the fixings. He kissed her and asked. "How are you doing it?"

Gina smiled. "Numb, but better than I was."

"What about the kids?"

"Hard to tell. Josh stays in his own little world either playing games on his table or watching movies. I guess it's his way of coping with everything." Josh was sitting on the couch watching a Star Wars movie.

Jim chuckled. "I guess there's worse things he could be doing?"

"True?"

"What about Audra?"

They both looked in the bedroom as Audra was till organizing things. She was a neat freak. Loved everything in the proper order. Gina replied. "She's a tough girl. I haven't seen her cry since that night and even then, she did a good job fighting back the tears. I don't know if it's really hit her yet. Or she is just being brave for her little brother, which I suspect she has had to do all of his life."

Jim replied. "Audra is probably more resilient than her own mother gave her credit for. She will have her moments of grief. The best thing you can do is just be there for her. Let her know that she is loved…that she has a friend."

"It's all I know how to do because I don't know how to be a mother."

"Did you get a hold of their father?"

Gina took a big gulp of wine. "Yes, I did… he's a fucking asshole. I see why his ex-wife hated him. He's in Europe with his young girlfriend. Supposedly he's working over there and won't be back to the states for a while."

Jim was stunned. "What…he's not coming back for his kids?"

"No! In fact, part of the ongoing battle, he had with his ex-wife, was getting a paternity test. He claims that the kids aren't his because she cheated on him a lot and wasn't on birth control or used protection. And until the issue can be solved, he's not claiming responsibility for them anymore."

"Wow, what a fucking dick. A perfect excuse to run out on your kids and the worst part is with him being out of the country, we can't enforce his duties as a parent. However, I do think they are better off with you. Better to be with a good friend than a shitty father."

Gina smiled, then she kissed Jim. "I don't disagree." The two of them set her small dining room table that was just big enough for an apartment. It comfortably seated four, but no more than that. Gina asked Jim. "So how is your investigation going?"

Jim replied. "We have a few leads. One of them even fits the profile of a potential killer; the problem is she's been missing for almost a year."

Gina replied. "Really...you think she's running."

"Don't know that for sure, but it certainly looks like she doesn't want to be found. Right now, she's just a person of interest. That's all we have to go on."

"I hope you find her...sounds like she just might be your killer."

Jim nodded. "We have a long way to go before we can prove that, but we'll see." Jim finished taking out the boxes of food from the bag and setting them on the dinner table." He said. "I also have some other news and you're not going to like it."

"Oh, more bad news...it seems to be the trend the past few days."

Jim laughed. "The guy you beat up, which I'm still impressed with by the way. He's getting out of jail."

"What, why?"

"He was arrested for assault and since the witness is dead, the DA's office can't prosecute so they have to let him go."

"That's fucking bullshit. She's dead, can't they hold him for that."

"No, because she injected the drugs herself that caused her death... unless there's evidence that he injected the drugs into her, there's nothing the police or DA can do. They can build a case, but they can't hold him without evidence. They have to let him go...it's the law."

Gina gave him a dirty look. "It's a fucking stupid law and you know it."

Jim shook his head at the comment. "Even the scum of the earth have constitutional rights, that's what great about the constitution...everybody is protected by it."

Trying to crack a smile, she replied. "I know, but its still horseshit."

"I agree. However, I did find out that Dallas PD will be investigating her death and seeing if they can link him to it. They might be able to get him on second-degree murder or even manslaughter."

Her halfhearted attempt at smiling didn't work, she was just too angry. Gina poured herself another glass of wine and called the kids to the dinner table. Maybe just having a nice dinner would help her get over everything, she thought to herself. It was worth a shot, at least. The kids had met Jim before and didn't seem to mind him so that was something, she told herself. Gina knew that they weren't really a family, but if only for the night, pretending to be, made them forget all the bad shit going on in their lives, then it was worth it. The thought finally brought a smile to her face.

Jim was getting to the task force office later than usual. He had to make a stop, first thing in the morning. It was the only time he could meet with the Private investigator hired to find Amy Henderson. The PI office was on the south side of Dallas in the Oak Cliff Area of the Metroplex. It was a dainty office that didn't look as if it was occupied by a professional business, but when Jim walked in, he saw where most of the money went. There was a great deal of equipment used for investigation, expensive equipment by the looks of it.

The investigator's name was Tom Graves. He looked as if he had been doing it for a while and didn't have much to show for it. Jim could tell he spent most nights at the office sleeping on the old shaggy couch that was clearly made in the 1970's. But Graves had a good reputation and sometimes that's all you needed to keep the doors open. When Jim walked in the office, Graves was trying to make coffee on the old beat-up coffee machine in his office that hadn't made a decent cup of coffee in twenty years. He saw Jim and said. "You must be the Detective I was told would stop by."

"Yes, sir, Detective Jim Summers."

"And you want to know what we have found on Amy Henderson."

"Yes."

"Yeah, her sister called and said to help you if I could. Normally, I don't share information with the police, unless they share with me and they never like to share."

Jim laughed. "Most of the time that's true."

"I don't suppose you can tell me what this is about?"

"All I can say is that she is a person of interest in a crime."

Graves gave Jim a dirty look. "You mean she's a suspect."

"Person of interest for right now."

Graves laughed. "Yeah…she's a suspect."

"Look, I really need to talk to her, can you help me?"

"Depends…is there a reward for her. Because if there is and I help find her, it's mine, I mean, I do have a business to run."

Jim shot back a dirty look. Dicks always ask about the money first. He replied. "If there happens to be a reward, I'll put your name down for it. So, what do you have on her?"

Graves pulled out a folder with the Amy Henderson's name on it. "Not much I'm afraid. I pretty much followed the money; I looked at her transactions… standard stuff."

"And?"

"She sold her Condo about a year ago. She didn't owe anything on it and got $175,000 for it. And then she withdraws it all from her bank account and then closed the bank account."

Jim thought it was strange. "Okay, that's a bit odd."

"Yeah, normally banks frown upon that thing, most small Chase Bank Branches don't have that much cash on hand… she had to go to the Main Branch in downtown Dallas. Then she got a re-loadable Green Dot Visa Card and loaded $140,000 on it…that popped on my radar because the company thought it was fraud and reported it. Took ten days to clear."

"Did she make a purchase with the Card?"

"Nope."

"Really?"

Graves laughed. "I know sounds strange, right! But it's just been sitting on the card for almost a year."

Jim paused for a moment, trying to think of scenarios where she would use a reloadable VISA card with $140,000 on it. "What do you think she's waiting for?"

"It's my experience that people who use re-loadable cards, can't get a bank account or don't want to. Plus, they're always trying to hide something, and they never think reloadable debit cards are traceable, but if it's a transaction made with a credit or debit card, we can always find it. Cash is the only true currency that can't be tracked unless it's in large denominations."

"And what do you think she's hiding…what's your theory?"

Graves smiled. "I think she's going off the grid. She did get involved with that survivalist group and I think she's moving somewhere where those kinds of groups thrive."

"Seriously!"

"Yeah. Here's something else. It's the last contact I have from her. She bought a car in Colorado a month after she closed her bank account and put the money on the re-loadable card. She paid cash for it, but because she bought it at a dealership, she had to register the car and put her name on the title."

Jim thought it was peculiar, if she was trying to go off the grid, then buying a car at a dealership was a big mistake. Or was it misdirection? Was she still in Texas just to kill the man who had harmed her so long ago? There were still too many questions. But he responded. "Sounds like she's moving west, someplace remote. I doubt Colorado was her final destination or she at least wants us to think she's not in Texas."

"You think it is misdirection, but it was almost a year and there's no telling where she's ended up if she went off the grid."

"Meaning she could have come back to Texas. For example, I know she sold her car in Lincoln, Nebraska and then bought a plane ticket to Oregon… why buy a car in Colorado if you're flying to Oregon that's only one way?"

"I think when people are looking for you and you're trying to go off the grid so no one can find you then everything you do is misdirection."

"Exactly. So, the truth is, no one really knows where she's at, which also means she could be back in Texas."

"Is that what you're hoping for?"

Jim got up out of the seat in front of Graves' Desk. "Right now, I just need to find her. Do you have any other leads?"

"Afraid not…she's a ghost."

"Are you still getting money from her sister?"

Graves gave him a dirty look. "It's an ongoing investigation…you know how it is. I'm not doing anything illegal."

"Maybe just unethical, but I'm not here to bust you on it, however, I have a favor to ask."

Graves, still giving him a dirty look replied. "Sure, I'm all about helping the police."

"If you get any new information about her, I'm your first phone call, but that also means, you need to still be looking for her instead of just sitting on your ass extorting money from a client."

Graves shook his head. "That's not what I do, sometimes the leads dry up and the trail goes cold, but it's my experience that people always turn up. You can't get off the grid completely. She'll pop up somewhere."

Jim tried to crack a smile. "Try and find out something more for me this week if you can. It would be greatly appreciated."

The young girl sat in the corner of her room shaking. She didn't want to think about what was going on in the next room. It's not like the intruder was mean to her, all they did was tell her stay in her room and not come out until given permission. But still, there was an intruder in the house, a stranger that she didn't know anything about. Of course, it was scary for a ten year old. It was the screams that frightened her the most, but even the silence from the other room scared her. All she wanted to do was go to school…for it to be a normal day without her father bothering her. School was her safe place. Unlike most kids her age, she loved being at school. Everything made sense when she was at school and it was no surprise that she was a great student, well mannered, and liked by teachers and fellow students. It was very different from her home life.

In the next room a man was laid out on the bed in the shape of a cross. In fact, his hands and feet were nailed to the foot and headboard of the bed. He was still unconscious as the mysterious person, dressed all in black and wearing a thin ski mask stood over him. All that could be seen was the person's eyes. It was time to wake him up. He was given smelling salts and quickly snapped back into consciousness. It took a few moments to full register what was going on, but the pain from being nailed down rushed to his head and he started screaming. The girl in the next room heard the screams and started crying.

The person standing over slapped the man in the face a few times and said. "Shut up…your screams are not going to help you."

He was frightened and tried to stop, but the pain was too much. The person injected him with morphine… a lot of it. He got an instant high from it and calmed down for the most part. He tried to move, but the nails were too strong, and it just caused more pain. The person standing over the bed said to him. "I need you calm so you understand me. I have given you some pain killers, but they will only last for a little while."

He replied. "Who the fuck are you?"

"I'm your reckoning. You've been a very, very bad man and you have the chance to be forgiven."

Still scared, he replied. "What did I do?"

"You know what you did; you know what you've been doing probably since she was a toddler."

A pale sheet washed over his face. His worst fears had come true. Somebody knew what he was. He tried to make some excuse, but the other person in the mask cut him off. "Don't tell me you didn't do anything…I can see it on your face that you did and you know that I know the truth about what you are, you child molesting mother fucker. She is your daughter… not your plaything."

Through the pain that shot through his hands and feet, and the fear resting in the pit of his stomach, he somehow managed to reply back. "Don't kill me, I'll stop. I will get help."

"You tried that before, Joe, and you quit the therapy. You should be a registered sex offender by now, but then you were never convicted on two separate occasions when your wife reported you. And then you disappeared with your daughter so you can continue with your evil ways. You don't sound like someone that wants to stop."

The tears started flowing from his eyes. "I promise, I will do better this time."

"I know you want to think that, but we both know that's not true. You know that you will just keep doing it. "

He tried to scream this time. The mystery person stuffed a gag down his throat to shut him up. "That wasn't cool. You're not showing me that you want to live." He was crying like a little girl who had just scraped her knee on the playground. The person standing over the bed responded. "If I take the gag out, are you going to scream?"

Joe shook his head, no. The masked person wasn't sure whether to believe him or not but took the chance anyway. The gag was pulled out. "Now, you understand that you have to be punished for that." He was scared but didn't try to argue. He just hoped that the punishment wasn't too severe. He wasn't completely naked, lying on the bed. He still had his underwear on. They were pulled halfway down his legs. A hunter's knife was placed underneath the shaft and the scrotum, and with one swoosh, his genitals were cut off. He started to scream again. The pain was excruciating and that's when the gag was put back in his mouth.

The other person replied. "I know it hurts, but in order to find a reckoning, we have to endure a little pain or sometimes…a lot of it! Now, do you believe in forgiveness?"

Joe tried to say something, but the pain was too much. He nodded, yes. The other person replied. "Good, because even though you have to be punished for your sins, you can also be forgiven, if you truly want to before you die..." Joe heard that word and started to struggle. The masked person held him still and said. "Stop it. You will die someday, could be today, could be tomorrow, but what's important is that you seek forgiveness for the bad things you've done so when death comes for you, your soul is ready."

The masked person looked over at his left side right below the chest. It was slowly bleeding out. Joe saw it too and started to cry. The masked person said. "You don't have much time before you bleed out. When I'm done, I will call an ambulance and we will let God decide if you live or die today, but only after you ask for forgiveness, and we perform the ritual. "

For the next few minutes, Joe's daughter didn't hear anything. She kept her head down the whole time hoping that it was all a bad dream, but then she saw the sun peeking through her window, so she looked up. The masked person was standing over her while the sunlight covered their eyes. The daughter started to cry and then heard the person say. "It's over, you're free...he won't bother you ever again."

The daughter was relieved in a way, but still scared of the mysterious individual dressed all in black and wearing a mask. She wanted to say something...anything, but the words just weren't there. The other person handed the girl, her father's cheap prepaid cell phone...it wasn't even a smart phone and then said. "Call 911 and tell them to hurry because your father is dying. " The girl should have been more scared when she heard the part about her father dying, but there was a calmness that fell over her. Somehow, she knew everything would be okay, now. Even when she walked into her father's bedroom and saw him on the bed, nailed to the head and footboard, blood running down the side of the bed. He made no sound. The girl knew he was dead, and it didn't bother her one bit. She wasn't afraid anymore. Once upon a time, she was always afraid, but not anymore.

12

Jim went straight to the task force office after his meeting with the private investigator. More and more, Amy Henderson was starting to look like the killer. She had the motive and from what he could tell, the skill set. Maybe she didn't fit the religious profile, but everything about her said she was capable of killing someone. However, it was Detective James Cross who would throw a wrinkle in that idea and make the others rethink their working profile of the killer.

Detective Cross was waiting for Jim at his desk when he walked in. He had a stack of files for him. Jim was amused and even replied. "Cross, you look like you're about to give me a pile of homework."

Detective Cross laughed. "Could be. If nothing else, you won't be short of reading material on the can. I found 12 murders over the last ten years that might fit the profile of your killer. Not as elaborate as the three murders that you think are linked, but they were staged so to speak, and each murder has something in common."

Jim was certainly intrigued. Nobody else has found anything matching the killer's MO. He responded. "What do they have in common?"

"People who were accused of a crime, but not convicted. They all got away with it. Now, not all of these cases involved men who were accused of sexual assault, but they were all what I call crimes against humanity. You can read through them and see what I am talking about."

"Do you think our killer could have done all of these murders?"

Detective Cross shook his head. "Probably not. Take the one that is my personal favorite, what they called the *Dinner Party Murders*. A former CEO of a Bottle Water company was poisoned along with his wife at a dinner party with some of the Investors and Board Members, Everybody died right there at the table and then the killer staged it with each of them, holding a bottle of the companies water."

Jim sat back in his chair and replied. "I remember that murder. Only one person was arrested, but never convicted. Police concluded that it was done by members of an environmental group who had accused the company of using materials to help clean the water which made people sick to the point that it was life-threatening."

"That's right and the CEO had been accused of covering up the findings so they couldn't be sued. They even had a whistleblower who mysteriously ended up dead. Anyway, I threw this one in there because of the way it was staged. Probably isn't the killer...that was a murder with a political statement and our killer doesn't strike me as someone who cares for such things.
"

Jim laughed. "That's a good observation and I agree. It occurs to me that after thirty years on the job, you've probably seen a lot of strange shit!"

Detective Cross laughed. "You have no idea. I've learned that most murders are committed over love or money. I've seen more than one guy kill his wife and the man she was having an affair with, and then stage it like it's some kind Romeo and Juliet suicide pact."

"Really, more than one guy."

"Yeah, believe it or not...that MO is popular when it comes to crimes of passion."

"I guess men and women do some pretty fucked up things when it comes to murder as if the act itself wasn't fucked up to begin with"

Detective Cross laughed. "You got that right. My personal favorite was the wife who had killed three husbands, all for the insurance money. Not very original, but she claimed that she had been abused in each of the marriages and that it was self-defense. The first one she buried in the backyard and then had a pool put over the spot. I guess if its self-defense there's no need to call the police and you're allowed to bury the body how you see fit or so she thought. The last one she shot with his hunting rifle, but again, claiming self-defense, said he grabbed the frying pan she was using to cook their dinner and came after her with it. But the funny thing is, she never bothered to dump the food out when putting it in his hands as he was laying on the ground, bleeding to death. I guess he never thought the food would go flying out of the pan when swinging and trying to hit another person."

Jim laughed. "She didn't really think the physics out on that one, did she?"

Boisterously laughing, Cross replied. "No, she didn't, but it just proves that people do a million stupid things when they commit murder and never realize it. You just got to find what they are so you can catch them. It's no different for our killer even if we can't see what they did wrong."

"Well, the killer has been perfect. No physical evidence at the crime scenes. Nothing that points to a definite suspect so all we have are theories that are hard to prove."

Cross took a sip of his coffee. "I have a theory for what it's worth. We are looking for murders that fit a certain MO, right…but what if that's a waste of time."

"What do you mean?"

"Maybe it's not about other murders that can be connected to this killer. Perhaps it's about these three murders. They're very deliberate and there's a message behind them. I think the killer doesn't care if we find anybody else, they want us to know why these three people were killed.

Jim was taken aback by the very notion. It was very interesting, and he even said something to that effect. Detective Cross continued. "The religious aspects behind Don Bennett's murder, got me thinking. I was reminded of something my mother said to me when I was kid. She was Catholic."

Jim was surprised by the last statement. "Really, you don't strike me as someone who is Catholic."

Cross laughed. "Oh, I'm not... I was raised Methodist. My mother was a Catholic and even though she converted when she married my father, she still went to Mass every once in a while, at a local parish not too far from us. There was a priest from there who did a couple of years in jail for fraud and got excommunicated. You see, he was a gambling addict and stole church funds to support his habit. Claimed that he was trying to raise money for the church, if you can believe that. Anyway, he got clean and when he got out, started a homeless shelter, which mostly catered to battered women. Turned it into one of the largest shelters in that city. My mother even volunteered there and when I asked her why, she said that even though a Priest might get kicked out of the church, he doesn't stop being a priest or a man of God. No matter how far they fall, that part of them will always remain."

Jim replied. "I've never been very religious, but I can see that about so-called men of god...by nature, we are what we are and that never goes away.

"Think about it...once a priest, always a priest, so maybe that's what we are looking for?"

"A priest...an actual priest?"

"No...someone who probably used to be one and considers this doing the work of God."

Jim cracked a little smile at the thought. It wasn't a bad assumption. Jim replied, "An excommunicated priest sadistically killing sinners in the name of God...well, I have seen stranger things."

Cross smiled back. "Like I said, it's just a theory, but if it was me, I would try and find out how many former priests live here. Catholic Churches should have records. "

"It's a good idea."

Cross took another sip of coffee. "Also, even if it's not some former priest, it's still someone who's devout. I bet they go to Mass or Confession, at least a few times a week. Either way they go to church a lot. If you stake out Catholic churches, you'll see the people who go a lot. I bet we would find someone who fits our profile and who could possibly be a killer. I know you have a suspect in mind, but it doesn't hurt to look at other possibilities."

Jim thought about it for a moment. "I don't disagree, but that's also a lot of manpower. I don't know if I could get that okayed."

Detective Cross nodded. "I understand…it's not easy being the head cop and being expected to solve the impossible without enough resources to do the job, but good cops always find a way."

Jim laughed. "Is that your idea of a pep talk…coach!"

Sarcastically, Cross replied. "Sure…that's what old guys like me are here for." And then he walked back to his desk and went back to work. He didn't have any more advice… just simple truths based on his own experience as a homicide detective for twenty years and in Texas of all places, which was its own special category of hell.

As had been their custom since the task force was put together, Jim and Maisie stayed late, going through old cases and trying to narrow down their suspect list. Even thought they had someone they both liked for the murders, it was far from certain and like good investigators they would exhaust every possibility before narrowing in on their main suspect. Jim had been staring at the same file for the past half hour. Maisie looked up and asked. "Have you found anything? You've stared at the same file for a while."

He smiled. "Not really, I just think this particular case is interesting…The Dinner Party Murders."

"I remember that case. Police concluded that it was environmental terrorism because the bottled water made people sick. You don't think it's connected to our serial killer?"

"No…not the same MO. But it was a staged murder and that's why it ended up in Detective Cross' pile."

Before Maisie could say anything, a visitor walked in. It was the Plano Medical Examiner, Dr. Vanessa O'Connor. And she brought dinner. Smiling, while looking at the two detectives, she said to them. "I figured you'd be working late and might need some dinner so I brought Chinese Food."

Jim returned the smile. "This is a pleasant surprise, what brings you to downtown Dallas. It wasn't just to bring us dinner."

"No, I was curious. This case has intrigued me ever since we talked. Just wanted to know what you had found and if I could help." Jim took the food from her hands and thanked her. Maisie was curious about the woman. She didn't necessarily like the idea of strangers walking into the task force office. So, Jim introduced them and told her about their previous conversation and how she also had a background in Criminal Psychology. Maisie was less suspicious of her now and replied to her. "Ah, you're the one who figured out that the wings were fairy wings!"

Vanessa smiled. "Yes...the benefits of a Catholic Education mixed with being taught Celtic Mythology by my Irish Father."

Maisie laughed at her sarcastic comment. "That was a good catch. I don't think anybody around here would have gotten that." Vanessa smiled back. Jim was getting out the food and seeing if there were still some paper plates left from the last time the task force ordered take-out when Vanessa walked over to their investigation board. She looked it over and seemed to be impressed with the clues that they had cobbled together so far. But there was one particular item that stoked her curiosity. She looked at Jim and Maisie and asked. "The Sin Eater...who came up with that?"

Jim nodded in Maisie's direction. Vanessa looked at her and replied. "Really, how did you come up with that one?"

Maisie finished a bite of her egg roll. "It was just something that I thought of after discussing the religious aspects of the killer's MO. We know the killer is punishing them, but what if, it's more than that. What if they're trying to absolve the victims of their sins."

Vanessa smiled. "Interesting!"

"Well, like you pointed out to Jim, if a Fairy is considered a fallen angel or anti angel, if you will, still doing the work of God, then what's the opposite of a priest who can absolve you of sin...."

Vanessa finished Maisie's sentence. "A Sin Eater, because they don't have the same rights as a Priest when it comes to absolving sins, but they still do it anyway... it's the union of opposites philosophy."

"Exactly. That's what I was thinking too. I remembered something about it in a philosophy course I had to take."

"Good theory, but why the show? Why stage the murder if you're going to punish them and then absolve them of their sins?"

Maisie shrugged. "That I can't figure out unless I'm dead wrong about the Sin Eater aspect and the killer is just punishing the victims for the sake of punishing them. "

Vanessa replied. "I don't think you necessarily wrong about killer thinking they're a type of Sin Eater...it's a good theory. But as investigators, you always have to figure out the "why" in order to find their true motive."

Jim finished his bite of food and replied. "Ego...the 'why' is ego. It's about killing these men and punishing them...the killer thinks they're the only one who can deliver justice. The only reason to make a show of it is because of their ego."

Maisie replied. "What if it's meant to be a warning?"

"That could be true. But I'm curious about something...a Sin Eater performs a ritual, right?"

It was Vanessa who responded first. "Yes, while it may be a little different in certain countries...the purpose is the same. The Sin Eater places a piece of bread or bread-like substance on the body of the person they are performing the ritual on. It symbolizes the body of Christ. Then they will usually take a few sips of wine to represent the blood of Christ. The other person is supposed to confess their sins and then the Sin Eater eats the bread, therefore eating the sins that have been confessed. The Sin Eater's job to take the sin away and they do it by eating the body of Christ, which as you know was sinful when he walked this earth and didn't become pure again until he rose from the dead and ascended to heaven."

Jim replied. "So, the Sin Eater performs communion on the victim? I thought it's the victim who eats the bread to consume the sin."

Vanessa laughed. "Yes, and No…the Sin Eater is supposed to be the one consuming the sin on behalf of the person confessing, but it's not unheard for the confesso to eat the bread as well similar to communion. Each Sin Eater performs the ritual differently. The whole ritual is supposed to cleanse the person of their sins by eating the sin. And in some cases, they will pour wine over the bread and person's body to symbolize it being washed in the blood of Christ. "

"Interesting!"

"It's a very Celtic ritual, but also has its roots in paganism." Vanessa chuckled. "Then again, a lot of Christian traditions come from pagan traditions."

Okay, the reason I ask the question, the murders seemed ritualistic and from what you're telling me that's true. If we go with Maisie's theory that the killer is trying to absolve the victims of their sins, then maybe the murder itself is some weird version of a crucifixion where you also have to die to truly be absolved of your sin… and for justice to be served. Jesus had to die so he could rise again and be transformed, right? I might be grasping at straws here,"

Vanessa smiled. "What you're saying is, everything about the murder is a ritual."

"Yeah. I mean, even the victim's side was pierced with a sword so the victim would bleed out just like Christ did on the cross if I remember correctly from when I was in Sunday School."

Vanessa smiled at the astute observation. "You're not wrong."

"Good. Now it brings me to something interesting that Detective Cross said. Even if a priest were to be kicked out of the church, they are still a priest at heart. You don't stop being a priest just because they tell you, you can't be one. Is it possible that we are looking for an excommunicated priest still doing God's work?"

Both Maisie and Vanessa were taken back by the theory. None of them had even considered that. It seemed unfathomable. Whoever heard of something that crazy? But then again, it was unthinkable at the time that Jack Ripper could be an educated man...even a gentleman as some have suggested. However, all things are possible when it comes to murder. Vanessa replied. "That's quite a theory. I think it's unlikely, but you ask if it's possible...yeah...it's possible."

Jim tried to crack a smile but responded in kind. "I don't like the idea. I mean the last thing we need in Texas is a psychopathic priest killing people."

Maisie Replied. "Sure, but it would be worse if he was a Baptist." They all laughed at the notion; after all, she wasn't necessarily wrong. But then a thought hit Vanessa...an idea that nobody had come up with yet. She spoke up. "Why has no one suggested that the killer could be a woman?" Maisie was stunned, not at the notion, but that she had not suggested it first. She replied. "Yeah, why hasn't anyone suggested that....is it possible that the men I work with can't fathom that our killer could be a woman?

Jim gave her a dirty look. He didn't consider himself a sexist, but then again, most men don't. However, he didn't like the implication from two people he respected that he was a sexist and he himself couldn't believe the killer was a woman. "Look, before you get all bent out of shape, I'm not saying that isn't possible the killer can be a woman. Anything is possible short of aliens committing these murders. But is it likely, no?"

Both women shot him a dirty look, but it was Vanessa who asked the obvious question. "And why not, give me one good reason, why a woman couldn't commit these murders?"

Jim shook his head. "First, a woman could do it because she has the ability to do it...I say that so there is no misunderstanding with my words. However, it's unlikely because the statistics don't support it. Most serial killers are male, between the ages of 35 to 50, fit enough to be able to move bodies over 200 lbs. They're patient, they're meticulous, and usually have families. And they were probably abused as a child and came from a broken home."

"And where are you getting these statistics?"

Jim smiled. "These are FBI statistics, of course. Even here in the State of Texas that's what we go by."

Maisie replied. "And you think those stats can't apply to a woman?"

Jim shook his head. "I'm not going to debate this... of course, they can, but I'm talking about what's most likely. It's probably a man committing these murders. And let's not forget, there is no evidence to support that a woman committed these murders."

"But we have a female suspect unless she's magically been ruled out!"

"True, but she's only linked to one murder." Maisie, not liking his answer, gave Jim another dirty look. He responded. "Let me give you one more fact and this one is the most important one. There has never been a female serial killer in Texas."

Vanessa sarcastically replied. "One that's never been caught. To think that there hasn't been one in Texas is a little naïve and narrow-minded."

Maisie replied before Jim could say anything. "That's not completely true. What about Genene Jones, the nurse who murdered all those kids in the early 80s? She's a serial killer."

Vanessa replied. "Oh yeah...I forgot about her...she's still in prison, right? They never executed her."

Jim replied to her statement. "It's true, she is still in Jail, but she's not classified as a serial killer. A murderer, yes, but not a serial killer."

Maisie asked. "Why do you say that?"

"According to the FBI classifications on killers, she doesn't fit the criteria. Jones wasn't actually trying to kill the children, it wasn't premeditated...she poisoned them so she could revive them. They were accidental deaths resulting from her assault upon the kids. Also, here's an interesting fact, when she was evaluated by a psychiatrist, she was diagnosed with a form of Munchausen Syndrome by Proxy..."

Maisie interrupted. "Are you talking about the attention disease where a parent will intentionally make their kids sick so they can make them better?"

"Yes, and why she wasn't a parent. They say she took on the same characteristics which is why it's only a form of the disease."

"Many believe that it's not real because it's so rare and finding actual people with the disease is impossible."

Jim cracked a smile. "That may be true. The other issue regarding Genene Jones is the State of Texas doesn't have different degrees of murder…it's all one capital crime. But by federal standards, it would have only been second-degree murder, which doesn't carry the death penalty. Serial Killers commit first-degree murder because of the premeditated and planned method of the murder. And that's why she isn't classified as a serial killer. So, Texas has never had a genuine female serial killer." Vanessa gave Jim a dirty look and so he corrected his statement. "Sorry…a female serial killer that has ever been caught. So, before we actually say that it's a woman who committed these murders, we better have concrete evidence, or the notion won't even be considered."

Vanessa asked. "Are you afraid that you will be laughed out CID for suggesting that this serial killer could be a woman."

Jim laughed. "I don't give a shit about appearances as long as I am right. They can laugh all they want, but if my superiors are going to take me serious then yes, I have to have concrete evidence and if we don't, then it doesn't matter what I suggest."

Vanessa shook her head in disbelief. "The men in this state drive me nuts. You can't even take the good ole boy attitude out of honest police work."

Jim nodded. "It's a sad fact, but true. However, not all of us are like that. I for one, consider all possibilities when identifying a killer."

Maisie replied. "That's good to know, but where do we go from here….looking through old cases and ruling out victims that these men harassed or assaulted is one thing, but how to we find the killer?"

Jim sat back in his chair and took another bite of noodles. "We know a few things for certain. The killer is religiously devout, probably Catholic, and a creature of habit."

"What do you mean?"

"They would go to church on a regular basis and being Catholic, they would go mass, probably a few times a week or perhaps confession, right! My point is, they would be seen at church regularly."

Maisie gave him a curious look. "What are you saying, we start staking out Catholic Churches."

"Yes."

"Really!"

"Yes, I'm dead serious and we start with the ones in the Metroplex, maybe the killer's devotion to God gives us a break in this case? That could be how we catch our killer."

Both women looked at Jim with satisfaction. They couldn't argue with his logic. Perhaps he was right, even, a killer who was religious wouldn't lose their devotion to God, especially if they thought what they were doing was justified. Even the Bible had some justification for murder with the notion of "eye for eye." But with most religiously devout people, they still seek God's permission for their actions and that's what Detective Jim Summers was counting on.

13

There was a loud knock at the door. Gina was expecting it, but not for another twenty minutes. The social worker was early for her routine visit, but Gina suspected that's what they liked to do in order to catch foster families by surprise and see how they were with the children in their care. Gina wasn't frazzled by this…her apartment had been clean for hours and the kids never caused problems. In fact, they were both getting their homework done so they could actually have fun this weekend. Most kids in their situation would probably act up or rebel as a way of dealing with the grief of a parent dying.

Gina let the social worker and said. "Hi, Rhonda…you're early."

Rhonda smiled. "We like to do that to catch you off guard."

"I figured… but I've been ready for a while."

Rhonda looked around at the clean apartment and the kids sitting at the small dining room table, doing their homework. "I see that. Well, let's get to it." She looked around the apartment, especially the extra bedroom to make sure it was habitable. Rhonda had certainly seen worse, and this was far from a trailer park, which she always hated going to. It didn't take long to inspect the place. Everything seemed fine. Next was the Interview. That was short because it had only been the first week. Gina was allowed to slide on a few things, but all in all she had done more than expected, considering how quickly everything had happened. Normally, social services would have placed the kids with a more experienced family, but this was an unusual circumstance.

Finally, Rhonda and Gina had a chance to talk outside of the typical caseworker interview. Gina walked with Rhonda to her car and asked. "I know you're responsible and having been friends with Audra and Josh, there wouldn't really be a problem with you fostering them for the time being. But how are they really doing."

Gina kind of laughed. "I guess we're all putting up a pretty good front, but truth be told, Audra is one tough girl. I think she's had her moments of grief, but even more glad to have a more normal situation if that makes sense."

"It does. After having looked at the file on her mother and all the shit she was into, I can see that about Audra. What about Josh?"

"I think he traps himself in his own little world as a way to shield him from everything. That's why I think he hasn't really grieved and like his sister, glad for something normal."

Rhonda smiled. "That makes sense, but we do want both of them to see a psychologist who specializes in grief counseling. It will be good for them and I would like to get their assessment on the kids. Just routine."

"I understand. Probably be good for them."

"I set up an appointment for next week."

Rhonda was about to get in her car when Gina stopped her. "There's something I want to ask…it may be too soon to ask, but I made up my mind."

"What is it?"

"What do I need to do to adopt Audra and Josh?"

Rhonda was surprised by the question. Most folks just wanted to foster kids so they could get the check from the state. This was different. She replied. "Are you sure. Fostering is easier and you can keep them for years with the State of Texas' help?"

Gina cracked a little smile at the notion. She knew some folks only did it for the money, but she didn't want to be one of those people. They deserved more than that after everything they had been through. Gina replied. "I know, but adoption is the best option, they need stability and not having to fear that they will be dumped off on someone else."

"I don't disagree with you, but this is a big step. Are you absolutely sure?"

Gina smiled. That was the one thing she was sure of these days. She wanted to take care of those two kids. She responded with joy. "Yes…absolutely sure."

Rhonda smiled back. "Good…this will make things easier on everybody, but there are a few things you are going to have to do to be approved. The first thing is you have to get a bigger place. A two-bedroom apartment won't cut it. You need at least three bedrooms since it's a brother and sister, you are considering adopting."

"I can find a bigger place that's affordable."

"Within the next 30 days?"

Shocked at the time frame, Gina replied. "I guess if I have to."

That will be the most important thing, right now. The rest, we can work on. So, I will follow up next week, with the next step."

Gina was happy to hear that. It was better than hearing, no. She didn't know why she did, but she gave Rhonda a hug. It might have seemed strange, but Rhonda didn't mind. It was comforting and that's what Gina needed as she was about to take this huge step. It wasn't just about her anymore now.

The room was packed with cops. Trying to cram everybody in the Task Force Office was a bad idea, Jim thought to himself, but he had asked for manpower. And he got it. The room was wall to wall with cops, some who were just patrol cops and some who were detectives, all of them from different cities in the metroplex. Jim was going through some paperwork while they waited for him to speak. Finally, he asked everybody in the room to look at him.

Jim spoke. "Thank you for showing up today. All of you have been assigned to this task force for some extra duty, which means you will get some overtime. I know you weren't given a few details on the assignment so let me tell you the full story. We are doing a mass stakeout of all the Catholic Churches in Dallas/Ft. Worth. We are looking for a killer, one who is deeply religious and probably goes to a Catholic Church a few times a week. You were given a memo with details on our profile of the killer. This is the person who killed the former Senator, Don Bennett. Now, this killer might be connected to some other murders, but we are focusing on the Don Bennett murder. Before anybody asks, no, you won't be making any arrests. We don't know what the killer looks like. However, we are looking for a pattern. We are looking for any person that attends these churches at least three times a week, whether it be for mass, confession, or just stopping by and saying a prayer."

One of the cops in the room spoke up. "Are we supposed to identify these people?"

Jim nodded at him. "I was just getting to that. You will be taking pictures or video. We capture an image of everybody who goes in and out just like an old fashion stakeout. Then we catalog everything by days and match the pictures to anybody who is going to church more than three times a week. And finally, we get their names and start doing background checks. Hopefully, we can narrow it down and find someone who fits our profile."

Another cop replied. "Sounds like a lot of work and could take a while, how do you know this killer hasn't left town or won't leave town while we're looking."

Jim replied back. "We don't know, but this is what we have to go on when it comes to find the killer. And as for it taking a while, this is why we have more manpower. Our goal is to find possible suspects in the next couple of weeks. However, included with your memo is a picture of Amy Henderson, she is our prime suspect right now and has been missing for almost a year. I want all of you to look out for her. You can read more about her in the memo, but she was the first victim Don Bennett was accused of sexually assaulting and the only one to win a civil suit against him. If she is spotted at one of these churches, you are to call for backup and then detain her. Do not arrest her…only detain her. She is wanted for questioning."

Another police officer spoke up with a condescending tone. "So, you think, the killer might be a woman?" Pretty much all the male cops snickered and silently jeered at the notion. Maisie who happened to be standing in the back near Jim shot the officer a dirty look. How dare he belittle the idea that a woman could be a serial killer in Texas she thought! Jim paused for a moment, collecting his words so he could fully be understood.

Jim responded. "For you guys out there, let me be very clear. Both men and women are suspects. I know most of you guys don't believe a woman could do something like this, I mean we've never had a female serial in Texas. And to be honest, I thought that too in the beginning, but we don't rule out the possibility no matter how implausible you think it is. You have to take pictures of both men and women."

The same police officer replied. "So, she's an actual suspect."

Jim was annoyed by the question. "Yes…a legitimate suspect." They hadn't actually said Amy Henderson was a suspect, but there was no denying it at this point. She was the main suspect for now and a small part of Jim hoped that she was in Dallas and they could catch her. It would make things easier. Jim continued. "If I find that any of you didn't take pictures of men and women, then you will be off this assignment quick. Detective Cross will be handing out schedules, which will include the location of your stakeout and who you will be paired with. That's all for now."

The other officers started to file out of the room as soon as they got their schedules. Maisie walked over to Jim with a file. It was the full report on the Don Bennett crime scene. As she handed it to Jim, she said. "According to CSU's report, they found breadcrumbs underneath the dining room table. Nobody thought anything about it because it was a place where people eat and it's natural to find food crumbs underneath it."

That sparked Jim's curiosity. He replied. "Looks like your theory was right, but what kind of bread did they find?"

"What do you mean?"

"Was it leavened or unleavened bread?"

"I still don't understand the question."

"Did it have a rising yeast agent or leavened bread? Was it a flatbread or unleavened like a communion wafer?"

She was surprised by the question, but responded. "Oh, not exactly for sure, why?"

"If it's unleavened or the killer used a communion like wafer, there's only so many places that would sell something like that so maybe we can track them down that way. It may be a long shot, but it's worth looking into."

Maisie thought for a moment. "Do you know how you would go about making unleavened bread? What I mean is most people buy bread making kits and use a breadmaker so…"

Jim cut her off before she could finish her last sentence. "You're thinking if there is a kit for unleavened bread, then maybe we find the places that sell it and try to track who's buying it because it's probably not a popular item."

Maisie smiled. "Exactly!"

"Okay, it's worth looking into. I would think only places like a Whole Foods, or a Central Market would sell something like that, any natural food store really."

"I will do that."

Jim looked up from the forms he was having to sign asking for more manpower. A task force always brought more paperwork. It was the worst part of the job, especially for Jim because it seemed he spent half of his time filling out forms. It took away too much time…time he could be spending catching bad guys. He used to complain when he first got to CID, but he learned quickly that those complaints always fell on deaf ears with his superiors. But unlike some of the folks he worked with, he never got used to it.

He looked at Maisie and said. "I've got some bad news for you. I won't be with you tonight…I've got a thing."

She replied. "Oh, that's okay; I can play nice with others. Who am I with?"

"Detective Jackson."

Her good mood quickly disappeared like the winds of West Texas. She said. "Why…am I being punished for something?"

"No...not at all. Detective Cross had something going on with his youngest daughter that just leaves you and Jackson who's not paired off."

Maisie still had a look of shock while waiting for Jim to say he was joking. She expected to be some kind of prank...the kind of thing that cops often pull on one another. But that was not the case. She didn't like Detective Jackson and found him to be annoying. He reminded her of the same simple good ol'boys she had grown up with that only had a narrow-minded point of view and rarely could be objective. Maisie liked to think she could play well with any fellow cop, but some just rubbed her the wrong way. Detective Jackson definitely fit the bill.

Jim responded to her look of disappointment. "I'm sorry, it's just for the night."

"It better be just for the night, and I can't guarantee there won't be a little drinking on the job."

Jim laughed. "Well, don't do that. He's not worth getting in trouble over. I will make it up to you by paying for our dinner tomorrow night."

She laughed as she rolled her eyes at him. "It's the least you can do. And I mean that." Jim always found her wit amusing. It made working with her easy.

Later that night Maisie and Ron Jackson got assigned to St. Thomas Aquinas Catholic Church. Maisie had only been there once but knew the area since she didn't live that far away. Ron Jackson has never been to a Catholic church in his life. He had been raised Baptist and still thought Catholics were filled with a lot of old-world superstition. It was fair to say that he just didn't understand Catholics, but even worse, he didn't want to try and understand. They arrived about forty minutes before six o'clock mass and started taking pictures of the people going inside. They tried to get as many face pics as possible.

Detective Jackson thought the assignment was stupid. Mostly because he had his own theory about the killer. He asked Maisie, who hadn't said a word to him since they greeted each other right before they got into the car. "Do you really buy that the killer would go to church?"

She gave him a strange look and replied. "Yeah, I do. I helped come up with the theory."

He was a little shocked. "Really!"

"Yes."

"Okay…I can see we're not going to agree on anything."

Maisie shook her head. "You apparently think this is a bad idea…why?"

Detective Jackson took a couple of more photos. "I've never met a killer that went to church. Christians don't usually murder people."

She chuckled. "You think Christians are perfect?"

"Not perfect, but certainly not murderous psychopaths."

"Does that go for Ku Klux Klan members who would lynch black people because they thought it was the Christian thing to do since God only cares about white people. They still went to church didn't they. Or about the idiots that bomb abortion clinics and kill doctors who perform abortions because they think God commanded them to do it."

Ron gave her a dirty look. "Those aren't real Christians. And they shouldn't be called a Christian."

"The killer isn't one either, but they think they are. And that's the point."

"What is?"

She smiled. "By trying to understand the way the killer thinks, then we can catch them. This killer would go to church."

"We don't know that for sure?"

"That's why we call it a theory Detective Jackson."

He laughed at her sarcastic comment. "Yes, I know the definition of the word theory, but let me ask you this. If it's really an ex-priest doing the killing because they think they're doing

God's work, wouldn't they stay away from a church because they can't cross the threshold of a church as a sinner?"

Maisie was stunned by the comment. It was insightful. She may not agree with it, but she marveled at the fact that Detective Jackson could have that kind of insight. She replied. "Let me understand this, you think that a killer ex-priest wouldn't' be able to walk into a church because their purity has been tainted too much that they can't cross the threshold of the church."

"Yeah...don't you?"

"I think that it's an interesting theory, but they would also have to know that what they're doing is wrong. And I don't think they believe what they're doing is wrong... the killer thinks their actions are justified by God."

Detective Jackson reflected. "Let's say you're right, with all these people going in and out, how do we tell who could be a killer? It's not like an ex-priest is wearing a sign that says I'm an ex-priest.

Maisie laughed. "True. But we're looking for a self-righteous type. Someone who thinks they are morally superior to others and have a breaking point."

"What do you mean?

"The kind of person who could be pushed to violence if they thought it was the right thing to do based on their moral code...no matter how misguided it could be. An ex-priest could fit the bill."

He didn't disagree with her assessment. No argument could be made that she was wrong, it was a good theory. He responded. "In that case, we should check the backgrounds of our potential suspects. Chances are the killer would have had some violent incidents in their past... either they would have been the cause of those incidents or just involved somehow. Either way, violence is in their past...enough to cause a breaking point as you so put it."

She was amazed again at his assessment. He was right. Maybe he wasn't so dumb after all? And she commented on that fact. "And here I thought you were some dumbass redneck who couldn't figure out an MO to save his life."

He smiled at her sarcasm. Some might be offended by her comments, but it didn't bother him...he had been called worse. He said. "Who says I'm not, then again, I have my moments."

Maisie laughed. "However, just because I agree with you doesn't mean I like you."

Again, not offended by her insult he said. "That's okay...we don't have to like each other to get the job done." Damn Right!" It was the most honest thing he had ever said since meeting her the week before.

Jim hadn't seen his sister for a while. It was hard when he lived in Austin and she lived in Dallas especially when he was working all the time. When a case brought him to Dallas, he always tried to at least grab lunch with her, but this case, was one of the most time-consuming cases that he'd ever had. Finally, he got some time, but more than that, he needed something from her. And with her being an FBI agent in Dallas, right now she was the best person who could help. Instead of lunch, they met up for a drink at a local Irish Pub in Dallas that seemed a little out of place in that particular city, but it had the best collection of Whiskey in the city. A love of whiskey was something they had in common. Something that they both got from their father. He got there first and ordered a 12-year Macallan Scotch.

Finally, his sister Hannah showed up. She looked at her brother and didn't say "hi," instead, sarcastically she responded. "What, you didn't get me a scotch! Fucking asshole!"

"You can get one yourself...you can afford it on your government salary...I hear you're getting raises anyway."

She smiled. "Only if congress approves them. But you know those fucking democrats...they don't want government employees to have raises, they will vote to increase welfare benefits for every fucking illegal immigrant."

He gave her a dirty look. He never considered himself political, but he always got annoyed at his sister's comments about how only one side was to blame for everything. However, he loved her anyway. So, he ordered herself a scotch.

Hannah said to her brother. "So, saw you on TV, I get why you haven't seen me until now. Pretty big case you're working."

Jim rolled his eyes at his sister's understatement. "Yeah, you can say that?"

The bartender poured Hanna's scotch in front of her. She asked her brother. "Have any leads?"

"A few, but mostly just theories." He pulled out of his jacket pocket a copy of the profile memo that he handed out to Taskforce explaining what they were looking for when it came to suspects and gave it to Hannah. She looked through it and then commented. "Wow, you have one dark and twisted killer here. So, it's not just about torture, it's religious in nature?"

"Yes, we're pretty sure it is and one of the working theories is that it might be an ex-priest or even a former minister that's performing the murders."

Hannah took a sip of her scotch. "Not a bad theory."

"We also have another one. And that's where I need your help."

She gave him a dirty look. It wasn't the first time he took advantage of her being an FBI agent and having access to more extensive databases. Laughing, she replied. "I knew this wasn't just a social call."

"It is...I do want to know how you are, but I also need your help."

She couldn't help but be amused at the situation. Her brother always did this because the way he saw it, social calls could also be a good opportunity to get something from family and make it harder for them to say no. It was Jim's way of killing two birds with one stone. Hannah would get annoyed by his actions, however, he was her brother and she loved him. She would end up helping him anyway.

Hannah responded. "You know you're paying for my drinks tonight because you're asking for help."

Jim laughed. "I was already planning on it."

Hannah ordered another scotch. "Okay...how can the FBI help you?

"It's not like that."

"Of course, it is...you've never asked for my help unless you needed FBI resources."

"I've asked for your help before that didn't involve the FBI."

Hannah laughed. "No, you haven't. You're too much like Dad, you never ask a woman for help unless you absolutely have to or you really need something from them."

Jim was caught off guard by the comment. Their father was a typical Texas good ole boy, a misogynist prick who thought women were second class citizens and never asked for their help unless they couldn't do it themselves. Both of them never really got along with their father. And for Jim, being compared to the man was a bit of an insult. He replied to his sister. "Yeah, I don't think I've ever been that bad, but say what you want. I still need your help. Can I have it without you harassing me?"

She laughed. "No, because harassing you is half the fun. But I will still help you if I can."

He could never be mad when his siblings harassed him, at least he had family that did that. Jim certainly knew people who didn't have that in their lives. He said. "Thank You. What I need is help finding someone... a woman who has gone off the grid." Jim told her the backstory on Amy Henderson, everything they knew so far. It piqued Hannah's curiosity. She asked him. "Is she your prime suspect?"

"Right now, we are just treating her as a person of interest, but she sure as hell seems like the type of person who could brutally kill these men."

Hannah chuckled. "Just because she has become one of these survivalist types, doesn't mean she graduated to murder. I mean, according to the FBI criteria for serial killers, it's always the least suspecting that become sociopaths. They're good fathers or mothers, go to church, pay their bills, and are usually involved in their community."

"I know, hence why she is only a person of interest. I don't know for sure if she really is cable of killing these men, that's why

I need to talk to her. I need to get a sense of who she is and let my instincts give me an answer."

Hannah nodded in agreement. "You do have good instincts…always did. But if she has gone off the grid then it makes it near impossible to find her."

"I understand that, but I figure if she hooked with some patriot group, maybe she's under surveillance. Maybe the feds actually know where she's at."

"It's a possibility, but even if she is, the FBI or Homeland Security team watching her isn't going to blow their cover so you can talk to her."

"I know, but if I know where she's at then I bump into her accidentally and say that I'm a private investigator her family hired to find her, maybe that's a good way of talking to her without tipping off she's being watched by the Feds."

Hannah took another sip of scotch and pondered her brother's plan. "It's a risky move. If I find out where she is for you, they are going to want to know why. Then, if you show up asking questions, especially with one of the groups that are already over suspicious of the government, it can easily tip off the people she's running with. That gets both of us in trouble and I shouldn't have to remind you that when it comes to crimes on the federal level compared to ones in Texas, the FBI will let her do whatever she wants in Texas just to get her and her group on more serious federal charges."

Jim rolled his eyes. He knew what he was really asking. It was a huge favor. Homegrown terrorists were always considered more serious than murderers in Texas despite the brutal nature of these crimes. He replied. "I get it, but I need to find her."

"Okay, but let me also explain something to you. If the feds find her and link her to the murders because if she was found across state lines, they can take over the investigation and I know you don't want that."

Jim shook his head "no." He replied. "Yeah, I figured, but it's still worth the risk."

"Really."

"Yeah. We've ruled out most of the potential suspects, but we don't have anybody that would be considered a prime suspect.

She's the last one on my list and to be honest, at the rate we are going this could turn into a cold case sooner, rather than later and that I definitely don't want to happen."

Hannah smiled back at her brother. "Alright, I had at least warned you of the risk of what you're asking,"

"I know and I appreciate it."

Hannah finished her second scotch. "Okay, I will make some phone calls and see what I can find out." They each had one more round and spent the rest of the time catching up instead of talking business. It was good to catch up. It had been longer than before, since they last talked and a lot of had happened in their lives. Jim even told her about his divorce and the fact that he had met someone, here in Dallas. Hannah actually liked hearing about his relationships, mostly because she loved giving him advice. She was a good FBI agent, but she was even better at giving him relationship advice. It was annoying at times, but in the end, it always made him laugh. That's how it could be with brothers and sisters.

14

Gina got home early. She had only worked a half day. She wanted to be home when Audra and Josh got home from school. It was a big day. She had big news. Life-changing news. Gina was nervous and rightly so. She had never thought about doing something like this until Audra and Josh came along. Hell, she had never thought about having kids at all. Her career had always come first, and she had never really made room for kids. Wanting to adopt two kids was a big deal. Gina was happy to do it, that she was sure of, but would Audra and Josh want her to adopt the?!

She got their favorite kind of pizza for dinner. They had weird tastes. Josh liked just pineapple and cheese. Audra liked the barbecue chicken-style pizza. Gina wasn't sure if you could really call it pizza, but the one thing they could all agree on was that a big chocolate chip cookie with icing was out of this world. She got one of those too with soda. It wasn't exactly healthy, but it tasted wonderful and she wanted the kids to feel good while discussing the adoption. Finally, the bus dropped them off. Josh and Audra both had keys to the apartment now so as they walked in they found the small dining room table spread out with pizza and pieces of the big cookie as if they were having a party. Both were surprised. It wasn't a special day that they knew of, but both kids had the biggest smiles on their faces when they saw everything.

They pigged out, almost to the point that they nearly all got sick. But it felt good. Gina ate more pizza than she usually did, way beyond her calorie limit since she was always watching her weight. She still had that actress mentality, even though she hadn't appeared in so much as a commercial in a few years. Josh let out a huge burp that even the neighbors could hear, which made everybody laugh. Finally, Audra asked. "What's the occasion… is there something going on." Gina smiled at her intuition. Audra was smart and definitely wasn't fooled easily.

Gina replied. "While I just wanted to be nice since it's been a big adjustment staying with me after your mom passed… there is something I want to talk to you about. Something important."

Audra replied. "It's about our dad; he's not coming back to America, right?"

Gina laughed to herself. She was always amazed how nothing ever really got past Audra. Somehow, she always knew what was going on. She could see Audra in the future, getting herself into trouble for being too smart for her own good, in a good way of course. But it was also a source of pride taking care of someone who might be too smart for their own good. Gina replied. "I promised that I won't lie to you, and I certainly won't do it now. Your father isn't coming back." Audra knew it, but it still felt nauseating to hear it out loud. Gina continued. "The truth is he doesn't think he's your real father because apparently, your mother cheated on him throughout the marriage?"

Audra asked. "Is that true?"

"I don't know, a DNA test would give you a conclusive answer, but he won't take one.

"Why?" Tears started to well up in her eyes. Gina paused for a moment and put her hand on Audra's hand to try and comfort her. She replied. "The only thing I know for sure is he just doesn't want you and probably never did. I wish there was a nicer way of saying it, but it's the truth." Josh had a horrified look now on his face. Hearing that didn't sit well with him, after all, he was still just a boy who wanted a father.

Gina wanted them to know the truth and she also wanted to be reassuring…god knows both kids could use some reassurance these days. She didn't know if she could come up with the right words to make the kids feel better at that point. Most of the time, the truth hurts. Gina said to Audra and Josh. "It doesn't matter if he wants you…someone who doesn't want you shouldn't get to be a parent. So, what if he doesn't want you, it doesn't mean you're not loved. I'm here and I'm not going anywhere. And that's why I want to adopt you."

Audra was stunned but happy to hear the news she had always felt a kinship with Gina. She liked staying with her and didn't want to leave. Audra replied. "Really, like getting full custody of us?"

Gina smiled. "Yes, that's usually how adoption works." Smiles started to return to Audra and Josh's faces. Gina continued. "I want to adopt you…not just be a foster mother, but actually adopt you. If that's what you want."

Audra began to cry, but not because she was sad. This was the happiest news in she couldn't remember when. She replied. "I would like that." Then she looked at her brother and asked. "How about you?" Josh didn't say much, but when he did, it was usually profound, even if it was just a one-word answer. He replied. "Cool!"

Audra laughed at his comment. "That's all you have to say?"

"I like living here…I don't want to live anywhere else." That's all he had to say to show his approval. Audra and Gina smiled at the same; they were both happy to hear him say that. But Audra one more question. "If you adopt us, do we have to call you, mom?"

Gina was taken aback by the question. She hadn't really thought about it. Legally she would be their new mother, but a replacement mother at best. Gina tearfully replied. "You can call me anything you want. Truth is I can't replace your mother. Maybe all I can do is be a really good friend. However, I know that I can be your family and that's what I really want to do." The kids didn't say anything; they both got up and hugged her. Words weren't necessary this time. Gina became an instant friend the first time she met the kids, especially the first time they had to spend the night, to get away from their drunk and drug-addicted mother. But when they hugged each other, it was in this moment that they truly became a family, at least in Gina's mind.

The last two weeks had gone by quickly since the task force started staking out catholic churches. The list of potential suspects grew more than any of them could imagine. As Jim was putting photos of people who went to church three or more times a week, he even commented to Maisie. "I didn't realize Catholics in this city went to church so much! Baptists, I could see that…they live for church services."

Maisie smiled at the comment. "Church is church…it doesn't matter the religion if folks are super religious then go a lot. But if you think this is bad…nothing beats those who go to tent revivals. They go every day and happily hand over their money to con artists."

He chuckled. "You don't sound bitter at all. I guess you have some personal experience with this."

"Yeah, my mother was one of those people. We were mostly poor because she liked to give all of our money to churches, hoping to get some kind of salvation out of it. All it did was make our family more miserable."

Jim kept posting pictures on the huge bulletin boards they brought. By the time he was finished, they counted 878 photos, not including people who worked at the church. He was not happy and commented to that effect. "This is too many people to look at. It's going to take forever to get through the background checks…time we don't have."

Maisie replied. "Most of these are just housewives who don't have one violent bone in their body and probably have never committed a crime in their life. They should be easy to rule out."

Are we starting to make a list of names? "Yes. It took longer than expected because originally some of the cops were acting like they were getting names for a petition, but got accused of harassing people. Finally, after a couple of days, Detective

Cross suggested that they start taking down license plate numbers and running the plates to get their names."

Jim smiled. "That was a great idea."

"Yes, it is, but the problem is it's going to take weeks to do 878 background checks."

Jim sighed. She was right, it would take too long. There had to be a better way of narrowing down the list. He knew they had to check everybody out just in case, but only a handful was more important as suspects. He said. "Let's start with ones between 35 and 55. I doubt anyone older than that is our killer, but we'll check them out last."

"That will certainly make things easier. Also, one more thing. Finally got hold of directories from these churches going back fifteen years. "

Jim smiled at the good news…finally, a bit of luck, he thought. Government bureaucracy was bad, but the bureaucracy within a Catholic church was worst when it came to offering any information to the police. The church had become increasingly suspicious of law enforcement over the past few decades. Who could blame them when so many priests had been accused of sexual abuse and police were trying to prosecute. The church had a deep history of protecting their own and covering up whatever truth was necessary in order to do so. He asked her. "Did you have a chance to look through everything?"

Maisie replied. "I did. I found four ex-priests in Dallas."

Surprised, Jim responded. "Really and they're still living here now?"

"Not exactly! Two of them are dead. One of them is sixty-eight years old. But, the last one, he's the most interesting out of all them."

"Oh, why's that."

She showed Jim a police report and started to explain. "Father Daniel Merrick, age forty- three and excommunicated five years ago for assaulting a husband and father of three. Beat him so bad, it put him into a coma for a month. Police tried to get him on attempt of murder, but could only make felony assault stick. Father Merrick claimed that the dad was sexually abusing his two daughters and tried to help the mother leave him, but she stuck by her husband after the good priest showed up at their house and tried to play hero by getting them to leave. They wouldn't and he lost his temper and almost beat the guy to death. He ended up doing fourteen months in the Dallas County Jail. The church suspended him while he served his time but made it indefinite when he got out. I guess they didn't like the idea of a priest nearly killing a member of the church."

Jim replied. "Okay, now you piqued my interest. A history of violence with a sense of Justice…that fits our profile. I think we have a new prime suspect."

"You want to talk to him today?"

"I'd say he's our main priority. Do you have an address on the guy?"

"Yeah…he lives in McKinney and works as a counselor at rehab clinic and camp for at-risk youth up in that area."

Jim walked over to his desk and grabbed his coat hanging off the back of his chair. This was the first major lead they had since staking out churches and right now Father Merrick was a better lead than Amy Henderson. At least they knew where he was. Jim started to walk out the door and asked Maisie, "Are you coming?"

She was surprised. "We're going now?"

"Why not…no time like the present." He didn't want to waste any more time looking through photos when their killer could be just forty-five minutes away. He had spent too much time trying to solve these murders, anyway. Too many years wasted with nothing to show for it.

It was about midday as Maisie and Jim traveled the long stretch of highway up to McKinney, Texas Traffic wasn't that bad on Highway 75 except for a few construction spots. They made good time to the rehabilitation ranch. It was fairly new. Had only been open for a couple of years, but according to Google, got good reviews. Jim and Maisie arrived and found the main building. They asked for Daniel Merrick and were in luck. He had some free time since lunch had just started at the ranch. He usually ate his lunch outside, alone with a good book when the weather was nice. The woman at the front desk told the detectives where he would be and then found him on a bench beneath a tree near the cafeteria.

Jim said as they walked up to him with his eyes staring down at this large hardback that he was about halfway through. "Father Merrick…Daniel Merrick?"

Daniel looked up and replied. "Nobody has called me Father in a long time, but I am Daniel Merrick."

Jim pulled out his badge. "I'm Detective Jim Summers and this is Detective Maisie Green. We would like to talk to you, if that's alright?"

Daniel was a bit surprised to see two detectives. All they got at the ranch were juvenile police officers and usually only one at a time. He replied. "Sure, what's this about…one of my kids?"

"No, we wanted to talk about your days as a priest and what got you kicked out?"

His temper came through with his reaction. "Oh for fuck's sake. Why can't you people leave me alone about that shit…I did my time and the church kicked me out…end of story."

Maisie commented. "We struck a nerve, didn't we? I mean, you don't even know what we are going to ask. Do you often get this mad over a simple question?"

He gave her a dirty look. "Sure, I do, it's always the same story. One of the kids I'm counseling, complained to their parents, probably said I abused them in some way and the parents called the cops. And because I have a record, they send you guys out to harass me over some bullshit claim."

Jim replied. "Calm down, we're not here for that."

"Good, because until these kids stop blaming others like me, they are never going to get better. And this shit just gets old."

Jim chuckled. "I can imagine, but we have something more important to talk about."

"Oh, okay, what can I help you with?"

"Are you still religious, Father Merrick?"

The ex-priest gave him a strange look. "Well, first, you don't have to call me Father. Haven't been a priest in a long time. I'm just Daniel now. Second, I didn't quit believing in God just because the church won't have anything to do with me, but why do you ask?"

"I'm curious, how many times do you go to church a week?"

"Why do you care?"

Maisie responded. "We just want to know…it's a simple question."

Daniel paused for a moment, pondering the question and wondering whether he should answer it or not without a lawyer present. He did reply. "This feels like entrapment. Am I some kind of suspect?"

The detectives avoided the question, but Jim responded. "I promise this is not entrapment, but we still want to know how religious you are and how often you attend church?"

Daniel didn't want to answer, but he knew they wouldn't go away unless he played along and answered their questions. "I guess you're not going to tell me what this is about?"

"It's nothing bad, I assure you."

Sarcastically, he replied. "Why don't I believe you?"

Jim laughed. "It's true, we are investigating a crime and your name came up…"

Daniel interrupted. "As a potential offender because I have a record and a history of violence, right?"

"Yes."

"I guess I fall under a certain profile…right?"

"Unfortunately, for you…yes."

Daniel shook his head in disbelief. "You make one mistake and you're marked for life. You know, I'm not that violent, but sometimes I have a temper. I just lost my cool one time and didn't even realize what I was doing until it was too late. It's a poor excuse and you probably hear it a lot, but it's true, at least with me."

"We don't doubt that."

"Can I ask what you're investigating?"

"We can't tell you that at this time."

Daniel sarcastically smiled. "I guess I am a suspect then."

Maisie responded. "You're a person of interest. If you were a suspect, you'd be in handcuffs right now, if that makes you feel any better."

"It doesn't but thank you for trying to make me feel better. Sounds like you have some counseling experience, Detective Green." She nodded in agreement. Daniel continued. "I am still religious. I still believe in God, the same way I did before the church excommunicated me. And I try to go as often as I can. Maybe three or four times a week."

Jim with a surprised tone replied. "That's a lot."

"Compared to what, when I was a priest, and I went every day! Honestly, it's not enough, Detective… I wish I had the time to go more. I'm still a priest at heart; I'm still a man of God. The church can't take that away just because I don't wear the collar anymore…does that make sense, Detective!"

Jim looked over at Maisie acknowledging that they had heard that before. It wasn't just a coincidence. Jim replied. "I can understand that. Have you been in any fights or altercations since you got out of jail?"

Daniel took a deep breath. He was starting to get annoyed at the questions, but he continued to answer them anyway. "No, except for the times we have to get a little physical around her. Sometimes when kids first get here, they can be a little violent and we have to restrain them. But if you're asking, have I beaten the shit out of someone like before…no."

"Did you have any incidents before you got arrested or was it just a onetime deal?"

Daniel didn't answer for a moment. He asked a question of his own. "What is this really about?" But before the detectives could answer he said to Jim. "Wait a minute…I recognize you…you were on the news, not too long ago. You're the cop investigating that Senator's murder!"

Maisie responded before Jim could say anything. "That's true; we're part of the task force investigating his murder."

"So that's what this is really about. You think I had something to do with it because I'm here pretty much all the time and plenty of witnesses around that can testify to that."

Jim replied. "Calm down, father...sorry, Daniel. We are not accusing you of anything or you would already be in handcuffs. But you are a person of interest so we're going to ask you some questions. You can answer them here or at a police station."

Daniel shot an angry look his way. He didn't like the term, "person of interest" because it really just meant, suspect in his mind. He was jaded. He didn't trust cops just like any other criminal. And unfortunately, he had the experience of knowing how cops really operated when they zeroed in on a suspect. It was no surprise that he would get a little nervous. He replied. "Fine, continue to be intimidating, if it makes you feel better."

Jim laughed at his comment. "Do you think the Senator deserved to die?"

"Wow, you're really treading on my sensibilities as a former priest. I'm not God, it's not my job to judge whether a person deserves to die or not."

Maisie asked him. "Do you think he was a bad person? He did have a history of sexual assault on women."

Daniel sighed. He knew they were trying to trap him with his answers. "If he did all the things, he was accused of then yes, he was a bad person, but remember detective, we're all sinners."

"Sure, but we don't all go around raping women...unless you do...do you?"

He let out a chuckle. "Even if I did those things, what makes you think, I would confess my crimes to you?"

"Thank You."

"For what?"

"For really giving me a reason to investigate you. But then again, you were a priest... maybe little boys are your thing."

Anger boiled over with Daniel and it showed in his reply. "Fuck you Detective. I was a good priest except for one little indiscretion."

Maisie was going to say something, but Jim interrupted her. "Alright, enough...be polite...Father."

"You can ask your questions but take your bad cop bullshit and shove it. Not every priest is like that."

"We know that. Did you ever meet the Senator?"

"No."

"How did you feel when you heard what he was accused of?"

Daniel paused for a moment. He didn't answer the question; he had something else to say. "Now, I finally understand why you're talking to me."

"What do you mean?"

"I heard that the murder was ritualistic. If that's true, then there's some kind of religious symbolism behind the murder, which would make perfect sense why you're talking to me…I'm a priest with a history of assault. I make a good suspect."

Jim nodded in his direction. The former priest just figured it out and to Jim's way of thinking; he was too smart for his own good. Jim didn't like that about criminals. He replied. "That's a good assessment…how did you figure that one out?"

Daniel laughed. "I have a BA in Psychology from Boston College and a Master's in counseling. Did that before I became a priest. Put two and two together…it makes sense why you would talk to me."

Maisie responded. "Do you think you have the right to punish, what you call sinners if the law doesn't?"

"What you really want to know is if I'm capable of doing it and would I have any remorse?"

"Yes."

"I think every man is capable of violence if they are pushed to the right breaking point, but assault and murder are two different things. Besides, I don't have any connection to the senator and if you do a thorough enough investigation, you'll find that out." He got up from the bench he was sitting on. "If you're not arresting me, then I have to get back to work."

Jim replied. "We're not done talking with you. Where were you on the night of the 16th?"

Daniel turned around. "I understand you have more questions, but if you want to continue talking then it will be with my lawyer. However, I will answer one last question. The 16th was game night, I was here and at least a dozen people can verify that."

Jim and Maisie didn't say anything after that. What could they say, he "lawyered" up. Anything else would be breaking the law. Jim never minded bending it from time to time in order to catch a killer, but it was too early to play that card. Jim did comment. "You can go for now, but I'm sure we will be talking again soon."

Daniel didn't say anything. He simply smiled and started to walk off, but as someone who always loved to give advice, he had some for the detectives. He said to them. "I know you have your theories about what kind of person the killer might be. You have a working MO no doubt. That's why you think the killer is religious and if you truly believe that then you should know that there are three kinds of religious people."

Maisie sarcastically replied. "There are only three kinds…"

Daniel laughed. "Usually. The first kind isn't really religious. They use religion to have power over men and women. They can be cult leaders and politicians. "Jim and Maisie both laughed at the last part because it was very true in Texas. Daniel continued. "And make no mistake about it; there are a few priests who fit that description. The second kind is truly religious. They're devout in their beliefs even to the point that sometimes they can be blinded by their faith. But no matter what, everything they do is for the Glory of God so anything remotely evil isn't an option. The third kind is devout in their beliefs as well, but they don't have a problem doing anything evil for their beliefs. You see, these kinds of religious people justify their evil acts because they believe that what they're doing is so right that it doesn't matter if they have to do something wrong to make things right. Maybe they're even convinced that God commanded them to these things. They have empathy, but it's twisted and misguided. The DSM-V says they're sociopaths and maybe they are. But these people, they're the ones you need to truly be afraid of."

Jim asked. "Why?"

"Because they are willing to do anything for what they believe is right. And that's when people usually end up dead. I think that's the kind of religious person you're looking for." He paused for a moment, stared as the two detectives and then gave them an ominous warning that brought chills. "Be careful Detective, if you do find that person, you may not like the face you find." He paused and stared at each of the detectives for a moment. Then he said. "Ask yourself, are you truly prepared to see the face of the devil because it's just as seductive as it is scary and that's what you're going to find. You may not see what they're doing as all that wrong. And you may not be that scared at first because the devil can easily seduce you into believing in their cause but make no mistake… you should absolutely be scared. Daniel turned around, walked off, and never looked back. Maisie wanted to ask him some more questions, but Jim stopped her. They let him walk off. That was enough for now.

Maisie asked Jim as they were walking back to the car. "What do you think? Could be our killer?"

"My gut says no. That doesn't mean we shouldn't keep an eye on him, though. He seems too smart for his own good and I don't like suspects who are too smart for their own good. They either have a good alibi or know how to get rid of the evidence. True killers always fuck up somewhere."

Maisie thought the comment was funny and laughed. She couldn't really disagree. She did, however, reply. "You know, it's interesting what he said about different kinds of religious people, especially the third kind."

"I agree and it's easy to think about our killer is some kind of a psychopath without any kind of conscious, but the way this former priest describes them, which seems to fit with our profile, we actually have a religious sociopath on our hands. And I think that's worse."

"Why?"

"You know what you get with a psychopath, and it makes it easier just to put a bullet in their head! But with a religious sociopath, it's different…"

Maisie interrupted and finished his sentence. "It's about their beliefs and realizing that they may not be wrong. How do you catch someone that you may agree with?"

"Well, that's a moral conundrum that cops are not supposed to have and yet it happens with each one of us."

"Sure, I agree, but can you argue that the victims do deserve to die, they're sexual predators."

"We don't get to make those judgments."

"I know, but my point is, in order to catch a killer like this, we need to understand their belief system. We're trying to track this killer by the places we think they're going to be... maybe it's not about that. Maybe it's about whom they would target."

Jim replied. "In this case, sexual predators or deviants, but those who got away with it."

"Yeah, it may come down to actually catching them in the act if we can't find any physical evidence that connects them to the victims."

Jim paused for a moment, thinking about their next move. "Instead of staking out churches, we stake out potential victims that fit a certain pattern."

"And then we cross-reference it with our list of suspects...see if there are any connections."

Jim smiled. "It could work. We would essentially be making our own criminal database...it would take time, but maybe that's how we crack this case." They didn't say anything else for a little while, but Maisie kept thinking about something else the ex-priest said. She couldn't get it out of her mind. She said while they were driving back to the office. "Something else he said is bothering me."

Jim responded. "What?"

"He said that we should be afraid of this person. Do you think we should be afraid?"

"To be honest, I've never thought about criminals like that...I'm pretty simple, either you catch them if you can, or you kill them."

She laughed at his simplicity. She knew Jim was smart, but another part of him was still just a simple Texas Good Ole Boy playing cops and robbers. "You were the one that caught Billy Ray Petty, right?"

"Yes."

"He loved to cut people up while they were still alive. You weren't afraid he might catch you and do the same?"

"No. He was insane and like a rabid dog, sometimes, you just have to put them down. That's what I did. I knew he wouldn't go quietly if we caught him. The only thing I cared about was making sure that my aim was true." He had a serious look on his face. "Why are you asking me this?"

"It was eerie the way he said it. Almost like he was still a priest warning us of some kind of demon that could possess our soul if we keep looking."

"He was just being dramatic for the effect. I've never met a minister that didn't give into the theatrics when talking about God. I'm sure a priest or even an ex-priest is the same way."

"So, it doesn't bother you?"

Jim laughed. "Even if it turns out to be the devil herself…"

"Her?"

"The devil is her, also known as my ex-wife. But all kidding aside, even if our killer turns out to be the devil, they're just a criminal that we catch and put away, same as the rest."

"Except for the reasons why a killer does what they do. There's something very personal about these murders."

Jim paused for a moment searching for the right words. He understood what she was saying and didn't disagree with her theory. But he still was a cop with a single vision. His job was to catch a killer any way he could. But he did reply to Maisie's comment. "Their reasons don't really matter unless it helps us in some way to catch them. At the end of the day, they're just one more criminal we have to take off the streets. That's it."

Maisie shook her head, not at all agreeing with his assessment. She replied. "If you say so."

They got back to the office about an hour later. There was still more photos to go through from the stakeouts. It seemed as if they had only scratched the service with potential suspects that went to church at least a few times a week. There were more people than Jim had anticipated. So when they got back, he immediately went to his desk and started looking through more photos. Nothing looked out of the ordinary until he saw a familiar face among them there were three photos of Gina coming out of St. Thomas Aquinas Catholic Church.

15

Jim was excited to have dinner with Gina that night. He even looked forward to getting to know the kids more. It was a family dinner. Gina hadn't told him about adopting Audra and Josh, yet. But he was a cop with good instincts, he knew how much she cared about them, and that adoption was a real possibility for her. It was going to be a good night with dinner and games. Jim didn't want to spoil it, but the photos of her, to which he couldn't take his eyes off, bothered him. He simply couldn't let it go. Like an itch, there were too many questions that festered at his suspicious nature. He began to realize that he didn't really know Gina that well. Did she have a double life that he hadn't anticipated?

Jim knocked on the door to her apartment. He was earlier than expected. Gina answered the door and seeing him brought a big smile to her face. I guess you could say she was happy to see him. She said. "Hi, you're actually early. Dinner's almost ready so come on in."

He stopped her before she turned back out of the doorway of her apartment. "Before we sit down and eat, I need to talk to you."

"Oh...okay. Come on in. We can talk in the kitchen."

"No, let's do it out here, if you don't mind. Won't take long."

His response made her nervous. Gina had this sinking feeling that it was over with Jim and that's what he came by to tell her. I guess he was the old fashion type. He couldn't break up with someone on the phone like most people; he had to do it in person. She respected him for that. It made her like him even more because there weren't that many honorable men in the world anymore. She replied. "So, I guess this is where we break up. Thank you for doing it in person, at least."

Jim was taken aback by her assumption. But under the circumstances, he could understand why she would think this was a breakup. But he quickly put her mind at ease. "It's not what you think…I'm not here to break up with you."

"Oh…It feels like bad news, so I just assumed.

Jim laughed. "No, that's not what's happening here. Although, it may be a little bit of bad news, I'm hoping it's not." He pulled out the photos of her at the church and handed them to her.

Gina was shocked. She didn't really know what to make of it and the first emotion she felt was anger. "What is this…are you having me followed."

"No, I'm not."

"You don't have to spy on me to find out about me…just ask, you son of a bitch."

Her reaction was normal. That's what Jim told himself as he fended off her anger. "That's not what this is… let me explain."

"Fine, you have one minute before I throw you off my property or last the porch in front of my apartment."

"The photos were taken when you went to church this week. The murder, I'm investigating, we think the killer is deeply religious because of the ritualistic way the murders were done. So, we have staked out catholic churches looking for people that attend more than three times a week and fit a certain profile. It may be a shot in the dark, but we don't have much to go on except our profile of the killer. Anyway, you were spotted at St. Thomas Aquinas. It wasn't deliberate and I didn't take them."

Gina shook her head. "You think I might be as killer?"

Jim grabbed her hand, tenderly letting her know that he didn't think the worst about her. He replied. "No, I don't. But I have to ask about the photos and rule you out, Just like everybody else on my list."

"This is messed up...as a cop, you should already know if I'm a killer or you have terrible instincts. Besides, you wouldn't understand."

"Try me. I mean, I didn't think you were that religious so help me to understand."

Gina's anger turned to sadness. He didn't know the truth about her. In fact, they hadn't really gotten a chance to learn about each other's past. A lot had happened since they first met. She replied. "It's true; I'm not really religious anymore. I did grow up Catholic, but I wasn't at the church this past week for service. It's the anniversary of my mother's and my sister's death. They're only a few days apart, not the same year, of course, the dates they died are two days apart. I went to church to light candles for them. I do it every year."

Jim was a little stunned. The thought had never occurred that she would be there just to light a candle and remember loved ones. But he wasn't Catholic, and it wasn't common, where he came from. He said. "Oh, I didn't realize."

"You wouldn't though, you don't know about my family. The third time, I was at church was because I went to confession. Every once in a while I do that because it makes me feel better. Sometimes, it's good to talk to a priest who tends to have a better moral compass than your best friend. But up until last week, it's been quite a few years since I went to confession."

Jim smiled. "How did your mother die, if you don't mind me asking?"

"She died of cancer when I was sixteen. My dad was so grief-stricken and couldn't handle it that he just took off. Said, his daughters reminded him too much of her and that it was too hard to live with so that's why he had to leave. Can you imagine telling your own daughter that shit just before you're about to abandon them.? I found out he died about five years ago. When I go to church, I only light a candle for my mother and sister. He can rot in hell for all I care."

"I'm sorry."

"Nothing you can do. It's life...sometimes we lose loved ones too early. But I'll never forget them and that's part of the reason I go to church and light a candle on May 6th when my mother died and May 9th when my sister died."

"What happened to your sister?"

Gina's eyes started to well up. "It was a car accident about eight years ago. She and her husband and two kids were killed when a drunk driver in a truck ran a red light and slammed into them. Their car flipped a few times and all of them were killed instantly."

A sad look washed over Jim's face. Nobody deserves this kind of tragedy, he thought. "Holy shit, I'm so sorry. You shouldn't have to live with this."

"It's nice of you to say. But now you know more about me and why I was at church. I may not be religious, but sometimes it makes me feel better."

Jim smiled. "I can see that. And I'm sorry that I had to ask about the pictures."

"I understand, you're doing your job and I get how it looks."

"But I also have to ask, did you go to a Catholic School."

"Is that the detective asking me or the guy I'm dating?"

"Both."

She paused for a moment, starting to get annoyed by the questions. Asking about the pictures was one thing. But beyond that, she started to feel like a suspect being interrogated. However, she did answer the question. "I went to a Catholic school for middle school and my first two years of high school. After my mom died and my dad took off....the family couldn't afford it so I had to finish up at a public school. Does that answer all of your questions?"

Jim felt satisfied with her answers. He didn't suspect her anyway, but to do his job properly, he still had to follow up on her. It couldn't be ignored, especially when murder was involved. He replied. "Yeah, I'm done asking questions and I can cross you off our list of suspects."

Gina smiled and said. "Thank You. Dinner would be a little awkward if I was a suspect." He laughed at her comment. At least she could have a sense of humor about everything." Gina continued. "Speaking of Dinner... the Lasagna is probably ready by now...hope you're hungry."

He replied as they walked inside her apartment. "I'm famished and thank you for telling me about your mother and sister. It means a lot."

"I guess it's time we get to know each other a little more. It seems only right if we are going to date."

He smiled. "Yeah, I think we are beyond a one-night stand, now."

Gina kissed him. "You got that right!"

Whatever questions Jim had about Gina and her connection to this case, disappeared. His instincts told him, that there was nothing about her and he was usually very cynical when it came to people especially potential suspects. She made him feel at ease. There was something about it that he couldn't quite put into words. He was beginning to fall for her and unlike in the past when he fell for a woman, it didn't scare him. For the first time in a long time, he was happy.

It was halfway through dinner with Gina and the kids that Jim's phone started ringing. He didn't answer it, he was having too much of a good time. But the phone kept persistently ringing. After the third phone call, he couldn't ignore it anymore. It was Maisie. He responded to the call. "What, this better be good, I'm in the middle of dinner."

Maisie replied. "Are you near a TV?"

"Yes, I think so."

"Turn it on Channel 5...NBC has a story about our case?"

Jim asked Gina if she actually had cable. She did and then he turned on her TV to the news. The five o'clock news had the story, but it was already on their website. Maisie had texted him the link. The headline read...

"SENATOR BENNETT'S DEATH LINKED TO BLACK FAIRY SERIAL KILLER"

Jim was furious. How did they get this, he thought. He responded. "What the fuck, which came up with that name?"

"They wouldn't have come up with the name unless somebody deliberately leaked this story with the details of our investigation."

"Well, whoever did it; they're in a shit load of trouble. I will bring them up on obstruction charges."

"I don't blame you, but are you listening to the news?"

Jim turned up the volume as the news anchor began talking. Gina and the kids were watching intently as well.

The newscaster began to speak...

"Tonight, we have chilling details about former Senator Don Bennett's Murder. According to police details, it has been linked to a Serial Killer that has committed murders dating back, the past four years. This killer has become known as the Black Fairy Killer because of the fairy wings that are found painted on the victim's body. According to a police memo, this killer is known to be deeply religious and perform a ritualistic style killing of their victim. The victims are tortured first and laid out in some form of religious symbolism. According to sources, Texas State CID and the Dallas Police department have been staking out Catholic Churches in Dallas/ Ft. Worth, hoping to find the killer they think still attends services because of their devout religious beliefs. It has even been suggested that the killer might be a former priest. From what we know so far, this killer is linked to the murders of Oil Barron, Jack Perry two years ago and film producer, Hugo Blackmon, who was found dead in his Austin home four years ago. No motives have been announced yet and Texas State CID or Dallas Police could not be reached for comment. Details are forthcoming, but we will keep you updated on the investigation into the Serial Killer, known as the Black Fairy Killer."

Jim replied to Maisie who was still on the phone. "Shit, this is bad. And I'm definitely, not crazy about the name."

"Texas Tabloid journalism, that's all it is and they couldn't come up with a clever name if they tried."

Jim let out a small laugh at her comment about journalism. He couldn't agree more. He said to her. "Be at the office early tomorrow. We got a lot of work to do." He turned around to Gina and the kids who were giving him a strange look. Or maybe it was fear...he couldn't quite tell. Gina asked him. "Is what they are saying true?"

Jim didn't want to answer the question. Too much information hadn't gotten out already, but he knew it would be worse to lie to them. And the kids had already had too much disappointment in their lives, lying wouldn't help; they didn't need that from some man they were finally starting to trust. He responded to her question. "Part of its true, but they don't have all the information."

"Like what?"

"It's true, we're looking for a serial killer, but the ritualistic nature of the crime has been exaggerated. It's more complicated than that. I really can't say anymore, it's an ongoing investigation."

Audra asked. "Did the killer really paint Fairy Wings on them?"

Jim tried to smile and ease the situation of not wanting to answer questions, but still maintaining their trust. He replied. "That's been exaggerated by the news, that's all I can tell you." Suddenly, he was let off the hook when his phone started ringing again. This time, it was his boss from Austin. He excused himself and took the call outside.

Jim Answered. "I bet I know what this is about."

His boss, the head of CID, Robert Walker replied. "Are you trying to be funny?"

"No, just trying to ease the tension on what I'm sure is going to be an angry phone call."

"How the hell could you let this leak to the news?"

"We didn't let this happen deliberately, but I have over forty cops working on this thing with all the stakeouts we've been doing… it was bound to happen."

"That excuse isn't going to fly. You know how bad this is right?"

"I get that, sir, and I am working on damage control."

"Good, you can fill me in on your plan when I get there in the morning and before the press conference."

Jim was surprised to hear that. But also curious about the press conference that his boss just mentioned. "What press conference?"

"You don't think we can just ignore this, we have to talk to the press and try to keep the public from panicking over some religious nut job on a killing spree. We can't have them make up their own details about this case. We control the story no matter what."

Jim shook his head. "Yeah, I know how this works; we have to set the record straight." He hung up the phone and went back inside to try and enjoy the rest of the evening. A peaceful evening before the shit show started tomorrow! But for Jim, he just got reminded that when it comes to murder in Texas, nothing stays a secret.

16

Jim was up early. He wanted to be the first one into the office, especially before his boss arrived. It didn't happen that way. Maisie got there at the same time as Jim. It was just a little after 7am. And when they walked into the office, Jim's boss, Chief Robert Walker had been already there looking at the crime boards. He wanted to see where they were at on the investigation and to see if there was anything new that Jim had not included in his email reports. Jim responded. "Hello sir, did you just get in?"

Robert replied. "Yeah, drove straight here from Austin. I wanted to be here when you got in."

"I'm sure you want to be brought up to speed?"

"That would be nice, but before that happens, "he looked at Maisie. "Who are you?"

She walked over to shake his hand and replied. "I'm Detective Maisie Green, I was the original detective assigned to this task force."

"Nice to meet you. Okay, let's start. Do you have a prime suspect yet?"

Jim took a sip of his coffee. "We have suspects, but I wouldn't characterize any one of them as being a prime suspect?"

"So this Amy Henderson…the victim who actually won a lawsuit against Senator Bennett, she wouldn't be considered a prime suspect. I mean, according to your report, sounds like she should be."

"She could be, but since we haven't talked to her, we don't know if she has an alibi so we just keep her as a person of interest."

"Except the fact that she has disappeared and her behavior over the last five years fits the profile of someone who would get revenge on a person that harmed them. I have to ask... are you afraid to say the killer might be a woman because we've never had a female serial killer in Texas?"

Jim rolled his eyes. "That has nothing to do with it."

Robert Smiled. "Good! Personally, that sexist bullshit drives me nuts. Only narrow-minded people think a woman can't be a killer. And I don't have time for those people in my division."

"Finding her is one of our priorities?"

"And what are you doing about that?"

"Well, besides keeping tabs with the Private Investigator who was hired by her sister to find her, I called someone at the FBI to see if she had popped up on any federal watch list."

Robert was surprised. He knew Jim didn't like to call his source at the FBI unless it was absolutely necessary. He replied. "Really, you called your sister, uh?" Maisie was a bit shocked that his sister worked at the FBI. She said. "Your sister is a FED!"

Jim nodded at her. "Yeah, I have a sister in the FBI, and it's always a huge pain in the ass when I have to call her...she definitely loves to lord it over me." Then he looked at Robert and replied. "Yes, I called my sister, Amy Henderson is a priority, need all the help we can get, right?"

"Good for you...has she found anything?"

"No, not yet."

"Keep me updated. "Now, what about this ex-priest who went to jail for assault?"

Maisie fielded this question. "We talked to him yesterday. He fits our profile but has more than one alibi the night Don Bennett was killed. Apparently, he doesn't really leave the rehabilitation ranch he works at. But there was something strange about him."

Robert replied. "Like what?"

"He seemed a little overconfident like he knew what was going on and what we were going to ask him. Plus, he gave us this very eerie warning."

"Do you think he killed the Senator?"

"I don't know, but I get the feeling, he might know who did it."

"Kind of like a priest who knew that a fellow priest was molesting kids and didn't say anything." Maisie shot him a dirty look for the analogy, but it was also right on the money. She nodded yes.

Robert poured himself another cup of coffee from the pot of coffee he had made when he got in. It was his third cup. He asked. Is there any other suspects?"

Jim replied. "We are still running background checks on the people we took pictures of from the churches, but nothing out of the ordinary pops up."

"Is there any connection between the victims?"

"One of the detectives found out that Don Bennett and Jack Perry knew each other. In fact, Perry donated to his campaigns. But that's not out of the ordinary either."

Robert chuckled. "So, all you have after weeks of investigating are a few suspects, only one has a connection to the one of the victims, but no physical evidence that ties the suspects to any of the victims. And you still don't know how they're being targeted."

"That's about it, sir."

Maisie said Robert. "We do know that the victims have one thing in common…they were all accused of sexual assault and got away with it. No jail time and only one person had to pay out and that was only one time. We do know that."

Robert gave her a serious look. "But you still don't know how they are being targeted, the one thing you need to know in order to catch the killer. At the end of the day, you don't have shit and that's all the press will see, which will make our jobs ten times harder as they love to scrutinize every little thing we do on the internet."

Sarcastically Jim replied. "Yes, sir, we're fucked, but at least we have each other." They all laughed, even the chief as he said.

"Very funny smart ass, but in all seriousness, you have to do better."

"Do you have any suggestions?"

"We should tell the press that Amy Henderson is our prime suspect and any information on her would help. The press needs a name to stop the feeding frenzy that's about to ensue."

Jim shook his head. He didn't like the idea, but sometimes it could be hard disagreeing with his boss. Jim replied. "I think that's a bad idea."

"Why?"

"If she's underground, it makes it that much harder to find her. We tip our hand too early with her as a suspect, she goes underground for good and then we never find her. And the last thing we need is another unsolvable case. I would also wait to see what my sister finds out."

Robert thought about it for a moment. Took another sip of coffee and then replied back. "Okay, for now we don't mention her name, but if we don't have another suspect in a week then we tell the press she's a suspect. That gives the FBI a week; let's see if they can actually help us." Robert was a Texan through and through. He never trusted the FBI or any federal agency if he could help it. As far as he was concerned, Texas had enough resources to solve their own crimes.

Jim's boss told them he was done for now and went back looking through everything they had so far. Maisie pulled Jim aside and asked. "Do you really think that's what's going to happen if we float her name to the press or are you just afraid to tell them that a woman is the prime suspect?"

He gave her a dirty look. It was the second time she was suggesting that he might be a sexist. "I don't care if the press thinks we're crazy for suggesting a woman could be the killer. Told you before, I don't give in to all that sexist bullshit. I don't want to lose a chance of finding her and making her disappear for good. We need to talk to her. And I need to look into her eyes to get a sense if she could be our killer."

"Look into her eyes!"

"Yeah, interviewing a suspect is like playing poker, you don't know if they're bluffing or telling the truth until you look into their eyes... the eyes always tell the truth."

Maisie laughed. You men always think you can tell everything about a woman if you look into her eyes. And yet, we're still a mystery."

Jim smiled. "I won't argue with that, but killers are all the same, their reasons for it may be different, but they can't hide their guilt, or shame... or whether they enjoyed doing it because the eyes don't lie."

The press conference was at 9am on the dot. Most people would have waited until noon, but Robert wanted it done early. He wanted it out of the way so they could get on with their day and hopefully after feeding the beast that was the press, the frenzy would be over quick. Jim and Robert both agreed, they would give a brief statement and only take a few questions. They would be straight to the point and then get the hell out of there. The press conference was being held outside of the main police station. It was nice outside so perhaps the sun shining could bring a cheerier mood with the press. Perhaps, it was too much to ask for.

There were a lot of reporters there, more than last time. Jim jumped right in and said. "Well, I know what you are all here for so, let's get to it. We have a statement and then we will take some questions."

A reporter interrupted. "So, the leaked memo from your investigation, are the details true?"

Jim shook his head. "I can already see some of you aren't really listening. Again, we have a statement and then we will answer questions. The leaked memo, you are referring to, yes, it is true, but so that you are not taking it out of context, let me just say that they are just notes. These are ideas we have in building a profile."

The reporter from the Dallas NBC TV station interrupted and asked. "Are you saying that everything in the memo is false?"

"No, I am just trying to put this into context. Let me tell you what we know. We can confirm the former Senator, Don Bennett's murder is the result of a serial killer who has been linked to at least two other murders over the last four years. The Oil Barron, Jack Perry, and film producer, Hugo Blackmon. All of the murders were done in a similar fashion, meaning they were ritualistic and had some religious symbolism."

Another reporter asked. "Is that the reason for the fairy wings left at Senator Bennett's crime scene?"

"We don't know for sure if they are fairy wings or angel wings. Probably angel wings, but we floated the idea that it could be fairy wings, it was just an idea we had, that's all."

The same reporter asked. "Are you saying that this isn't the Black Fairy killer?"

"Well, that's a name you, the press, came up with. I guess to sensationalize the murders. I wouldn't characterize the killer that way. But the wings were only found on one victim. I wouldn't even call this, the killer's calling card. Just want to point that out before any of you exaggerate everything in your reporting."

The reporter from the Dallas Morning News asked the next question. "Is there a connection between the victims or are they chosen at random?"

Jim gave her a serious look. "We haven't found anything yet. However, we do know that Jack Perry and Don Bennett knew each other. Jack Perry donated to his campaigns."

The same reporter asked a follow up question. "Do you know how these men were targeted or what they have in common?"

"As far as we can tell, they were all excused of sexual assault and never convicted."

The reporter from WFAA, Channel 8 chimed in. She had an angry tone when she spoke up because she was getting tired of what she considered softball questions by other members of the press. "Look, Detective Summers, your statement and the questions asked so far are all well and good, but there's a more important question that you need answer...why has the police been lying to the public? Don't you think we all have the right to know if there is a serial killer on the loose?

Jim was ambushed by the question. It pissed him off, but he tried hard to not let show in his voice when he replied. "We're not trying to hide anything, but we're not going to tell you every little theory we have. We only report what we actually know."

The reporter from Channel 8 responded before anybody else could. "The memo that was leaked is weeks old, you've known about this serial killer for a while and the only reason, you're talking about it now is because your memo was leaked, so again, why the need to lie to the public. And what else are you lying about when it comes to your investigation?"

Jim didn't answer the question. This one Robert responded to and the anger in his voice definitely showed. He didn't like the press and wasn't trying to hide his disgust with them. He said. "Ma'am, we are not trying to hide anything, but we are also not going to tell you everything. You don't think when the Redskins come to town they tell the Cowboys their game plan just to make them safe and secure."

The reporter was taken by surprise with the comment and didn't know how to respond. But she did ask. "I'm sorry, who are you, sir?"

"I'm Chief Robert Walker. I'm the head of Special Investigation Services within Texas CID. And whether you people like it or not, we're just not going to tell you everything, while it may sound silly to you, we don't want to tell you anything that might tip off the killer with the details of our investigation and stop us from catching them. You're not exactly known for keeping secrets."

She replied. "Sir, we are just trying to keep the public from panicking. That's why we have the right to know what's going on with your investigation."

"If you're trying not to cause a panic, then I guess you shouldn't have reported the details of our memo. This press conference is over now. The task force here in Dallas will keep you up to date on the pertinent details."

Another reporter tried to get in one last question. "What do you have to say to the fact that you have been staking out churches, looking for this serial killer...can you give us any details on that."

Jim replied. "We don't have any comment on that." He and his boss started to walk away. Everybody was trying to get in one last question, but nobody could hear anything over everybody trying to scream over each other. Jim said to Robert as they were walking back the task force office. "You know what they're going to write about tomorrow, right, the headlines are going to say, we're deliberately lying to the public."

Robert laughed. "I don't care; they can write what they want about us. They'll probably take everything out of context anyway. We addressed the issue of the leaked memo and told them we're looking for a serial killer, that's all they get for now. We continue doing our jobs."

"Are those our orders?"

"You better fucking believe it. The press is just a damn nuisance anyway. There should be a law that says they can't report on police investigations until after we've solved the crime."

Maisie walked up to the two investigators and said. "That was brutal. Jesus, they're like sharks in the water after smelling blood."

Robert replied. "Believe it or not, I've had worse from the press. And I've learned how to quickly shut down their feeding frenzy."

Maisie laughed. She thought it was bad, but then again, she had never been through a press conference before after a murder. It probably could be worse. All of sudden they were interrupted by a reporter who came rushing down the hall and flagged them down. The reporter never got to ask a question and she wasn't going to let the press conference being over stop her from doing so. When she was determined, there was no stopping her.

She said. "Detectives, I'm Chloe Keller from the Lone Star Examiner. I've got a source that says Amy Henderson has been missing for a year and you don't consider her a prime suspect, why?"

Both Jim and Robert were annoyed. Not that she asked a question, but that it was about Amy Henderson. They hoped that the press wouldn't catch on to her scent and ignore the fact that they had lied about her being a suspect. Jim responded and his annoyance with the reporter easily showed within his tone. "What source? Who told you that?"

"Is it true that her sister hired a private investigator, and no one has found her, yet?"

"Did the sister tell you that?"

"So, it is true?"

"That's not a confirmation. Tell me your source and I will tell you if it's true."

Chloe Laughed. "Oh, I'm sure you'll do just that after I tell you my source because, cops never lie!"

"Try me."

"My source, his information is solid so you might as well confirm it for me."

Jim smiled. "So it's a him, which means it's probably the private investigator, Tom Graves…right!"

Chloe gave him a dirty look. She had a healthy distrust for cops and especially hated when they turned out to be right. Most of her journalism career had been spent reporting on corrupt cops. She replied back. "I'm still not going to tell you who he is, but its solid information and I have a story. You can comment and try to explain why you're lying, maybe people will understand because of your investigation, or I just run the story and say cops didn't care to comment. Our readers will probably just think more corrupt police officers, deliberately misleading the public."

Jim paused, giving her a sarcastic smile. Then he answered her with a threatening tone. "Let me explain what happens next, you print a story without any police confirmation while making up facts that can hinder our investigation, and then we can arrest you for obstruction of justice. How much reporting can you get done while sitting in jail?"

"Your threats don't scare me, especially when I have a solid story. You'll just make me a martyr, which is what every journalist loves to be."

"Do journalists love to print stories when they have their facts wrong and then end up having to print a retraction. How do you know for sure he's giving you correct information and not just trying to get his name in the paper so he can get a little free advertising for his business? You better be damn sure that's not the case before you use his information for your story…it would be a terrible, terrible thing if you were wrong."

Chloe stood there for a moment, not really knowing how to respond. The worst thing for a journalist is to be wrong about the facts. The Lonestar Examiner may not be the most reputable newspaper in the state, but Chloe prided herself on being a reporter with integrity. After all, she was looking forward to making the leap to a better paper. And she couldn't afford to be wrong on this. It's not like Tom Graves wasn't sleazy and it was possible he was lying to her. She didn't say anything, but Jim said one last thing to her. "I hope we understand each other, you don't have the luxury of being wrong with the story."

The detectives walked off. Chloe knew she had something but was it worth publishing. That was the bigger question, and the choice wasn't easy. For now, she would hold off and just write about the press conference. At least, now, she knew those facts were correct and it was one hell of a story. A serial killer who used religious symbolism to commit murder. That was a huge story in Texas, no doubt about it

17

It was raining, which made it hard to get inside the house with the groceries and try to stay dry. There were no lights turned on. He usually kept the kitchen light on since he usually came in through the door that led from the driveway to the kitchen. He couldn't see anything as he got the final bag of groceries in the house. He couldn't see the person within the shadows in the corner of the kitchen. He accidentally tripped over one of the bags and a couple of cans of spagettios rolled out. As he bent down to pick them up, he didn't see it coming. A blow to the head that put him on the floor. And before he could turn around and see what was happening, everything just went black.

Finally, his eyes started too slowly open. He was groggy and had a terrible headache from being hit on the head. It was dark so he couldn't see anything. But even worse, he couldn't move. His left arm was tied in an upward position. The other arm was numb to where he couldn't move it. He finally noticed that he was kneeling in a weird position. That's when the fear rushed in. He tried to scream, but not a sound came out of his mouth. His mouth was dry…too dry to scream. Or was his mind playing tricks on him. He couldn't tell, but somehow was able to whisper, "Who are you and what do you want?" No one answered back, but he knew someone was there. He could hear the slight sounds of footsteps whisking over the hardwood floors as they creaked with each step.

Since it was too dark to see anything, he kept trying to call out, but even the small sounds of his voice disappeared because of how dry his mouth was. Then a small desk lamp was placed in front of him and turned on. It was the kind that bent, which made it easier for the other in the room to point the light on the man's face, nearly blinding him in the process. It made it harder for him to see the other person in that they were dressed all in black and wore a mask. The only thing he could see was the blurred outline of the person's eyes, but to him, it looked like a demon lording over him. He wondered if it really was a demon coming to take possession of his soul. Finally, the voice spoke and asked. "Do you think you can hide from your sins?"

With fear in his voice, he replied. "What are you talking about?"

"You're a pedophile, who disappeared so he wouldn't have to register as a sex offender."

"You must be mistaken?"

"That's what you would like for me to believe, but we both know that it's true. You are Henry Frankston...you did three years in prison for molesting two little girls. And then when you go out, changed your name and disappeared so you wouldn't have to register as a sex offender."

Panic set in. He had been found. It had been so long since he used his given name, Henry Frankston, that he felt a sting when heard it. It was a sharp reminder of the person he was trying to escape, but knew that his urges were too strong to ever truly escape the dark alter ego of whom he wanted to be. Once he got a taste for it, he just couldn't let it go. He would keep doing it and he knew he would never stop. And after enough years had gone by, he just liked it way too much and it was that desire that consumed his soul. He replied. "What do you want?"

"To save your soul, if you want it."

"I haven't done anything...I quit that stuff a long time ago"

The person leaned in and looked at Henry directly in the eyes. He still couldn't make out the face, but he was still scared as hell, that much he knew for sure.

"You did, uh; do the two children you have locked up know that?"

Henry started crying. The crying turned to pleading. He didn't think anybody knew. The police who had been looking or the missing kids certainly didn't have a clue. But somehow, this mysterious demon like presence. He wondered if he was really dead and if this was the devil playing mind games with him, just part of a master plan to torment him. He tried to make the other person in the room stop what they were doing.

The mysterious person answered. "Pleading will not save your soul, but there is still a chance at forgiveness by God…are you ready to find out if you can be forgiven?"

Trembling, Henry replied. "Yes, is it going to hurt?"

The person smiled. Henry could barely make it out, but he could tell the person was smiling. "Yes, but only for a little while." Then Mark felt the sharp object pierce his side as blood started slowly pouring out. The process had begun.

Two days had gone by since the press conference. Jim's boss stuck around just to see if he could help with case…maybe he could see something the others did. He had been working in CID and Major Crimes in Texas for over twenty years. He had more experience with the worst crimes committed in Texas than anybody in his office. If there was anybody who had seen it all…it would be him.

Jim stared at the same crime board that he had been staring at for two days. He was hoping something would change, but to his dismay, there was nothing new. No new leads. No new ideas. They were nearly done with all the background checks they had performed from the photos taken of people scene at the Catholic churches they had staked out. Nobody stood out as a possible killer. It was mostly deeply devout mothers and fathers who happened to attend church more than once a week but did not have a history of violence. There was one guy that Maisie liked. He was a parole officer who seemed to have a large amount of cases of former convicts who had a history of violence towards women and children. He even had a more than the usual amount of sex offender cases. It just seemed out of the ordinary as if he was trying to be some kind of ultimate moral authority for these degenerates of society. At least that was her theory. They checked him out, but he had a solid alibi for the night that Bennett was murdered.

Jim hadn't taken his eyes off the board for the past hour. Not even for a bathroom break for all the coffee he had been drinking all day. Maisie walked up behind him and said. "Maybe, you need to walk away and come back tomorrow with a fresh pair of eyes."

"And then we would lose another day. Besides, there's something, I'm not seeing...some kind of clue that just hasn't popped out yet, which could lead us to the killer."

"If you haven't seen it by now then you probably won't tonight. Go home, get some sleep, and come back with fresh eyes."

Jim shook his head. "No, it's too early to go home."

"Its 6:30, you've been here since 7am and put in a full day."

Jim was stunned. Was it really that late? He replied. "Wait, what time is it?"

"6:30, damn, I need to be somewhere by 7pm."

Maisie smiled. "Hot date tonight?"

"Not exactly, I'm supposed to watch Audra and Josh tonight. Gina had a film editing gig in Austin today and tomorrow, so her friend Lori and I split time watching the kids."

"Wow, must be getting serious if you're watching the kids."

Jim laughed. "I don't know if it's that serious, but she asked me for a favor."

"If a woman trusts you around her kids, then it's serious. As a single mother, I can tell it's true."

"I don't know how serious it can be if she lives here and I'm only here for a short time."

"Well, however you want to look at it, it is a big deal." Jim was going to comment by then the phone on his desk rang. Even though he was packing and about to walk out, he answered the phone. This is Detective Summers."

The voice on the other end answered. "Detective Summers, this is Daniel Merrick, the former priest, you questioned."

"Yes, father, what can I do for you?

"You don't have to call me father; I'm not a priest anymore."

Jim laughed to himself. "Sorry, force of habit."

"I called because I saw the press conference. Is it true that the wings drawn on the victims were Fairy Wings?"

"Only on one victim, but yes, that's what we think they are…not angel wings."

"Hence the name Black Fairy Killer by the press?"

Jim smirked at the name. He still hated it, but he replied. "Yes, but not a fan of the name, personally."

"Based off the questions that you were asking me and why you think a priest might be the killer because of the religious background, I'm assuming you think the killer had a Catholic Education?"

"No offense, but I can't talk about it, especially with someone that we haven't completely ruled out."

Daniel laughed; he completely understood the truth in that statement. "Sure, I get it. Makes sense. But I wanted to offer some information that might help. I'm sure you are aware that fairies in Celtic mythology are considered fallen angels, pushed out of Heaven by God after Lucifer's fall."

"Yes, I did know that after doing some research."

Daniel smiled at the Detective's cleverness. "What you probably don't know is that when it comes to a Catholic Education the studying of fairies is limited."

"How so?"

"While fairies in folklore are briefly touched on in an English Class, the teaching of their mythology and symbolism in course work is an elective. Not everybody who goes to a Catholic School in Texas would take a course like that. It's not even a standard course in Catholic Universities. It's a very specialized type of coursework."

Jim paused for a moment, pondering what he just heard. "You're telling me that only a small group of people would learn about the mythology of fairies in a Catholic High School?"

"Yes, each class would only have 10 to 12 people and the class is only once a year at any school. Some smaller schools wouldn't even have the class. I had to substitute for those who taught the class a few times. Get the records for who were in those classes at each school, wouldn't be that difficult, if you wanted to cross reference suspects."

Jim cracked a small smile. "You know that you and those who taught the class would be on our list of potential suspects as well."

"I know, but I'm not worried about it. I'm not your killer and no amount of evidence you think you could find would prove that."

"Then why help me?"

"Because someone using religious symbolism to murder people is not very Christian and goes against everything we stand for. No matter how much they think they're justified in their actions…they don't get to play God…none of us do. And that's why you get a little help from an ex-priest."

Jim couldn't tell if he was being genuine or just trying to throw the cops off the scent when it came to the former priest being a suspect. As a cop, he was a skeptic; it was part of the job. However, the information was helpful when it came to the police's profile of the killer. It was worth checking into at the very least. So Jim politely thanked him and then left the office for the day.

Jim was running late. These days he was hardly on time for anything. That's how it could be with the job. He finally arrived at Gina's apartment about fifteen minutes after 7pm. Gina's friend, Lori, took the first shift with the kids, which meant she took them to school and picked them up. It was Jim's turn to do the same. As he walked into the apartment, Lori gave him a scolding look for being late; she actually had plans that night. Not really a date and she hadn't gone on one since her assault, but she had plans with a guy friend that night and was now running late.

Jim replied to her look. "Sorry for being late. It's hard to keep regular hours with the case I'm working."

Lori liked him. He was good for Gina, which was the main reason she liked him, so she wasn't too mad. She said. "Well, I'll overlook it this time, only because you're a nice guy and treat Gina well."

Jim laughed. "Thank You, I'm a cop so it's not too often I get called a nice guy." Lori smiled at his sarcastic comment. He asked her. "How have you been? I'm sorry I haven't followed up since your incident."

"It's okay, I know you're busy. You're working a pretty big case. I'm fine, I've had some rough days, but getting better. It's still hard to trust men, but one day at a time, right."

Jim smiled. "I can't really blame you. What happened to the guy who did it?"

"Oh, you didn't hear…"

"No."

"I guess his wife found out he was cheating so she shot and killed him. Then she killed herself."

"Holy shit, really!"

"Yeah, Karma is a mean bitch."

Jim laughed. "I would say so."

Lori smiled and then grabbed her purse, chit chat was over and she was late enough so she rushed out the door and left Jim to figure out dinner. He said "hi" to the kids and then set his briefcase on the dining room table.

Audra asked in a very precarious voice. "So about dinner… don't suppose you know how to cook?"

Jim sarcastically laughed. "Not anything you'll probably want to eat. Let's just say, I make a mean Venison Stew."

Audra winced at the idea. "You're right, we wouldn't like that…any other ideas?"

He laughed. "What kind of take out do you like?"

Both kids simultaneously replied. "Pizza."

"Pizza it is. May not be healthy, but at least they deliver." Audra and Josh smiled. They were both big fans of pizza, especially exotic pizzas like barbecue chicken or dessert pizzas such as chocolate chip, ff you could even call that a pizza. But nonetheless, Jim ordered what they wanted because he was like a cool uncle that gave into a kid's every whim just to make them happy.

The pizza arrived in about twenty minutes. The kids just gorge themselves in from of the TV, watching some nonsensical movie that had lots of CGI. Jim went back to work, looking through background checks on people they had taken photos of at the churches they had staked out, hoping something out of the ordinary popped out that gave the task force another possible suspect.

Audra and Josh had been watching a movie while Jim worked, but Audra being the inquisitive type, got bored with the movie and wanted to know about what Jim was working on. She walked over to the dining room table and glanced at the photos he had laid out. Audra wasn't really supposed to see them, but Jim was so engrossed with his case files that he didn't tell her to look away. She responded. "Gina said you're looking for that serial killer they call The Black Fairy."

Jim looked up. "Yes, that's why I'm here in Dallas. And I for one don't care for the name. It makes it sound like the killer is some kind of mythical beast."

"Is it true, that the people who were killed have fairy wings?"

"Well, I can't really talk about the case with you, but I will say that the press gets it wrong most of the time and just speculate about a serial killer. The only facts they really have is what the police actually gives them?"

Audra nodded as a way to say she understood what he was saying. Then she replied. "If it were true, it would be the first time that a killer used wings as a symbol?"

Jim was stunned by the comment. It wasn't something a thirteen-year-old girl should know. He put down his reading glasses and asked her. "How do you that?"

"I have been researching serial killers on the internet."

"Why?"

"I was curious ever since the news said we had a serial killer on the loose. And they're fascinating."

There was a shocked look on his face. He never imagined a normal thirteen-year-old girl would say that. Then again, he didn't really know what a normal thirteen-year-old girl was like.

"That's usually not how people describe serial killers, but why do you find them fascinating?"

Audra thought about it for a moment. "Because of why they keep killing people. I read that some people have the urge to kill and can't control it."

"That's true. It's a psychological disorder."

"Others do it because they just like killing people."

"That's also true. Some killers get a taste for it and they keep killing it because they like it."

"Do you think a serial killer is bad if they only kill bad people that do horrible things to others?"

Jim gave her a curious look. Audra asked him a though-provoking philosophical question and there were no easy answers to the question, just a matter of perspective. But before Jim could give her an answer, he responded. "Why do you ask?"

She replied. "I read a news article that talked about it. The article said the men whom the Black Fairy Killer murdered had sexually assaulted women, is that true?"

"The victims were accused of those crimes but were never found guilty in a court of law. And technically they are innocent until proven guilty."

"But if they did do those things, then they're bad men and deserve to die so is the Black Fairy Killer a bad person for killing these men?"

"The answer is complicated. First, whether they deserve to die or not, that's up for a court of law and a jury to decide, not one person taking the law into their hands. Second, vigilante justice is illegal and it's my job to stop them. Whether the killer is a bad person is or not, that's a philosophical question, one that I'm not here to answer and you're too young answer."

Audra gave him a dissatisfied look. She clearly didn't like the answer and it showed in her reply. "I'm not that young. Old enough to know you're being an asshole."

Jim laughed, couldn't help. It was funny and she was right, but he also didn't believe in sugarcoating the truth, especially to someone who was too smart for her own good. "Audra, I'm not trying to be mean, it's just not black and white when it comes to a serial killer, but my job as a cop is pretty straight forward. I catch the bad guys and stop them from hurting innocent people. Let the lawyers and judges debate the morality of it all."

"Well, I don't think this killer is really bad if they only kill bad people."

Jim gave her a strange look. "You may be right, but I think you're a little too smart for your own good." Audra replied with a dirty look. Jim laughed and then replied. "Now, that's not necessarily a bad thing. It just means you'll do great things."

"You think so?"

"I have no doubt."

She smiled. "Do think it's bad that the killer you're trying to catch would kill my father."

Jim was surprised by the comment. But he understood why she would say it. It's not uncommon for a girl to hate a father who abandoned her. He replied. "I can't say whether it is or not, but I do get it. From what I understand, your father is a piece of shit for not wanting you and Josh."

"I know, I shouldn't think like that. "

"It's okay…it's natural to think that after what you've been through. But it doesn't mean you stop loving your father."

Audra seemed confused by the statement. "What do you mean?"

"Fathers can be real sons of bitches, mine certainly was, but that doesn't mean you stop loving them, even if they don't love you back." Audra was still confused; how could you love someone that didn't love you back. But she wasn't old enough yet to understand an undeniable truth, love is complicated, and we don't always get to choose whom we love especially shitty parents. Jim continued with a story. "You don't know this about me …well, not even Gina knows, but my father was a Texas Sheriff and wasn't a very good man, mostly because he was a drunk. He was abusive and I can't say for sure he had any ounce of love in his bones. My dad used to hit my mom a lot. Never knew why she put up with it, but she did. When I was about your age, he was drunk one night while on the job and just shot a guy in a bar who was giving him attitude as he put it. The guy didn't have a weapon or anything. Just mouthed off to my dad and he got shot for it. A Grand Jury indicted him on murder charges and he got suspended. There was a witness whose testimony had just enough evidence to indict my dad. Well, he wasn't going to take that. He found the guy. Then he shot and killed him. Also, shot his wife who witnessed my father killing her husband."

Audra was shocked by the story. She asked. "Did your dad go to Jail?"

"No, he killed himself, right after he shot the man and his wife."

"Oh, sorry."

Jim tried to smile and let her know, it was okay. "Thank You, but my father wasn't a good man. However, that doesn't mean I didn't love him."

"Why?"

"Because he was my father and no matter how bad he might have been, he did some good things and some of them were with me. My point is despite all of his faults, I could still love him for the good inside of him. You can still love your dad for the good things he's done for you and Josh and that's what you hold onto if decide to have a relationship with him in the future. Don't throw all that way by wishing he was dead at the hands of a serial killer. And you never know, he may regret abandoning you two and want to have a relationship. Hating him makes it harder to realize that everybody deserves a second chance. "

Audra didn't respond. She simply smiled at Jim's kind words. As she got up from the table to go back and watch the movie, she had another question for Jim. "Do serial killers always know their victims?"

"No…not always"

"So, they can just randomly pick people to kill?"

"The method for how a killer chooses their victims is different with each killer. There are patterns and tendencies, but no set way of choosing victims."

"Oh, okay. I guess I don't understand how serial killers think because it doesn't make sense to just randomly pick victims. Shouldn't there be a reason why a killer would pick someone to kill even if they didn't know them?" Audra didn't give it another thought as he she sat back down on the couch. Jim, however, couldn't get what she just said out of his head. It was unlikely that Audra realized just how profound she was being. Like Jim said before, she was too smart for her own good, even if she didn't know it. But it was Audra who posed a question that his team had not asked yet. It was an important question that would eventually identify the killer.

Jim got on his laptop and clicked on the internet. He did a Google search for Black Fairy Killer. It was the first story that pulled up. The Lonestar Examiner's top story was and an editorial titled, "Black Fairy Killer: Serial Killer or Savior?" The article questioned whether the Black Fairy should be considered a murderer or some kind of savior for killing a few sexual predators who had never been caught or convicted. Jim was not amused. This was the kind of article that could turn the killer into a hero or worst, a martyr if they were ever caught. And what kind of Justice would that be?

18

Jim got the kids off to school and on time, believe it or not. He was shocked by that because he had always heard that it was almost impossible to get kids up and at school on time. But his married friends with kids who had told him such things always seemed to exaggerate how horrible it could be with a family and kids. Of course, those were also the ones that didn't know how to discipline their kids and they were bad to begin with. Audra and Josh were pretty good kids, considering all the shit they had been through. It wouldn't have been that big of surprise if they acted up all the time.

He got to the office to find more background checks that needed to be looked through. He was still hoping to find another plausible suspect other than Amy Henderson. He has not forgotten what the ex-priest had told him but hadn't had the time to start gathering old school records on who had taken a class about mythology and symbolism. When he walked into the office, Maisie was waiting for him. She was annoyed and wanted to talk. She said to him. "Did you see it; tell me you saw it!"

Jim rolled his eyes at the thought. He had a pretty good idea about what she was talking about. He replied. "Are you talking about the article from the Lonestar Examiner?"

"Yeah...fucking bush league!"

"I know, but we can't arrest them for an opinion piece."

"You're not mad?"

"I didn't say that. I'm just not going to let it bother me? We have too much work to do, anyway. Why are you bothered by it?"

She gave him a dirty look. Maisie wasn't really mad at him, just mad at the question the article posed. She responded by saying. "I'm mad because they made the very question we were discussing, public, and they can influence public opinion. I understand that the victims might have been bad men and maybe they deserve to die, to pose that question on the front page of the newspaper where they can influence what people think of the killer, it's just sloppy journalism."

"I agree, but the only thing that needs to be understood is that vigilante justice is illegal and our job is to find those who do it so they can receive a fair trial. A jury can decide if they should go to jail or be set free. And that's all we need to say. But for the press, we say. "No Comment!"

She tried to crack a smile. "Okay, but its times like this; I think Freedom of Speech is a crock of shit!"

Jim laughed at her comment. He didn't disagree, as a cop; freedom of speech is good when it worked in your favor. Not everybody had gotten to the office yet, but Detective Jackson had been there for a couple of hours following up on a lead. He was on the phone when Jim arrived. Finally, he was done with the phone call. Jim was pouring himself a cup of coffee when Detective Jackson walked over with a file folder. He said. "Jim, you got a minute, I got a lead on a potential suspect."

Jim was surprised, but also glad. It was good news because they needed a break in the case; something that didn't focus on a suspect they couldn't question or even worse, find. He replied. "For a good lead, I have all the time in the world."

Ron smiled. "I think you're going to like this one. Remember how you told me to look into relatives of female victims who had accused any of these guys of sexual assault!"

"Yeah."

"I found one...Aldo Martinez."

"That name sounds familiar."

"He is the brother of Alena Martinez, one of the rape victims from the so-called rape party that Jack Perry ordered to scare off families in that neighborhood he wanted to buy in order to build another oil rig. She was one of two victims that ID'd him being there and also said that a man fitting Don Bennett's description was there."

"Okay...what makes him a good suspect?"

"A number of things." He started to layout out things from the case file he had created on Aldo Martinez. Then he started pinning photos on one of the crime boards. Maisie was curious and walked over to see what he had discovered. Detective James Cross walked into the office and immediately became curious about the presentation as well, so he walked over to where the rest of the detectives were and started to listen. It was the first real lead they had, had in weeks; it would change everything about the investigation of the Black Fairy Killer.

Ron pulled out a copy of Aldo's employment file and pinned it on the board. "Each of the three victims had the same security company...Highland Security. Aldo Martinez has worked for them the past fifteen years. First, as an installer, then as a project leader, and now as a project inspector"

Jim replied. "Okay, but a lot of people work for the second largest security company in Texas, what ties him to the victims?"

"He was the project leader five years ago when the security system was installed on Hugo Blackmon's house in Austin. I understand that it was a year before he was killed, but Aldo Martinez had been to the house and knew the layout."

"What about the other two...was he the project lead for those installs?"

"No, four years ago, he got a promotion. He became a Project Inspector, which requires traveling to different job sites all over the state and inspect installs, especially large jobs. He would have inspected the security system installations at Jack Perry's home, which he knew one was installed at his house about eight months before he was killed. He would also have inspected the installation at the Don Bennett's house, which that system was installed, one week after Jack Perry's house."

Jim was stunned... in fact; they were all surprised at the coincidence. And in this job, rarely are there coincidences! Jim replied. "No shit so he would have been on site at all three places at some point, giving him easy access!"

Ron nodded. "Yes, sir."

Maisie responded by asking the obvious question. "Is there any way to verify whether he was in Dallas the night, Bennett was murdered?"

Ron smiled as he replied. "I already checked. He drives a company car and they have GPS. Came in that day and left early in the morning. The only thing, GPS puts his car near the house during the day and at his hotel for the rest of the night."

"Well, I doubt he would take the company car to a crime scene. He probably just took an UBER or more likely a taxi since they can't be tracked on your phone through an APP."

"Probably, but he was in Dallas that night, on another inspection job."

Jim replied. "And still makes him a likely suspect for at least one murder. But is there anything that would put him at the Jack Perry crime scene within 24 hours of the murder."

Begrudgingly Ron replied. "No, Highland security doesn't keep GPS records going back that far. But according to work records, he was back home in Midland on the day the murder occurred, so he wasn't that far from the house."

"He was in the same city, but there's no way to prove he was anywhere near the house."

"No."

Finally Detective Cross spoke up. He agreed with everybody's assessment of Aldo Martinez so far. But there was something else that tugged at his curiosity more than else. He asked. "Midland police were the first to investigate Jack Perry's murder, why didn't they consider him a suspect, being the brother of one of the rape victims and working for the company that installed the security system? Wouldn't he be at the top of a list somewhere as a primary suspect...I mean, he did have motive!"

Ron looked through the case file. He remembered seeing something about him being questioned by Police. He found it and then replied. "Actually, he was questioned about the murder. Detectives thought the same thing, but he had an alibi…he was at a party and over a dozen witnesses saw him there."

"They all saw him at the party the entire night?"

Jim looked over at Detective Cross. He knew where he was going with the question, and he was right to ask it. Ron looked through the file and responded. "No, I can't find anything that people said he was there all night…just that he was there."

Detective Cross said. "So, it's possible that he was only there a little while and then left so he could go kill Jack Perry."

"Yes, sir, I guess it is possible. But here's the kicker. After they questioned him, he helped them when it came to how one could get past the security system. There's a note from one of the detectives that Aldo Martinez was very helpful."

Detective Cross shook his head in disbelief. "Fucking Christ, sounds like they barely questioned him and never gave him a second thought, without ever really following up."

Jim smirked and responded to Detective Cross. "I've never known Midland Police to be all that smart. And they probably don't realize that it's not uncommon for serial killers to want to help the police."

Detective Cross replied. "In the old days, if I missed something like that they would have had my badge. Sloppy police work like that is inexcusable."

Jim chuckled at Detective Cross' statement. He certainly wasn't wrong. He looked at Ron and asked. "Is that all you have?"

Ron shook his head, "no." He replied back. "Actually, no, using the profile, you came up with about a religious or Catholic education, I did a background check. Aldo and Alena Martinez went to St. Mary's Catholic school in El Paso from middle school through High School. Both were honor students, but it was this that stood out in Aldo's school records." Ron had copies of an essay that Aldo had written in high school. As he handed each one of them a copy of the essay, titled, Michael the Archangel: God's Hired Gun, he said. "Aldo wrote this for some kind of

Catholic Scholarship, which he won. I know it's not talking about Fairies, but it's the symbolism that caught my attention. He writes about how the Archangel is basically used for God's own vengeance and that revenge is okay when you're an Archangel. How far of stretch would it be to go from an Archangel to a Fairy or a fallen angel as a symbol."

Jim replied. "It wouldn't be." He was about to say something else before he was interrupted by Detective Cross reading a passage from the essay. He said. "Listen to this. *If God didn't condone vengeance or even revenge, then why would he need an Archangel? They do God's dirty work. They carry God's blood on their hands. Where there is mercy, there is also vengeance. You cannot have one without the other. God has the avenging angel do the dirty work that needs to be done so that God can remain pure. But most importantly, the Archangel is proof that God will allow certain souls to commit vengeance without it being a sin*"

Detective Cross put down the paper and said with a sarcastic tone. "Anybody feel like this guy shouldn't be suspect!"

They all laughed at the comment, but it was Jim responded. "I think it's very clear that we need to talk to Aldo Martinez." He may not have liked Ron very much, but he was not above giving him praise when it was earned. He said to the detective. "Well done, Detective. You just found our prime suspect, at least for now." Then at the same, he looked at both Detective Green and Detective Jackson and said. "Both of you pack a bag; we're going to Midland tomorrow so we can interview Aldo Martinez."

It had been a busy day for Gina. It seemed as if she had been playing catch up all day since she had gotten back from her film editing gig in Austin. It was a big job and too much money so she couldn't really turn it down. But there was always too much work to catch up on, not only at home, but at her day job too. It was one of those nights that she just didn't have the energy to cook so she just got burgers for her and the kids from Jake's Burger's, a Texas Institution.

When she got home, she found the kids doing their homework. Audra and Josh had been taking the bus home, so they got back to the apartment before Gina did. Most days, they had their homework done before she got home so they could all hang out. Some nights they played games like a family. Some nights they would watch a movie or even go to the movies. Sometimes Jim would join them. But they did things as a family, and it was certainly different for the kids. They had never really known that with their own mother, especially after the divorce when they were on their own. Both kids were happy for the first time in a long time.

Audra usually finished her homework early. She was smart and had an uncanny ability to get things done early. When she was done with homework, she usually surfed the internet for interesting things that she could learn about on her mother's old laptop. Audra was curious girl and never stopped trying to learn something new. These days, it was all about serial killers. It may have been a little demented for a thirteen-year-old, but when the news sensationalizes a serial killer with name, Black Fairy Killer, it's hard not to be curious.

Audra was looking up more stuff about serial killers when Gina walked into the apartment with dinner. She walked past the dining room table as she made her way into the kitchen and saw what Audra was looking at. It surprised her to say the least. She asked Audra. "Why are you looking up stuff about serial killers…you're too young for that kind of stuff!"

Audra, smiling, replied. "I'm not that young anymore and I've seen a lot in my thirteen years."

"That may be true, but you shouldn't be in such a rush to lose your innocence. It's okay to still be a kid and not be exposed to such disgusting things."

"But it's fascinating. Did you know there are different kinds of serial killers?"

"I did not. I thought they were all just people who hunted people down and killed them because they liked it."

Audra replied. "That's a simple answer; it's more complicated than that." She started reading from a website about FBI statistics when it came to serial killers as Gina got the burgers out of the bags

"An anger-motivated serial killer is one that's driven by an intense hatred of a group of people. This anger can be based on religion, gender, lifestyle, or race, and could be fueled by something from a life-changing event to the irrational development of racist views. Some profiles also call this type a "mission serial killer," as they believe it is their purpose in life to rid the world of a certain type of person.

Ideology can also be a very powerful motivator for some types of serial killers. These are the people that also tend to target a single group of people, but it's to further their own cause and ideals rather than to rid the world of a very specific type of person, as in anger-motivated killings. Terrorist groups are often ideology-based.

Some serial killers are motivated by financial gain. These are the killers that ingratiate themselves into a household, and then perhaps kill for their inheritance, and they're the ones that take out insurance policies and then kill to receive their payoff. Robbery-homicides are also an example of crimes with a financially motivated serial killer. These killers are also known as comfort-oriented serial killers, and many female serial killers fall into this category.

Some serial killers commit murder because they're driven to do so by their own psychosis or mental illness. Also called visionary serial killers, they often suffer from delusions and hallucinations, thinking that something is telling them to commit murder. These are serial killers that are usually found incompetent to stand trial, as they often truly believe that demons, gods, or other otherworldly influences are pushing them.

Power or thrill killers simply do it for the rush. These people are often aware that they're going against what's socially acceptable, but the feel of power and domination is too great for them to pass up. Sometimes the dominance can take on a sexual aspect, but here it's more about the feeling of power than about the actual act itself.

There are also those that kill because of their own perverse sexual desires. Unlike power or thrill killers, it's about the act instead of the power that it imparts to them over their victim. In some cases, this might not even be reflected clearly in the crime scene, and it may only be later, at home or in an environment they feel is safe, that they can fulfill their fantasies.

The other main type of serial killer is someone ho commits multiple murders in conjunction with another criminal element. Examples include a member of a drug or a street gang committing gang violence, an enforcer for organized crime."

When she was done reading, Gina had already laid out the dinner on the dining room table. Gina replied to what Audra had just read. "Do you know what all of those types have in common?"

"What?"

"There was a breaking point that drove them to kill someone else. Maybe they get a taste for killing and can't stop. It becomes a compulsion or maybe some kind of tragedy drove them to where they feel the need to kill. If you want to try and understand a serial killer, then you try and understand their motivation."

Audra thought it was a strange thing to say or maybe she just didn't understand the point Gina was trying to make. She responded by saying. "Do you think we should feel sympathy for a serial killer?"

"No, not necessarily. They are still murderers, but I don't think it's so black and white with serial killers. Just like it's not black and white with someone who is mentally impaired, and they commit a crime. They should still be punished, but Jail isn't the best place for them. I think law enforcement needs a better understanding of serial killers."

"What do you think of the Black Fairy Killer?"

"I don't like the name. It sounds ridiculous, like something out of Lord of the Rings. They couldn't come up with something better?"

Audra smiled. "I think it's cool. It's dark and mysterious. And a bit gothic, which I find cool."

Gina laughed. "If you say so. The only thing I can say is the killer probably had a tragic life that drove them to all of this and it makes me feel sorry for them. And what about you."

Audra thought for a moment, not wanting her answer to be misunderstood.

"I don't know if I would call him a murderer. Maybe he's an avenging angel of some kind. He only kills bad people."

"How do you know it's a him…could be a woman did you ever think about that?"

Audra nodded, acknowledging the possibility, but then she commented. "According to FBI statistics, it's probably a man between the ages of 35 to 45 who likes the thrill of killing powerful men who got away with it."

"And I bet those statistics were made up by men. It may be more likely, but not completely impossible that it could be a woman. Just saying."

"Do you think it is?"

"I don't really care. Just want you to look at a different point of view, especially if your fascination with serial killerss turns into wanting to be a cop or FBI agent one day who profiles serial killers. Our curiosity can turn into dreams of what we want our life to be someday."

Audra smiled. "I still don't know what I want to be when I grow up, but it could be cool to a cop one day like Jim."

Gina smiled back. It was touching to hear her compare herself to a good father figure for a change. And that's what Jim was whether he realized it or not. Gina said. "I think you have the brains to be a good one, but for now just be a kid and don't read such disturbing material…in my opinion." They hugged then called Josh over to the dinner table so they could eat dinner as a family. Lately, that had become the best part of Gina's day.

19

Maisie kept looking at her watch. He was late and their flight was in half an hour. These days, Jim always seemed to be running late. She looked over at Detective Jackson, who shrugged at her as if to say, he didn't know what to do. Jim was the lead investigator, and they couldn't leave without him. Finally, he came rushing into the office and grabbed his briefcase with the case files they were taking with them. He looked at the detectives and said. "Alright, let's go. We have a flight to catch."

As they were walking out of the office, Maisie asked. "Where have you been? I mean we're cutting it a little close for our flight, don't you think?"

Jim smiled. "Trust me, they're not leaving without us…we are on a private plane reserved for state law enforcement."

"Oh, I thought we had to take a commercial flight or something."

"Nope, we're important enough to get a private plane."

"Why are you running late?"

Jim pulled out a piece of paper and showed it to Ron and Maisie. "I was getting a warrant from a friendly district Judge."

"A warrant?"

"Yes, so we can search Aldo Martinez's home. I didn't want to wait so I went ahead and got a warrant based on the information we already had. I couldn't get one to tap his phones so hopefully we will get more evidence for that warrant after today."

Ron replied. "Good thinking, but does the warrant include his work vehicle as well."

"Yes, I made sure to include that. Also, just so we are clear. We are only interviewing him as an expert on the security system. I don't want him to think he's a suspect right off the bat. If he thinks we need his help, hopefully he'll keep his guard down and let something slip that incriminates him."

Ron asked. "Do we talk to him first or search his home first?"

"We talk to him first. The game is up if we serve the warrant and search his home…he'll know he's a suspect and will probably lawyer up and then we'll never anything out of him."

Ron didn't argue with the strategy. He knew that even though, he found the connection with Aldo Martinez, Jim was still the lead investigator, and they were going to do it his way. So for now, he would just follow his lead. The flight took just over an hour. A flight from Dallas to Midland, Texas was always longer than it seemed to be. But then again, West Texas was a lot further from civilization than most people realized. It was a world all unto its own where a man could get away with pretty much anything because the only three things that seemed to matter where God, Football, and Oil in no particular order. You would think seeing dead bodies would be the worst part of the job for Jim, but really, it was having to investigate anything In West Texas.

The three detectives didn't plan on staying the night, so they went straight to the regional office of Highland Security where Aldo Martinez worked instead of checking into a hotel. Maisie had called ahead to make sure he was still in the office so they wouldn't miss him. When they arrived, they seemed to catch him off guard, which is what Jim wanted. Surprising a suspect when it came to questioning, always got better results. At least that had been Jim's experience.

Jim showed his badge to the front desk receptionist and told her that they needed to speak with Aldo Martinez. He was surprised to see the police in the office, but after the three detectives introduced themselves, he brought them back to his office without hesitation. He asked. "What is this about?"

Jim said. "We actually needed your help?"

"Oh, what with?"

"Questions about your security systems. Two years ago, you assisted Midland Police in the Jack Perry murder investigation about his security system, which you were the Project Inspector for."

Aldo was a little surprised. He thought that the investigation was over. He replied. "Yes, I oversaw the installation of his high-end security system the year before and they wanted to know how someone could get past it. Basically, needed some technical advice."

"Was there a way to get past it?"

"Not really, it was one of our top of the line systems. The normal way cutting or rerouting the phone line wouldn't have worked; our systems have a firewall of sorts that prevents that from happening. But it wouldn't have mattered anyway"

"Why not?"

"That system had a biometric feature on it. It took a thumb print to deactivate the system."

All of the detectives were surprised to hear that. None of them had heard of a security company in Texas offering such high-end stuff. Ron replied. "So Midland Police concluded that someone had snuck into the house while the victims were there?"

Aldo said. "I guess, that's the only I can see somebody getting in and killing that guy. "

Jim segwayed the conversation into asking about Don Bennett's murder as if it was a nonchalant conversation. He was trying to make Aldo think that he couldn't possibly be a suspect, at least until they searched his apartment. He asked. "I'm assuming you heard about the murder of former State Senator, Don Bennett?"

Aldo nodded. "Of course…it's been on the news. It was a serial killer who did it, right!"

"Yes sir and we think it's linked to the Jack Perry murder. That's why we are here. I understand you oversaw the installation of the security system on his house too?"

"That's right?"

"Just like with Midland police two years ago, we needed your help regarding the security system…how would someone bypass it?"

"Honestly, I don't think anybody can…he virtually had the same system as Mr. Perry including the Biometrics. If you were to break in then you would have needed Don Bennett's thumb print."

"Without using the actual thumb pressing down on the scanner, is there another way to get a copy of the thumb print?"

Aldo sat back in his chair, pondering the question. Even he wondered if there was a way to do it. He thought of possibilities, but Biometrics can be tricky. He answered." We do have to scan the print into the system, which means we have a copy of it on our server and technically it can be printed, but you would have to print it on some of three-dimensional surface that had a the right texture to completely outline a finger print. I personally don't know of anything that would work."

Maisie chimed in. "What about a 3D printer? Couldn't you take the print and apply it to a three-dimensional vector of thumb and then print it in a 3D printer?"

Aldo thought for a moment. "I suppose so, but don't they normally print plastic! Hard plastic wouldn't work on a thumb print scanner; you would still need some kind of soft, squishy surface for the print to be on and something that could be pushed flat on a scanner."

"But it would be possible if you could create something from a 3D printer other than plastic."

"I suppose so."

Jim asked the obvious question. "Do you guys have3D printers in your offices?"

Aldo replied. "No, we don't have a use for them."

Maisie asked. "How many people can remotely login to your server?"

"Why?"

"Just curious to see how many employees can do that and who might have a 3D printer in their house!"

"Aldo thought for a moment. "We have a lot of employees who can remotely login into our server, but having access to the part of server which contains fingerprints for our biometric systems... there's not many who have that kind of access."

"So the list is small! That would certainly narrow down the list of suspects."

Jim nodded in agreement. He was impressed with Maisie and the questions she asked. But since he was in charge it was his job to ask the one question they were sure to get a "no." He asked anyway. "Can we get a list of employees who have access to that part of your server?"

Aldo sat back in his chair. "Unfortunately, I can't just give it to you. It's private employee information; I would need a court order before giving you the information."

Jim replied. "I understand, but we are going to need it and keep in mind, because the nature of the crime, Texas CID could file obstruction of justice charges against Highland Security."

Aldo certainly didn't like being told that. He was smart enough to know, that it had to be a cop's trick in order to get him to comply. And it was, but he wasn't going to be swayed that easily. He responded. "You can try, but I'm sure out legal department would have something to say about it and they like a good fight."

Jim laughed. "Then I guess we let the lawyers fight over the issue. In the meantime, thank you for your help, we may have more questions so we will be in touch." Jim shook his hand and then the detectives walked out of the office. Maisie was surprised and as they were walking out asked Jim. "Why are we leaving...don't we have more questions...I know, I did?"

Jim answered as they walked out of the building. "I don't want to tip our hand, right now, he's thinking that we suspect one of his employees and that's what we want him to think. By the way, great question about the 3D printer. Maybe our theory is wrong about the killer sneaking into Don Bennett's house by riding in the trunk."

Ron asked. "Why didn't you at least ask him about the paper he wrote or that scholarship?"

Jim, frustrated by the question, gave him a bit of a dirty look and replied. "Because that would have shown him our hand.

There's no way he thinks he's not a suspect after we explain how we got a hold of the paper. It's not time to ask him about it yet."

Ron could tell Jim thought it was a stupid question. He was going to respond and try to redeem himself by showing Jim he actually knew what he was doing, but he was cut off before he could say anything. Jim said. "At this point we need to search his home and see if we can find anything that ties him to the crimes. Detective Jackson, I want you to stay here and keep an eye on him. Follow him and see where he goes."

Ron was a little bit pissed and it showed on his face. "You're putting me on lookout duty!"

"Yes, is that a problem?"

"This is my lead; I should be searching his home with him"

"And I'm still the supervising officer here. You get lookout duty and instead of thinking of it as shit work, maybe you're the one who catches him destroying evidence, which is what we like to call within law enforcement, catching him red handed." Ron tried to act like that was a better deal than it really was, but he still figured it was shit work. And in all honesty, it was. Jim did that on purpose because he didn't want to deal with him while they searched for evidence. He still thought Ron was just a dumb redneck cop getting by because he was one a star in high school. He wasn't necessarily wrong, but Aldo Martinez was a good lead. He couldn't deny that.

Ron stayed back and sat in the McDonalds across the street watching the Highland security building. Jim and Maisie went to his condo with local sheriff's deputies to execute the warrant and search his home. As with Texas law, a local Sheriff's deputy had to be present executing a warrant if the police officers serving it were from another jurisdiction. Jim picked the lock so they didn't have to break the door down. As they entered the place, Jim and Maisie's first impression was that he was clean. Aldo Martinez was a neat freak. Everything had its spot... everything was in perfect order.

They walked around and nothing seemed out of the ordinary. Maisie was the first to notice the big iron Gaelic Cross hanging above the fireplace. At first, they thought it was just decoration until they walked into his bedroom and saw a Catholic

Cross hanging above his bed. Aldo was still religious. Apparently his faith was important to him. As they deputy stood by the door, the detectives did a thorough search looking for something that could tie Aldo to at least the latest murder.

Maisie looked in the hall closet and found his rifles and other hunting gear. Aldo had a few rifles, but it was the collection of knives that caught her eye. She showed Jim. There were at least a dozen knives and daggers in his closet. They were different sizes and some of them didn't look like hunting knives. Aldo Martinez didn't seem as if he was some great collector of knives or old-style weapons so it was curious that he would have these.

Maisie asked Jim. "Do you think any of these could be a murder weapon?"

He replied. "The question is whether it's our murder weapon!" He reached for his cell phone and found the person he was looking for in his contacts. He made a call to Dr. Vanessa O'Connor. She picked up and he said. "Dr. Connor, Jim Summers, I have an interesting question about Don Bennett's murder?"

She was pleased to hear from him. The Black Fairy case really interested her, and she hoped that she could assist more with it. It was the strangest case that she had ever done an autopsy for. Vanessa replied. "What can I help you with?"

"The cut in the abdomen, how big would the object be to make that cut?"

"Well, it depends. Whoever did it, could have used small dagger and just kept cutting to the right or left to make the incision bigger. But if they used some kind of dagger that fit the actual size of the cut, then it would be about two inches"

Jim was a little stunned. "That's a pretty big dagger or knife."

"True, but if your killer is really trying to mimic the Roman blade that pierces Jesus' side when he was on the cross, then he would use a dagger about the size of a Roman Pugio or Roman Dagger."

"How big are they?"

"About two inches wide? Sounds like you have a lead."

Jim smiled. "You can say that. We might have a murder weapon."

Vanessa was excited for the break in the case, but there was caution in her voice. She wanted to make that whatever they found was the right weapon. The smallest detail they got wrong could allow the killer to go free. She said. "Just make sure that whatever you find is double-edged. The cut was made by a double-edged object."

Jim looked at the collection of knives. There were a few that fit the bill. He replied to Vanessa. "Thank You for the information, I'll be in touch." As soon as he hung up, Jim got another call, it was his boss. Jim was shocked when he heard the news from his boss. There has been another murder in Houston.

20

Jim and Maisie were waiting at the small landing strip by the private plane they had flown on when someone driving a black sedan for UBER pulled up. Ron had to hitch ride from where he had been staking out Aldo Martinez. He was annoyed that he had been pulled off the stakeout and it reflected in his tone when he got out of the car and asked them what was going on.

Jim answered his question. "Sorry you have to abandon your stakeout, but we're on our way to Houston and that takes priority."

Ron's look on his face showed that he wasn't pleased. He responded. "Okay, why are we going to Houston?"

"There's been a murder that fits the profile of our killer. It takes priority right now. But I've asked the local sheriff's department to keep an eye on Mr. Martinez. Wherever he goes, we'll know about it."

Ron was curious about the murder. He asked. "What kind of murder...is it just as gruesome as the others?"

"We don't know many details yet, just that Houston police found the body this morning and it looks like he's been dead for the past few days. My boss said to drop what we were doing and get our asses there ASAP. A Houston CSI team is on the scene now."

"So, it's bad?"

"That's a good assumption. Usually when my boss says to drop everything and get to a crime scene, it's pretty bad."

The three of them got on the plane. It was only an hour flight from Midland to Houston. And didn't take them long drive to the crime scene when they touched down. It was a small house on the outskirts of Tomball, away from the bustling parts of the city. The house was hidden from the road, hiding behind big oak trees so that no one could tell where it was really there. To most cops, it looked like a good place for a drug den. But it was the perfect place to commit a murder and it was only by pure accident that the mailman discovered the bodies from the smell coming through a cracked window.

The house was filled with cops and technicians. There was barely any room in the front yard with all the cop cars and CSI vans there. Jim noticed that they had teams of cops walking the one acre property, which was never a good sign. Jim's instinct told him that it was worse than the others and after the lead investigator on the scene walked the three detectives into the house to where the body was still in its original position; Jim saw why he was right. The scene was horrific. Shocking to most. Maisie nearly lost it and broke down when she saw it. The victim was a man cradling a baby with one hand and holding a knife in the other with a stabbing motion towards the child. The knife's blade pierced the baby's skin as it looked as if it was going into the baby's heart. Now, a child had been killed, it was definitely worse than the other murders.

There was a lead detective on the scene from Houston PD. She found Jim and is the other detectives and gave them the rundown of the crime scene. Detective Summers," she responded, "I'm Detective Martha Rains."

"Nice to meet you. He Replied. "Let's start with who discovered the body."

"It was the local postman. He said he hadn't dropped off any mail in days, but had some today and the smell tipped him off that something was wrong."

"So this was done in the last three days?"

"That's what we figure. It appears that they have been dead for at least 48 hours."

Jim knelt to take a closer look. They were just past the rigor mortis stage as serious decomposition started to set in. Jim replied. "I estimate more like 60 hours since they died, but we will need to do a full autopsy to really determine that."

Detective Rains asked. "I have to ask since State CID was called out here…is this a Black Fairy Murder?"

He didn't know how to really answer that with any certainty. The murder was gruesome, but it was different than what they had seen so far so he was hesitant to call it a Black Fairy murder. He simply replied. "We don't know yet, but we are here to find out."

"Would this serial killer actually kill a child?"

Just the phrase was shocking to hear. Killing sexual predators that got away with it was one thing, but killing an innocent child was a whole new level of demented. Jim responded. "Have you determined an actual cause of death for the child, I could be wrong, but it doesn't appear that the knife killed the child. Looks like, it barely grazed the kid."

"Maybe you're right, we don't actually have a cause of death, but it looks pretty clear that the man is stabbing the child."

"Let's not jump to conclusions yet." Maisie started to feel sick. The crime scene was getting hard to see. She couldn't help it, tears started to fill her eyes. Jim looked at her and said. "Detective, if this is too much, you can step out of the room."

She gave him a cold look as if to say, *how dare you question my professionalism at a crime scene* and said. "I'm fine…it's nothing I can't handle."

That was far from the truth and Jim could see it written all over her face. He replied back. "Maisie, it's okay, step outside for a moment and get some air. That's an order." She was going to say something snarky, but his look shot that idea down. Maisie walked out of the room angrily staring as she walked away. It might have been embarrassing for her, but it was the right thing to do to maintain the integrity of the crime scene.

CSI was still photographing the scene Jim and Ron looked around, trying to examine every little detail, no matter how gruesome. Jim asked Detective Rains. "Have you pulled prints yet?"

She pulled a tablet out and replied. "Actually, we did. His name is Henry Frankston. He came up pretty fast in our system since he's a sex offender that's been missing for two years. Apparently, he got out of prison after doing a three-year bit for molesting his sister's kids. When he got out, he failed to register as a sex offender and disappeared. Cops have been looking for him for a while."

"What about the kid?"

"Nothing yet."

Detective Jackson replied. "Maybe the kid was never fingerprinted and that's why you can't find him. It's not uncommon for really poor families to not have their kids fingerprinted or families that travel around a lot, especially if the kid wasn't born in a traditional hospital."

Detective Rains responded. "Good call."

Jim smiled. "I agree, so maybe somebody filed a missing person's report with the description of the child, and we get lucky that way. Somebody has to be looking for him."

Jim didn't say anything for a few moments as he walked around the display of bodies. The scene was too different than the other murders, yet, just as horrific. But why? What was the true meaning behind this, especially involving a dead child. These were the thoughts that consumed him, for he had never seen anything like this before. Then he noticed something and had one of the CSI technicians shine a black light above the head of the dead man looking for fibers. It was faint and not visible to ordinary eyes. Jim asked the technician to go back. There writing on the wall. Was this some kind of DA Vinci Code style message from the killer? The technician sprayed a substance over the message so it could be seen by everyone. It read "GEN2212."

Jim responded. "What the hell is that?"

Detective Rains replied. "The killer appears to have left a message."

"Perhaps, but what does GEN2212 mean...sounds like a password."

"To what," the Detective asked.

Ron looked at it closely while the other two kept asking the obvious questions. Excited, he said. "It's not a password...it's a bible verse." Both Jim and Detective Rains surprised by the answer. Ron said the verse out loud. And he said, *Lay not thine hand upon the lad, neither do thou anything unto him: for now I know that thou fearest God, seeing thou hast not withheld thy son, thine only son from me."*

Jim looked at the writing on the wall and then looked at Ron. He was stunned and it showed in his tone. "Holy shit, you're right Detective, makes sense now. This murder symbolizes the story of Abraham and Isaac."

Ron asked. "But why...Abraham didn't murder Isaac and even if he kills him in the story, it wouldn't have been murder, but a sacrifice unto God.

"Maybe just like in the story, this is about testing the man's righteousness and what he would be willing to do for God. Make no mistake about it, this is a serious message."

"Does the killer think they're God?"

Jim looked at Ron and replied. "Or they think they're the alternative to God so that a deviant like this can get salvation."

Just the notion mad Ron shake his head in disbelief. "That's sacrilegious!"

"Our killer doesn't think so and that's what makes them dangerous." Jim ordered the technicians to finish up and to get lots of pictures. Then he turned to Detective Rains. "When the bodies get to the city morgue, they're not to be touched."

She replied. "A Medical Examiner has to do an autopsy to determine a cause of death to complete the death certificate."

"I understand, but I'm going to fly in our own Medical Examiner to do the autopsy."

"By law the autopsy is performed by a Medical Examiner from the county where the murder occurred."

"Unless it's superseded by tactical command like State CID...we have tactical command over this crime scene since it's linked to a series of murders we've been investigating. We can call in our own Medical Examiner to the autopsy and that's what I want." Detective Rains didn't like hearing that, but she didn't argue. Like most cops in Houston, she didn't like outsiders coming into her city and taking over an investigation. There was no love loss when it came to State CID. She had always thought of them as stuck up "know-it-alls" who looked down at city cops. She wasn't necessarily wrong. Many of them were like that, but never as bad as the FBI or even the DEA. When it came to taking over an investigation, they could be real assholes.

Jim took some photos of the crime scene with his phone and then walked outside. He looked for Maisie who he assumed would be around the car, but found her walking around the outside of the house especially the back yard. She was trying to make herself useful and see if there anything else to the crime scene. Jim found her and before he could say anything, she said. "You didn't have to send me out…I can handle the scene."

Jim nodded. "I wasn't trying to insult you, but you looked as if you were about to throw up and I didn't need you contaminating the crime scene."

With a dirty look, Maisie replied. "How is that not insulting! Do you want to disrespect me some more or tell me what you came to say?"

"You wouldn't be the first to throw up at a crime scene, it happens to every seasoned detective."

"Even you, I suppose."

"You don't have to be so bitchy, but yes, it's happened to me before. Now if you can stop taking it so personal, then I have something to show you."

Here anger turned to intrigue. Jim said. "We found writing on the wall above the male victim in invisible ink." He showed her the picture on his phone. "Do you recognize it…it's a Bible verse?"

It didn't take her long to figure out the symbolism. "Abraham and Isaac…it's the story of how God asked him to sacrifice his son in order to test his faith."

"Yeah, that's what we think too. The real question is why this form of symbolism…it's completely different from the other murders."

"Maybe there's something unique about this victim...something that makes him different from the other sexual predators that were murdered."

Jim replied. "He's a pedophile, his perversion involves children" and then he told Maisie who the victim was and how he had been missing for two years. Maisie commented that it made sense. A different kind of predator required a different form of symbolism. She said to Jim. "Maybe the symbolism has to do with the type of victim, meaning the murder is unique to their particular perversion. And the commonality is that it's biblical."

Jim thought about it for a moment. Her answer was intriguing. "So, each murder is committed to a particular Biblical theme ... I would buy that, but at the end of the day, how does that help us capture the right person."

"We look for somebody that knows their Bible and understands the symbolism within it. That's the profile we're looking for..." She didn't finish her sentence because she noticed something odd. Because of where she was standing in the backyard, Maisie was at the perfect angle to notice how strange the backyard looked. Jim asked. "What is it...you didn't finish your sentence?"

"Do you notice how the shed looks bigger than it supposed to be?"

"No."

"It looks as if goes deeper in between those two trees and is closer to the fence line."

Jim looked. "I don't see anything."

"Guess I'm the only one that sees it. Let's check it out."

Jim didn't argue with her hunch. He always trusted a good cop's instincts more than facts. The two detectives entered the shed. It was unlocked. There was nothing unusual about it. It had all the things you would expect to find in a garden shed, old gardening tools, pots, potting soil, and seeds. And it looked as if none of the stuff had been touched in ages. But Maisie noticed something else. There was another door behind a shelf. It was hard to see, but because the shelf did not have a back to it, she could see the outline of the door. She and Jim moved the shelf. This door was locked and there was no reason it should be unless you were trying to hide something. Jim took his pistol and hit the padlock with the butt of his gun. It took a few tries, but the lock broke. There was no light and both of them used the flashlight part of their cell phones to shine some light in the room.

The smell hit them first. It was nauseating and almost made Maisie throw up again. The little room smelled like death. Because there was no light, they didn't see anything right away, but they shined their lights in the other room and found it. They were both shocked to find two raggedy blankets and pillows, and two dishes. This is where the pedophile kept the child. However, there was two of everything. Jim responded. "There were two kids in here."

Maisie replied. "If that's true, then what happened to the other one?"

"That's a good question…we need to get a dig team in here and see if he buried the other child." It was a horrifying thought for Maisie, but the detectives couldn't discount the possibility that there was another dead child on the property and their killer might have had something to do with it. There would be no sympathy for someone who could do something so vile as to kill a child. Justice for the killer would be more severe.

It had started to rain as Detective Summers was standing outside at the small municipal airport, waiting for the small private plane to arrive. The rain was the perfect end to a shitty day. Finally, the plane landed. There was only one person besides the pilots, Dr. Vanessa O'Connor. Jim has called her and basically drafted her on behalf of State CID. She didn't even have time to go home before two detectives in Plano fetched her and drove her to an airport so she could get on a plane. She was a bit annoyed and it was understandable. However, she never turned down a job, which made her husband angry, but it was a small price to pay for being considered an expert in her field within the State of Texas and being called on to consult in murder investigations.

Vanessa got off the plane and didn't even say hi before responding to Jim waiting for her. "Okay, what the hell is so important that I had to fly immediately to Houston."

Jim could tell he was a little angry and he let out a small laugh to try and ease the tension. "A murder…I need you to look at the body."

"No shit…I figured that part out. But you didn't give any details. Why is this one so important?"

"Because it involves a kid." Vanessa was stunned by what he just said. He must be telling a bad joke, she thought. But Jim handed her a tablet with crime scene photos so she could see that he was telling the truth. Vanessa never lost her composure when it came to dead bodies. It was one of the things that made her good at her job. This made her wince. It was shocking. "I guess I'm doing an autopsy on both."

"Yes, but mainly the child. We need to know how he died."

Vanessa paused for a moment to collect her thoughts. "You need me to tell you if your serial killer did this or if its natural causes."

Jim nodded. "Yes, it becomes a whole new ball game if our killer is murdering children and I need those answers before this leaks."

"Leaks?"

"A child murder doesn't stay a secret very long when it comes to the police. It's only a matter of time before the press has it and then becomes a media frenzy. Then it will be harder to find the truth when we have to investigate every bullshit lead or we put the wrong man in prison because the powers to be, want us to arrest someone for the murder and they don't care who it is."

"That's why you wouldn't give me the details over the phone or send me photos. You think someone would hack our phones."

Jim laughed. It did sound crazy, but he said to her. "It's not uncommon these days. It's happened before and we can't let it happen this time."

"I understand." Vanessa replied. She took a closer look at the photos when they go in the car. "The crime scene is very different, but I see similarities."

"You're right. The victim bled out from someone piercing is side just like the others. No word yet if there is traces of bread crumbs and we can't find fairy wings anywhere."

"You think this might be a copycat?"

Jim nodded at the possibility, but his instincts said no. He replied. "I don't think so. The symbolism is different, but…"

Vanessa cut him off and finished his statement. She knew exactly what he was going to say. "But the symbolism is still biblical. In this case…the story of Abraham and Isaac."

"Yep. We may not be able to find Fairy Wings, but the killer left a bible verse. Our killer is now starting to preach."

Vanessa was stunned. The bible verse made the crime even more disturbing. She commented. "Or the killer is finally displaying their full ego as… serial killers can't help it… their ego will always have to be displayed within the details in the crime."

Jim laughed at her comment. After all, she wasn't wrong. He opened the door to the standard police Chevy Tahoe that he drove in. As she was getting in, he got a text message with a link to a news website. He cursed when he saw the headline. "Young Boy and Man Latest Victims of Black Fairy Killer."

He showed Vanessa. She cursed too. Then Jim said. "We don't have any more time. I need answers to put a stop to the leaks and misinformation." Vanessa nodded. "It will probably be early morning, but I will have answers for you." With that said, the Chevy Tahoe raced through the streets back to the main hospital in Houston where the bodies had just been delivered about an hour earlier.

21

Audra was surfing the internet when she came across the news article about the murder in Houston. It was the same article Jim was texted a link to. She was still fascinated by the Black Fairy Killings and was always checking the internet for more news. Audra pointed out the article to Gina. It surprised her and then her feelings turned to concern for Jim. What madness did he have to deal with? She called him.

Jim was sitting in a conference room with the other detectives when his phone started ringing. Normally he would ignore phone calls when he was in the middle of an investigation. But it was Gina, and he could use a friendly voice. He answered. "Hey Gina…good to hear your voice."

She smiled. "I know that I probably shouldn't call. You're busy."

Jim walked out of the room. "No, it's fine. A welcome distraction."

"Audra showed me an article about the murder in Houston…is it true?"

"Partially true, but I can't say anything else."

"This Black Fairy killer murdering a child and having to see that…I can't imagine."

"Yeah…it's a horrible thing to see, but we're not sure how the child died yet. An autopsy is being performed now."

Gina tried to smile but could anyone smile when an innocent child was dead. She replied. "Well, whatever the truth is…I hope it leads you closer to finding who the killer. I guess that's all I can really say since you can't tell me anything about your investigation."

He smiled. "Wish I could. It would be nice to have someone to talk to about it…other than cops."

"At least you're thinking of me." She missed him and it showed in her voice. She tried to smile as she said. "I'll let you get back to work."

"Thank you for calling…hearing your voice made my day. It was more than just screwing around or even dating with Gina. He was starting to fall for her. Weirdly, it didn't scare him one bit. He couldn't recall the last time that had happened.

The detectives had been sitting in the conference room at the main police station for the last couple of hours looking at photos of the crime scene. Pizza boxes sat on the table with scattered paper plates and plastic cups. They still needed to eat. Jim had been staring at the same photo for the past ten minutes. He couldn't take his eyes off it. It was the portrait shot of the victim stabbing the knife towards the child. There was just something about it…the way the victims looked in the scene. It was like the Mona Lisa of crime scene photos where you couldn't tell if they were smiling or crying out in agony. They were almost expressionless. Was that point? Was there some kind of meaning within their expressions?

Maisie finally asked. "What is it…do you see something we don't in that photo? God knows, you've stared at long enough."

Jim looked up from the photo. "There's no expression. You can't see what they're feeling… why?"

Ron asked. "Why does it matter they were murdered, how do their expressions help us catch the killer?"

"It matters Detective Jackson because every crime scene has been about symbolism. What's the symbolism behind the expressionless faces? If it's done on purpose...why?"

"Maybe there's no meaning behind it at all!"

Jim kind of rolled his eyes at the thought. It was possible, but unlikely. If nothing else, the killer was meticulous with the murders. There was meaning in everything. Jim replied. "You may be right, but I think the bigger question is why change the MO? Why this particular biblical theme? That's what I want to answer. If that's what we can figure out, then maybe we can predict where the killer is going and that's how we catch them."

Ron didn't seem to buy it. He didn't believe in asking why a criminal does what they do...he didn't care. He replied. "I think you're reading too much into this, but this whole crime scene reminded me of a story this preacher I once knew told me regarding Abraham and Isaac. He said it wasn't about God testing Abraham's faith in him, he already knew Abraham had faith. It was making Abraham see how true his faith was by asking him to sacrifice what he truly loved so that Abraham would never doubt himself. God didn't need reassurance because he already knows everything."

Maisie was the first to respond as Jim sat back in his chair, pondering the little parable that they were told. She asked. "Are you saying the killer was testing the victims' faith by asking him to kill his sex toy...that's the message the killer is trying to send?"

Ron replied. "If that's how you want to look at it!"

Jim interrupted. "No, our killer is making the victim see that he is too weak to give up his toy by making him kill it and that's why he has to die. This scene is not about absolving him of his sins in some fucked up ancient ritual. Like I said before the killer is preaching...they want the victim to see his sins and know that he isn't capable of repenting. It's like holding up a mirror in front of you to show all of your dirty deeds. It's actually kind of clever."

Maisie was taken back. The killer's message made sense. She replied. "If that's true, perhaps the victims are carefully chosen… they're not random sexual predators being killed. Each victim is specifically chosen to deliver a specific message."

Jim smiled for she was on to something. Nothing was random in this case. It was specific and knowing the specifics was how they were going to catch the killer. They were getting closer; Jim could feel it. He was about to say something when Detective Rains came in the room. He looked at her and said. "Detective, do you have any news?"

She handed him a file folder. "We found out the identity of the kids through fingerprints. They were in the fingerprint system. I guess they got fingerprinted at school the past year."

Maisie, shocked at what she said, replied. "Kids…you said kids, right?"

"Yes. It appears that your theory was right. Henry Frankston kidnapped two kids and kept them locked up. A brother and sister. Well, not exactly kidnapped…more like he bought them."

Jim, Maisie, and Ron were all stunned by what Detective Rains said about buying the kids. What did she mean! Jim replied. "You said bought them…did I hear that right?"

Detective Rains nodded. "Yep. The father is a meth addict. Cooks it too. Mother died a few months ago in a meth-related explosion. Anyway, the father, desperate for money, apparently sold his kids a week ago to Frankston for $2,000."

They were all horrified to hear that, especially Maisie. How could anybody just sell their kids? It was inconceivable to think such a thing would happen. Jim had seen the worse of the worse over the years during his investigations but had never come across something like this before. He asked. "I am assuming you got the father in custody?"

"Yeah, picked him up a few hours ago. Guy is a mess. Actually broke down and cried when we told him what happened and didn't even deny what he did."

Angered about what this guy did and what she was hearing, Maisie replied. "How can this piece of shit, cry for his kids after what he did! That's fucking messed up." Jim nodded at her while agreeing with her assessment, but their personal opinions didn't matter when it came to asking objective questions.

He steered the conversation away from her condemnation so they could get back on point.

Jim asked Detective Rains. "Do you know how the kids we targeted?"

"Frankston worked as a janitor at the boy's elementary school. That's how he also targeted the father and took advantage of him being an addict, needing money. He was working under an alias and the school never bothered to do a background check because it cost too much money."

Maisie angrily replied. "What kind of school doesn't do a background check on their employees."

Jim answered her. "A school that is seriously underfunded. This is Texas…money for the public schools is not a priority. But that's beside the point. "He looked around the room and continued. "What about the girl…what happened to her?"

Maisie looked at Detective Rains. "Before, we try and answer that question, what are their names? I think it's important that we know their names."

The Detective looked at her copy of the police report. "Jack and Heather Tyson."

Jim nodded in agreement. He understood why she would want to know; it made them more human instead of just a case number. He tried to be more objective about the whole thing, but agreed their names were important. He said. "If the girl is dead, he would have had to get rid of the body to keep from getting caught. He couldn't just dump the body unless it's a place where he knew no one would find it."

Ron replied. "He lived on a whole lot of land, maybe he buried the body."

"Maybe, we should get some cops out there to search the land and see if there is any place that resembles a grave or place where the ground was dug up." Detective Rains made a phone call to make that happen. Jim also had another possibility. "If the guy has the money to buy kids, perhaps he has the money to get rid of them. What if he found a crematorium to burn a body off the books? We should check around and see if anybody would have done that the past week. There are probably only so many places that would do it. Maybe we get lucky and find a body or find out who got rid of it. Either way, we take another scumbag off the streets." It was worth looking into and that's what the Detectives did while waiting for an autopsy report.

It was late. Gina couldn't sleep so she decided to get some work done. She hasn't updated her IMDB.com page in a while. Audra couldn't sleep either. She tended to stay up late reading about serial killers to feed her fascination. You could say she was consumed with the subject matter. Gina was having trouble accessing her old IMDB.com account when Audra came out of her room.
  Gina asked. "What are you doing up? It's late."
  She replied. "I couldn't sleep."
  "Probably because you stayed up reading more about serial killers."
  Audra laughed. "I only read a little bit. What are you doing?"
  "Fixing my IMDB.com page. I can't get into the old one. Guess I'm going to have to make a new one."
  "I didn't know you had a page on there."
  Gina cracked a smile. "Yes, it's a necessary evil in the entertainment industry. I don't need it for acting credits since I don't really do that anymore, but it's nice to get credit for all the editing projects I do especially for trying to get more work."
  Audra changed the subject. She had a question that she could never ask her mother without some drunken judgmental answer. She asked. "How do you know if you like someone?"
  Gina was surprised by the question. She didn't exactly know what Audra meant by it. "Do you mean like someone as a friend or do you mean like, like someone."
  "Like, like someone."

Gina smiled at her. "Is there a boy you like…or a girl?"

"A boy, but I don't know if I like him enough to kiss him. Some days he's sweet and some days, he's annoying."

"Teenage boys are like that. Their raging hormones make them seem bipolar. And every woman feels that way about men, no matter their age. One moment, we think men are sweet and the next, we are so repulsed that we don't want to be anywhere near them. That won't ever change."

Audra laughed. "When he's just with me, he's sweet; he's even written me a couple of poems. But when he's with his friends, he's an asshole."

"Well, there you have it."

"What do you mean?"

"If he's sweet with just you, then he likes you. But most teenage boys are assholes when they are with their friends because if they are vulnerable with women then they look weak. It's a pride thing. One day they grow up and don't feel so insecure where they can be sweet towards a girl in front of their friends."

"When does that happen?"

"Usually when men hit their 30's…sorry to say. Since this is the first time you have asked me a question about boys, let me give you an honest answer and not the teen beat one. If you like the guy then go out with him. Enjoy his company if it's just you two. And when he's with his friends, just ignore it because you can't change it anyway. He will grow out of it. Now if he's an asshole to you all the time, then run away… he's not worth it and definitely not good enough for you."

Smiling, Audra hugged Gina. It was good advice, better than anything she would have gotten from her mother. Audra went back to bed, but before she got to her room, she turned around and asked. "Do you miss Jim when he's away?" It was a curious question for most people, but not for Audra. She couldn't remember a time when her mother ever missed her supposed father when he went on business trips. It was like she never cared for him…only his money.

Gina replied. "I do miss him. What can I say, I like him and you tend to miss the people you like when they're away. That's how it works." Audra smiled and went inside her bedroom.

She was still at the age where she didn't understand much about boys, but somehow she understood what Gina was saying. The boy she liked; she missed him when she didn't get to see him at school. Perhaps, that's how liking someone really starts. You just miss them.

It was close to 2am when Dr. Vanessa Connor got done with the autopsies. She wasn't completely done, but enough to determine a cause of death for both victims. One of them was a big surprise. She quickly finished her report and then rushed to the main police station where the Detectives were waiting. Most of the time something like that could wait until the morning, but this was different. Time was not on their side when it came to quelling the rumors about this particular murder. Vanessa walked into the conference room. Both Jim and Ron were propped up in chairs against the wall snoozing and trying to get a little sleep. It had been a long day and the morning would come too quickly.

Maisie responded as Vanessa walked into the room and saw the file folder the was carrying. "Is that it…the autopsy report?"

Vanessa laughed as she replied. "What no small talk!"

Maisie smiled. "It's 2am, I think we are all out of the small talk."

"Well, in that case…yes, I have an autopsy report. Or at least part of one. Still waiting on a Toxicology report. That will take more than a few hours."

Maisie slammed the table as hard as she could, trying to wake the guys up. It worked. Both Jim and Ron nearly fell out of their chairs when as they were startled awake. She said. "Time to wake up…the doctor is here with the report."

Jim, who was trying to awaken from the deep sleep he was actually having, got a jolt of joy when he heard the news. He was happy, to say the least, about finally getting some answers about the latest murders. He avoided the small talk as well and asked. "Finally, what did you find out?"

Vanessa nodded. "First off, the boy wasn't murdered...not by Frankston or your killer. The official cause of death is an asthma attack. Most likely he was dead before the murder scwas ene created."

Maisie replied. "Holy shit. I wonder if Frankston even knew that the kid has Asthma."

Jim responded to her. "I wonder if the father even knew or even cared before he sold his kids for drug money." Looking at Vanessa, he asked. "Did being in a darkened room, kill the boy?"

Vanessa replied. "Most likely, sheds don't have really good ventilation and if he spent a long time in there, which it appears he did, that would cause serious problems for anybody who has asthma and could kill them."

"At least now, we can put a stop to the rumors that the Black Fairy killed a child. One less headache for us."

Vanessa spoke up. "That's not the biggest surprise I found while performing the Autopsy.

"Oh?"

"Henry Frankston wasn't murdered. He died of a heart attack about an hour before he was pierced in the side and his blood drained out."

Everybody was surprised to hear that. Did that really happen! Why stage the scene if the victim wasn't really a murder victim? Everybody in the room was pretty much thinking the same question. Maisie responded. "If that's true, then why go through this and change the MO? I mean there's no reason for it, right."

Jim replied. "Sure, there is... because the message is more important than the death. It's what the death symbolizes that's more important."

Ron was intrigued by Jim's answer. He added another thought. "It's like Jesus' death on the cross. What his death symbolized for mankind was greater than all of his suffering. His death represents salvation for all mankind. It doesn't matter how he died, but what he died for."

The rest of the people in the room stared at Ron for a moment. His thought was precise and probably the most profound analyzation of the killer. It gave the rest of them something to really think about. Jim said. "I think you hit the nail on the head. That's why our killer is preaching. Their message is more important than how the victims died. But I wonder…" He paused in mid thought. The silence in the room felt like forever, so Maisie spoke up.

She asked. You wonder what?"

Jim came out of his trance. "Sorry, I was just thinking, perhaps the killer doesn't even like killing?"

"What do you mean?"

"We assume that every serial killer, once they get a taste for killing, they can't stop. It's a craving for it. For some it's a compulsion. For others, they do it because they're curious to see how it feels to kill someone. What if this one is different? They don't like killing, but spreading their message is their craving."

Vanessa replied. "Then that means they could be squeamish if they saw the crime scene up close and personal, like seeing it the same way we do. The confidence they have with what they're doing is seen in the message itself."

"Yeah. And that's something we can use when interrogating a potential suspect. What will their reaction be when we make them look at the photos. Scared or filled with pride at their glorious work."

Maisie replied. "You want to set a trap so you can get a better read on the suspect?"

Jim smiled. "Yes. I still trust my instincts more than potential evidence."

"And is Amy Henderson still your leading contender for the Black Fairy Killer or Aldo Martinez?"

Jim nodded. "They're both good suspects, but I won't know for sure until I talk to them, that's the only way it works for me." That was all he said as he got up from his chair. He was done for the night. It had already been a long day and the only thing left was to set up a press conference later in the morning. They had to address the media. It couldn't be avoided unless they wanted more rumors getting around. People in Texas were already on edge the more the Black Fairy Killer remained at large and the rumor that the killer might have killed a child could push the state over the cliff of mass hysteria. Jim wanted to make the press conference quick, but would he really be that lucky. It was a safe bet, no!

22

The press conference was at 9:00am on the dot and the huge conference room at the main police station in Houston was filled wall to wall with reporters. Most of them were local, but a lot them were from places like Dallas, San Antonio, and Austin. There were even national reporters there too from CNN and FOX news. This case had taken on a life of its own now, it was national news now. Why wouldn't there be when you had a catchy name like The Black Fairy killer.

Jim walked to the podium. There was no small talk. He got right to it. He said. "Thank You for coming today. We will only answer a limited number of questions after we make our announcements. Now the main purpose of this press conference is to correct some of the rumors that have been going around or should I say, written." A local reporter tried to ask a question. Jim replied. "I am going to get to that, please, no more questions until I'm finished."

Jim paused for a moment as he collected a file folder that contained the autopsy report. He said. "First, the murder victim that was found is named Henry Frankston. He is a sex offender that didn't register when he got out of prison two years ago and went missing. And before anybody asks, yes, we suspect him to be a victim of the Black Fairy Killer."

A reporter from the Houston Chronicle tried to ask a question. "Is it true that a child was also found murdered?"

Jim gave her an icy stare. "Looks like some of you can't follow the rules, which means you won't be allowed to ask questions. We'll let your competitors get to ask them instead." He could hear a few silent jeers from the crowd, but he wanted them to understand who was in charge. Jim continued. "Now for the second thing I was about to tell before I was interrupted. A child was found on the scene. A seven-year-old boy by the name of Jacky Tyson. He was kidnapped along with his sister Heather by Henry Frankston. He was not murdered by the Black Fairy Killer despite reports and rumors. The cause of death was an asthma attack. Probably brought on by being held in a dark room without much ventilation. We have concrete evidence of his cause of death from the autopsy report."

Another reporter interrupted. "Where was Jack Tyson found? It's been reported that he was part of the crime scene."

Jim was annoyed by the question, but he answered it anyway. "That part is true. The boy was part of the crime scene. He was put on display along with Henry Frankston. That's all we can say this time. In addition, we do not know the whereabouts of his sister, Heather. There's no evidence of foul play so she is categorized as a missing person. Her photo will be circulated, and we will declare an amber alert for her with an 800 number that will be used as a tip line. We would like your help in getting the word out so we can find her."

Jim paused for a moment, trying to remember if there was anything else he wanted to say. There wasn't, so he opened the floor to questions, even though he just assumed not to. A reporter from the Dallas Morning News asked the first question. "How did Henry Frankston acquire Jack and Heather Tyson?"

Jim replied. "They were sold to Frankston by their drug addict father. Apparently, he needed money for supplies so he could cook another batch of meth. He is currently in custody with Houston PD."

The reporter had a follow up question. "Is there any evidence that the father was a part of the murder?"

"No... the evidence suggests that the Black Fairy Killer works alone and doesn't have any accomplices."

Finally, a local Associated Press reporter asked. "This is the second murder in a month and at least the fourth that we know about from the Black Fairy killer over the past couple of years…do you actually have any suspects."

"As I have mentioned before to the press, we're not going to tell you who we're looking at so you can tip them off that we're looking at them. Call me crazy, but I just don't trust any of you to help the police out and keep it a secret."

Most of the crowd laughed at his statement, but the reporter didn't appreciate the answer. She responded. "You think this is funny, there's a serial killer out there, that's killing kids now, and the police can't seem to do anything about it…I think we would all like to know what you're doing to stop this killer."

Jim was pissed. And rightly so. His biggest pet peeve about the press was when the go the facts wrong or took general statements from the police out of context to shape the type of story that would sell more newspapers or get more views. He saw the press as the biggest hindrance to a police investigation. His anger was evident in his tone when he responded to the reporter. "It's easy to judge us, especially if we don't solve crimes as fast as you want. This is a thankless job and we do it anyway, especially when the press rarely praises us when we get it right but has no problem splashing our mistakes all over the front page. You're better at turning the public against the police instead of working with us to solve heinous crimes like this. Why, because all you care about is more views online or newspaper sales. And even when I've given you the facts, you'll still twist them just to fit your own agenda as evidenced by the AP reporter's accusations. So let me be very clear…we will catch this killer no matter what lies you tell about our investigation. Any reporter that reports false stories that impedes our investigation…you will be arrested for obstruction of justice, and we will prosecute you to the full extent of the law. That's all the questions we will be taking today."

The AP Reporter, angered by Jim's subtle insults that she was nothing but a hack of reporter, got one more question in. "Detective Summers… are you threatening the press?"

Smiling back at her, Jim replied. "Absolutely!"

And that was it, the press conference was over. Jim cut it short to avoid anymore, what he deemed, asinine questions. Pretty much every reporter in the room tried to ask one more question as he walked away from the podium. He never looked back and hastily walked out of the room. Maisie asked. "I thought you were going to give them a little more than that."

He sarcastically smiled. "I was if they had played nice, but I am not going to answer stupid questions or be their punching bag as they accuse us of not being good at our job. Besides, with all the leaks to the press regarding this case doesn't matter what I say anyway…they seem to form their own conclusions and print their story from there."

Maisie laughed. Jim wasn't necessarily wrong. The press could be an uncontrollable beast and feeding them just made it worse. Jim, Maisie, and Ron went back to the conference room. When they walked in, Jim's boss, Robert was waiting for them. Jim was a bit surprised to see him, but then again, shouldn't have been given the magnitude of the latest murder and its impact on the Black Fairy Case. Robert said hello to everybody and then asked if he and Jim could have the room to themselves. Maisie and Ron walked out of the room after he offered to buy Maisie a cup of coffee. And for Jim, it felt like he was about to be scolded in the principal's office. He was half right.

Robert said to him. "Nice press conference, but not a good idea to antagonize the press, especially threatening to arrest them for obstruction of justice."

Jim laughed. "It may be a little overkill, but they need to be called out for running false stories. We can't have that bullshit!"

"I agree, but it happens with every major investigation. The press usually only gets it half right."

"Aren't you tired of that crap? I mean, for once, can we have them help us instead of trying to scare the public."

Robert smiled. "In a perfect world, sure, but as long as we catch the bad guys, I don't care what they say."

Jim asked. "What are you doing here? I didn't expect you to come to Houston, I mean, we have this handled."

"Is that so?"

"Yeah...we got the autopsy report back pretty fast. We know the cause of deaths. And it looks like this was done by the Black Fairy killer."

"But what about suspects? Do you have a new suspect that you haven't told me about or is it looking like Aldo Martinez might be out killer?"

Jim paused. He knew his boss well enough to know what he was getting at. What were they waiting for? Why hasn't there been an arrest yet? There wasn't a right answer to those questions. It was complicated. But Jim responded. "I don't have any new suspects and we didn't talk to Aldo long enough for me to get a sense that he might be the primary suspect."

Robert looked confused. From what he understood, Aldo Martinez looked pretty good as a suspect. At least that's what he was led to believe from the email reports. He said "I read the paper that he wrote in High School...pretty serious stuff. And the timeline of his inspections in different cities coinciding with the murders. Plus, he had enough motive to kill the oilman. That's enough to at least bring him in. Why haven't you?"

"We've been a little busy with this current murder."

"That doesn't mean you couldn't have called Midland PD and have them hold him."

Jim gave his boss a funny look. He often did that when he disagreed with his strategy. He liked Robert but didn't think he was all that smart when it came to being an investigator at least not as smart as him. He was better at being middle management... the type of job where you don't ask a lot of questions and you certainly don't have to think outside the box. Jim responded. "I get what you're saying, but I think it's the wrong move."

"Why?"

"Because we don't have anything concrete yet. It's all circumstantial."

"But it is enough to get him in a room and interrogate him!"

"Probably, but right now, he doesn't think he's a suspect, which makes him less cautious and prone to mistakes. And that might cause him to slip up and give us the actual evidence we need to convict. Right now that's not the case."

"That's why you interrogate him and get a confession."

Jim rolled his eyes. "We do that and we tip our hand…he'll know he's a suspect. He will lawyer up and then we will have to release him because we don't have evidence. And that's when he disappears. We have one chance to get this right if he truly is our killer. That's why I think we should wait. We gather more evidence and see if we can actually tie him to the murders."

Robert was frustrated. Jim could see it on his face. Taking their time with the investigation was a nice sentiment, but it rarely worked out that way. He replied back. "If we had the luxury of time, sure, maybe."

"What does that mean?"

"We're out of time and under too much pressure. We need to make an arrest."

Jim was stunned a little bit by his comment. What was he really abdicating? Sir, are you saying that it doesn't matter if a suspect is really guilty…we just need to make an arrest?"

Robert gave him a dirty look. "Of course not. But what you have never understood are the politics involved with a murder investigation. The longer it takes the catch a murderer, the less trusting the public is of us and that's when all hell breaks loose. Criminals think they can get away with anything. And with this one, you don't even want to know the calls I've been getting, asking us why we can't solve this. I even had the governor call me personally and if the head of CID is getting calls from the governor, that's bad news for everyone."

"I don't give a shit about the pressure from bureaucrats; I care about catching the real killer and doing this investigation right."

"I know, that's what you should give a shit about. But when you're the chief, you have to worry about the politics too. And that's why time is up. He's a good suspect; it's time to bring him in unless you found Amy Henderson."

"No…still no word."

Robert nodded. "Then he's our main suspect…pick him up and get him in a room."

Now Jim had a look of frustration. "Sir, let us hold off…please."

"What are you afraid of…that it will happen again. Because if that's it, stop beating yourself up. Every cop gets it wrong at some point."

Jim sighed. Yes, Robert was right. Even good cops aren't perfect. They do get it wrong sometimes, but it doesn't make it hurt any less, especially when your mistakes get somebody killed. Jim only had one response. "I get what you're saying, but this case is too important to be wrong."

Robert laughed the comment off. He didn't disagree. However, he was the boss and that came with making difficult decisions. Most of which, were unpopular. He said to Jim. "You disagree and are reluctant, so I'll make it easy. I'm ordering you to get him and bring him."

"Are we arresting him?"

"No, just bring him in for questioning, but you lean on him hard. See if you get a confession or gives you something for an arrest."

Jim got snarky. "A false confession," he replied.

"I'm not even going to dignify that with an answer. The only thing I will say is this, I want Aldo Martinez in custody today." That was it. The meeting was over. Robert walked out of the conference room, leaving Jim to swallow his pride, go against his own instincts, and do something he knew he shouldn't do. But orders were orders.

Before walking out of the conference room and getting on a plane back to Midland, Jim called his sister. Surprisingly, it didn't go to voicemail. She answered after the second ring. Jim didn't have time for the pleasantries, he simply asked. "Sorry if this is too blunt, but I need to know right now if the FBI has located Amy Henderson."

His sister was a caught off guard and asked. "Why, what happened?"

"There's another suspect and I'm sure, we're about to arrest him."

"That's a good thing… right!"

"It would be if he was the actual killer, but I doubt he is."

"You sure about that?"

Jim laughed. "Maybe not 100%, but he doesn't feel right. So, before this turns into something we can't walk back. I need to know, if Amy Henderson has been found."

Jim's sister paused for a moment, not wanting to add to the bad news, but there wasn't any good news anyway. She replied. "I did find out, her name is part of an ongoing investigation, I can't tell you any more than that. Apparently, it's a high-priority investigation; I wasn't even given all the details."

"So basically, no chance of getting to talk with her."

"I don't think the Agents involved in the investigation know where she really is. At this point she may be in the wind. But if they did know, you still wouldn't get to talk with her. My advice, go with the suspects you do have."

Jim didn't like the answer, but what could he do at this point. You play the cards you're dealt, simple as that.

23

The Captain at the Midland Police station walked out of his office and flagged down two patrol cops. He had an assignment for them. He said. "Ramirez...Briggs, got an assignment for you. We got a request from State CID to pick up a guy and bring him in for questioning." He handed the request to the two officers. As they were about to leave, a Detective walked over to the Captain.

The Detective asked. "Hey Captain, somebody faxed over a copy of a Warrant, I think it's from CID."

The Captain was surprised. It was strange to get a fax on a warrant and too much of a coincidence that it would be from CID when they just got a request from them. With a strange look on his face, he had to ask. "What's the name on the warrant?"

The Detective replied. "Aldo Martinez."

"What, I just got a request by email to pick him up."

"Why would we get faxed a warrant too?"

The Captain shook his head. "It's CID; they're not the most organized bunch. They probably just updated the request right after they sent the first one and decided to Fax it. It happens sometimes. Hell, I probably have another email with the update."

"Don't you think that's a little strange?"

The Captain rolled his eyes. It probably was, but he didn't care. "Look, it doesn't matter, we serve the warrant. Detective, you and your partner, go arrest the guy." He looked at the two uniform cops and said. "Ramirez…Briggs, you back him up. As soon as he's in our house, I'll notify CID." The Captain went back in his office and the Detective, along with the uniform officers left the station so they could serve the warrant. It was supposed to be routine, however, it would be anything but that.

They were back at the airport, heading back to Midland. For Jim, Maisie, and Ron, it had been a brief stay in Houston that still didn't yield any answers on the true identity of the Black Fairy Killer. Could Aldo Martinez really be the killer, Jim highly doubted it. It didn't feel right and it was that feeling that he just couldn't shake. But he was a good suspect and it was time to rattle the tree a little bit and see what it produced when questioning him. Maybe he was wrong…maybe they had seen the face of the killer…the face of the devil himself.

As they were boarding the plan, Jim stopped and looked at the other two Detectives, especially Ron. He said. "Before, we go, I want to make this very clear, we are not arresting Aldo Martinez. We are only bringing him in for questioning."

Ron asked. "Why not arrest him?"

Jim gave him a dirty look. "Because we don't have enough evidence. It's all circumstantial."

"It's enough for an arrest, though!"

"But not enough to convict. Any halfway decent defense attorney could get him off with what we have especially without any physical evidence tying him to the crimes. And when CID arrests someone, we make sure we have them cold, so there's no chance they can be found not guilty or get off with a technicality."

Ron shook his head. "I think this is bullshit. We have him."

"No, we don't, but we will after we question him. We're going to lean on him and if he is the Black Fairy killer, he'll confess if for nothing else, to inflate his own ego. A killer like this wants to tell the world what they did and they're right." Ron didn't respond. He didn't really hear what Jim what was saying except for the part of getting Aldo Martinez to confess. He was thrilled with that part.

As they were getting seated right before takeoff, Maisie had to ask. Her curiosity was boiling over. "Jim, I couldn't help overhear you and your boss in the conference room, what was he talking about with you being a little gun shy...if you don't mind me asking?"

Jim chuckled. Some people may not like to talk about their past failures, but Jim was different. He was never embarrassed by his mistakes. He never thought of himself as some kind of investigative god. He didn't always get it right, but most of the time, his mistakes only made him better. He said. "I don't mind you asking. The last serial case I worked was just a little over a year ago. I got it wrong with the main suspect. We suspected this husband and father of 3. He was killing his mistresses or so we thought. The killer liked rough sex, especially choking. He would get his victim as close to death as he could while fucking them. That's how he got off."

Maisie had a disgusted look on her face. "Jesus...that's fucking sick."

"Yeah, he was a Grade A psycho. Anyway, there wasn't any physical evidence, he didn't cum inside the victims, always used a condom, and then cleaned everything up. But we got sweat secretions from the Condom getting stuck in one of the victim's vagina, especially when he tried to remove it. So we got partial DNA. The victim was the main suspect's sister-in-law and he had a history of cheating on his wife. So, I was absolutely sure, he was the killer. But I was wrong."

"How? Sounds like he would be the killer?"

"Exactly, but as it turned out, it was the guy's father. DNA was so close to each other based on the Y chromosomes that it was a near-perfect genetic match. His 62-year-old father had been doing this for a while, mostly with underage Hispanic girls who had been trafficked so there wasn't any kind of registry on them and we couldn't find a pattern or in most cases the bodies. We figured he killed about 30 girls. Anyway, we arrested him. The stupid Judge set a small bail amount, so he was able to get out, but the damage was already done. When he got home, the wife already filed for divorce and was in the process of changing the locks. He flipped out at what he considered her overreaction."

"Yeah, but her sister had been killed, her reaction is understandable."

Jim softly laughed. "He didn't see it that way and bashed her head in with a big stone from one of the flower beds, in front of their kids too. Left her lying in her own blood right there on the front lawn. Then he went inside, got the small 38 revolver he kept in his nightstand, and blew the back of his head out."

"Fucking hell!"

"Yeah! I was so stuck on him, I didn't even consider other possibilities. We eventually figured out it was the guy's father. He killed himself when police when he figured out the police were on to him. Even left a note saying that he was sorry for making his son look guilty. But it didn't matter, my bad assumption got a woman killed."

"Any cop could have made that mistake. You only followed where the evidence took you."

"True, but you understand if I'm a little more cautious now...or gun shy as my boss put it."

Maisie was about to respond when Ron briskly walked over to the two of them and showed a news alert he just got on his phone. It read, SHOTS FIRED AT POLICE IN MIDLAND!

Aldo Martinez was getting ready for a business trip. He was heading back to Dallas and wanted to get an early start. It was one hell of a long drive from Midland to Dallas. As he was answering the last of his emails, he got a phone call. It was his direct line. Normally, the customer service reps took inbound calls at his Highland Security Branch. Only when it was really important did he get a direct call. He answered the phone. "This is Aldo, how can I help?"

The voice on the other end of the phone replied. "Call 432-595-1120 on your other phone." They didn't mean his regular cell phone. They were referring to the other one he carried with him.

Aldo quickly got the prepaid cell phone out of his briefcase. It was a cheap prepaid smartphone that only had the standard Android Apps installed along with a VPN app. The sole purpose of the phone was to disguise who he was and to keep him from being tracked by those who were overly curious about his other life. He called the number. He didn't even have to say who it was that called. Aldo simply responded. "What's the emergency?" He knew it had to be one if he was getting a call, telling him to call a secret number.

The voice replied. "You have to get out of there immediately. A warrant has been issued for your arrest. Cops are on their way right now."

Aldo was shocked. What would they be arresting him for? He had been careful. Very careful. There were no crimes that the cops could tie him to. He was almost sure of that fact. He asked the Voice on the other end. "What are they cops trying to arrest me for."

"Murder...our guy at the station called a few minutes ago when he saw the warrant come across their system. The cops already left before he saw it so we don't know how much time you have."

"I don't understand...how do they have me on a murder charge?"

"Aldo...it doesn't matter. Get out of there now. We will text you a rendezvous location."

Aldo hung up the phone. He packed anything that could be considered sensitive documents in his briefcase and then he unlocked the bottom drawer of his desk. That's where he kept a silver Desert Eagle 50 Caliber Automatic pistol. It was a powerful handgun and could take a man's head clean off if needed. It was the kind of pistol you needed when you weren't messing around. Aldo rushed out of his office and didn't even say goodbye to anyone as he made his way to the front door. It was too late. An unmarked police car and a Midland PD patrol car pulled into the parking lot.

Aldo thought about trying to escape through the back, but he knew there wasn't time, and he wouldn't get far on foot that way. It was just open desert-like ground for miles behind the building. He panicked. There was only one way out of this. He was going to have to shoot his way out. But there were four cops. Could he get them all and get away? As the police walked to the front door, Aldo walked out towards them. He fired his gun. Catching all four police officers by surprise, he was able to shoot one of the detectives in the head. He wounded one of the uniform cops before the other two police officers drew their weapons and fired off some rounds. Aldo didn't make it to his car. The gunfire pushed him back inside the office. But now it was a whole new ballgame. He had hostages. There were eight people in the office. All of them cowering in fear over what they had just seen. Their boss had just killed a cop. And now they were his hostages…the situation couldn't get much worse.

The building was surrounded. Nothing was going to escape the Highland Security branch. Aldo was pacing inside while looking out the window about every five seconds. His hands were sweating as he tightly held his gun. Understandably, he was nervous. He had never taken hostages before. In fact, everybody in the office was pretty on edge. Maria, the office secretary asked. "Sir, what do you plan on doing with us?"

Aldo quickly turned around. "Hopefully, nothing, but that's up to the cops. "He checked the window again, more police cars were coming. He figured it was the hostage negotiator Midland PD was sure to send out. It was, sort of. Detective Jim Summers and his team finally arrived on the scene after rushing from the airport in what looked like a high-speed chase on Interstate 20 towards Midland. When Jim got out of the car he immediately started asking who was in charge. He found the man and the cop introduced himself to Jim. "I'm Sgt. Miller. I have tactical command right now."

Jim shook his hand. "Nice to meet, State CID is taking over now." Sgt. Miller rolled his eyes. "Whatever man, but if we take this guy down, he's going to our jail."

Jim nodded in agreement. "Let's get him out first. Has anybody talked to him?"

"No…we keep calling and the office phones are wired now so if they place a call, it comes to us."

"What about a hostage negotiator?"

"We have one on the way, but he was at a conference in San Antonio so we don't exactly have an ETA."

Jim looked around at all the cops who were there. It was like the entire police force was on the scene, but he wasn't surprised. One of their own had been killed. He asked. "What's the latest on the officer who was injured?"

With a solemn tone, Sgt. Miller replied. "He's still in critical condition."

"Sorry about your men?"

The Sergeant nodded. "Now that you're here, do you have a plan? Do we take this asshole dead or alive?"

"My plan is to take him alive. We were only coming here to question him and that hasn't changed."

The Sergeant gave Jim a stern look. "With all due respect sir, my officers came here to serve a warrant for murder and now he's killed one of them. If we get a clear line of fire, we're going to shoot the fucker. You don't kill a cop in Midland and then get special treatment."

Jim got in the sergeant's face. "Let's be clear. State CID has command here. You're going to do what I say if you want to keep your job and avoid jail time for screwing up my investigation. Now my instructions were to only bring him to your station for questioning. We didn't issue a warrant for his arrest."

"We had a copy of the warrant faxed to us."

Jim shook his head. It was hard to believe a colossal mistake like that could happen. Murder warrants never got faxed. Not even a copy would be sent that way. They are usually delivered in person. But Midland as big as it is, was still just a podunk Texas town that didn't have much sophistication when it came to police work. At least that was his opinion. Jim replied. "We will get into the mistaken warrant later. Right now, we have to get this guy out of there without killing any hostages and that starts by actually talking to him."

"How, he won't answer the phone!"

Jim pulled out Aldo's business card that he took from him a couple of days ago. It had his cell number on it. If Aldo wouldn't talk on the phone, maybe he would text him. Jim texted his cell phone, hoping that Aldo still had it on him. He said. "I have his cell phone, maybe he will respond to a text message."

Jim texted. "Aldo Martinez, I am Detective Jim Summers with Texas State CID, we talked a couple of days ago. Here is the situation, you're surrounded, but I'm sure you already know that. We would like to talk to you and try to resolve this situation, peacefully. I'm sure everybody in there is getting hungry, we can arrange for some food. Would you be willing to talk to me?"

Aldo was stunned to get the text message. He was maintaining radio silence until he received instructions from the man he had talked to earlier on his other phone. He didn't think that he should respond, but if this was going to go on for a while even he knew that people were going to need to eat. He texted back. "Food would be good."

Jim smiled when he saw the response. There were some light cheers among the other cops when Aldo responded back. Jim said. "Alright, now we're getting somewhere." He texted back. "Great, but before we go forward. We need to talk on the phone…will you talk to me?"

Aldo knew what he was doing. They weren't just going to give him food for nothing. He paused, thinking about all the consequences that would happen if he actually called the police. Right now he had the power and if he called, he would lose part of it. Aldo looked at the scared faces around the room, wondering if they were going to make it out of there alive. Food would definitely help calm their nerves. He decided to risk it. Aldo called the number that had been texting him.

Jim looked at the Sergeant and smiled. So far, his plan was working. He answered the phone. "Thank You for actually calling me."

Aldo replied. "We could use some food."

"And we can help you with that. How about some pizzas?"

"Pizza is good. Get us four pepperoni pizzas, two cheese pizzas, and two supreme pizzas."

Jim wrote it down and then asked. "What, no sausage pizza."

"No self-respecting Texan orders sausage pizza. Not even Mexicans." Jim couldn't help but laugh. He wasn't wrong. Sausage Pizza was considered Yankee Pizza. Jim replied. "We will get those ordered. Should take about 45 minutes."

Aldo asked. "So, you're the Hostage Negotiator?"

"No, I'm not…I am, however, the guy in charge. This is my investigation."

"Why am I being charged with murder?"

"Actually, you're not, the warrant was a mistake…. sorry about that. The cops who came to your office were to only bring you in for questioning, that was it."

Aldo shook his head, not wanting to believe the horseshit he was hearing. He just killed a cop over a mistaken warrant. "So, what now?"

"We have a pretty serious situation, don't we? And now innocent people are involved."

"I guess you want my demands. That's how this works, right!"

Jim had the call on speaker phone. The rest of the police standing around could hear the conversation. Jim looked around and they all pretty much had the same look on their face, immense curiosity, what was Jim going to give Aldo to get him out of there or release the hostages? Then Jim stunned them all with what he said to Aldo.

Jim, in an authoritative tone, said. "No, I don't care about your demands. A Hostage negotiator might say different, but I don't. I'm not here to bullshit you; I'm here to tell you the truth.

You're pretty much fucked. You killed a cop and in Texas, we usually just put you down for that. We don't waste time on trials."

Aldo was caught off guard. "What the hell, are you saying that you're just going to come in and shoot me."

"No...just telling you how we treat cop killers. So let me tell you what your options are. You kill any hostage; we come in and kill you. If you even harm any of them, we kill you. The only way you get out of this alive is to give yourself up."

"Aldo's mood quickly turned to anger. He was furious at this point and it showed in his voice. "Give myself up and go to prison, fuck you. You get the death penalty for killing cops and I won't die in Prison."

"I understand, but what if you didn't have to go to prison? What If you could escape the death penalty?"

"Bullshit, you're just telling me what I want to hear."

Jim paused for a moment. He didn't want to lie. He was still trying to as honest as possible and build a rapport with him. "Maybe you won't have to do time or if you do, what if you were only charged with manslaughter? That is minimal time...maybe probation, but it isn't the death penalty."

That piqued Aldo's curiosity. He was ready to hang up his phone and take his chances. But replied back. "Keep talking."

Jim continued. "It's what we call an accidental death. You were provoked and that's why you shot the cop. You were provoked because the warrant for your arrest was false. It was our mistake...it was our fault and that backed you into a corner. That's what could be argued. So instead of getting arrested for murder, maybe it's just manslaughter with a little bit of time. Hell, get the right judge and maybe you get like 10 years' probation. Hell, you can probably sue the police department for a false arrest and make some money. "Sgt. Miller gave Jim a dirty look. He was about to say something when Jim waved him off.

Aldo replied. "Is that even true? That seems like Bullshit."

"Of course, it's true...you can ask your lawyer, but the only way this works is if you give yourself up."

Aldo laughed to himself. "There's always a catch, isn't there."

Jim laughed too. "You're right, there's always a catch."

Aldo looked around the room at the hostages. He had a hard decision to make. Truth is, he didn't want to hurt anybody in the room. Some of them were even his friends. The choice was too hard to make so he simply replied. "We'll talk about it after we eat."

24

It felt like forever since the last time Sara went to confession. Maybe not forever, but it had been a while. She tried to remember; maybe the last time she went was in college. Going to a church, lighting a candle, and saying a prayer had been good enough, but for a while now, she felt as if she needed more. Sara wasn't confessing anything as much as she just needed to talk to someone. She could talk to a therapist but something inside of her said that she neede a priest. She went to St. Thomas Aquinas in Dallas. It was closer to where she lived.

As luck would have it, a confessional booth was open. She went inside and soon after, a priest by the name Father Kieran sat on the other side of the masked wall. Sara spoke first. "Bless me father, it's been a long time since my last confession.

Father Kieran replied. "What matters is that you're here now, what would you like to confess?"

Sara smiled. It was comforting to hear that. "I don't know if I really have any sins to confess…don't know if I've really done anything wrong, but I needed to talk. I've been feeling trapped."

"What do you mean?"

"Like nothing I do, makes a difference…am I really helping anyone?
Would it really matter if I was around?"

Father Kieran smiled. "You're not the only one that feels that way. We do too. Every priest here at the parish has felt that way, even to the point of questioning our own calling. "

Sara was surprised. "I never thought a priest would admit to questioning their own calling."

"I know the church tries to make a priest as some invincible being once they become ordained, but we're still human, filled with the same self-doubts as the people who come through the doors of a church. But let me ask you this, has there been at least one good thing you feel you've done over the last week."

Thinking about it, brought a smile to Sara's face again. "I saved a girl from the abuse of her pedophile father not too long ago."

"That's very heroic. It shows that you have compassion."

"I don't regret what I did even if some think I was wrong to interfere, but there's a lot of things I've done that I seriously question if I made the right choice. I can't say for sure what I have done is wrong and the Bible doesn't exactly have clear answers. "

The priest replied. "Here's the thing about the Bible, is only meant to be a guideline when it comes to morality. It's not absolute as some men of God would have us believe."

Sara laughed. "Should a priest really be saying that?"

"Not everybody will agree with me, but it's also the most honest answer you will get from a priest. Everybody has to figure out their own version of morality. Hopefully the Bible will be their guide. Look at it this way, the Bible says *thou shalt not steal*, but if someone steals food to feed their family because they don't have money, is it really a sin? Should we not show compassion for their situation instead of some form of punishment?"

Sara commented. "How about murder? The Bible clearly says it's wrong, but yet it justifies it with *an eye for an eye*."

Father Kieran laughed at the notion. "You're right, it's not exactly black and white when it comes to killing. However, revenge isn't something holy either and there's an argument to make that *eye for an eye* is simply just revenge. So with that said, are you thinking about murdering someone?"

"No, but I do want to see certain people die. I do think that the world would be better without them. Is that wrong?"

"Yes, it does fall under the category of impure thoughts, but we're all guilty of those kinds of thoughts."

"Even priests"

"Yes, even priests, although some don't like to admit it."

Sara was surprised to hear that. But like the man said, they we human. Father Kieran asked. "How did you rescue the girl?"

"It doesn't really matter, but I know they're safe now."

"Then you did a good thing."

"Even if how I did it may be bad?"

Father Kieran thought about it for a moment. "Only God can judge you for your actions. I don't think it's important how you do it as long you save a life. I would think even God would take into consideration, the greater good."

"So what's the answer if you keep feeling trapped?"

"Prayer. And to keep trying to do what is right. That's what keeps you morally centered. That's what keeps you from being trapped. You may not feel it today, but eventually, you will and for the impure thoughts say five Hail Marys. I'm betting, you'll feel better."

Sara smiled. She did feel better, believe it or not. She left the confessional booth and headed home. On her way, she thought to herself, perhaps she should do more than just light a candle next time she went to church or go to the occasional mass. Maybe what she needed was to attend on a regular basis. It worked for other people, why not her?

When Jim got off the phone, he immediately told one of the officers to get some pizzas ordered, it didn't matter from what place. But he couldn't get past the icy stares from the police officers standing around who were looking at him as if he just botched the hostage crisis. Sgt. Miller responded. "No offense, what the hell was that? How can you tell him that he could get off with just manslaughter? That can't be fucking true."

Jim gave him a dirty look. "Of course not, but he doesn't know that. He killed a cop...he's going down for it."

"Then why tell him that shit."

"Because I'm trying to get him to give himself up peacefully and if he thinks he's not going down for Murder, he might just do that."

"And telling him that he could win a lawsuit, what's that about!"

Jim smiled. "This is America, winning a lot of money without having to earn it can be a powerful incentive. Maybe that gets him out too. And if he were to win a lawsuit, then I think that's worth saving the hostages' lives....don't you!"

"You're a terrible hostage negotiator."

"Probably, but if it works then who the fuck cares. Let me know when the pizzas get here." Jim walked off. He sure as hell wasn't going to be lectured by some local sheriff's deputy who'd never dealt with a serious crime like this before. Detective Jackson seemed to agree with the deputy, but he didn't exactly get along with Jim anyway.

Maisie followed Jim. She had never been through anything like this before in her career. It was a little overwhelming. She asked Jim. "How does a warrant mistakenly get sent from State CID?"

"It doesn't happen unless someone forges the document."

"Are you saying..."

"Yes, someone forged that document and faxed it."

"Holy shit, who would do that?"

Jim nodded. "Don't know for sure, but I bet the list is small. Anyway, it doesn't matter at this point. We have a hostage crisis to solve."

"So, what's the endgame, here?"

Jim shook his head. "To be honest, I don't know how this plays out? I don't think anybody thought Aldo Martinez would just up and shoot a cop."

Maisie tried to laugh to lighten the mood. "Yeah, talk about a big surprise. Do you think, he will give himself up?"

"In a perfect world, yes. However, I don't think we're going to be that lucky. I think SWAT will end up having to go in."

"You still don't think he's the guy, do you?"

Jim paused for a moment so he could collect his thoughts. "My instincts still say no, but there is evidence to suggest he is. Won't know for sure, unless we get to talk with him a little bit."

Maisie tried to be somewhat joyful. "You never know, we might get lucky." Jim smiled but didn't say anything. Maisie continued. "I'm going to try and see if I can find some coffee, want one?"

"Sure. That would be great."

Aldo, kept checking his watch. They said 30 to 40 minutes and he was counting. People were getting hungry. He looked out the window again. It was the exact same scene of cops just milling around waiting for something to happen. Finally, one of the sales guys asked. "What happens after we get food?"

Aldo shot him a dirty look. He didn't really know. It's not like this could go on for days. They weren't equipped for that. He replied. "We're going to play it by ear."

"That's it. What the fuck are you even going to do with us?"

Aldo pointed his gun at the guy and replied in anger. "You'll either fucking die or get out of here alive…that's what's going to happen."

"How long are we doing to be here?"

"That depend on the cops."

The sales guy was about to say something else but was interrupted when Aldo's other cell phone rang. He answered it and the voice from earlier was on the other end. He asked. "Do you have a plan for getting out of your fucked situation?"

Aldo thought about it for a moment. "I'm working on it. They're supposed to be bringing us food. That's the current situation. "

The voice replied. "Well, we do have a plan for getting you out. We can't let the police have you."

"Okay…what's your plan?"

"Wait for the signal."

"What signal?"

"You'll know it when it happens so be ready." Aldo hung up and looked around the room. Everybody was still scared, not knowing what was really going to happen. Aldo had to admit to himself, even he was nervous. But he knew that whatever was going to happen was going to happen soon.

About twenty minutes later, a pizza delivery guy showed up at the scene. Nobody thought much of it since the police had ordered pizza for the hostages except for the fact, they didn't have it delivered. The police would have gone to pick it up themselves. The pizza guy was simply a distraction. Five black SUVs drove up from around the back of the Highland Security office, using the back roads from behind the building to mask their entry point. The cops standing around didn't even see them coming before it was too late. One man got out of an SUV and went to the trunk. He pulled out a Military Grade Rocket Launcher and fired into the crowd of police officers. One of the squad cars exploded, causing some of the officers and deputies to be blown back. Two were killed instantly by the explosion. It was the signal Aldo Martinez was waiting for.

25

Audra had been surfing the internet looking up more stuff about serial killers when a breaking news notification popped up. She had her laptop set to receive news updates, local and national news. She was naturally curious about the world around her, which was very different from most girls her age. The item that popped up was about a police shootout in Midland, Texas that was still going on. She clicked on it and read a little bit of the article. Wanting to know more, she turned on the TV in the living room and turned-on Channel 8 WFAA. Their local affiliate was live at the scene, covering the shootout at the Highland Security office.

They didn't show much as it was too disturbing for viewers, but she saw something familiar in their coverage of the shootout. Audra saw Jim on TV, firing his gun. She felt the tightening in her stomach as fear grabbed hold of her. Jim was in a gun fight and there was no way of knowing if he would make it out alive. Gina finally got home. She found Audra almost in a panic attack watching the news. She asked. "Are you alright, what's going on?"

Audra replied. "There's a police shootout and I saw Jim on the TV in the middle of it."

Now Gina Panicked. "What, are you sure it was him?"

"Yes."

"What's the shootout over?"

"The news said it was a hostage crisis that turned into a gun battle; it's in Midland... that's all I know."

Gina did the catholic cross and said a prayer to herself. She prayed for Jim's safety. And then for the next hour and a half, Gina and Audra stayed glued to the TV, hoping to see just a glimpse of Jim or get even the slightest news that he was okay."

Gunshots were flying through the air like rain. Jim, who had only ever been fired upon twice in his career, had never seen so many bullets fired at the police. It was like something out of an 80s action movie. When the squad car blew up, everybody found cove . Jim and Maisie found cover behind the SWAT team where they had been getting a cup of coffee. Bullets kept whizzing by and they didn't seem to stop when the men in the SUVs had to reload. They weren't really trying to hit anything, just keep the police at bay so they could accomplish their true goal.

Squatting down, Maisie asked. "What the hell is going on...who's shooting at us?"

Jim pulled out his gun. "I don't know."

Maisie got out her gun as well. "Why are they here?"

"I think they're here to break Martinez out."

"That's a lot of firepower to get one man out of a hostage situation."

"Yes, it is which means they aren't fucking around."

Bullets continued to spray across the crowd of police officers. Some of them were trying to fire back, but to no avail.

Even the SWAT team was having a hard time getting shots off and they had AR-15 Assault rifles. Most of the bullets being fired came from the men in SUVs. There was no real strategy for the police other than fire back and not get shot in the process. Finally, Jim saw some of the men with guns heading towards the back of the building. He commented to Maisie as he pointed to the men. "Looks like, they're going to try and get Aldo out the back."

She was surprised at first, but then it made it sense. It was the best option for an escape with the police pretty much pinned down from gunfire. Maisie replied. "What do we do?"

Jim looked around. If they were going to stop them, they needed better weapons. Jim and Maisie went inside the SWAT van. It had enough weapons and tactical gear for a small army. He grabbed two bulletproof tactical vests, handed one to Maisie, and said. "Put this on." Then he grabbed two AR-15 assault rifles and handed one of them to her. "I'm assuming, you've fired one of these before?"

In a nervous tone, she replied. "Yeah, but not at a person."

Jim cracked a smile. "Good enough. Just aim and point it in their direction." Jim looked around the van. He was looking for something specific but having a hard time finding it. Finally, he saw them, flash-bang grenades. Just what he needed. He hooked two of them to Maisie's vest and then grabbed two of them for himself. Maisie gave him a strange look. He responded. "They're for distraction…if we're lucky, we can catch them off guard and take them down without getting shot."

Maisie replied. You got to be kidding. Isn't this a job for the SWAT team?"

"I think they're a little busy right now." She gave him a dirty look. The SWAT team captain walked into the van. He said. "Oh good, you found extra weapons. Time to get into the fight."

Jim replied. "They're trying to break Aldo Martinez out the back, so that's where we are headed to stop them.

The Captain replied. "Really!"

"Yeah, how many men do you have down?"

Bullets hit the side of the van, causing those inside the van to duck for cover. Fortunately, the van was made with heavy metal and bullets weren't getting through. The Captain said. "I got two men down, but we can't seem to advance on those fuckers...there's too many of them and they have heavy assault rifles as you can see."

"You have air support?"

"That would be nice, but we're not big enough to have such nice things. We have two small, armored assault vehicles with 50 Caliber 'Modified Browning' Machine Guns on top. I've ordered them here. They're not too far away so they should be here any minute. "

"Good. Now, I need a couple of guys to follow behind us and lay down some cover fire as we make our way to the back of the building. I figure we're about 70 or 80 yards away." The Captain nodded in agreement. He then peeked outside and yelled to a couple of his men. "Morris...Johnson, get over here. "Both of them ran up to the van, avoiding any stray bullets that could hit them. " The Captain said to them. "Follow the detectives and lay down cover fire. And try not to get shot." Both men nodded.

Jim looked at Maisie. He could tell she was nervous. She had never been in this kind of situation before. She had only ever faced off with one man who had a gun pointed in her direction...not even directed at her. This was a whole new ballgame and it was no surprise that she felt like throwing up. Jim said. "Look at me. Take a deep breath. You're going to stay right behind me. Move when I move. And shoot when I shoot."

Maisie took a deep breath and said. "Okay."

"When you shoot, aim true, and go for a headshot in case they're wearing Kevlar. Just like our police targets at the range. Can you do that?" Maisie nodded, "yes."

Jim smiled. "Okay. Let's go!"

They started to make their way towards the back of the building. The SWAT guys gave them cover fire. Bratatat...Bratatat. Jim and Maisie ran 15 yards and dove down, laying down cover fire the for the two SWAT officers so they could make run the 15 yards. Bratatat...Bratatat. There wasn't much cover since it was pretty much an open field leading to the back of the building so they took turns shooting covering fire so the others could make it. Some of the men from the SUVs saw what they were doing and shot back. Both SWAT officers were able to kill at least one of the men doing that. Jim, Maisie, and the two SWAT officers ran and lay down cover fire five times, crossing the 75 yards from the SWAT van to the back of the Building. They made it without anyone being seriously injured. Maisie was bleeding from a bullet grazing her arm. Her adrenaline had kicked into overdrive, she didn't even notice until Jim pointed it out. But she wasn't going to quit, they had come this far.

When the gunfight started, Aldo was looking out the window. He saw the Squad Car explode and cheered. He said to himself, "The cavalry has arrived." Most of the people in the office, found some sort of cover when they heard the gunfire. They were scared before. Now they were terrified, except for one person. The sales guy who had been asking questions saw it as an opportunity. He rushed for Aldo, who for a split second wasn't paying attention. He didn't make it before Aldo shot him. He got close enough that Aldo shot him close up and pretty much blew his chest wide open with his 50 Caliber Desert Eagle Pistol. The sales guy died instantly, causing more panic with the other hostages

Aldo looked at everybody and said. "Listen up; this is what happens to stupid mother fuckers who try to be heroes. Stay down, it will be over soon." That's what he thought at least. But it didn't matter; he heard the clanking at the back door. That's also when he saw the text message on his other phone…*go to the back door; we're coming to get you out.* Aldo shot his gun a few more times just to scare everybody. He hoped that would keep everybody from getting up and trying to take him down. Turned out, he was right.

    Gunfire was still buzzing over their heads when they reached the back corner of the building. The back door was located on the side which looked as if somebody had built an addition to the overall building. Jim, Maisie, and the SWAT guys had some cover in the corner of the backside of the building that the extra edition created. They were also covered a little bit by the dumpster area as it masked them from the men in the SUVs who were firing. It was easy for Jim to look around the corner and see 3 men standing by the back door as if they were guarding it. They had already breached the back door and were starting to move Aldo Martinez out.

    Jim pulled one of the flash-bang grenades from his vest and motioned for Maisie to do the same. Then he signaled that on the count of three they would pull the pins and throw them in the direction of the other men with guns. He also whispered to everybody. "We take Aldo Martinez alive…no matter what….NO MATTER WHAT!"

    Jim and Maisie threw their flash-bang grenades. Bang! They went off like clockwork and easily distracted the three men. Jim was quick to react and killed the one closest to him. He then killed the one furthest away with a head shot as the guy was trying to get his gun up. Maisie got a good aim on the other one and nailed him with a head shot as well. There were three guys inside the building trying to collect Aldo. Jim threw another flash bang grenade inside the doorway as one of the other guys was firing. He was able to move out of the way with only a bullet grazing his shirt…no bodily harm.

    The men inside were disoriented. So were the hostages for that matter. Jim and the two SWAT guys moved inside. Each one of them was able to fire their weapons and take the bad guys out with one shot like a great tactical team with precision. In the midst of all the confusion, Aldo tried to make a run for it out the door. Maisie was making her way inside and saw him. She put a stop to it by taking the butt of her AR-15 and bopping him the face with tremendous force. She easily knocked him out. Jim couldn't help but laugh; after all, it was a pretty cool move.

Jim quickly got Aldo handcuffed, but they weren't out of the woods yet. There were still plenty of men outside with guns trying to get Aldo. More of them might be trying to come through the back door. Gunfire was still going off repeatedly like a constant war zone. It showed no signs of letting up. As Jim and Maisie got Aldo to a secure place in the building and checked on the hostages, Morris and Johnson, the SWAT team officers guarded the back door waiting for any "unfriendlies" that might come in. That's when they heard it; the armored assault vehicles finally arrived and opened fire on the men around the SUVs. It evened out the odds. Finally, the police were able to take out more of the bad guys with their huge 50 Caliber 'Modified Browning' Machine Guns. They even took out one of the guys trying to shoot off another rocket launcher. The police were now winning.

All in All, there were about twenty guys who rolled up in SUVs. The police were able to take out fourteen of them. When it was clear that their little jailbreak wasn't going to work, the remaining men drove away. The voice on Aldo's other cell phone had lost communication with the men who were supposed to extract Also, he knew they must be dead, so he ordered everybody who was still alive to abort the mission. If he was lucky, Aldo was dead, and it wouldn't be a total loss. He wasn't that lucky.

This had been the biggest gun battle in Midland since the Texas Rangers had been defending the area against Comanche Indians in the late 19th Century. The death toll: 14 bad guys dead and 6 police officers killed in Action. For Detective Maisie Green, it was the first time she had ever killed anyone…an experience that would haunt her for the rest of her career.

26

The dust had finally settled and there were more dead bodies at the scene than most Midland Police Officers had seen in their lifetime. The scene outside the Highland Security building could have been any war zone. The hostages were being treated by EMT's, but there weren't really any injuries among them. They were mostly in shock from everything that had transpired. The Press were swarming the area, especially local TV stations, trying to get any comment they could from the police. National News outlets were taking an interest as well such at the Associate Press, CNN, and FOX News. It was chaotic, but they got their man, that was the main thing.

Jim found Maisie. She was getting patched up by the EMTs, but unlike the hostages, she needed a few stitches. Jim smiled at her and asked. "How are you feeling?"

She sighed. "I'm still shaking."

"It's shock mixed with adrenaline…it's normal and it will wear off."

"I don't think this should be normal…at least I don't want it to be normal in my life."

Jim laughed at her sarcasm. She had a point. "I want you to know, you did good out there…very good. I loved your move knocking Aldo Martinez out as he was coming out the door."

"Thanks, but I don't feel like I did a good job today. All of this was too much, not exactly normal stuff for cops."

"True, what happened today is rare. Of course, it also occurs to me…you've never killed anybody before in the line of duty before…correct"

Maisie almost welled up with tears. It was a sickening feeling taking a life. She said. "No, I haven't."

"I won't patronize you by saying that it gets easier because it shouldn't. You just get better at ignoring the terrible feelings that come with killing a person."

"How do you ignore those feelings?"

Jim laughed. "I drink good scotch… nothing less than 12 years."

"I can see that. Do you mind if I ask how many people you've killed in the line of duty?"

Jim thought about it for a moment. "I killed three today, so that would make it a total of seven."

"Holy shit. I can't imagine doing that."

"Don't try, hopefully, you'll be luckier than me and this will be the only one for you. But I'm glad you're okay."

"Thank you." The EMT finished up wrapping her arm and gave her a shot for the pain. The bullet only grazed her, but it did cause her to bleed a lot. Jim continued. "I do have a favor to ask and then you can fly back to Dallas."

"What is it?"

"I want you to accompany Aldo back to the station and make sure he is sent straight to an interrogation room. I don't trust Midland PD not to beat the hell out of him for killing cops. We need him conscious so we can question him, if you get my drift."

She nodded. "I can do that and probably good thinking."

"Also, I know you don't like him, but take Detective Johnson with you…this is his prime suspect so I wouldn't expect him to be a typical good ole boy cop in this situation and let them beat him. Would take away from his glory!"

Maisie laughed at the last part. Jim wasn't necessarily wrong. She replied. "I think I can stomach him for a little while longer."

"Great. I won't be too far behind. And once we get to question him. The Jet will take you and Ron back to Dallas…CID can take it from here with the investigation." Maisie nodded, letting him know that she understood. She asked. "Why can't you do it?"

"I need to take care of some things here, CID business. But I will be at the station shortly." He smiled and walked off. Maisie got with Ron and they put an unconscious Aldo Martinez in the back of a police car. Only one Midland police officer accompanied them since they couldn't take the car themselves and to ensure they had the greater numbers in case some of the Midland PD tried to send Aldo to the morgue before he ever got to the station.

Jim found Sgt. Miller. The sergeant was still mad as hell about how everything went down, and he definitely didn't like Jim or the way he handled things. Jim said to him. "Sergeant, sorry about your men." Miller didn't respond he just gave Jim a disapproving look. Jim asked. "What was the final death count?"

Sgt. Miller replied. "Six officers killed in the line of duty today, not including the one Martinez killed earlier."

"I'm sorry."

"No offense, nobody cares whether you're sorry or not.

That scumbag better pay for this. If he walks or gets a lighter sentence, I'll put a bullet in him myself."

Jim nodded in agreement. He was sympathetic to Sgt. Miller's anger. Jim said. "I agree and make no mistake, despite what I told him on the phone, he will be going down for murder one. As far as I am concerned, cop killers get a one-way trip to death row."

"You make that happen or it may not be that pleasant for you the next time you come to Midland." It wasn't really a threat, more like a friendly reminder of what could happen. Jim understood that. He didn't necessarily disagree, especially if he were in the Sergeant's shoes. He smiled. "Understood, but you won't have to put a bullet in him because I will do it first."

Sgt. Miller nodded."

"Before, I forget more CID officers will be here tonight to go over the crime scene and to help with trying to identify the shooters. It is our investigation, but we want to work with your station to get the job done. So, it goes without saying, we appreciate your cooperation."

"It's not like we have a choice, right!"

"No, but we still like to ask nicely."

Sgt. Miller gave him a dirty look. Jim was about to respond, but he got another text message from Gina. He had gotten about a dozen text messages from her asking if he was okay. Even got a few phone calls. In all the chaos, he forgot that she might have seen the news and would be worried about him. It was a comforting to know she cared. He excused himself and walked away to call Gina.

He clicked on one of her messages and called her. She saw his name on the Caller ID and immediately picked up. She said. "Oh, Thank God...you're alive."

Jim softly laughed. Not the exact response he expected. He replied. "No need to worry, I'm alive."

"Audra and I saw the shoot out on the news or at least what they could show."

"I'm glad they didn't show everything...it was pretty messy, but I'm alright."

"Are you hurt?"

"No, one of the Detectives who were with me was grazed by a bullet, but that's all the harm that came to us."

Gina smiled. "Then my prayers have been answered."

"God was certainly looking out for me today."

"The news hasn't confirmed anything yet...did you get the guy who took those people hostage?"

"We did...he's in custody now."

"Good. You should know, Audra has been glued to the TV since they started reporting the incident, I think you scared her."

"Tell her, she doesn't have to be scared. I promise, I'm alright. Thank You for checking on me...it means a lot."

Gina smiled as a few tears ran down her cheek. The sentiment was not lost her. It felt good to receive it. She asked, "Do you know when you'll be back in Dallas?"

"Honestly don't know. Probably, at least a few days depending on how his investigation goes down here. But I will be back as soon as I can. Would be nice to have dinner with you and the kids."

"Agreed, it would be nice." Gina heard someone over the phone calling for Jim. She knew he had to go so she told him before he had to rush off. "Jim, just come back when you can."

Jim smiled. It was nice to hear something like that. "I will and I'll be back before you know it." It made her happy to hear that. After all, she was falling for him…falling for him hard. And no one was more surprised than she was.

Jim's boss had finally arrived at the scene in Midland. He was accompanied by a dozen CID officers and a few Texas Rangers who could help with the investigation. It was big time now. It wasn't just about hunting a serial killer. The biggest shootout in over a hundred years happened in Midland, leaving about twenty people dead, both cops and criminals raised a lot of questions. Why did it happen, that was the big question! Robert greeted Jim by saying. "What a huge fucking mess."

Jim chuckled. "Don't disagree."

"What the hell happened?"

"Looks like a murder warrant might have been falsified and when Midland PD tried to serve it, Aldo Martinez opened fire."

"Do you know who created the false warrant?"

Jim shrugged. "No, and we haven't had time to look into it."

Robert replied. "We'll conduct an investigation once we're done with all of this."

"What's with the Texas Rangers?"

"Just here to help...they're going to try and ID the men who tried to break Aldo out. They may have links to drug cartels."

Jim was a little shocked to hear that. "Really...are we sure about that?"

"They may be. That's what the rangers are here to find out along with our guys. Plus, they're going to be tearing Aldo's life apart and trying to figure out how this happened."

"This is still my case, right?"

Robert gave him a serious look. "Yes... but like I said, this is bigger than hunting a serial killer...you get more manpower. He's a cop killer now and a small army tried to capture him so we couldn't.... we need to know why." Jim nodded. Robert also said. "By the way, congrats on the arrest and saving the hostages. You did a good job."

"We didn't save all the hostages, unfortunately."

"True, but not because of anything we did. Aldo killed a guy who tried to be a hero. There's no way you could have stopped that."

"Yeah, tell that to the guy's family."

Robert winced. He could see Jim's point, but they couldn't do anything about it now. There were more important issues. Robert asked Jim to ride with him to the station. They had some things to discuss before Jim got to interrogate Aldo Martinez. As they were driving to the station in one of the unmarked Ford Crown Victoria's, Robert said to Jim. "You should know the Governor called me before I flew out here."

"Holy Shit...when was the last time he personally called State CID."

"It's been a while and it was definitely bad. He never calls unless it's bad."

"What did he say?"

Robert chuckled. "He basically let me know in a not-so-subtle way that we needed to stick these murders with Aldo Martinez."

"You're kidding me...he was actually giving an order to charge him with the Black Fairy murders."

"He wouldn't come right out and say it like that, but he in his so-called influential way, was saying that we have the guy and charge him with what we have."

Jim shook his head. Never once had he been a part of an investigation where the state's own governor was pretty much ordering the arrest and prosecution of a suspect. It was ballsy considering he could get impeached for that sort of thing. Jim replied. "But we still don't know for sure if he's the Black Fairy killer."

"You still have doubts after this... somebody sure as hell didn't want him to be caught by the police."

"I think he's guilty of something, but being a serial killer, we don't know that for sure. And I won't pin some murders on someone. You can have my badge before I do that."

Robert gave him a dirty look. "No one is saying to do that. But I warned you about dragging out this investigation; we need to end it as fast as possible, especially after this shooting. The public won't stand for it."

"What do you know that I don't?"

Robert laughed. "I know a lot more than you do...that's why I'm the boss."

"Then what are you really trying to tell me...no more riddles...just say it."

"Alright...we're going to need a confession from Aldo Martinez...something iron clad...we can't let the courts fuck this up. And no bullshit insanity plea, either."

Jim paused for a moment, giving Robert an ominous look. Finally, he replied. "So, I guess you want this confession by any means necessary, uh?"

Robert shot him another dirty look. "I'm not telling you to do anything illegal, I'm just saying, work your magic and get a confession. "

Jim knew the signs. He knew what his boss was asking. He felt the pressure to solve this case and help get a sure-fire conviction. But it was never that simple. He was one of the few cops in Texas that didn't see things in Black and White. The evidence was still circumstantial. There was still too much coincidence with the timeline of the murders and him being in those cities at the same time. Jim had to be sure before he could push a suspect hard to get a confession and he wasn't sure of anything in this case. But at the end of the day, he still had a job to do and Aldo Martinez was guilty of something, that he was sure of. All those dead bodies proved that.

27

The Midland Police station was crowded with spectators, waiting to see what was going to happen with Aldo Martinez. He was a cop killer now and despised by everyone in the station. Any one of them would have been happy to get it over quick and just shoot him. That's the sense Jim got as he walked past a parade of Midland Police Officers on his way to the interrogation room. The Captain was standing near the doorway along with Robert, Jim's boss. He had curious look when he spoke to Jim. "Your boss just told me the real reason you wanted to talk to this guy. The Black Fairy Killer, uh. You think it's him?"

Jim cracked a smile. "I guess we're about to find out." The Captain nodded and then moved out of the way so Jim could get inside the room and do his job. Detective Jackson was right behind him. Jim said to him. "You can come in the room since this is your lead, but I'm asking the questions. "

Ron replied. "I don't get to ask anything, this is my guy."

"Only if I let you…this is still my investigation, and you follow my lead." Ron wanted to say something, but Jim cut off. Jim's stern look lets him know that he shouldn't even try to talk back. He wasn't the one in charge. Before they went in the room, Jim saw a soda machine down the hall and walked to it. He got a Dr. Pepper from the machine. Everybody gave him a strange look except Robert; he knew what Jim was doing. It was an Interrogation tactic. A simple gift to make the suspect feel more at ease and hopefully get them talking.

Jim and Ron entered the room. Aldo was awake, courtesy of the smelling salts Maisie had given him earlier when was put in the room. He was also handcuffed to the table. It was to prevent any violent outbursts that could hurt somebody's body. Nobody had talked to him since he got to the station. Nobody would answer his questions, but he didn't really have any since he knew what was probably going to happen being a cop killer and all. But the night was still full of surprises.

Aldo looked up at the two men. He asked. "Is someone going to tell me what the hell is going on here, why I am in this room?"

Jim replied. "Don't worry Mr. Martinez, we're going to get to that soon enough." He handed Aldo the can of Dr. Pepper and two Motrin pills. "Getting knocked out with a gun can be painful…this will help." Aldo quickly grabbed the soda and started drinking. He was thirsty. He took the pills as well for his massive headache."

Aldo asked. "Who are you?"

Jim replied. "I'm detective Jim Summers from Texas State CID…we spoke on the phone earlier today." Aldo was a bit surprised, but he acknowledged that he knew who Jim was. Jim continued. "This is Detective Ron Jackson, he's part of our task force."

Aldo was curious. "Task force? You already have a task force for today's incident."

"Not exactly. But we are here to ask you some questions."

"You were there today, you know what happened."

"Not about today…"

Aldo interrupted. "So I guess, we're not going to talk about getting manslaughter for killing that cop."

Ron rolled his eyes at the notion. Jim cracked a smile. "No…I'm afraid that ship has sailed after 20 armed men tried to break you out and more cops died including the other one you shot."

"I guess what you said on the phone was a lie?"

"I wasn't lying at the time, but that was before the shootout. You should know that you're looking at Death Row now, but is there is a way to avoid that."

Aldo with curiosity asked. "What do I have to do?"

"Answer my questions about some other crimes."

Jim had a file folder with crime scene photos of four murders, Hugo Blackmon, Jack Perry, Don Bennett, and Henry Frankston. He laid them out in front of Aldo and didn't say anything for a moment. He wanted to see Aldo's reaction and he certainly got one. Aldo was shocked. He had never seen something so grotesque. He had seen dead bodies before and not the kind at a funeral. But this was something else, like something out of a slasher film, only worse. At least with movies, you knew it was fake. Aldo knew the photos were real. He looked them over out of curiosity like a person who sees a car wreck, but can't look away. However, where most people would pick up the photos to look at them, Aldo could not. Touching them would make him unclean. Touching them would let in the darkness from these heinous crimes. Aldo did not look at them very long before he turned away to stop the nauseating effect of seeing them in the first place.

Aldo asked. "What is this?"

Jim sternly looked at him. "You should already know. Don't you recognize your victims?"

"What...what are you talking about?"

"Murder. The people you killed and then used to stage these horrific crime scenes."

"You're joking... you think I killed these people. I've never killed anybody until today."

Jim cracked a confident smile, trying to make Aldo think he knew more than he did. "That's not entirely true, is it?"

Aldo started to get agitated. "That's what the warrant was for. Look man, I didn't kill anybody. I don't even know who these people are."

"That's definitely not true. You know at least one of the victims. The second photo is Jack Perry. The man accused of organizing a rape party to which your sister was a victim."

Aldo looked again and it turned out, he did recognize him. He got mad at the mere mention of Jack Perry's name, but after looking at the photo again, he smiled. He was happy to see him dead. He responded. "Yeah, I know who that is. Fuck that guy. I hope he's burning in hell."

"You didn't like him too much…did you?"

"Of course not, my sister was raped because of him trying to scare families out of their homes so he could put up another oil rig."

Jim nodded. "So, you wanted him dead?"

"Wouldn't you want the man who raped your sister dead. Rapists don't deserve to live."

Ron couldn't help it, he interrupted. "That's why you killed him, uh?" Jim shot him a dirty look and said. "Detective…keep your mouth shut." But Ron's question was enough to get a response from Aldo. He replied back. "Wanting him dead and killing him are two different things. I wasn't the one who killed him."

Jim continued his questioning. "Are you sure about that?"

"Detective, do you want me to say it a different way…I can, but the answer will still be the same. I didn't kill him."

"Okay, tell me what you think of those crime scenes…they're pretty elaborate…even artistic, wouldn't you say?"

"They're horrific, but artistic…not at all. They're symbolic, though."

Jim eye's perked up; he thought his response was interesting. "Why do you say they're symbolic?"

"I'm catholic, we think everything is symbolic."

"Make sense. You had a strict catholic education didn't you?"

"I guess."

"You and your sister went to a private catholic school all your life?"

"Okay."

"You got a pretty good education, didn't you?"

"Sure."

Jim softly smiled. "You don't have to hide that fact, be proud of it. Not everybody gets that kind of opportunity. I also hear, you're a pretty good writer?"

"Better than some, I suppose."

Jim pushed the photos closer to Aldo. "Do you know anybody else in the photos? You can look at the names at the top of the photos if that helps."

Aldo didn't even look at them before he answered. "No, I don't know who they are, but I believe, I already said that."

"You did, but then you said that you did know Jack Perry. Just want to see if you're lying about any of the other victims. And you should know the Senator."

"I don't know anything about any Senator."

"Really, you don't recognize the name Don Bennett?"

"Oh yeah, the State Senator who was always being accused of Sexual Harassment. So what!"

"What, you didn't know that Don Bennett and Jack Perry knew each other or that Jack Perry donated money to his campaigns." Aldo tried to look stunned. Jim continued. "You see, I think you did know that and the reason you killed the Senator along with Jack Perry is you heard that the Senator was at the rape party…maybe he was the one who raped your little sister."

Aldo got mad. Instinct kicked in and he jumped up, trying to get out of the handcuffs. "Fuck You!" He replied.

"Does that make you mad? Is that the kind of anger you used when you killed these men and staged the crime scene?."

"Fuck you…you can burn in hell with those pigs."

"You already said that. Now that I really have your attention, answer this question truthfully, tell me what you know about fairies, especially dark fairies?"

Aldo was confused by the question. It was strange and nothing like the other questions he was being asked. Jim was looking for Aldo's reaction so it could tell him if he really knew anything or was bluffing just like in a game of poker where the only way to win was to read the man in front of you. Aldo responded. "What are you talking about, the woodland creatures found in mythology?"

"Sounds like you know a little bit about mythology, did you study it in Catholic School."

"We learn a little bit about stuff like that within literature courses in school, but what does this have to do with anything?"

"You know what I found out...sometimes fairies are considered fallen angels in mythology, but you probably already knew that." Again, another confusing look by Aldo. Jim thought, either, he was a damn good actor, or really didn't know what he was talking about. Aldo glanced at the photos again, especially at the names on the photos. Finally, it was starting to make sense.

Aldo replied. "Wait a minute, I saw something on the news about it. There's a serial killer on the loose called the Black Fairy Killer. You think I'm him?"

Ron spoke up. "We know you're the Black Fairy Killer so you might as well save us a lot of time and confess." Jim threw a disapproving look his way. "Detective, I won't say it again , shut the fuck up."

Aldo responded with his two favorite words. "Fuck you...fuck the both of you."

Jim got back to the task at hand and said to Aldo. "My partner there may not know how to keep his mouth shut, but he isn't wrong. We have you cold. Confess now and you just might save yourself from Death Row. Might even get yourself declared insane and get sent to some cushy medical prison."

Aldo replied. "You've been trying to get me to confess to these murders since we've been here, what makes you think I'll do it now!"

Jim had a confident smile. "Because of what we have on you."

"I think you're bluffing, you can't really tie me to these murders."

Jim pointed to the dates on the photo. "See those dates, that's when they were murdered, and you were in the same city where the murders took place on those dates working for Highland Security. As a project inspector, you were traveling through the cities on those dates, inspecting Jobsites. We checked the timeline of your travels over the last four years. Plus, you were the project leader for the security installation on Hugo Blackmon's house. Found that out too. I bet you know how to get past one of those security systems since you used to install them."

"All of that is a coincidence. Do you have physical evidence that puts me at those crime scenes or any witnesses?"

"I guess you know a thing or two from watching a few episodes of CSI . You can get the answer to that at your trial. But we also have motive. Don Bennett and Jack Perry were part of a rape party involving your sister…there's no one more who'd want to get revenge on those fuckers other than your sister, but you're more capable of killing them than she is. I hear she's pretty much catatonic these days and rarely leaves the house since it happened."

Aldo erupted with anger hearing more about his sister's rape. He said. "Fucking pigs. That's all you are…nothing more."

Jim laughed. "Call us what you want, but you know we're right.'

"Wanting them dead doesn't mean I did it. And what about the other two assholes, why would I kill them? What motive do I have there?"

"That's what we couldn't figure out, until we found this. "Jim pulled out the essay Aldo had written for a college scholarship about God, Angels, and revenge. He showed the essay to Aldo just to remind him of what he apparently believed. "We found what you wrote twenty years ago. That's some serious religious shit there…symbolic too."

Aldo started shaking his head. "I was a stupid kid just trying to make some waves and be unique just to win a scholarship, it doesn't mean anything."

Jim Shrugged. "I think it's much more than that. Like for instance, this is my favorite part of your essay. *If God is a vengeful god, then revenge is required to make a just and peaceful world. God even has his own instruments for revenge such as the archangels, Michael in particular. For if all things are to be just in the eyes of God, then revenge is necessary for those who go against God's plan for his children. Would God call upon us to seek revenge? Would we be willing to answer the call to help make the world in his image.* Jim looked at Ron. "What do you say Detective, sounds like God is telling him to murder people for revenge?"

Ron laughed. "Yep, he thinks murder is okay as long as God commands him to do it." Aldo gave him another dirty look. Shaking his dead again, he replied to both of them. "Because you don't seem to get it… you make up a bunch of bullshit to get me on the hook for 4 murders. "

Jim replied. "Then tell us what we don't get."

"This paper is nothing. It's the ramblings of an 18-year-old kid, too smart for his own good. I don't even believe most of the shit in that paper. I'm telling you, you have it all wrong, it's nothing."

Jim stared him down, trying to male Aldo feel uncomfortable and let him know that he was not buying into his bullshit. He said. "Or it's your Manifesto…your Mein Kampf before all of your evil deeds."

Shaking his head, again, in disbelief, Aldo replied. "You couldn't be more wrong, Detective Summers."

"We can let a jury decide that."

Aldo paused. There seemed no way of convincing them that he wasn't the Black Fairy Killer. They were hell bent on pinning the murders on him, there was no escaping it. And every plea Aldo could make for them to think any different would change that fact. Finally, he said the last thing he was going to say. "I'm done talking, I want my lawyer."

Jim smiled. "You're going to need one, but this is your last shot to avoid Death Row." Jim placed a legal pad in front of Aldo with a pen. "Write out your confession now and we'll make is so that at most, you get life in prison."

Aldo looked at the legal pad for a moment. At first, he wasn't going to do anything. But after thinking about it for a moment, he picked up the pen and started to write something. It wasn't long; just three words…*Go Fuck Yourself!* Jim continued to read from the essay for the next few minutes, hoping to get a reaction out of Aldo and possibly make him talk again. Then all of sudden there was a knock at the door. It was Aldo's lawyer, but not the one he usually used. He had never seen the man before. The lawyer instructed Aldo not to say anything else…he was done talking. He looked at the Detectives and said that the interview was over. And because even cop killers have legal rights, they couldn't argue with that. So, for now, they were done interrogating Aldo Martinez.

28

As Jim and Ron walked out of the interrogation room, they were congratulated by the Midland PD Captain. He said. "Great work, it was fun to watch. I think you almost had him." Ron smiled at the compliment even though he didn't do much. Jim replied. "Thank you, we'll see what happens." Jim and Ron walked with Robert out of earshot to those who might listen in on their conversation. Maisie was with them as well. Jim was surprised to see her still around, but also a little glad that she was sticking it out.

Robert said to Jim. "The Captain was right, you did a good job. And I have to say, you picked a great quote from his essay… got his blood boiling with that one."

Jim cracked a bit of a smile. "Thank You but didn't exactly accomplish what you wanted. "

"Don't worry, we'll get him. If his lawyer is smart, he will convince Aldo to write out a confession and take the death penalty off the table."

"Even if he really isn't the killer."

Ron was surprised to hear that and commented. "What are you talking about? The paper, the timeline, working at highland security…this is our guy. And people who aren't guilty don't lawyer up, which is what he just did."

Jim had an angry look on his face. He was getting tired of Detective Jackson's simplistic bullshit. He replied. "First of all, he didn't ask for a lawyer until the end. His pleas that he was innocent were for real. After we showed him the photos and he knew we had him cold, he would have asked for a lawyer then and didn't But that's not why I believe he isn't the Black Fairy Killer."

Even Robert was getting frustrated with Jim's theory. Aldo Martinez was a good suspect...almost perfect. He asked Jim. "After talking to him, you still don't believe, why?"

Jim said. "Because of the way he looked at the photos. He was shocked and grossed out by them."

Ron responded. "They're horrific; anybody would be shocked by the scenes in the photos, especially the one with a dead child."

"That's true of most people, but not the killer. They would be proud of their work because it's their work of art. We would see that pride on his face from a simple smile or a joyful smirk. The killer would admire everything in those photos...did you see any of that on Aldo's face. No...because he's not the killer. He was truly horrified by what he saw as if he was seeing them for the first time."

Ron replied. "He could also be putting on an act."

"True, but our killer wouldn't do that. They want us to know what they're doing and why. Remember, the killer is preaching, and you don't put on an act when it comes to your message to the world."

"I still call bullshit on that...this is our guy."

"Just because you want him to be the real killer, doesn't mean it's true. However, I think Aldo knows who the killer might be."

Robert asked Jim. "What do you mean?"

"I don't know, I haven't really fleshed out the theory yet, but it feels like somehow there's a connection with Aldo and the real killer. There's something about that essay that eerily feels connected to our profile."

Ron replied. "Because he's the killer, why can't you fucking see that?"

Jim in an angry tone responded. "No, that's not it, but perhaps, he knows the killer or knew them years ago. My instinct tells me that the real killer has read this essay and it helped formulate their way of thinking. Anyway, I would like to talk to Aldo Martinez again."

Robert nodded at Jim. "I don't know if I necessarily believe in your theory, but it wouldn't hurt to talk to him again…if his lawyer will allow it."

Ron rolled his eyes. He couldn't believe what he was hearing. He thought to himself, was he the only one who wasn't crazy, Aldo had to be the guy killer. Robert told them to take a break and he would see what he could do about having them talk to the suspect again. For Jim, it might be the only chance he got to find the connection between Aldo and the real killer. It might be the only chance to prove his theory was correct and to know that his instincts weren't wrong since he had been questioning them for a while now. Maybe Jim was still a little gunshy when it came to his certainty about a suspect.

Jim and Maisie left and went to get something to eat. Jim realized that they really hadn't eaten that day except for a light breakfast. Both were famished. It also gave them a chance to call loved ones. Maisie called her son. Jim gave Gina another call just to hear her voice. He even talked to Audra and Josh. It was nice to talk to them. He wasn't a father, but it was comforting just like it would be for a father. They took a break for almost an hour.

When they got back to the station, Jim could tell there were more people at the station than when they left. There were more people in suits, which could only mean one thing. Feds. The desk sergeant told Jim that his boss was waiting for him in the main conference room. It had windows and Jim could see the men in suits within the room with his boss, Robert. He had a sick feeling that he wasn't going to like what came next.

Jim slowly entered the room as if he had been summoned to the principal's office. He felt that bad news coming. Robert said to Jim. "Detective Summers, welcome back…have a good break, get something good to eat."

Jim didn't know what to say and never liked small talk. "It was fine, food was good too." Jim looked around the room, especially at the three men wearing suits. He asked. "I'm sorry, but what is going on here? Am I in trouble for something?"

Robert replied. "No, Detective, you're not in trouble. These men are from the DEA and US Customs. They're here to talk to us."

The DEA Agent walked over and introduced himself. "I'm Agent Bryan Coleman. He pointed to the US Customs agent. "This is Agent Remi Douglas with US Customs. We are part of a joint task force investigating drug smuggling and trafficking operation that has come through Midland for the past few years."

Jim responded. "Okay, what does that have to do with us?"

"Your investigation into a serial killer interrupted our main investigation with Highland Security." Jim was stunned and this is where the other shoe was about to drop. In his experience when the Feds got involved, it never turned out well. Jim asked. "What do you mean?"

Agent Coleman handed him a folder filled with photos and a DEA surveillance report. "We have been watching them for over two years. We believe they're a front for the Chamero Cartel and a pipeline for smuggling Cocaine and Heroin but have never been able to prove it."

"You can't be serious?"

"Detective Summers, I couldn't e more serious. And we know for a fact that Aldo Martinez didn't kill Jack Perry or Don Bennett. Or Henry Frankston for that matter because he's been under surveillance. We have photos of him that go against your timeline for the murders. Your boss showed us the forensic report while you were gone so we could confirm the details."

Jim looked at Robert. "Well, I guess that proves my theory he's not the real killer." Then he looked at Agent Coleman. "Thank you for confirming that fact, but why are you really here?"

"Because now that Aldo has killed some cops and caused a shootout, we find ourselves in an interesting predicament. We've never been this close to having an informant especially this high up in the cartel."

"Aldo Martinez is a part of the Cartel?"

"Yes and he knows a lot about their operation. That's why they sent 20 men to break him out of the hostage situation. Plus, his uncle is Pablo Chamero, one of three brothers who are head of the cartel. They can't afford to have him talking to the police so we're here to cut a deal and make him our informant in the prison system where the cartel does a lot of smuggling."

"If you put him in prison, won't they just kill him to keep him from talking?"

"Not necessarily, we allow him to pick the prison, he wants to go to, one whose drug operation is controlled by the Cartel. He gets word to his associates that as part of pleading guilty to murder, he can pick the prison he does his time in and therefore still be useful."

Jim smiled. "Sounds like a good plan."

"But we also want him to be transferred to a federal prison at some point."

"Okay, but he hasn't committed a federal crime."

"He will after he confesses to the murders of Don Bennett and Jack Perry."

Jim looked confused. "What are talking about, even if he confessed to murders he didn't commit, they happened here in Texas, which is a state crime."

Agent Coleman handed him a case file. It was a murder case. Jim started to look through it as Coleman explained their plan. "What you have there is a murder that happened in New Mexico about six years ago. As you can see from the way it was staged, it's similar to the murders you're investigating and even has some religious symbolism in the murder. Now, we don't know if this is done by the same killer, but we want Aldo Martinez to confess to it so it becomes a federal crime…"

"And that's how you get him into a Federal Prison!"

"Yes."

Jim shook his head. He couldn't believe what he was hearing. "Well then…that's a bunch a fucking horseshit!"

Agent Coleman got angry. "I don't like your tone Detective."

"I don't give a fuck. You want him to confess to murders that he didn't commit while the real killer is out there. What are we supposed to do about the real Black Fairy?"

"Keep investigating if you want, but they will have to be a copycat killer."

Jim laughed. "Of course. But you know the only way that works is if they kill again, we can't call them a copycat killer until they murder someone."

"So what!"

"You're essentially letting an innocent person die to make your plan work."

"It's a small price to pay for helping us take down a Drug Cartel. And if you haven't noticed, innocent people die every day in the war on drugs."

"But that shouldn't justify you letting an innocent person die."

Agent Coleman cracked a sarcastic smile and then got angry. "There's a drug war going on, Detective, in case you haven't noticed, and we will use any means necessary to take down a Cartel and help win the war on illegal drugs. Aldo is more important to winning that war than killing a few perverts in Texas."

Jim laughed. "Important to a failed drug war, where nothing has changed in the last forty years and will never change. I think you're smoking or snorting some of the product you confiscated."

"Fuck You, Detective."

Robert responded before anybody else could. "Jim, I know you don't like it. It's a shitty deal, but there's a bigger picture here."

Jim replied. "What do you want from me? You're taking this case away, are you expecting me to like it and say thank you."

"No, but the lead investigator has to sign off on the deal just like me, the District Attorney, the DEA and Mr. Martinez."

Jim was stunned; he had never had anything like this happen before. He was not one to do deals especially with the Feds. He was a simple cop, he investigated a crime, caught the bad guy, and put them away so they could never get out of prison and harm innocent people again. He said. "I'm not fucking signing off on this...you want to make this deal, you can have it, but you don't get my consent."

Agent Coleman replied. "I guess you're not really a team player after all, but here's the skinny...we don't really need your consent. I can hand the file of the New Mexico murder along with your case files to the Black Fairy murders and they'll take over in a heartbeat. Then the FBI won't think twice about making this deal with us. Either way, this going to happen. Agent Coleman placed the folder with the details of the deal and signature lines on the conference table for Jim to sign.

Jim looked at the folder and then he looked at Robert. He said. "I can't believe you're going along with this…you hate the Feds."

"True, but if you ever want my job, then you have to learn how to play politics even when you don't want to. Just part of the game. I don't like the deal either, however, in the grand scheme of things, it is a good deal. We take a bad guy off the streets and perhaps take down some drug dealers too."

"But you're okay with the fact that somebody will have to die before we can go after the 'so called' copycat killer."

Robert gave him a dirty look. "I'm not going to have that conversation with you."

Jim rolled his eyes. It seemed like everybody, but he was okay with an innocent person dying and the worst part, he couldn't do anything about it. He just had to take it. Jim asked. "What if I don't sign this document?"

"Two weeks suspension pending a formal review to determine whether you get to keep your badge. But you don't really want that…don't be stupid, just sign the document and be done with it."

"Has Aldo Martinez agreed to this?"

"His lawyer is presenting it to him now. I'm sure he'll take since it takes away the death penalty."

Jim nodded to say okay. Aldo Martinez would have to be crazy not to take the deal. Jim asked. "When is the press conference?"

"Probably tomorrow morning, but you don't have to worry about it. I'll handle it with Midland PD and the Attorney General, you've done enough."

Jim was about to say something but decided against it. He had said enough already and nothing he could was going to change the deal at this point. He walked over and looked in the folder with the agreement he was supposed sign. He cracked a smile after looking through it and said to Robert. "Now, I see why you really wanted me to sign this…the Non-Disclosure Agreement."

Robert smiled. "Yes, standard procedure, especially if someone wanted to leak the details to the press or tell anybody they're not supposed to."

"And a legal way to take their badge?"

"Among other things!"

As Jim was signing, he said. "Nothing like a simple, subtle form of intimidation to keep cops on the straight and narrow. But don't worry, just because I think the deal stinks doesn't mean I would leak it. Never done something like that before…never will."

Robert nodded. Jim was expecting him to say, "I know you wouldn't," but he didn't. Maybe his boss didn't completely trust him, after all. Maybe he had a right to, Jim, for a brief moment thought about leaking it to the press, but it would be out of anger and tried not to do things out of anger. Jim finished signing and handed the folder to his boss. Robert did say. "Despite what happened, you did a great job with this investigation."

"That would actually mean more if we caught the real killer."

"True, but nonetheless, take a two-week `vacation and come back refreshed."

Jim smiled. "Maybe I'll do just that after we break down the Dallas office." And that was it, he walked out, didn't say anything else about the deal. He and the two other detectives headed back to Dallas. All Ron and Maisie knew was that Aldo finally confessed to two of the murders. It was supposed to be a big victory for State CID, maybe it was in some way, however, for Jim it felt like he lost the championship on some bullshit penalty that everybody knew was wrong but couldn't be reversed. That's always a worse feeling than just losing.

29

It was tomorrow already. For the first time in months, Jim slept in. He hadn't had more than a few hours of sleep since the investigation had begun. Last night he got almost nine hours of sleep and that was after passionately making love to Gina for a couple of hours. Jim was never good at going on vacation, especially just sitting around and relaxing. Never one for just sitting still, he always had to be doing something. But it felt like he was on vacation already. He had one last thing to do before going back to Austin.

Jim arrived at the task force office in Dallas. Most of them had already gone back to their regular units once they heard that Aldo Martinez had confessed and the investigation was over. Maisie, Ron, and James Cross were the only ones left packing up the office. When Jim arrived, the press conference had just ended down in Midland. Jim didn't want to watch the charade. Who could blame him!? Ron was not really helping with the packing. He only came to get his things. He was walking out of the conference room as Jim came towards the doorway. He said to Jim. "Better late than never, you missed the press conference."

Jim shrugged. "I didn't need to see it. Already knew what they were going to say."

"Why weren't you there, it's a big victory for you?"

"I disagreed with how they handled things and didn't need to be talking to the press."

Ron gave him a strange look. "You still don't think he's the killer, do you?"

"I know he's not the guy, Detective."

"Wow, you just can't handle the fact that somebody else found him, can you?"

Jim laughed at the notion. "I can see how a simple mind like yours would come to that conclusion. But you're not even close. My ego is not so fragile that I have to get the credit. I don't care who scores the win as long as we get the win."

"You tell yourself that all you want, but I think you're a bitter old dinosaur who doesn't like the fact that I found the killer."

Jim shot him a dirty look. "Wow, you're a fucking idiot. I thought that the first day, I met you and you've done a great job confirming that every day since. "

"Spoken like a sore loser. He's the Black Fairy Killer. He confessed and innocent people don't confess to crimes."

Jim shook his head in disbelief. "Actually, innocent people confess to crimes all the time. You know how many serial killers have taken credit for murders they didn't commit…if that's your criteria for thinking he's guilty, then you're a bigger idiot than I took you for."

Ron smiled. "Whatever man. I hope you're not this bitter when I transfer to CID and we might have to work together again. "Jim was stunned. Was he serious? Would Detective Jackson actually transfer to his division? Would they actually accept his transfer? Jim replied. "You can't be serious."

"Oh yeah, turns out I have a knack for this kind of investigation, and working for CID will look great on a resume when I run for Sheriff of Tarrant County someday. Oh, and make sure you spell out my full name when you sign off on my commendation for helping you solve this case." Ron turned around and walked off, confident, and full of himself, but blind to the fact that his intelligence was no higher than that of a simple beat cop. He would make a perfect Sheriff one day; he would never have to do any real work but could take all the credit.

Jim replied as he was walking off. "Ron, if you do transfer, here's your first lesson…there's no room for football stars. It truly is a team effort and no one man gets credit for the victory. The whole team does and that's why you will never hear one person singled out. Could your sensitive ego really handle that? You should be honest with yourself before you take that job." Jim ignored what Ron was saying in response and walked into the conference room. It didn't matter what Ron was saying, Jim had already moved on to more important things and it was the only way to best Detective Jackson in this kind of situation.

Maisie gave Jim a solemn look as he walked into the conference room. It felt like the last day of school where nobody was going to see each other for a while or ever again. He nodded to let her know that he understood how she felt. She said. "I'm sorry for how everything went down, but at least we caught him."

Jim cracked a sarcastic smile. "Well, we did catch a killer, but not the one we've been looking for. It doesn't matter now, the investigation is officially over and we all get to go home."

James responded. "I take it you know more than what they said in the press conference."

Jim shrugged. "I do, but I can't say anything more. Let's just get all this stuff packed up and you two can go."

Maisie who was always curious and couldn't just let it go had to ask. She wanted to know what he knew like it was the latest gossip that you just had to hear from friends. She asked. "What is it... what happened with his confession?"

"Really... I can't talk about it. As part of his plea deal, I had to sign off on it as the lead investigator and that included an NDA."

James replied. "Must be pretty serious, if they made you sign that."

Smiling, James replied. "You can say that."

Trying to kid around a little bit and lighten the mood, Maisie said. "Sounds like to me, you think what you know shouldn't be a secret."

"I wish it were that easy." Jim started packing up more files into boxes. After about a minute, he said. "Fuck it...Aldo Martinez made a deal with the DEA. Apparently, Highland Security is a front for the Chamero Drug Cartel and their smuggling operations. Aldo is the nephew of one of the three heads of the cartel."

Maisie, shocked, asked Jim. "Are you serious?"

"Yep. His deal in order to avoid the Death Penalty for killing those cops is to become an informant for the DEA about their smuggling operations in prison. But he had to confess to two of the Black Fairy murders to get the deal."

James replied. "Holy shit. I guess the DEA had been watching Highland Security for a while."

"Yeah, but here is the real kicker. They had a file on a murder in New Mexico who fit our profile. It was done in a similar fashion as the ones here. The DEA will get him to confess to it at some point…"

James interrupted. "So they can put him in a Federal Prison as an informant."

"Yep, which also means that if we were to find the real killer then they would just be a copycat killer and in order for that to happen…"

Maisie answered before he could finish his sentence. "The Black Fairy has to commit another murder because a copycat killer couldn't possibly commit their murders before Aldo did his."

Jim gave her a thumbs up and said. "Bingo. An innocent person has to die before we can investigate again and actually try to catch the real killer."

"Fucking Christ. And they're willing to let that happen."

"Yeah, because it's a small price to pay in the War on Drugs. That's the really fucked up part of this deal and there's nothing we can do about it."

James responded. "I agree that it's fucked up, but the deal makes sense, at least for Aldo… If I were facing the Death Penalty, then I'd probably make that deal too."

"True, but what I am really pissed about, is I think we were close to finding the real killer and now they'll probably just go dark to where we'll never find them."

"I wouldn't be so sure; the real Black Fairy killer is not done yet. There's still more to do…more to say with their murders. Even if Aldo Martinez could kill one of these victims, it would only be for revenge and the murder certainly wouldn't be so deliberate."

Maisie asked. "What do you mean?"

"These murders are very specific based on the victim and their crime, hence deliberate. And if the killer is preaching as has been suggested, then they must have a lot to say. I just don't think they're done preaching. I could believe Aldo would kill Jack Perry and Don Bennett, but for revenge and it wouldn't be so elaborate."

"He did write that paper about God using Archangels for tools of revenge."

James smiled. "That thing! It's not the manifesto of a serial killer…just a kid trying to make waves by playing devil's advocate with a different point of view. Nothing more than a little teenage rebellion… my daughter used to do it all the time when she was in high school and college just to piss me off. Of course, now it serves her well in her career."

Jim asked. "What does your daughter do?"

"Criminal Defense Attorney…if you can believe that."

Jim laughed at karma's sense of humor when it came to Detective Cross. He said. "I guess your daughter is still playing devil's advocate with you and your job."

"True, but she's a good kid. And it's not really that important just like that guy's high school paper."

"The press and the public won't agree with you. It will be poured over and researched until the end of time trying to find answers about why he did it as if it were the writings of Charles Manson."

James smiled. "We'll, that guy is a fucking moron. And the same goes for the public. Let them say what they want to say."

"I wish it were that easy to ignore."

"It is that easy. You go home at the end of the day, have a drink if you prefer, and ignore the bullshit. Find something to take your mind off everything. It's an old cop's trick. For me, it was my family…we love to play games. I would go home and play games with my wife and kids and forget about everything with the job."

"I don't have those things."

"But you have a girl that does have kids. My point is you find something to take your mind off the job, especially if you have a bad day."

Jim smiled. "Sure. You've learned a lot about how to deal with the job over the years."

"You have to in order to keep your sanity." Jim nodded in agreement. James told Jim something else that he wouldn't forget. It would stay with him for a long time. James said. "Last piece of advice I have for you, take a vacation. Go somewhere and clear your mind because you're not done with this investigation. The real killer will have to kill again, and you need to be at your best when you come back to this investigation."

Jim didn't say anything. He took the advice to heart. He had to admit, it was pretty damn good advice. The three of them finished packing the remainder of the files. It didn't take that long, but it was Jim who had to stay behind and make sure they were sent back to Austin properly by State CID's preferred delivery service.

Before Maisie and James left, Jim made sure to thank them for their service. He said to Maisie. "Thank you for everything, especially your insight. You're a good Detective, better than most."

She smiled. "It's been interesting, a little too real at times, but interesting. Glad, I could help." He reached out to shake her hand, but she hugged him instead. It was more appropriate considering they survived a shootout together and then she walked out.

Jim said to Detective Cross as he reached out to shake Cross' hand. James laughed and said. "Yeah, I'm not going to hug you… I'm an old-fashioned cop; a handshake will do just fine. "Jim laughed. " Fair enough, I want to thank you for your help. Your insight and experience were truly valuable."

"It was my pleasure. By the way. There were a couple of cases that came in while you were down in Midland that you should take a look at. One of them fits the killer's MO. A guy was tortured and laid out on his bed in the form of crucifixion. That's also how he died. You should read the file when you get a chance. It might help you to identify the real killer." Jim nodded. He made a mental note to look at it before it was packed away with everything else and only made available to the lawyers involved with the case. After today, he wouldn't have the clearance to look at the case files since he was not the lead investigator, and they were only available to lawyers and federal agents involved in Aldo Martinez's case. Despite his looming questions, the case was finally over Detective Jim Summers…for now.

30

Jim was on his way back to his hotel room to pack up when he found himself in a strange place. He would never go there for anything personal, but this case had him going there looking for answers. Not the kind of answers that most people went there to find. The clarity he needed was coming from a different place; it was the ever-consuming desire to know, "why." And that's how Jim ended up walking through the doors of St. Thomas Aquinas Catholic Church.

It was late in the afternoon, over an hour away from the 6 o'clock mass. The church was fairly quiet except for housewives and old women who usually came in the afternoons to pray or to do confession. This was something Jim noticed as he was looking around the church and he found it interesting. He thought to himself, that different kinds of people went to church at different times. People who worked were often found later in the evenings. He wondered if the killer visited a church during the day or at night. It would say a lot about them.

Jim sat down. He didn't pray and it made him stand out a little bit. He looked around the church as if he were staking out the place, again. He was curious about what was going on inside the church, but it also made someone curious about it. Jim was sitting in one of the pews towards the back of the church when a priest walked up. He asked. "How are you today?"

Jim smiled. "Fine, thank you."

"I can't say that I've ever seen you in here before."

"I don't come here for church."

The priest was a bit surprised. "You're not Catholic, are you?"

"No, I'm not...it's okay that I'm in here, right!"

The priest replied. "Oh yes, it's perfectly fine. Our church is open to everybody, including non-believers and Protestants." Jim laughed at the amusing comment. The priest introduced himself. "I'm Father Kieran."

Jim reached out and shook his hand. "It's nice to meet you, I'm Jim Summers

"What brings to our church today?"

"Curiosity, I guess."

"Some form of curiosity is what usually gets us through the doors; it's what we do with it that counts."

"Jim smiled. "It's a nice sentiment, Father."

"Most Priests like to be philosophical. Guess I'm not much different. Now, if you don't mind me asking, what kind of curiosity brings you in here?"

Jim thought for a moment. How direct did he really want to be? "Father, what would you do if someone confessed to you a crime they committed?"

Father Kieran was a little stunned at the question. "Are you here confessing to a crime?"

"No."

"I guess it would depend on the crime."

"Such as?"

"Please understand that we deal more with what is considered a sin than a crime. The Bible is very clear about impure thoughts and yet is not a crime in the real world. You can't prosecute someone for having impure thoughts. It is a sin, though. The Bible also says stealing is wrong, it's one of the Ten Commandments, but I wouldn't report anybody that was so desperate that they had to steal food to feed the family. I would try and help them, and hope that they would seek forgiveness."

"That makes sense, but what if the crime is murder? I seem to remember the Ten Commandments is pretty clear on that being a sin and we do prosecute people for murder."

Father Kieran smiled. He knew Jim was dancing around what he really wanted to ask. "Now we get to the real question, so I have to ask, is this just 'you' asking, or you as a police officer, asking?"

"How do you know that I am a police officer?"

"Well, I figure only a police officer would ask a question like that, plus I did see you on the news. You were investigating the Black Fairy murders."

Jim laughed. "Well, so much for future undercover work. Guilty, I am a police officer."

"Why don't you ask the question that you really want that ask."

Jim tried to crack a smile. At this point, he couldn't hide his true intentions or what he really wanted to know. "Over the last couple of months, have you had anyone confess to anything that sounded like a murder?"

"No."

"Would you tell me if they did?"

"No. Because the sanctity of the Confessional Booth prevents me from doing so.

"We're talking about a serious crime."

"Please understand, the moment a priest violates the sanctity of confession we cease to have a purpose in the church. We can never be trusted again, and trust is the most important thing to have in order to be a good priest. Can you understand that?

Jim nodded, letting him know that he understood, but it wasn't as simple as that when trying to find answers. He replied." I get trust, in my world if you can't trust your partner, they pretty much cease being a partner. But don't you think you have a duty as a priest to respect and uphold the law? Wouldn't that compel you to report a heinous crime?"

Father Kieran paused. There have never been simple answers to that question, but he did have a response. "I think we should respect man's laws, but I'm also a priest and I follow a higher law. And we should never put man's law before God's. Part of it is being able to confess your sins and seek forgiveness without fear of retribution."

"Are you okay with someone getting away with murder?"

"That depends…do you believe in God."

"Does it really matter if I do?"

Father Kieran smiled. "Yes, it does because if you believe in God, then you also believe that it is only God who judges us in the end. We can never truly escape our misdeeds. Maybe on earth, we can, but not when it comes to how our soul will be judged for eternity."

"That's not really an answer."

"Sure, it is…just not the one you're looking for."

Jim rolled his eyes. The conversation was becoming frustrating. He wanted a simple and straight-to-the-point answer, but all he seemed to get from the priest were riddles masked as a common philosophy. He responded. "I get the sanctity of confessions, but you know, I can get a court order that would compel you to tell me any information you had about a murder."

Father Kieran gave him a stern look. "You can try, but we are not required by law to tell you someone's confession. Texas House Rule of Evidence 505 protects men of the clergy… we have the same privilege as Lawyers and their clients."

Disbelief came over Jim as he also shook his head. "Damn, I was hoping you didn't actually know that law, and I could scare you into telling me."

The good Father smiled. "Sorry about that, I know the law, but even if we were not protected by state law, there is still church law. I would be excommunicated. But more importantly, as a priest, I would be glad to sit in jail and be a martyr so I can protect the secrets of my flock…every true man of God welcomes that because it would be our own lion's den if you know my meaning."

Jim understood the reference from his days in Sunday School, Daniel in the lion's den. He replied. "I get it. But I am trying to find a killer and will use any tactic I can, to do that."

"I thought the Black Fairy Killer had already been caught."

"A killer was caught…but not the real one. There's still one out there."

"I see, that explains why you're really here. You think the real killer is Catholic and would have come to confession."

"Something like that."

Father Kieran remembered something. "I seem to remember the police staking out Catholic churches for a couple of weeks, I'm assuming that was you.

"Yes, and I'm sorry about what happened. It must have made your parishioners nervous."

"Yeah, that kind of thing doesn't put a whole lot of trust in the police among our parishioners, but I understand why you did it. I probably would have if I were in your shoes."

"My intention was not to offend you or anybody in your church, I'm just trying to catch a killer."

Father Kieran smiled. "I still can't tell you what somebody may have confessed, but I will at least tell you this, only because it wasn't really a confession. A few days ago, I talked to someone who was very troubled. That's the best way I can describe it. They needed someone to just tell them everything was going to be okay…that they were still a good person despite the bad things they may have done."

Now Jim was really curious. "Do you think this person wanted to confess to a crime, but couldn't?"

"I don't know for sure, but what I do know is they were in a dark place and needed some guidance."

"That's all well and good, but if they actually told you about a crime they committed, you still wouldn't tell me because you can't do that."

Father Kieran shrugged and smiled at Jim. "Honestly, I'm not trying to lie to you. I probably shouldn't even be telling you this much, but we all have a role to play regarding the killer you're looking for."

"What do you mean?"

"You're a police officer; your role is to craft their doom by catching them and putting them in jail. My role is to help save their soul when they're finally judged for their sins."

"You know that you can't stop them from being sentenced to prison if they're caught or even save them from the death penalty."

"I'm not talking about that. Yes, every criminal is judged by man and a jury of their peers. But I'm talking about saving their soul for when it's judged for eternity."

"That's assuming that they can be redeemed."
What makes you think they can't? If we are to truly believe in the power of forgiveness, there has to be forgiveness for even the worst sinners."

Jim shook his head. He didn't share the same thoughts." I can't say that I agree with you, some people are beyond redemption. For example, when I was younger and had been on the job for about a year or two, I got called to an armed robbery and the guy who robbed the place was surprised to see us. He ended up taking one of the store clerks hostage. The rule book says to try and negotiate so that no harm comes to the hostage. Maybe I was too gung-ho, but all I saw was a guy harming an innocent person so when I saw an opening, I put him down. Shot him dead and to this day, I don't regret it. Maybe it could have turned out differently and I wouldn't have to take a life. However, if it's between a potential killer an innocent person, all the philosophical questions of right and wrong and looking for a different alternative right out the door...you put the fucker down to save the life."

The father softly smiled, trying to show Jim he understood where he was coming from. "In your situation, I can see that, but in my line of work, I have to believe that people can be redeemed. But I'll pose another question because I've heard that the victims of The Black Fairy were bad men who preyed upon women."

"That's partly true."

"What if it was God's will that they die and he found an instrument to carry out his plan."

"If you're honestly going to make the defense that God is commanding this person to kill people, then you're crazier than most of the religious people I encounter."

The father nodded. "I'm not saying that God is really doing that. But God could if he wanted to, and they say that he does work in mysterious ways. Personally, I don't think God would do that, but what I know about this killer, they think they're doing the will of God and from where I stand it's hard to find fault in their logic."

Jim gave him a dirty look. He understood, but the priest wasn't thinking of things in black and white. Ideas were never that simple. As a police officer, it had to be that simple... It had to be right or wrong for him to function in his job. He gave the priest a stern look as he replied. "I don't care what they believe it's still a crime and it's my job to catch them."

"A crime, according to the laws of man and I'm not arguing that what they're doing is a crime according to you, but all I am saying is we look at a bigger picture... It's the battle for their soul, so we take into account their true reasons in order to help their soul."

"And as you said, that's the role you play in all of this if you were to encounter the real killer."

"Yes, another reason why I can't tell you any more than what I've already said. You do strike me as someone who wants to know more than just the identity of the killer and why they do the things they do, so I'm going to give you something to ponder that will help you to understand their beliefs.

"Another philosophical antidote?"

"Call it whatever you want." Father Kieran paused for a moment, trying to think of something inspirational or heartfelt that could make Jim see it from his point of view. He said. I'm sure you've never heard of him, but in the 20th century, there was a famous theologian by the name of Thomas Merton. His writings are well renowned among Catholics, especially since he was a Trappist Monk. His teachings are brilliant and some even called him a mystic. But one of his most famous writings is what we call the Prayer that Anyone Can Pray. It says, *My Lord God, I have no idea where I am going. I do not see the road ahead of me. I cannot know for certain where it will end. Nor do I really know myself and the fact that I think that I am following your will does not mean that I am actually doing so, but I believe that the desire to please you does in fact please you. And I hope I have that desire in all that I'm doing.* There are some like myself who believe that the very act of trying to please God does please him and it's what drives us in all that we do. Because trying to please God should be a good thing."

"Are you saying that because the killer is trying to please God and because of that, it's okay to do what they do?"

Father Kieran had a sympathetic look on his face. "Whether it does actually please God or not remains unseen. I believe your killer does what they do because they think they're pleasing God. Maybe it's some messed-up interpretation of Christian faith, but there's power in belief. And sometimes that can be a very dangerous thing. I'm not condoning what they're doing, but maybe this will help you to understand why. And if you do catch them, maybe what I'm saying will help you to have some sympathy when crafting their Doom. And hopefully, you let somebody like me try saving their soul. If nothing else, think about everything I've said."

Jim thanked Father Kieran for his input and then the good father walked off to continue the rest of his duties in the church, especially praying with parishioners and hearing their confessions. He had given Jim a lot to think about and it wasn't like Jim would stop thinking about this case anytime soon. How could he when the real killer was still out there? And his instincts told him that the Black Fairy Killer had more to say to the world. The deaths would keep coming, maybe not tomorrow, maybe not for a while, but there would be more someday. Jim was sure of it. But the looming question that had been there since day one was still there…could they figure out the identity of the Black Fairy Killer in time before there was another death? Only time would tell.

31

Four Years Later...

Four years is a long time, but not nearly enough to forget. While it had been that long since the Black Fairy murders, Jim had never forgotten that they had caught the wrong killer and the real one was still out there somewhere. Enough time has passed that people weren't thinking about the investigation anymore. Aldo Martinez certainly didn't give them a reason to remember. He had never given one interview since his confession. Plenty had been written about him and why he did it. Plenty of journalists had speculated if he would ever confess to the rest of the murders, but he'd only confessed to the one in New Mexico. Just as predicted it was the one that made his case a federal one. Now, Aldo Martinez was sitting in a Florida federal prison.

The biggest question surrounding Aldo Martinez and his murders had always been, "why." What was his motive? What was his message to society?" His paper about God and Revenge offered some insight, but not enough to quell the public's fascination with The Black Fairy. Two books had been written about him. One offered some half-assed psychological explanation that boiled The Black Fairy down to a simple psychopath with a grudge, some modern-day form of Taxi Driver. The other book looked at The Black Fairy as an avenging angel that shouldn't be locked up and let loose to kill the worst of society without constraint because it was God who made The Black Fairy and it was his will. People seemed to be split on whether The Black Fairy was truly evil or not. The only thing for certain, no one had a clear picture of the true motives of The Black Fairy. And with no definite answers, the public was left to make up their own, especially when trying to answer why he did it. However, while some had forgotten the case and others could never forget.

Jim may not have forgotten about the case, but he had moved on. The same for those who investigated the Black Fairy case. Detective Maisie Green didn't work homicide anymore, she works juvenile drug crimes so that she could be home at a reasonable hour and nobody shot at her. Detective James Cross was now retired, but retirement never suited him, so he went to work for a Private Investigation Service. He worked part-time at one of their new offices in Round Rock. Detective Ron Jackson end up working for State CID, he wasn't good enough to work for Special Investigative Services so Jim rarely had to see him which was a good thing. And finally, Dr. Vanessa O'Connor took a teaching position at the UT Southwestern Hospital and College of Medicine.

In moving on, Jim had built a pretty good life for himself, he never stopped seeing Gina. He had gone back to Austin right after the investigation and spent time on the weekends seeing her and the kids. So, it was only natural that after a month of doing that, when she was offered a job in Austin, he moved her, Audra, and Josh into his house. Even though he'd not said it out loud, he loved her. And with that, they became a family. Although Jim and Gina never got married, they made a family and Jim also became legal guardians for Audra and Josh. They had a good life. Jim had, had only one big case since the Black Fairy murders and most nights he was home by six.

It gave him plenty of time for family. He was there to see Josh come out of his shell and turn out to be kind of a prodigy with computers and game design. Already in middle school, he was taking classes in game design for a special program. Audra was a junior in high school and precocious as ever. She had grown into a fiercely independent and outspoken, young woman, smart as a whip with talents that she was just beginning to discover. One of those was her ability to play basketball. She seemed to have an almost natural jump shot and rarely missed. Audra made varsity at the end of her freshman year. Jim was happy, and they all were when it came to their new life in Austin. Jim had wanted something like this all of his life. It brought him a peace that seem to elude him most of his life. However, peace doesn't last and four years is almost enough time to forget the darkness. Today was the day Jim would be reminded.

He was running late to Audra's basketball game. Jim was up to his eyeballs in paperwork that needed to be done before he could leave for the weekend. Finally, he left the office but knew he probably wouldn't make it in time for the opening ttip-off at least not in the Friday Austin traffic. However, he made it earlier than he had anticipated, only five minutes after the game had started. Jim found Gina and Josh in the stands. He walked up and immediately kissed her. Jim had kissed her every day since she had moved to Austin. It was the best part of his day.

Gina smiled after they kissed. "You're late, but I'm glad you made it."

"Sorry about that, although all my paperwork is done. And now our three-day weekend can begin. So how is she doing?"

"You missed it. The reason they're up by six is because of Audra. On her first possession, she was coming off a pick and roll and three defenders surrounded her so she couldn't get a shot."

Jim laughed. "I guess the other team knows she's the star."

"Well, she got mad and decided to just stand back and shoot three-pointers. Nailed two of them in a row from NBA distance."

"Nice. I see her long-distance shot training is working. Audra's been trying to make three's from that distance for a little while, but had only been able to do it about 20% of the time."

Gina smiled. "So far, she's got two of them tonight." That put a big smile on Jim's face and like a proud parent, he was happy for her. And it was that joy that made him cheer, maybe a little too loud for her at times while annoying other fans. But he was unapologetic. She was the star of the team and he was extremely proud of here.

They made it through most of the first half when Jim got a phone call. He looked at the Caller ID. It was his friend with Austin PD, Mike Lester. Gina gave him a dirty look as if to say don't answer it. However, Mike never called him directly when it was a social call, he texted. If he called, it was for work and it was important. Jim told Gina that he needed to take it. He walked out of the stands and answered the call. "Mike," he said, "I hope it's important, I'm at Audra's basketball game."

Mike had a serious tone. "Sorry buddy, it is important."

Jim was standing in the foray outside of the gym now. "Okay, what's so urgent?"

"I have a murder that you need to look at."

"Afraid I can't. I have a three-day weekend with my family. Happy to consult on it next week when I'm free." "You don't understand Jim; I need you to take a look at it because you've investigated this kind of murder before. The murder is staged, and we've never seen anything like this… you have. I knew you were getting a three-day weekend and believe me; I wouldn't have called unless it was important. "

Jim got nervous. A sick feeling in his stomach hit like a dagger to the gut. He asked if Mike could text a photo. His friend sent one. Jim always seemed to have nerves of steel when it came to gruesome crime scenes. He almost threw up when he saw the photo. He replied. "You're right buddy, I've seen this before. Text me the address. I will be there soon. "

Jim knew Gina would be mad and Audra would be disappointed that he couldn't stay, but he couldn't sugarcoat it. This was bad. And he was probably the only expert who could lend the proper consultation to Austin PD. He walked back in and told Gina what had happened and that he had to go. She was mad, but she had learned to truly understand the nature of his job in the last four years. They may not have been married; be she was pretty much a cop's wife. Gina certainly understood what that entailed better than his ex-wife.

The crime scene was at a warehouse in Daffin, just outside of Austin. It was in a more rural part of the Austin area, out of the way from most people. From the looks of the area, Jim estimated that the killer didn't expect t the body to be found for a while. It was found quicker than expected as he was about to find out why. Austin PD had surrounded the area, Jim could see the red and blue blaze from the patrol car lights a half a mile away. CSU was already on the scene as well. He flashed his badge to the cops outside and then proceeded inside the warehouse. It took only a few steps to see the full outline of the crime scene. The picture he was sent was horrific, but the real thing was even worse. Detective Mike Lester was standing near the body when he saw Jim walk in. He walked over and greeted his friend.

Mike said. "Thank you for coming. I'm really sorry about the timing." Mike pointed towards the body. "As you can see, the photo doesn't do the scene justice. I wonder if there has ever been such gruesome symbolism."

Jim replied. "Oh, you'd be surprised." Jim stared at the scene. The victim was a man. He was naked. But the most bizarre thing was the way he was laid out. He was nailed to a large cross. He had been crucified just like Christ, although not exactly. The cross was upside down and his side had been pierced by a sharp object with blood slowly dripping out of it into some kind of ceramic. The cross was mounted to the warehouse railing on one of the back walls. Jim stared at it for a moment and then he noticed something. He commented. "Check it out, the killer even made a crown of thorns."

"Mike replied. "Yeah, whoever did this was very detailed. It's drilled into the victim's head and silicone was used to make it stay in place."

"Shows that the killer wasn't rushed. They had plenty of time to make this scene."

"Is that the reason the warehouse was used?"

"Probably not, if it's the same MO of the killer I'm looking for, the warehouse is something personal to the victim. Probably should find out who owns this warehouse and see if there's any connection, which by the way, do you have an ID on the victim?

Mike grabbed an electronic tablet from one of the other Detectives. "We do, he wasn't hard to find after we got fingerprints. Popped up in the system from an arrest where he was accused of molesting a little girl, his name is Reverend William Staples."

Jim had a shocked look on his face. "Reverend?"

"Yep, he's a Baptist Minister. He was an associate pastor at that big church that isn't exactly a mega church but should be because that's where all the pretty people go, you know, Clearwater Baptist. He was let go over an inappropriate incident with a minor."

"What do you mean, inappropriate?"

"We didn't find out much because there weren't any formal charges. But supposedly, he molested a young girl."

"Any lawsuits against him from the parents of the child."

"No, they pretty much swept it under the rug. But there was something else; he was arrested for filming two minors."

Stunned again by the news, Jim replied. "He made a snuff film!"

"Supposedly, but he was acquitted because there was no evidence in the film that he was there or even behind the camera."

"They didn't get him on child pornography?"

"The tape wasn't found in his possession. Somebody he knew had the video and told police that William was the man behind the camera. It came down to his word against the Reverend's, so the charges were dropped, and the other guy went to jail for child pornography."

Jim looked more closely at the other part of the scene. There was a small stool on the left side of the cross. It had a laptop opened and playing a video on a continuous loop. Jim didn't really notice the video until he got a closer look. It was a snuff film containing two little girls and a masked adult. He watched it and almost threw up. Blood and guts didn't make him squeamish, but that certainly made him sick to his stomach. Any decent human being would feel sick after having to watch that film. It was beyond disgusting.

Jim looked at his friend. "What the fuck, Mike?"

"Yeah, it's pretty much made us all sick, having to look at it. I was going to turn it off, but you needed to see it to really understand what we are dealing with."

"As if someone being crucified wasn't horrific enough." Mike laughed at his sarcasm. Jim asked. "Why did you call me out here, you think this is some kind of revenge killing and you want help with it?"

"No, I don't. I want you to tell me if this is a Black Fairy murder."

Jim gave him a dirty look. "It can't be because he is in federal prison."

"Or maybe it's a copycat?"

"I get that this staged scene has a lot of symbolism, but I won't confirm that it's a Copycat."

Mike was a little stunned he said that. "Really, you don't think so?"

"My first impression, no."

Mike held up a blacklight and pointed it toward the ground. There was an outline of something around the base of the cross. Jim saw it but couldn't tell what it was so he took a few steps back to get a better look. Finally, he saw it. The outline was Fairy Wings. They were drawn exactly the same as on the bodies of Don Bennett and Henry Frankston. That was the biggest shock of all when it came to the crime scene. The real Black Fairy killer had come out of hiding.

Jim responded to the wings. "Okay, that has my attention."

Mike replied. "So, this has to be a copycat killer, right? Or is Aldo Martinez not really the Black Fairy killer and just taking credit for the murders."

Jim couldn't really answer that. The only thing he said was. "Okay, perhaps a copycat killer is possible."

"So, what do we do?"

"I have to consult with my boss. Without an official request, CID can't get involved. We can consult, but that's it. In the meantime, I need photos of the crime scene. My boss will need extensive photos. "

Mike agreed to that. He said that Jim would get them in an hour. But then he asked. "There's just one thing I'm curious about, why is this guy crucified upside down? I don't get it."

"Jim paused and thought about it for a moment, trying to remember everything he knew about religious symbolism in order to give a sufficient answer. He said. "As a former pastor who committed egregious sins and was a sexual predator, he's not worthy to be crucified as Christ was so he's put upside down." That was the only thing he could come up with. Mike was stunned by the answer, but in a way, it made perfect sense. The message behind the murder, well, it was more profound than they realized.

32

It was late when Jim got home last night. Gina was mad and understandably so. He missed the rest of Audra's basketball game where she scored 37 points. Audra must have been disappointed too. Jim knew he screwed up, but it was unavoidable, and even worse, he knew they wouldn't understand. He apologized the best he could and promised to make it up to them. However, he had a job to do, and the rest would have to come later. They were supposed to do something as a family that day, but Jim left early so he could get the crime scene photos and talk to his boss.

After he got the photos from Detective Mike Lester, he headed to Robert's house. It was Saturday and this couldn't be done in the office. Robert was surprised to see Jim so early in the morning. He hated when his detectives showed up to his house unannounced, he was a man who liked his privacy, but he also knew that if Jim did it then it had to be important.

Robert did at least have to give Jim a dirty look when he arrived on his doorstep. He invited him and walked with Jim back to his home office. He even gave Jim a cup of coffee because even though he may be annoyed, he still knew how to be polite.

Still early in the morning, they both needed another cup of coffee. Robert had already been alerted to what had happened, but the photos told a different story. They always did. Robert flipped through them once and commented. "Jesus, I thought the other murders were sadistic."

Jim replied. "Yeah, the snuff film on a continuous loop is the most sadistic part of the scene…I nearly threw up when I saw it."

"Is there any evidence that this former minister shot the film?"

"No, but he's connected to it somehow."

"What makes you say that?"

"Because the staged scene is personal…maybe not to the killer, but the sexual crime is personal to the victim, especially if this follows the same MO as The Black Fairy"

Robert shook his head. "Okay, let's ask the obvious question because I know what you're thinking …is it possible that this murder really was done by a Copycat?"

Jim cracked a smile. "Of course, it's possible, but how much of a possibility is the real question. Do you honestly think it's a copycat? I don't, but there is only one way to absolutely be sure."

"Which is?"

"We need an autopsy, if there is soda bread or some kind of unleavened bread in his system then it's probably the same killer since that detail was never released to the public."

"You're referring to the Sin Eater ritual, right?"

"Yes, Don Bennett and Henry Frankston, both had that kind of bread in their system. "

Robert sat back in his chair. He started going through the photos again. He was thinking about what to do next. Then he spoke. "Okay, so what I'm about to tell you doesn't leave this room. Four years ago, I knew the Feds had Aldo Martinez under surveillance. I got a call from them right before you guys left his office after having questioned him for the first time. They really didn't give me any details; they just wanted to know why he was part of our investigation. When I told them why they told me that there was no way he could be the Black Fairy Killer."

"Why did you push so hard to get a confession out of him?"

"I didn't believe the Feds and I didn't want to lose jurisdiction of the crime. And before you say anything, yes, I know that I screwed up and innocent people got killed. So investigating this murder is a sensitive issue, we can't say it's anything other than a copycat or it screws up the federal investigation. It's a sticky situation, politically, so we can't just disrupt what happened. We also can't investigate this murder using old files from the Black Fairy murders as if we're looking for the real killer. Because it's a federal case, they can come in and sweep up this up in a heartbeat. Do you understand?"

"Unfortunately, yes."

This has to be done under the radar. State CID can't officially be involved unless the body count gets to two or three. I'm not saying that I don't want you to investigate this, but you can only do it as a consultant for the Austin Police Department. I believe that we need to catch this killer and whether we admit it's a copycat or not, at the end of the day this is a Texas Crime, the killer will be tried in a Texas Court, and will be executed in a Texas prison for murder. That's the way it needs to be if there's going to be any kind of closure."

Jim softly smiled "So basically I'm working with the detectives who are in charge of this murder and lending my advice, that's about as much authority as I'm going to have."

"Yes and no. You're only supposed to give advice to them, but you can still make an arrest... You have jurisdiction all over the state. And I will do you one better. We can provide resources so you can form a task force along with Austin PD and you can bring in outside help. If you want to bring in some of the people you worked with on the last investigation, you can. "

Jim got a little bit excited. "Well, there's only two that I would actually bring in and it sure as hell isn't Ron Jackson."

Robert couldn't help but laugh. "I figured as much. I wouldn't even put him on something like this. Personally, I can't wait till he decides to run for Tarrant County Sheriff, and we can get rid of him." Robert never thought much of Detective Jackson just like Jim. He would never have been hired on his own merits at State CID. Of course, the only way he could get a transfer there was because he knew someone with enough influence to get him the position and he was attached to a big case. Robert had always hated how people got the jobs they weren't qualified for, mainly because of politics. It was worse than Affirmative Action."

Jim nodded as a way of saying thanks. "I appreciate the resources, but we need to get the autopsy first and there's only one person that I want to do it."

Robert nodded back. "I figured as much. Dr. Connor is teaching at UT Southwestern, right."

"Yes."

"Well, since it is a College of Medicine, it won't be too hard to have the body shipped up there. Better to have it done up there than to raise suspicions with CID and the Feds while having her flown down here to look at the body."

"Really."

"You haven't been there as long as I have…that place has a lot of ears and information has a suspicious way of getting into the hands of outside agencies."

Jim laughed. "I'll take your advice on that. Besides, I need to go to Dallas anyway. Might as well kill two birds with one stone."

Robert handed the photos back to Jim. "I'll make the arrangements to lend you out to Austin PD and get a task force set up. And if I were you, I'd spend the rest of the weekend with your family, do something nice with them. It might be a while before you get to do that because there's no telling how long this investigation might take."

Jim didn't disagree with Robert. Everything would keep for at least a couple of days. And besides, Jim needed to make it up to Gina and Audra for leaving the game early the night before. This was his best chance since his vacation would be cut short as he would be going back into the Black Fairy investigation.

33

On Monday, Jim was back at work. In fact, he left early, before anybody else in the house was out of bed yet. Despite Gina being mad, he couldn't wait one more day to start this new investigation. There was a lot to do including a long drive to Dallas. The first thing he did after confirming that the body was shipped up to Dallas was call James Cross. who was living in the Austin area now. It didn't take much to convince him to help and join the task force. As he put it, retirement was boring, and he needed a good case to work on. Plus, there wasn't enough stimulating work at the Detective Agency he was helping to run. Missing person cases and wives trying to find out if their husbands were cheating on them just didn't cut it for an old homicide detective. James Ross was all too happy to join the team.

    The drive to Dallas from Austin was the usual three hours. It was a lot of time to reflect and come up with a few theories regarding this latest murder. What bothered Jim the most about the Black Fairy murders is there still wasn't a clear answer on why they did it. No clear motive. And trying to figure out the "why" was Jim's biggest headache, that's what kept him from truly letting go of the case. He knew that he had to find some kind of resolve or he would never be able to let it go.

Dr. Vanessa O'Connor had classes in the morning so it would be late afternoon before she could perform the autopsy. She didn't have any details; the only thing she knew was that someone in Austin PD had requested her for the autopsy. It was still Austin PD's case; Robert had used his influence with State CID to get the body transferred to UT Southwestern Medical Center in Dallas. Vanessa was always flattered when outside police departments requested her for autopsies or to consult on a case. After all, she had earned a great reputation as a consultant after the Black Fairy case after her morning classes, she headed back to her office and found Jim waiting for her. Vanessa was surprised. They hadn't spoken in four years. But she smiled when she saw him and used some of her charming wit to greet him. "I'm not sure I like the idea of cops just being able to barge into my office. It can create a hostile work environment."

Jim laughed and with a little sarcasm of his own, replied. "It's nice to see you too."

"And what do I owe the pleasure…I'm sure it's work-related, right!"

"I did want to see you too, maybe catch up because it has been a long time. But yes, it is work-related too."

She smiled. "Thought so."

"You're the best medical examiner in the State of Texas. "Can't trust anybody else with this."

Vanessa gave him a curious look. "Ah, this explains the request I had to do an autopsy. But I thought it was from the Austin Police Department."

"It is I am assigned to them as a consultant. But it's the nature of the murder as to why I am consulting with Austin PD and I requested you for the autopsy."

Vanessa paused. It wasn't for curiosity's sake. She was nervous and that rarely happened to her when it came to dead bodies. She responded. "It's a Black Fairy murder, isn't it?"

"Why do you say that? You didn't ask if it's a copycat murder."

"Because I never thought Aldo Martinez was the real killer despite his confession. And I suspect you wouldn't really be here if it was just a copycat murder. I mean, I can see you consulting on something like that, but you wouldn't take the lead in this investigation unless you thought it was the real killer doing it again."

Jim tried to smile without giving too much away. He never had a good poker face. "You are perceptive; I can't say anything about Aldo Martinez or his confession. What I can say is this murder may not be a copycat and that's why I need your help. You're familiar with forensics from the other murders and you know what to look for. I need you to tell me if this is a copycat or the real Black Fairy."

Vanessa smiled at Jim. "Sure, but you already know the answer, don't you?"

"Maybe, but let's see if I'm right."

Vanessa nodded. "I don't suppose I can look at the crime scene photos?"

Normally a Medical Examiner or the doctor performing the autopsy wouldn't get to see the crime scene photos so they could remain objective while doing the autopsy. Dr. Vanessa O'Connor was different and because of her insight when it came to creating a profile of the killer, Jim had no objection. He valued her opinion, which he couldn't say about most people when solving crimes. He had the photos in a folder and handed them to her. She started flipping through the photos and even winced a few times at the gruesome nature of the scene. She wondered if anybody had ever truly seen someone crucified before. Reading about what the Romans actually did and seeing it were two very different things.

There was one thing that stuck out at least to her. She was the only one who really noticed it and understood its true meaning. The large vessel that the blood from the body had drained into had a unique symbol on it. Vanessa commented. "The symbol on the large bowl is really unique…it's not something you see every day."

A curious look washed over Jim's face. "What Symbol?" He asked.

"It's a Celtic Symbol called a Triskele, but it's not the traditional design of the Triskele."

"I'm not following."

Vanessa had an electronic tablet with her. She got on the internet and Googled "Triskele" so she could pull up some images of the symbol and show them to Jim.

"This is the traditional design; it's more of the Celtic Irish Symbol that we see in design." Then she scrolled through Google images and found the one that was on the vessel.

She pointed to the symbol and said to Jim. "This is the Pagan version or commonly known as the Celestial Celtic design. They have very distinctive meanings."

"Such as?"

"Basically, Triskeles are one of the most common elements of Celtic art; they are found in a variety of styles in both ancient and modern Celtic art, especially in relation to depictions of the Mother Goddess. They also represent the Celtic concept of the domains of material existence- earth, water, and sky, and their interrelations. Sometimes the symbol can be spiraling lines to represent the continuity of time. It's a Pagan concept. But what makes the Celestial version different is the concept of life. It represents the Sun which gives life or means birth, then you have the afterlife and reincarnation. You see the Triskele within this design is these three concepts woven with those domains of material existence- earth, water, and sky. All of them are enclosed within a circle representing one realm…one celestial body. You're mixing Celtic and Pagan ideology when it comes to the idea of life and how it connects to all things in a physical world or material existence, the afterlife, and then reincarnation. Do you follow?

Jim shook his head. "A little bit. I get the three concepts of birth, the afterlife, and reincarnation. But what does this have to do with the large vessel? The killer is using some kind of Irish or Celtic design…so what!"

Vanessa chuckled a bit. Jim wasn't really seeing it, but then again, most people she knew couldn't see the hidden meanings within things as she did. She always thought their interpretation was limited. But she responded. "I just think it's interesting that the Celestial version is used. It's like the killer is saying that after death on the cross to prepare for the afterlife, the blood must be purified in order to be reincarnated. I mean, there's no reason to use that design unless you're trying to say something."

"Or preach."

Vanessa laughed. "If you say so."

"Reincarnation… I thought that was only a Buddhist thing."

"Not necessarily, Pagans believed a soul could come back into something else. Plus, isn't Jesus coming back from the dead, just a form of reincarnation, he was a man when he died on the cross and then came back as a godly being."

Jim sarcastically smiled. "I don't know any Christians that would see it that way."

"Maybe not, but my point is, it's not just an eastern philosophy."

"Good point. Now, you said this is a very unique symbol, right!"

"Yes."

"Where would you get a bowl like that, Ireland?"

"That's the thing, you can't just buy a bowl with that particular design…maybe with the common form of the Triskele, sure, but this design would have to be specially made."

Jim thought about it for a moment. "Really! Then it might be easy to track down the company who would make something so specific."

"Maybe."

"Thank you… that give me something to go on.

Vanessa smiled. "Sure, thing and you should be aware… this scene is very specific in its meaning. I think the killer is trying to make us understand something. I wouldn't be surprised if some of the victim's blood after it's been purified in this so-called Pagan ritual was used as some form of symbolism in another murder."

Jim nodded. He understood what she was saying, and he knew that this particular murder shouldn't be dismissed so easily as if the killer was just being theatrical. There was something they were meant to see, something in the darkness that still remained hidden. The blending of the Christian, Celtic, and Pagan ideologies was truly unique, but after hearing Vanessa's explanation about the Triskele's meaning, there was one word that came to mind, transformation. Isn't that what birth to the afterlife to reincarnation really is, a transformation from one thing to another? As always, her insights were incredible. He always learned something new after talking with Vanessa.

So that was the end of their conversation…for now, Vanessa told Jim that it would be the end of the day before she was done with the autopsy. Jim didn't mind the wait, he had someone to see, anyway. Someone who had good insights as well and whose help he needed to finally solve this case. But would she want to help. This case was filled with darkness. Could she go back into the darkness again? It was not an easy thing to ask of anyone. But there wasn't anybody else he could trust to bring this case to a natural conclusion.

Detective Maisie Green came out of the restroom after her third cup of coffee in an hour went through her like a waterfall. She had, had a long night and still suffered from insomnia from time to time. Today was one of those days where she would pretty much drink a pot of coffee to stay awake. And it's not like her job in Juvenile Crimes was all that stimulating. As she was walking back to her desk, she noticed a visitor sitting next to her desk. Although, she didn't recognize him right off the bat, Maisie was surprised when she did. Jim smiled at her when she sat down and came face to face with him.

Maisie responded. "Hi…this is an interesting surprise."

Jim laughed. "Good surprise or bad surprise?"

"I don't know yet…I guess it depends on why you're here. I'm assuming it's not to catch up."

Cracking a smile, Jim replied. "It's partly to catch up with you."

She raised an eyebrow at the facetious comment. "Ah, ha," she replied back. Then her suspicions kicked in. She hadn't spoken to him in four years, there was only one reason he would come and see her. Maisie asked. "There's been another murder, right?"

Jim didn't just come out and say yes, but he did confirm her suspicions with the look on his face. Maisie felt the same sickening feeling in her stomach just like the first time she saw Henry Frankston's murder scene. Jim said. "Let's grab a cup of coffee or maybe a beer if being on duty doesn't bother you anymore. "

Maisie couldn't help but laugh at the small bit of sarcasm regarding their professional nature as law enforcement. She usually followed the rules, but not so much in the last four years. She was still a good and honorable cop, just not like she used to be. The Black Fairy case had definitely changed her. She said. "I figure this isn't going to be an easy conversation so let's grab a beer."

There was a small bar around the corner. It was an unofficial cop bar because the beer tended to be cheaper than most places in Dallas. That's where they went. Jim and Maisie found a small cocktail table away from everybody else and ordered two Lone Stars. Maisie didn't want small talk even though she was happy to see Jim. She asked. "Can you tell me what happened?"

Jim took a sip of beer. "There was a Murder in Austin a few days ago…the way it was done looks like a Black Fairy murder."

Maisie looked at the file folder Jim had on the table. She pointed at the folder. "Are those the crime scene folders?"

"Yes." He took them out of the folder and handed them to Maisie. She took a deep breath, trying to prepare herself for the horror she was about to see. As she flipped through the photos, Jim continued to talk. "This is not an official CID investigation. It's Austin PD's case, but I have been asked to consult because of the nature of the crime."

Maisie finished looking through the photos. She had to turn away a few times because of how gruesome the murder scene was. She asked the same question others had. "Is this a copycat murder or do you think this is the real killer?"

"I think it's our killer come out of hiding, but the autopsy that's being performed will confirm it for sure."

"Autopsy?"

"Yeah…I had the body shipped up here to the UT Southwestern College of Medicine so Vanessa could do it."

"Really!"

"Yep. She's the only one I trust, and she knows what to look for."

Maisie nodded, she agreed with Jim's assessment of Vanessa. "Good Choice."

"I thought so. Anyway, because the Black Fairy case is technically a federal case now, we're trying to fly under the radar of the Feds so as far as everybody knows, this is a copycat case. But I have been given resources to form a task force along with the Austin Detectives who are working the case."

"Do they know that Aldo Martinez isn't the Black Fairy?"

"They don't know everything, but my buddy Mike, who is one of the Detectives asked me about it, so I figure he already suspects that Aldo's deal wasn't exactly legit. "

"You are going to tell them the truth?"

Jim shrugged. "Probably, when I get the full task force put together."

Maisie took a sip of beer and softly laughed. "So that's what this is about you want to get the band back together."

"Well, only the good members of the band…some of them are not being asked back."

That made her laugh. She knew who he was talking about. "I guess Ron is not being asked back."

"Hell no."

"Heard he went to work at CID."

Jim rolled his eyes at the thought. Unfortunately, it was true. "He did, but he's not good enough to work in my department. However, you are, you're a good investigator and that's why I want you to be on this task force."

Maisie tried to smile, it was a nice compliment, but the idea of investigating a crime like this again, frightened her. She replied. "You don't need my help."

"Sure, I do…you know the material…you have good instincts. And more importantly, I value your insight."

"You flatter me. But no, I can't."

Jim took a few more sips of beer. He was confused. He was sure, she would say yes. He asked her. "Why not?"

Maisie sighed. The truth was complicated, and she didn't want to look weak in front of Jim after he paid her such a wonderful compliment, but she wasn't the same detective that she was four years ago. It wouldn't be a stretch to say this case had messed her up a little bit. "Please understand, it's not that I don't want to help you. I just can't."

"You're going to have to give me more than that."

Maisie rolled her eyes. Of course, that wouldn't satisfy Jim. She continued. "After the shootout four years ago, I couldn't sleep for almost 2 years... Insomnia and the occasional panic attack. Anytime I heard something that sounded like gunfire I have a panic attack. I was good at hiding it for a long time and then I had a panic attack after looking at a dead body which has never happened before. I finally started seeing a therapist and figured out combination of dead bodies and associations with violence were causing them. That's when I transferred out of homicide."

"Are you okay, now?"

"I still get insomnia from time to time like last night, but the stress of not having to deal with dead bodies or shootouts have definitely helped. I do take some medication, which helps. I just don't know if I can go back into a case this horrific."

"I get it, you're not the first cop to experience panic attacks after a shootout. But what happened four years ago is very rare even for homicide detectives. It wasn't just some guy with a gun shooting at cops, it was a small army."

"I know, I've been told that before, but I just don't think I could go through it again."

Jim took another sip of beer. "Are you having a panic attack after seeing those photos?"

"No, they're just photos and not the real thing."

"True, but it's still pretty gruesome. Also, it's pretty rare to see something like that even with a homicide cop. You seem to be doing fine so how do you know you can't handle seeing something like that with the medication?"

"I don't know, but I do know that I don't want to be exposed to something like this again."

Jim smiled at her trying to offer some kind of comfort the best way he knew how. Normally, he just had a few glasses of good scotch and that's how he would get over something like this. He replied. "I'm not asking you to be involved in a shootout. I'm not really asking you to be in the field. What I need is someone who can look at all of the evidence, and photos, and offer a different perspective. I have people who can take down the killer...but I don't have enough good people to sit in an office and analyze the evidence or see patterns that I'm not seeing. That's what I really need from you."

It was hard to say no to that. Maisie had to admit that she was still fascinated by this case and sitting in an office drinking coffee analyzing data sounded like a cushy gig. She said. "Okay, that would be more ideal, but I'd be away from my kid and I got married last year, so banging away on an extended assignment is not exactly that good for a new marriage."

"Well, I could tell you that if he truly loves you, he'd understand, but that may be over the top."

"Perhaps that's true, but there is something else. I don't necessarily disagree with what the Black Fairy is doing. The victims are horrible people. Frankly, they deserve to die. I know as a cop I shouldn't say that, but that's the way I see it."

"Let me guess, you read the vigilante book about The Black Fairy!"

Maisie laughed. Jim seemed to know her all too well. "I did, in fact, but even before that book came out, I had the same opinion."

"Fine, I'm not going to debate the morality of what this killer is doing. I'm a cop and it's not my job to have a different take on vigilantism. But don't you at least want to know who it is and hear in their own words why they did it?"

"Sure, I would love to know their identity, but do I need to help catch them…no."

"Are you really sure about that?"

Laughing, Maisie replied. "No, not entirely."

"Okay, that I can work with." Jim told her what Vanessa had said about the symbol and its deeper meaning. He explained Vanessa's theory. This case had always been about symbolism, about a message, that the killer wanted the world to know. At least that's the theory that they had come up with four years ago. Jim hoped that this would pique her curiosity enough to come on board and join the task force.

Her response was, "wow, that's definitely interesting. You know there is a word that comes to mind about the killer with each murder they commit..."

Jim replied. "Transformation!"

Maisie was stunned at his response since it was the exact same thing she was thinking. She replied back. "Yeah, I think transformation is the perfect word."

Jim smiled. "You see, you're curious and I bet you haven't been that curious about anything in four years."

Maisie gave him a dirty look. "That's not fair; you're placating to my natural curiosity anyway."

"True, I'll do whatever works. If you don't really want to do this, that's fine, I do understand. But I need good investigators to help solve this case and you're one of the best detectives I've ever worked with. I'm going to see about the autopsy and give you some time to really think about it. You can let me know at the end of the day, then that'll be it. But do me the courtesy of really thinking about it before you say yes or no."

Maisie nodded. Then she finished her beer. Yes, it was true, she hadn't been as curious about a case in four years. Jim knew her well enough to know what strings to tug. But she kept thinking to herself if she did it and went back into the darkness with this case, who would she be when it was over? he had just gotten to a place where she liked herself again and was happy. Part of that had to do with finding a good man to marry. But the other part was forgetting most of what she had seen and experienced with a case like this so she could move on with her life, and with the help of a therapist. She didn't know if she could live with herself if she didn't help this case reach a conclusion. She would at least think about it. Maisie owed Jim that much for keeping her alive years ago during that horrendous shootout.

34

It was a short trip to Dallas. Less than a day in fact. Jim arrived back in Austin and still didn't know if Detective Maisie Green would take him up on his offer, and just in case, all the arrangements have been made for her to do a special assignment with CID and consult alongside Jim with Austin PD. About the only thing Jim had accomplished in Dallas was getting an autopsy done and confirming what he already knew. The real Black Fairy was no longer in hiding. Unleavened or soda bread was found in the victim's system, no doubt from the killer performing a sin eater ritual. But there was another interesting surprise from the autopsy.

By the time Jim had arrived back in Austin it was already too late to bring dinner for Gina and the kids. He pretty much got home just to say good night to all of them and would be up at the crack of dawn to get a head start on the new investigation. While he couldn't tell Gina all of the details, he at least let her know that he would be consulting on a sadistic murder with Austin PD. That was all he could say. Jim got up, made coffee, got a quick breakfast, and had just enough time to kiss Gina good morning before he was out the door. They wouldn't be working out of an Austin Police Station. CID had rented some space from the Austin branch of the Spade Detective Agency. Jim thought it was a clever name and highlighted the fact that it was run by retired police officers who didn't want to spend all day at home.

When he arrived at 7 am, James was already there, opening the office up. It was small. Just desks with computers and phones, and a small conference room. It was all they really needed, especially since there wasn't a whole lot of traffic going in and out. Most of the business was simple background checks that could be done from a home computer, serving subpoenas, and the occasional stakeout of a husband who was probably cheating on their wife. It was more like a part-time job for the retired cops you work there and a chance to drink beer and watch sports during the day or as James put it, the perfect retirement.

Jim walked in with James and helped set up. He had a few boxes with files in them. James thought it was strange since technically there weren't supposed to be any files on the old case. they would have been turned over to the Feds. He had to ask about them.

Jim replied. "Yes, these are all the case files of murders that we think were linked to the Black Fairy."

"You didn't give them to the Feds."

"No, we did, I just made copies of everything."

"Are you allowed to do that?"

"That's a bit of a gray area, but we have them and that's what counts."

James laughed. He wasn't surprised at all that Jim would have done that. "Somehow, I knew you would. You couldn't let this case go no matter how much you tried…not until there's a conclusion you're satisfied with."

Jim smiled. James knew him well, probably because they were more alike than they realized. Good Detectives usually are. He said. "You're right. I haven't stopped thinking about it over the last four years."

"That's enough times to come up with interesting theories."

"Maybe not more theories…I think I have more questions than I did back then…certainly more questions than answers." James smiled. He knew the feeling. Jim said. "By the way, the case file you handed me four years ago on our last day…the one you said, I should check out. I did."

"And?"

"It's a Black Fairy murder…I'm sure of it. I'll explain more when everybody is here."

James nodded. But he was also curious about something else, only because Jim hadn't said anything. He asked. "Is Maisie joining our team?"

"I don't know. She hasn't returned my phone calls after we talked yesterday. I texted her the details, so I guess we'll see."

"You didn't ask that Ft. Worth Detective to join us, what was his name…Ron."

Jim shot him a dirty look. "Fuck no…and that idiot, actually got a job at CID."

"Really…with you?"

"No, just because he worked this case, doesn't mean he's good enough to work homicide at the state level."

James rolled his eyes. "He did end up at CID so stranger things have happened." Jim laughed at how true that statement really was. The rest of the morning they made small talk about old cases and what he was doing with his retirement. Jim got files out of the boxes and organized them. About an hour later, the Austin Detectives walked into the detective agency. They may have been one short, but it was time to get started.

Detective Mike Lester walked over to the conference table and introduced his partner, Detective Michelle Morgan. Jim introduced James Cross to both of them. Mike asked. "So, is this it…kind of a small task force?"

"It is for now. Hopefully, we'll have someone join us later, but I only picked people who are familiar with this case…people that I worked with in Dallas. And more importantly, people that I can trust."

Mike cracked a facetious smile. "I guess things haven't changed much with you."

Jim laughed at the comment. "No, not really."

Mike looked around the room. "The office is small."

James responded to his comment. "It may be small, but it works just fine for a bunch of retired cops doing part-time detective work, so they don't have to be home annoying their wives. And we can always work out of the bar next door if we need to." Jim rolled his eyes at the notion. Retired cops didn't give the same shit they did when they were on the job and James could definitely get him into trouble.

Mike replied. "Whatever works, but how's the coffee around here?"

"Better than anything you have at your station...when you retire as a cop, you get better coffee...it's a rule." James showed them where the coffee station was in the office. Part of the detective agency's budget was having gourmet coffee in the office...they made sure it was part of their basic operating budget."

As Mike and James were getting coffee, Detective Morgan asked. "So where do we start?"

Jim pointed to the file folders at the end of the table. "You and your partner need to be familiar with the entire case?"

"Entire case...it's just the one murder...we're up to speed on that."

"There's something I need to tell the both of you, the truth behind the Black Fairy murders...only four people know the truth...you'll be five and six. "Mike walked back to the table, stirring the sugar and cream that he just put in his cup of coffee. He asked. "The truth about what?"

Jim was about to reply when the front door of the office opened, and a familiar face walked through. It was Maisie. Jim greeted her with a grateful smile. She said after walking in. "I guess, I found the right place... only had to turn around once. Sorry, I'm late."

Jim replied. "It doesn't matter, you're here now." He introduced the Austin Detectives to Maisie and told them both why she and James were such a big help four years before. Then he started to tell them about Aldo's deal with the Feds. Maisie asked if he should tell more people because of his non-disclosure agreement when signing off on the deal as the lead investigator. Jim simply replied. "It doesn't matter at this point; they need to know everything if we're going to finally solve this case."

The Austin Detectives were shocked to say the least, even skeptical, Detective Morgan more than anyone. She said. "Wait, I don't get it. He fits your original profile...someone deeply religious using Christian symbolism to exact revenge on sinners in the name of God. He wrote that paper about Archangels being God's instrument for revenge."

Jim said. "I know and that's what we originally thought too until we were given surveillance photos by the DEA confirming that he wasn't anywhere around at the time of the murders. He may have been in the same city, but not near the crime scenes."

"Not to sound like a conspiracy theorist, but couldn't the DEA have doctored their surveillance photos to convince you to go along with their deal?"

Jim sarcastically smiled. "I think Government Agents are capable of anything, but why only confess to two murders? Plus, he barely knew what a sin eater was when we interviewed him, at least not as much as the killer would. The paper was nothing more than a teenager being shocking for the sake of effect and to appear that he had an original idea to win a scholarship."

"I guess, I just don't buy it. And how do we know for sure that this really isn't a copycat murder?"

"I get your skepticism. It's hard to believe but its' the truth. And the autopsy report proves it. I hope you read through it carefully when I emailed it to you. The bread inside the victim's system was unleavened or soda bread...that detail was kept hidden from the public and never made it into the final report of how the earlier victims were killed. Only the real killer would have known that."

"Unless Aldo Martinez told someone like an eager disciple."

Jim shook his head. Her skepticism was amusing despite it being flawed. He responded. "His communication is heavily monitored. He is never allowed to answer any fan letters and the only visitors he can receive are close family members, where all conversations are monitored. If he was giving instructions on how to murder someone, we would have heard about it by now. Believe what you want, but I'm telling you, this is the real killer."

Detective Morgan shrugged at the idea. She just didn't want to believe it and it seemed as if there was no convincing her. It didn't matter, she wasn't going to dwell on it and decided to move on by asking. "How did you get onto him as a suspect in the first place?"

"We were looking for anybody that might have a reason to kill these people and who had a Catholic education. His name came up because of his sister Alena who was raped in a supposed rape party organized by Jack Perry. He fits the profile and in a background check, we found the paper he wrote."

Mike finally spoke up. "According to your report, he was traveling on behalf of Highland Security and in the cities where the murders occurred, when they occurred. If he really isn't the killer that seems like a very big coincidence or is he being framed?"

Maisie finally spoke up and gave her opinion. "You know I've always wondered that myself... It can't be just a coincidence that the murders were committed at the same time he was in those cities inspecting job sites."

James asked her. "You think the real killer would have known his schedule, maybe like an employee at Highland Security, thus making it easier to frame him?"

"Yes, but it would also have to be somebody that knew he wrote that paper. A friend that he confided in, or perhaps somebody he dated, which in this day and age could be a man or a woman. But my point is, what if the real killer and Aldo Martinez knew each other."

This is why Jim valued her insights. She had a knack for asking a question that others hadn't thought of. He said to her. "If that's true, then it's worth looking at employee files and looking more at Aldo's history, but we would have to do it quietly. It does tip our hand a little bit if we start asking questions about Aldo Martinez's past."

James commented. "I'll do it as a private investigator looking into an insurance claim or a lawsuit. And I can do it without asking any questions about the murderers as to not arouse suspicions."

Jim nodded in agreement. It was the best way to handle it. Agreed... We don't need any actual cops asking those questions."

Detective Morgan interrupted. "So where do we actually start? I understand if you want us to be familiar with all of the murders that are potentially linked to The Black Fairy, but Austin PD has been brought into this because of one murder... Shouldn't we be starting with that?"

Jim sternly replied. "Yes, we are going to start with that murder. We need to look into who saw him last and whom he associated with. We might get lucky and somebody might have spotted the killer knocking him out and moving him to where he was found. But we're also looking for discernible patterns with the killer, they haven't murdered anyone in Austin since Hugo Blackmon so why now.... Is the killer traveling through Austin or did they travel to Austin just to commit this murder or are they actually living in Austin. I'm wondering if there's a particular pattern to how the killer ends up in these cities where they commit their murders."

"Maybe there isn't a pattern and the victims are picked at random."

"Maybe, but my instinct tells me there's a bigger connection and we're not seeing it. I do want you and Mike to look more into William Staples background. You're more familiar with him than we are."

"We can do that. Besides the autopsy report, did you find out anything else like why there's no physical evidence?"

"It's true, we've never been able to find any physical evidence whatsoever at the crime scenes. We think the killer wears some kind of protective suit that doesn't allow any DNA to escape. And then they burn it after they're done and get a new one when they commit another murder. However, I did in fact learn something else. The Doctor that performed the autopsy, she's worked with us before and also helped create our profile of the killer. The vessel that the blood drained into wasn't a simple flowerpot with a cool design on it. It was designed specifically for this crime scene."

Jim passed out a memo to everyone explaining what Vanessa had told him about that particular Triskelion Celtic symbol. He explained to everyone the true meaning of the symbol when it came to life, the afterlife, and reincarnation. Be she told him a killer would probably be using the blood for something else. Then Jim revealed even something more shocking. The bread that has been consumed as part of the sin eater ritual did not have wine poured over it as with past victims. Instead, there was blood poured over the bread and consumed by Reverend William Staples before he died.

Everybody in the room was shocked when they heard about the blood. Detective Morgan and Detective Lester didn't fully understand what that meant, but for James and Maisie, it meant the killer was evolving with their symbolism. Maisie was the first to comment. "That means the killer used pagan and Christian rituals as a way to transform the soul or prepare it to meet God. The best way to do that is a blood transformation just like the pagans used to do."

Detective Morgan replied. "What, I don't understand... using Pagan and Christian rituals to kill someone, it sounds like a bunch of theatrics... what does this have to do with finding the killer?"

Jim replied. You're right, it is theatrics, but it's also about belief. To catch this killer, you have to understand why they're doing it and the meaning behind the way they're committing the murders. Then maybe we can anticipate what they're going to do next."

"What does the killer want us to see? To me, this is just someone trying to get attention... that's the only reason to do all of this."

"I'm not trying to be rude, Detective, but your thinking is limited. You don't go to the trouble to stage the scene with this kind of symbolism unless you are trying to say something to the rest of the world. You're trying to make them understand something from your point of view. If this was simply exacting revenge on sexual predators who have gotten away with it...the killer could have just shot them, stab them, or poisoned them."

"Okay, fine, let's say that you're right... How does this murder compared to all the others, help us in identifying the murderer?"

Jim smiled. "That's the right question to ask. We're going to do three things. The first is looking into the background of William Staples and like you said before checking with who might have seen him last. Second, because that vessel is specifically made with the Triskelion symbol. We're going to check with every company that could do that, figure out where it was made, and for whom.

And third, we're going to follow up on a murder that happened four years ago that we never got a chance to investigate before Aldo Martinez made his confession."

Jim handed out copies of the file that was being called the perverted father murder. Jim continued. This is Joe Teller, a pedophile father who sexually abused his young daughter before and after her mother died from a drug overdose. He was reported to the police twice, but they never considered the mother a credible witness because of her history of drug use and fraud. Apparently, the mother was fired from a job for fraudulent activity. Anyway, the child was removed from the home for about a week and after the investigation turned up nothing she was returned and that was it. The daughter never confirmed the mother's story either. That was the second time the wife reported him. So, as you can see from the case file. He was laid out on the bed in a crucifixion pose, his genitals were removed, and he was pierced in the side and bled out. Soda breadcrumbs were found around the bed, but police didn't think it was suspicious, just that he was eating bread in bed."

Maisie asked. "What happened to the daughter?"

"I was just getting to that. She was in the house when the murder happened. An anonymous call was placed to 911, saying that the man was dead, and the daughter was left alone. I got a copy of the transcript from when they questioned the girl.... They just asked if she had seen anything. She said that she saw a person dressed all in black, but she also said the killer spoke to her one time and then the cops never followed up with their questions, like was it a man's voice or a woman's voice. Anyway, the girl was put into foster care, only her last name changed, and then the records were sealed. That much I did find out and I've been trying to track the girl down the past four years."

"How, if her adoption records were sealed?"

"She was 10 years old at the time and would be 14 now. Since it was only her last name that changed, I've been trying to find any records on a 14-year-old girl named Monica here in Texas. I even put an alert out to all law enforcement agencies in the state. Well, something popped up about a week ago... a 14-year-old girl named Monica got caught for shoplifting and has to appear in juvenile court.... She matches the description of Joe Teller's daughter; Caucasian, blond hair, with hazel eyes. Because of the police report, I have her address, which I'm going to check it out later."

Maisie smiled and nodded in agreement. "That's a hell of a break. I hope it pans out."

"We'll see." Jim ended his briefing and gave out assignments they each had their own investigations that would hopefully help the bigger objective…finding the true identity of The Black Fairy. The gender wasn't that important to Jim, all it did was help them know what they were looking for. But if it turned out to be a woman, it would almost be too hard to believe and that would make her the most dangerous serial killer ever in Texas. Because belief is power. Just like the devil, having people believe you don't exist makes it easier to destroy their sensibility and plunge them into a dark abyss that they could never escape from. The Black Fairy had already become like some mythical boogeyman coming to punish sinners when God would not. That was the worst thing it could be. That's what Jim was trying to stop.

35

Gina had been staring at the computer screen for hours. Her eyes were beginning to hurt like hell. This editing project was a beast and the whole team was way past the deadline. Editing a TV show could be like that even if it was a streaming show on Amazon.com. She was taking a break and getting a cup of coffee when her phone rang. It was her friend Lori. Gina hadn't talked to her in a while, definitely not as much since she had moved to Austin four years ago. They texted a few times here and there. Sure, they were still friends, but even friends drift apart. Lori was calling because she was in town on business. She had left the County Clerk's office and had become an insurance fraud investigator with the State of Texas. It was better pay and better benefits and more importantly, she was happy in her new job.

Gina answered the phone. "Lori…it's been a while."

Lori smiled. "Yes, it has. How have you been?"

"Good, but busy. The editing job keeps me really busy…haven't had to do any court reporting."

"Sounds like that's a good thing. Anyway, I am in town… we should get together, have dinner or something."

"That would be nice. It would be great to catch up. But instead of going out, why don't we cook dinner at the house… a home-cooked meal and a good bottle of wine is always better than going out."

Lori softly laughed. She was thinking the same thing. "Sounds good to me. Would love to see Jim and the kids too you know I've always liked you two together."

"Jim may be late tonight. He's been consulting on a case with the Austin Police Department."

"Doesn't matter, it will give us more time to catch up and it's been far too long."

Gina smiled. "Yes, it has. I'm anxious to hear about your love life."

"And I can't wait to tell you. By the way, is Audra still interested in serial killers?"

Gina rolled her eyes at the thought even though Lori couldn't see her reaction. Gina didn't really like the fact that Audra had this fascination about serial killers, but she couldn't stop her either. There was no convincing Audra to stop once she set her mind to do something, she was stubborn that way. Gina hoped it was just some weird teenage girl phase. She replied. "Yes, she's still interested in them. I can't decide if it's truly unhealthy or not."

"I'm sure she's all right, but I do have a gift for her. A book about the Black Fairy that's pretty interesting."

"She's definitely interested in that one so I'm sure she will be happy to get the book. "

Lori was happy to hear that. And she was a little excited to discuss it with her. Lori, too, had a weird fascination with this particular serial killer. Lori and Gina made plans to start cooking at 6:00 pm. Lori would bring two bottles of wine in anticipation of a fun night.

Jim was heading to his car when he saw Maisie follow behind. He gave her a strange look, wondering what she was doing or if she needed to speak to him in private. She looked at him and said. "I would like to come with you if that's okay?"

He replied. "Are you sure, I thought you didn't want to be in the field. That's what you told me."

"I know, but I'm curious about the girl you found. I'd like to be with you when you interview her, if nothing else to satisfy my own curiosity. Besides, I don't think we're going to get into a shootout with a 14-year-old girl."

Jim smiled. One of the things he liked about her was her sarcasm. In another life, he might have even asked her out, but he never dated fellow police officers. "That's fine with me, but you never know this is Texas, everybody has a gun including 14-year-olds."

Maisie had to laugh at that idea. There was definitely some truth in his sarcastic comment. "I'll take my chances, but I'll be sure to wear a bulletproof vest just in case."

They both got in the car and started to drive. Jim didn't really have a chance to catch up with her since he last spoke to Maisie. It was a great surprise to see her walk through the door, but a happy surprise. He needed her. And even though she wouldn't admit it, she needed some police work that was more stimulating than her usual line of work. She had almost put her retirement papers in a couple of times over the last four years. She may have had panic attacks because of the shootout, but she still liked to investigate complicated cases like this and she always felt that she had a natural aptitude for this kind of investigation. So, Jim had to ask. "Why did you change your mind?"

Maisie paused for a moment, looking for the right answer.... not some bullshit answer to impress the boss. "The truth is you were right, I have to know who the killer really is. It will haunt me for the rest of my life if I don't know."

"Curiosity is a bitch, sometimes. It's too hard to let go of things were curious about and they can pretty much drive us nuts until we get the answers we're looking for... that's the way it has always been with me."

"Same here, the other reason I came is I kind of needed a break from my husband. I love him and he's a good father to my son, but he can be clingy at times and it's very annoying."

Jim laughed. "And I thought it was only women who could be clingy."

It would certainly make my life easier if that were true, except if I were a lesbian... But I guess I'd be screwed either way."

The two detectives drove to College Station. It turned out that the adoptive parents moved there a couple years ago because the father became a professor at Texas A & M. Jim was certainly glad for the short drive because driving to Dallas from Austin was tiresome. It's not that he didn't like the city, he just hated driving more than two hours to get somewhere. And as a police officer, he was not above using his sirens to get out of traffic. They had the Joe Teller file with them. The photos of his murder we're not as gruesome as some of the other ones they had investigated it, but it was still pretty shocking. Then again genital mutilation should be shocking. The daughter who was named Monica had, had her last name changed to Perkins when she was adopted. It was at the insistence of the Court that this happened so that she would not be associated with her pedophile father and his murder. The judge saw it as a way of protecting her from her past, even if she could never truly forget it. About an hour later they arrived at the house. By law they needed to talk to the mother before questioning the girl at school or if they got lucky the daughter.

They found the house with ease and knocked on the door. Cynthia Perkins, the mother was surprised when the detectives introduce themselves. Her immediate reaction was that her daughter had done something else worse than just shoplifting. In fact, she asked that very question in a belligerent tone. "Okay detectives, what else did Monica do?"

Jim responded. "Mrs. Perkins, it's not what you think, your daughter Monica hasn't done anything else. May we come in and explain?"

Cynthia Perkins let the detectives in and offered them something to drink. She offered water or coffee and they both asked for coffee. When she brought the coffee at the Jim and Maisie, Jim started to explain. "Mrs. Perkins we are investigating a murder that happened four years ago and we think your daughter can help."

Cynthia was completely surprised and then it finally dawned on her that they were talking about her father "This is about Joe Teller, isn't it?"

"Yes ma'am, it is."

"How dare you, hasn't she been through enough? My husband and I have provided a good and loving home for her. We have worked hard with her to forget what happened and what she saw. We tried to help her move on, what could you possibly ask her that wouldn't shatter all of that?"

Maisie replied to her. "Ma'am, we're not trying to make her relive her past. We understand what you guys have done and it's remarkable."

Cynthia snidely remarked. "I guess it's not that remarkable considering she got arrested for shoplifting and has to appear in court tomorrow."

"That can happen with any teenager. It's not like she got busted for selling drugs or something worse. But we do need to ask her one question regarding her father's murder."

"She told the police all that she knew four years ago. We got to see the transcripts from when they questioned her... she didn't see anything."

"Ma'am, that is true, but she also said that she heard the killer which, we believe, they actually spoke to your daughter. Police never followed up in their questioning. We want to know what she heard. Just one question, that's all we need to ask, can you please accompany us to her school so we can ask."

"Unfortunately, she's not at school, she violated the distance limit of her ankle bracelet. Police arrested her and put her in the Juvenile Detention Center until her court date."

Maisie responded before Jim could. "Ma'am, we don't actually need your permission to talk to her if she's in jail, but out of courtesy we would like for you to be there, if nothing else to show your support."

Jim interrupted before Cynthia could say anything. "Mrs. Perkins, I'll even do you one better, we can talk to the judge and see if they will dismiss the charges for her cooperation in our investigation. Would you like that?"

Cynthia slightly smiled. "That would be great, but I still don't like the idea of you dredging up her past."

"I know and that's why we're only going to limit it to one question."

Jim made a couple of phone calls and found out the name of the Judge who was presiding over the case. Her name was Mary Watterson and he found out that her rulings were always in the best interest of the child as well as also having a track record for giving Second Chances to wayward teens. There was a small mobile court at the Juvenile Detention Center which also included her Chambers. Cynthia followed the two detectives there. They found Judge Watterson's Chambers and she had just gotten back from court. Jim and Maisie explained why they needed to talk to Monica Perkins in regard to their investigation. That's when Jim asked for some courtesy in dismissing the charges after explaining who she really was and why they needed to question her. They were lucky that Judge Watterson had a soft spot for kids like Monica, so she agreed to the deal.

Monica was brought into the judge's Chambers wearing handcuffs, it made her mother sad and at that moment all she wanted to do was walk over and hug her to let Monica that everything was okay. Judge Watterson explained why she was there and the deal that she was going to make with State CID. She asked Monica if she understood and Monica answered yes, Jim walked over and introduced himself and also introduced Maisie. He was about to ask the question before he paused and thought to himself, maybe it would be better coming from a motherly voice so he asked Maisie if she would ask the question. She agreed.

Maisie walked over, she told Monica that she was a detective and wanted to ask a question about her real father's murder. Just the mention of her real father sent chills throughout Monica's body. If she was nervous before she was definitely frightened now. In fact, she began to cry, but the crying was more out of fear than sadness. Maisie said to her. "I'm sorry that we have to ask this question, I know that it doesn't bring back any good memories, but it's very important. Can you answer just one question?" With tears still in her eyes, Monica nodded yes. Maisie continued. "4 years ago, you told the police you didn't see the killer's face, but that you heard the killer, which means they spoke to you. Did you hear a man's voice or a woman's voice when they spoke to you?"

Monica paused for a moment, it was a simple question, but she still didn't know how to answer it. They didn't listen to her before, so why should anybody listen to her now? Maisie told her that it was okay. She wasn't in trouble and that they just needed to know whether it was a man's or a woman's voice. Finally, Monica spoke. "I heard a woman's voice. It sounded like my mother, but I think it must have been an angel talking to me."

Both Jim and Maisie were stunned by the response. It was a bit of a strange answer, but she had identified the gender of the killer. She may not be a credible witness in a court of law, but it would help Jim and his team to know what to look for. Jim almost wanted it to be a man because it would be easier to convict a male serial killer. This was still Texas and for most people, it was too hard to fathom that the real Black Fairy killer was a woman. And unfortunately, that's the kind of thing that could affect a jury when deciding whether to convict or not. Monica began to cry again and this time her mother couldn't help it, she rushed to her daughter's side and hugged her. Even Maisie put her hand on Monica to try and comfort her. Jim said to Judge Watterson that was all they needed and thanked her for helping them.

The judge quickly dismissed the charges and told the guards to get Monica processed out as soon as possible. But as Jim and Maisie were leaving the chambers, Monica said something else to them. She didn't think the Detectives believed her like the other cops who questioned her. Monica felt like she needed to make them believe her. She stopped crying and had a serious, deliberate tone when she spoke what felt like a warning. "I know that I talked to an angel, if you're trying to catch her, you shouldn't. Just leave her alone."

Both detectives were freaked out a little bit by the girl's ominous warning. On any other day it would have seemed strange that the girl thought she was talking to an angel, but then again with this case was it really that strange! As Jim and Maisie walked back to their car, she asked him if he recorded the conversation. Jim smiled and at the same time, pulled out his smartphone. "I put the recorder on just as we were walking into the judge's chambers. I got the entire conversation and now we have it for the record." They also needed the recording in case nobody believed the answer. They almost didn't believe it themselves. However, it also made sense when it came to their profile of the killer and that was the scariest part of this whole thing.

36

Gina poured Lori another glass of wine. They were having such a good time, she didn't know how many glasses they had, had so far, but they were already on their second bottle of wine. It was good to see Lori again and she had almost forgotten how fun it was to be around her. There was no shortage of laughter when she was with her friend. Unfortunately, they hadn't seen each other in over a year, so there was a lot to catch up on and they did just that as Gina prepared a simple enchilada recipe. Lori had a new man in her life and for the first time in a long time she was happy. She didn't date or even sleep with anybody for almost two years after her assault. And while there had been a couple of other guys that were nice, she wasn't crazy about either one of them. They were more or less, simple distractions. And then she met this current guy and never could stop thinking about him. She never got tired of being around him and always felt great when they were together. Lori told Gina all the gooey details and that's when Gina asked the obvious question. "Do you love him?"

Lori smiled. She had been thinking about it a lot but had never really answered that question with herself. But she did have an answer to her friend." I do, I'm not saying it's enough to get married or anything, but I do know that I love him."

"Every day! I'm happy every day that I'm with him."
"Well, it sounds like love to me."
"I guess it's what you and Jim have."

Gina smiled. She had never really thought of it that way, but she was happy with Jim...extremely happy! Lori commented." You know, to be honest, I'm surprised that it's lasted so long, don't get me wrong, I'm happy for you. But I've never known you to be in any kind of relationship that lasted more than a month."

Gina had a joyful tone when she replied to Lori. "I know, I'm surprised myself, but it just seems to work. I think a lot of it had to do with stepping in with the kids. But I can't really explain it, I'm happy when I'm with him and I know I'm a better person when I'm with him."

"I think you're in love, Gina"

She smiled. "Well, maybe just a little."

"How come you never got married?"

Gina thought about it for a moment. There wasn't a simple answer to that question. It's not that she was against marriage or that she didn't want to be married and have kids, had always wanted that someday. Jim, on the other hand, had always wanted to be married. He never liked dating and wanted something that his parents had... a long, happy marriage that seemed more like a fairytale than the real thing. Gina only had one answer. "To be honest, we just both felt that we didn't need to be married to be together. We're together and that's all we need to be. Labels aren't necessary. Besides, we're basically common law married anyway."

Lori laughed at the last part. "Then you're pretty much married anyway."

"I guess that's true... If the state of Texas wants to say that about us, fine by me. I just called Jim my love and my partner. Perhaps that's good enough."

"That sounds like a good life to me."

Audra finally got home from basketball practice. It ran later than usual because there was a big rivalry game coming up. She was still in her gym clothes when she walked in and found Lori and Gina laughing like they were still too silly high school girls. She gave them a strange look, trying to remember the last time she saw Gina that way. She couldn't remember. Audra said to both of them. "Hello, what are you two up to or should I ask, how much have you had to drink?"

Lori replied in a sarcastic tone. "Maybe a little too much, but definitely more than you, I hope. "

Audra smiled. She always enjoyed Lori's sense of humor. While Gina had always felt like the big sister she never had, Lori felt more like the wild sister she should have had to get her into just enough trouble to be considered a rebel. She said to Lori as she walked over to give her a hug. "It's good to see you, it's been too long."

"It certainly has… your mother has kept me up to date about all of your basketball exploits. I hear that one day we may see you play for the NCAA Women's championship."

"Maybe one day, I've gotten some letters from some big schools, but it's only a little bit of interest."

"Hey, at least they're interested. There are plenty of girls who aren't getting those letters. Audra smiled and hugged her again; she had, had a long day and needed a compliment like that. Lori started looking for her purse. She found it. "Audra. I got a surprise for you, I hear you still have a fascination about serial killers so I got you something… a collectible of sorts relating to a Texas Serial Killer."

Audra was intrigued. She never really considered herself a collector of anything relating to serial killers… she simply just wanted to know more about them and what made them tick. Lori pulled a book out of her purse. It was titled *The Dark Fairy*. The book was relatively thin, at most maybe a hundred fifty pages. It was simple in nature, just a red cover with a vector outline of fairy wings. The author was anonymous. She handed it to Audra and asked. "Have you heard about this book?"

Excitement washed over Audra's face. She looked like a little kid getting to open a Christmas present on Christmas Eve. Audra replied back. "Oh my God, I have heard about this book. Some say it was written by The Black Fairy himself detailing his original plan before he got caught. It's supposed to be his manifesto. The book was considered a myth until some rare, printed copies turned up on eBay. Where did you get this? It must have cost a fortune."

Lori was delighted that she liked the gift. "Actually, it didn't cost that much, it was published through Amazon.com.

That's how I got it. Somebody must have published an original copy of the book on Amazon."

"Really. I'm glad somebody did that. I've been wanting to read the book ever since somebody in a serial killer chat room told me about it a few months ago. Gina gave Audra a concerned look. She didn't like the idea of Audra chatting with strangers, especially about serial killers. After all, she was only 17 and there are a lot of sick people out there. She stated her disapproval, but Audra quickly reassured her that she had a VPN and nobody would know who she really was.

Lori responded. Well, I'm personally only halfway through it. I won't say that the writing is great, but the story so far is very interesting. It's like some mythical allegory. And the murder scenes are very, very gruesome, which I hate to admit, I kind of like."

"I can't wait to read it. I really hope he actually wrote the book because I feel like it wouldn't be as interesting if someone else wrote it with their own misguided idea of who The Black Fairy really is."

"I agree it would be kinda disappointing if it weren't true, but if he really did write this it's got to be the first time that a serial killer would allow anybody to get inside their own head outside of interviews. And that's pretty cool no matter how crazy they may be."

Gina was getting annoyed. She never liked Audra doing any research on serial killers and she certainly didn't like her talking about them. She figured this was a good time to tell her to get cleaned up and find her brother because dinner was almost ready. Gina disapprovingly looked at her friend. "I can't believe you gave her that. Couldn't you just give her a gift card to someplace like a normal friend?"

Lori softly laughed." Oh, don't be mad. You wouldn't be able to stop her from finding it and reading it anyway. Look at the bright side, at least her interest in serial killers is keeping her from fucking around with boys. I seriously doubt you and Jim are ready to be grandparents."

Gina gave her friend of facetious look, slightly amused at Lori's logic. "I don't even want to think about something like that.

Researching Serial Killers is definitely the lesser of two evils when the alternative is getting knocked up in high school."

Lori laughed. "I'm always here to help you find the lesser of two evils or look on the bright side whichever the case may be. They both took another sip of wine and just laughed at these wild notions they put forth. Gina could never really stay mad at Lori. She was always too much fun and more importantly, she was a very good friend in a world where they are hard to come by."

Jim played the recording again. It was even harder to believe a second time. The girl had said it, she confirmed the gender. In an investigation that was barely turning up anything about the identity of the real Black Fairy, this was huge. James, Maisie, Detective Lester, and Detectives Morgan all agreed that it should be played at least one more time because it was more than just hearing her confirm the gender, but it was also the way she said it and the warning she gave Jim and Maisie as they were leaving. James was the first to comment on the recording. He said to the rest of the group. "All this time, the identity that seems to elude us and now we finally know what to look for."

Detective Morgan replied. "She could be hallucinating; she says that she can hear an angel. An Angel."

Jim responded to her comment. "I don't think any of us can ignore the possibility that she could be hallucinating, but she didn't say that she saw an angel, just that the person sounded like one. I think it's a metaphor for what she is assuming is a good omen under the circumstances. She clearly identifies a woman's voice."

"This would never hold up in court. I think that girl is so traumatized that she would never be a credible witness."

"She doesn't need to be a credible witness; we just needed her to identify what she heard so we know what to look for."

"Honestly, after seeing her father murdered in such a gruesome manner, I don't think she can be sure about anything she saw or heard."

Maisie interrupted before Jim could respond. Even she was starting to get a little annoyed by Detective Foster's cynicism. It was one thing to be skeptical of a theory, but definitely not productive when you're cynical about every suggested idea from fellow police officers. Maisie asked. "Do you think it's possible that a woman could actually be the real killer?"

Detective Morgan gave her a disapproving look. "I think all things are possible, but not very likely. If we go just by statistics, it's not a woman committing these murders. It's most likely a man between the ages of 35 to 55 years of age."

"Forget about the statistics, after hearing that recording, do you believe the killer is a woman?"

"No, because I rely on statistics and evidence. Don't misunderstand me, I believe a woman is capable of multiple murders, just don't think a woman did these."

Jim replied to her comment. "We're all allowed to have our own theories, but I have asked you to at least entertain the possibility that it might be a woman. We have to consider that now and to be honest; I think it is more likely considering whom the killer is targeting. Wouldn't a woman be more likely to exact revenge on sexual predators who got away with it?"

Detective Morgan tried to smile and not make a big deal out of her indifference. She simply said. "It's a nice theory and I at least agree that we have to look at the possibility, but that's as far as I go."

Jim nodded towards her. "As long as you can entertain the possibility, that's all I ask. Now moving on, what did you and Mike find out about William Staples?"

Detective Mike Lester got out his notebook that he used to make notes. He said. "We didn't really find out that much. William actually worked at Wal-Mart...got a job there after he was dismissed as a pastor. He couldn't find any other work in the religious field. All in all, he had been a good employee and they never bothered to do a background check so they didn't know about his past. He had a shift the night before the body was found. According to the GPS records on his phone, he never made it home so whoever kidnapped him must have done it there or somewhere else. We do know that the killer drove his vehicle at least until it was dumped and burned."

Jim responded. "Okay, so the working theory is somebody staked him out at Wal-Mart and kidnapped him right after his shift, driving his vehicle from the Wal-Mart he worked at?"

"Yep. I think the killer drove his vehicle to the warehouse where he was killed and then dumped the vehicle somewhere else after they were done. At least that's the most likely."

"Did anybody see anything? "

"No eyewitnesses, which means somebody was in his car waiting for him or came up right behind him as he was getting in and then drove off. He got off at 7 p.m. so it was a busy time at Wal-Mart."

Jim thought for a moment. "Busy enough in a public place that people wouldn't really notice anything. That was smart."

Mike continued. "We asked if he'd had any problems with customers, maybe gotten into an argument with someone. Nothing! He seemed to be well-liked and has never had an incident while working there."

James chimed in. "What department did he work in?"

"He worked in the paint department, why?"

"Somebody could have been milling around and staking him out, maybe they were caught on the security cameras. We should probably look at the footage from the last three days before he was kidnapped. Like the hunter to its prey, I bet the killer staked him out to know his routine."

Detective Lester nodded in his direction. He said. "Good point, we'll go and get those from Wal-Mart and see if we find anything."

Jim asked Mike. Did you find anything else?

Detective Lester replied. "Not really. He was ostracized by friends and family. Lived a quiet life except for is dirty deeds. He didn't hang out with coworkers. He went to work and other than that, nobody can account for what he did. We've checked with his neighbors in the apartment complex he lived at. Mike softly laughed to himself. We checked with his neighbors and they didn't even know his name. One of them didn't even know anybody lived in that apartment?"

Jim replied. Found innocent in a court of law but deemed guilty by society and ostracized so nobody ever pays attention to him. Perhaps the only break we get is if we find someone on camera staking him out." Mike winced at the notion, he didn't like it any more than Jim did, but he was right, that was probably the only way they would get a break in William Staples' murder.

Jim looked at James and asked if he found anything. James responded. "I do think the vessel was made in Austin, but not by any pottery store or hobby shop that I can find. One guy did tell me after I showed him a picture of the vessel, that could have been made by an independent artist... somebody who would advertise on Craigslist and the only way to put that particular Triskele symbol on the vessel is to use an imprint on the clay as its drying. The brand can usually be made with a 3D printer."

"Okay, then how do we find someone who can do that?"

James smiled. I put an ad on Craigslist looking for someone who can make a flowerpot with obscure Gaelic symbols. Said I wanted to make a gift for my wife. I'm not going to look for them; I'm going to let them find me. Besides, I'm old; they should be looking for me, anyway!"

Everybody else in the room laughed at his sarcastic comment. His wit matched his experience. James replied. "Smart move. If you end up having to buy something, get a receipt and CID can reimburse you."

"Don't worry about it, if I buy something it'll be a gift for my wife. Our anniversary is coming up."

Laughing, Maisie had to ask. "Are you even Irish?"

James gave her a sarcastic smile. Who knows, but the Gaelic symbols are pretty on a flowerpot and my wife likes that sort of thing. Could give us a break in the case and my wife gets a nice gift... it's a win-win."

James made everybody in the room laugh again and Jim remarked that, that was the perfect way to end the day. It was late and he wanted to get home for dinner since they had a guest tonight. Everything else could wait until tomorrow. And chances are, they weren't going to get any bigger breaks in the case, than what they had just gotten. Short of finally figuring out the identity of the killer, Jim knew there wouldn't be any bigger earth-shattering news and that was pretty damn good for the first day.

37

It was late when Jim finally arrived home. He missed dinner, but that was to be expected. However, he was a bit surprised to already find Gina and Lori pretty much passed out in the living room. After surveying two open bottles of wine, he pretty much figured what happened. But he wasn't mad, he was glad that they had a good time and were able to catch up with each other. Jim had always liked Lori. He may not have known her all that well and despite their first encounter after she had been assaulted so many years ago, he found her pleasant to be around and loved her sense of humor. More importantly, she was a good friend to Gina and perhaps that's all he ever really needed to know about her.

Jim grabbed himself a beer out of the refrigerator. He was looking for some leftovers and finally noticed Audra sitting at the kitchen table eating and reading a book. Apparently, she had gotten into the leftover enchiladas. He walked over to see if there was anything left that he could steal for himself. He noticed the title of the book that she was reading. It caught his eye because it had the word "fairy" in the title. Jim asked her. "The book you're reading, what is it about?"

Audra was excited to talk about the book because she was really getting into it. She couldn't put it down. So much so, she was almost done with it. Audra said. "Oh my god, this is an incredible book. It's called The Dark Fairy, there's been a lot rumors that this book was written by the actual Black Fairy killer."

"What... are you serious?"

"Yeah... it's a story how about a fallen angel who becomes a dark fairy on Earth and tries to be redeemed by God. In order to become an angel again, the dark fairy must travel to nine sacred places and perform nine tasks for God. There are those who believe that the Black Fairy wrote the story as a way to tell the world what he was trying to accomplish, you know, his own personal allegory. "

Jim was a little shocked. "That's a little eerie. When was this book written?"

"No one knows for sure. Some say it was written before he was caught. A guy told me that only a few copies were printed many years ago and kept getting traded through used bookstores as well as being sent to libraries. But in the last year, somebody published it with amazon.com and now there are a lot more copies out there."

"Huh, interesting. What do you think?"

Audra shrugged a little. "At first, I thought it was basically just an internet rumor, you know something fun to talk about in serial killer chat rooms. But after reading this... I'm thinking it's gotta be true."

"Why do you say that?"

"The tasks in the book are basically killing people after being asked to judge whether they should be killed or not. God is essentially asks the character to make moral judgments and that in itself is a test. Plus the Dark Fairy is over narrating, by what I feel like is it's over-explaining why they must do the things they do. It's like they have to truly convince us that their journey is holy and righteous. Sounds like something a killer would do to make sure the audience understood their real purpose."

"Sounds more like a manifesto than a story. Manifestos are filled with a tremendous amount of ego."

Audra softly laughed. "This is supposed to be an allegory and there's no rule that says a manifesto can't be an allegory."

Jim nodded to her. "That may be true. I mean, I had a professor in college make the class read Mein Kampf and that's basically Hitler's manifesto, justifying why he was a psychopath. His ego is all over those pages. I guess it could be an allegory, but I prefer to look at it as an allegory of what not to do in society."

"I would say that whoever wrote this book put their ego within these pages."

Jim smiled. He certainly enjoyed how Audra looked at things and especially commented on them. She had a keen mind and a sharp wit. He asked her. "Do you mind if I borrow that book when you're done? I'm assuming you're going to stay up and finish it so I'd like to borrow it afterward if that's okay."

She didn't say no and he left her alone to finish it. When he got up the next morning to get his first cup of coffee, he found it on the kitchen table waiting for him. Whether it was a break in the case or not, an allegorical story that may have been written by a serial killer was certainly worthy of his attention. And as far as he was concerned, it was worth looking into, if nothing else, for more insight on the killer's true purpose as Audra so eloquently put it. This was something he would need to discuss with the task force.

Jim arrived at the office early, James was already there, but he was usually the first one in since he had to open the place up. When Maisie arrived, she found him sitting at the conference table reading a book and got curious. When you're on a task force investigating a serious crime, there is always something to do and rarely any downtime, so it was a little weird to just see him sitting and reading a book. She asked. "What are you reading?"

Jim looked up. "A book... Gina's friend, Lori, gave this to Audra."

"And you decided to borrow it and kill some time before we start today."

Jim softly laughed. "Not exactly, while it would be nice to have some time to read a book, this has to do with the case." James, who was getting himself another cup of coffee, looked from stirring in the sugar. Now he was curious. Maisie replied to Jim. "A book that has to do with this case, is it some kind of tabloid nonsense from an author who thinks they know what the Black Fairy killer was thinking?"

"No, it's not that kind of book. It's called The Dark Fairy and it's about an angel who falls from heaven or is kicked out and becomes a dark fairy on Earth, but God gives them a second chance. The Dark Fairy must travel to nine sacred places and perform nine tasks in the name of God. Some of those tasks involve killing sinners."

Maisie gave him a strange look. "Who wrote this book?""

"That's the thing, it's anonymous. Audra was telling me last night that there has been rumors for years that the Black Fairy wrote a book to explain their true purpose. At first it started with a few printed copies that floated through used book shops and eBay, but somebody decided to publish it through Amazon this past year."

Both James and Maisie were stunned to say the least. If the Black Fairy really wrote a book, it would qualify as earth-shattering news. James asked. "Is there a publishing date for the book?"

"No, all it is, is the book cover, the title page, and the story itself."

"So basically, anybody could have written this at any time?"

"That's true. But we know that Aldo Martinez did not write the book."

Maisie had a serious look for Jim. "Do you think the real killer actually wrote this book or just somebody fascinated with the case?"

Honestly, I don't know. But I do find it suspicious that the author is anonymous. If an actual writer wrote this book after being inspired by the Black Fairy case, wouldn't they put their own name on it?"

"So, you do think it's the actual killer?"

"This entire case has been filled with symbolism and hidden meanings and now we find there's a book out there about a fallen angel called the Dark Fairy trying to find redemption, I think we have to read the book and see if there are any clues that would give us answers."

James responded." I think it's very interesting that a serial killer wrote a book explaining why they did what they did. Some serial killers like to taunt the media by writing letters to the police or newspapers. Jack the Ripper did it, so did the Zodiac Killer, Son of Sam did too, and the BTK Killer wrote letters for years taunting the police. What if instead of writing letters to the media our killer wrote a book with clues to what they did and what they're going to do next. What if we're the ones being taunted by some weird allegory masquerading as fiction?"

Maisie responded. "Fucking Hell! The last thing I want to do is put together some book report that may or may not help find the Killer."

Jim said. None of us do, but we can't ignore it. I mean, if you really think about it what James said makes sense."

I agree that makes sense, at least a little bit. But I don't want to get bogged down reading some book that may just be pure fiction and lose sight of what we're trying to accomplish. If we can actually find the person who made that vessel, then it gets us closer to identifying our killer. I see that as a better possibility than a book."

"You may be right Maisie, I've always maintained that the only way we were going to capture this killer was to anticipate what they're going to do next. We don't have any evidence, especially physical evidence that ties anybody to these crimes.... four years later and we still just have theories that don't prove anything."

"Are you saying that we take this book at face value?"

Jim shook his head. "No, an allegory is the purest form of symbolism and when it comes to this case there is nothing but symbolism from our killer. I think the book gets us closer to seeing what we're supposed to see... what the killer wants to us to understand about her work. Even if it's not the real killer who wrote it, it's somebody with intimate knowledge of who she is. I believe there are clues in this book that will help us and that makes it worth reading."

"Maisie and James really couldn't argue with that. They still weren't any closer to finding the real black fairy than they were four years ago. I had to look at everything and consider every possibility. That was the most frustrating part because it was still hard to narrow down a linear path to the real killer. Maisie finally agreed. They would all read the book and examine if there are only four potential clues. Jim ordered a few printed copies and had them rushed. Thankfully, because it was somewhat of a popular book on Amazon some of them were already printed and can easily be filled from their warehouse so they could be picked up at an Amazon pick up center. He even had one sent the Dr. Vanessa O'Connor. He had a courier pick one up in Dallas and hand-deliver it to her later in the day. Jim felt in some ways that she would have the better insight on this book.

  Lori and Gina were finally up and trying to start their day. They both got up late and we're hung over. While it was good to see each other and share a bottle of wine again, they were definitely going to pay for it today. Gina could make her own hours so being a little late to get some editing done wouldn't be that big of a deal. Lori on the other hand would have to rearrange her schedule. Gina asked her what she had going on and if she was going to be in Austin another day. Lori replied. "Probably not. I have to ask a local judge about an insurance claim and then get some paperwork. I have stuff going on tomorrow so I should probably get back to Dallas tonight just to avoid a long drive early in the morning."
  Gina tried to smile, but she was a little disappointed that she didn't get another night with her friend. They didn't get to see each other all that often anymore and she would certainly suffer through another hangover just to have another fun night with Lori. But she responded. "I don't blame you; it's a shame because we haven't quite finished off my wine rack yet."
  Lori laughed. It was that sense of humor that she had been missing over the last four years since Gina had moved to Austin. "Well, you can always take a few days for yourself and come back to Dallas with the wine. Let Jim take care of the kids and let's do a girl's weekend in Dallas."

"I would like that and I get to meet this new guy of yours, make sure he's good enough for you."

"I think he just might be, one of the reasons I'm crazy about him."

"Gina poured Lori another cup of coffee and then asked. "You have time for some breakfast."

A disappointed look came over Lori's face. "Unfortunately, not. If I don't meet this Judge in the next hour, this will be a wasted trip outside of seeing you."

"I understand. We can't let it be so long before we see each other again, not when we're only 3 hours apart. I'm going to give you an extra-long hug in case I don't see you for a while, but let's definitely put something down on our calendars for the next time we see each other."

Gina hugged her and they held each other as if it was the last time they were going to see each other. Both were almost in tears because they both felt the same way and missed each other just as much. But it's funny how life turns out and where it takes you. Being in a relationship can do that. Gina gave her friend a to-go cup of coffee and then Lori rushed out. Everything had been rushed that morning from her shower to saying goodbye. And all that did for Gina was give her a sadness that she couldn't quite shake for the rest of the day.

38

Vanessa was finishing up her day. She was down to the last of the paperwork she had to sign off on. And as she was going through the last few emails that needed to be read, a courier dropped by and delivered the book that Jim had ordered for her. Vanessa even noticed one of her last emails was from Jim, letting her know that she would be receiving the book today. Jim explained in the email that the Black Fairy might have actually written the book. Like everyone else, she was intrigued by the idea that a serial killer would write a book explaining what they did and their true purpose. She needed to get home, but she wanted to start reading. Vanessa was a fairly good speed-reader and zipped through the first quarter of the book in the next half hour.

    The story scared her, but not in the way most people would think. Her fear came from the symbolism in the book, She immediately saw the allegory within the story and it reminded her of something else. A reminder of another famous allegory. Jim had called this book a manifesto when he talked to Audra about it, but for Vanessa it was much more than that, it was a life story. Yes, a story of redemption, but it was also a story of transformation from one celestial being to the next. This was much more than just killing people who have gotten away with a crime. The protagonist of this story was transforming into something more dangerous, something beyond man's control and limitations. A supernatural force if you will. She would finish the book that night, but before she went home she called Jim. When he answered she dispensed with the small talk and said. "I got the book, thank you for sending this to me. Whatever you think you have with this book, it's worse and anybody who touches this case is in trouble?"

Jim was stunned by her strange warning. "I don't completely understand what you're talking about?"

"I know and I'm not necessarily trying to scare the shit out of you, that's why we need to discuss this further. Is everybody on your team reading the book?"

"Yes, they're supposed to."

"Good, I'm coming down there tomorrow."

"It's that bad, uh!"

"We all need to fully understand what the killer is truly trying to tell us... But I also think it might be the key to catching the real Black Fairy."

Jim simply said, "okay." Vanessa didn't have anything more to say except they would talk tomorrow. She finished up whatever need to be done so she could take a day off including rearranging her schedule. And then she went home, poured herself a glass of good whiskey, and settled in to finish the book while also making notes. She had always loved investigating crimes. She had a fascination with the way criminals thought. And like many people, she also had a fascination about serial killers. Never once had she really been afraid, she knew there was evil in the world....pure evil. This was different. This made her truly afraid and it had nothing to do with some Catholic mysticism that she was brought up on. She was afraid of the true psychosis of this killer and their true goal. True belief in something could be powerful, but it can also be the scariest thing in the world.

It was the next day and the team had finally gotten security footage back from the Wal-Mart that William Staples worked at.

There wasn't much to go on, but as Jim, Detective Morgan and Detective Lester looked through it, there was one thing that stood out. There was a person who had been there three days in a row or at least a person that looked very similar. Jim was the first to point it out. He replied. "The same person has been there every day around the same time. They were there within an hour of his shift being over."

Detective Morgan replied. "I don't see the same person; two of them look like men and one of them looks like a woman with a ponytail."

"True, but they're wearing the same hat. We can't tell what the logo is on the front of the hat, but there's a small shape right above the hat adjuster. It's hard to see, but it is the same logo."

She looked at the footage again. "I can't tell if it's the same logo."

"We have people there around the same time with a hat that has a logo above the adjuster, so how many baseball caps have a logo there?" Here was the other thing he pointed out. "Two of them look like men and one of them is a woman, but all three of them are women, it's just for two of the days she has her hair up. What is the same detail, are the curved hips. Those are women's hips and she's curvy. Not even an overweight man would be that curvy."

Both detectives looked closer at the grainy footage. Detective Lester said. "Jim, I think you're right. They look like good childbearing hips, like the curves my wife had after our first child."

Detective Morgan responded. "Okay, I'll grant you they look a little curvy, I definitely won't say for sure that it's a woman, but more than likely it is."

Jim smiled. "I'll take most likely from any day with your level of cynicism. It looks like we have the same person there, staking him out and most likely it's a woman."

Detective Morgan nodded. She agreed somewhat, but she also pointed out. "Unfortunately, whoever that is knows where the cameras are and is looking away so we can't get a positive shot of their face."

"No, but we know they were there. And maybe somebody else working in the area might have seen the person's face. It's time to question more people at that Wal-Mart."

As Jim and the detectives finished going over the surveillance footage from Wal-Mart, the team had a visitor. Dr. Vanessa O'Connor has finally arrived. She walked through the door of the detective agency with a sense of urgency. James thought she had the look of some dame ready to hire a private detective to catch her husband cheating on her. She certainly got everybody's attention when she walked through the door. She had a big smile when she saw Jim and Maisie too. Vanessa liked Maisie from the first moment she met her and they started spitballing theories together.

Jim walked over and shook Vanessa's hand. "It's good to see you, I didn't think you really needed to be here, but I always appreciate your help."

"I'm glad to hear that, what I have to tell you is too long to put in an email." She looked around the small office, especially at the big crime board in the conference room with pictures of the victims, and nodded in approval of the place. This is a quaint little detective agency... It's kind of hard to find too. Definitely has the feel of some 1930s seedy detective agency, but I like it."

"It works well for us, we're a little misfit band of investigators."

Vanessa walked over to Maisie and said hi. She also told her. "I'm glad you decided to join this task force. The men may never admit it, but they definitely need you and your insights." Maisie smiled and said. "Thank you, it's nice to hear because you're right, they probably wouldn't say it."

Vanessa asked where the coffee was and James was nice enough to get her a cup. They all gathered in the conference room. She could see that at least some of them had been reading through the book, but highly doubted anybody had to read it twice like she did last night. She was at least hoping that they had read a good portion of it so they would be at least somewhat familiar with the story and she didn't have to explain every detail. Detective Morgan and Detective Lester introduced themselves. Morgan was curious as to why she was here and then Jim explained to her how she had been instrumental in the original case, especially how Vanessa was the one who pointed out that the wings were fairy wings on Don Bennett's body. Detective Morgan was skeptical and a lot of that had to with not really knowing anything about Vanessa. She asked her what her credentials were. Vanessa simply replied that she had a medical degree and also a degree in forensic psychology. She was certainly qualified even if Detective Morgan didn't believe it. After the introductions were done and they moved beyond the small talk, it was time to get started. Jim gave Vanessa the floor. She asked everybody." How many of you read the book all the way through?

    Jim and Maisie were the only ones who raised their hand. James said that he was almost done, but still had a ways to go. Both detectives had barely gotten through the first few pages. Mike didn't have time, but his partner, Detective Morgan didn't really see the point of reading the book. She thought it was just a bad lead that didn't really have anything to do with the investigation. Vanessa said to everyone. "I read this twice last night." It's some scary shit."

    Maisie asked her. "What do you mean?"

    "Because I believe that the Black Fairy wrote this book, telling us their master plan and why they're doing it. And if it's true, then even innocent people are going to die especially those trying to stop The Black Fairy."

    Jim responded. "What do you mean?"

    "I marked the passage in the book. Its right before the Dark Fairy in the story completes its final task. It reads... *And the archangel came down from heaven to talk with the Dark Fairy before she traveled to her final destination. The Archangel was sent to give her a warning. The final task would be harder than all of the rest combined. She would face many foes, be tempted by many familiar faces when walking this path. The Archangel warned the Dark Fairy that many Innocents would have to die and to not be afraid to kill them in order to complete the final task. The Innocents will try and stop your journey, for they want to see you remain in darkness. You will not want to kill them, but it is part of God's will. They will have to be sacrificed in order for you to complete your transformation and be redeemed by God. Do not be afraid. Have the courage and strength to do what must be done in the name of God, for it is his will above all others that you serve."*

Maisie replied. "Innocents, what do they mean by innocents?"

"The author is talking about us or anybody that would try and stop them from completing what they have to do. God through his Archangel is warning the Dark Fairy that there will be people that try to stop them and that they will have to be killed… sacrifice in order to complete the Dark Fairy's journey."

There was an uneasy tension that came with biblical like quotes It was a frightful warning. Serial killers choose their victims carefully, rarely was there incidental deaths involved in their murders. But this was very different; it was almost as if the Dark Fairy in the story was saying that innocent people were required to die while completing the final task.

Jim asked Vanessa. "Do you feel that with this killer, it's an absolute that the Innocents have to die?"

Vanessa tried to lighten the already gloomy mood in the room with a small smile. She replied. "Unfortunately, yes."

"Why?"

"It's about the power of their belief. That's what this has always been about." Vanessa looked around the room just to see the reaction on everybody's face after she said that. Nobody seemed to truly believe in her assessment so she asked. "How many of you have ever read Dante's *The Divine Comedy*"

Maisie replied. "You mean the long allegorical poem where the character travels through nine circles of hell?"

"Yes."

Detective Morgan asked. "What does that have to do with anything?"

Vanessa gave her a sharp stare. "It has everything to do with this book because the dark fairy has written in the same allegorical fashion as The Divine Comedy. The Divine Comedy is pretty much required reading in any Catholic School. Part of our profile is that the Black Fairy had a Catholic education. We talked about symbolism and hidden meanings within the way this killer performs the murders and then ask why, Referencing The Divine Comedy doesn't get any more straight to the point."

James responded. "Okay, let's say you're right, how is it similar and why is it important?"

Vanessa continued with her narrative. "Essentially The Divine Comedy is about the journey of one's soul to God. It's about the transformation in order to be closer to God and all that a person will have to go through. A person on this journey will be persuaded by sinners to turn away from their belief. They will be tempted, even by Lucifer himself. But if one is to complete the journey, they will be more powerful... they will go through darkness to find the light. This book, The Dark Fairy... It's essentially the same story. God is asking the Dark Fairy to travel to nine sacred places and complete 9 tasks...their own version of traveling through nine levels of hell."

James asked the question everybody was thinking. "What tasks is God asking the Dark Fairy to perform?"

"Murder, but they don't see it as murder. The Dark Fairy must kill 9 specific people and try to save their soul. That's what they're doing...there's nine specific people they are going to kill to complete their journey... or transformation as we have discussed before."

Maisie replied. "And the saving of their souls represents the sin eater ritual?"

Vanessa smiled. She agreed with the theory and that was one of the reasons that she felt that kinship with Maisie. She said. "Exactly. While in this story the ritual doesn't exactly play out the same way, it's very similar because the dark Fairy can't give sacraments.... they're still considered a fallen angel until they transform so they would have to do it in the same fashion as a sin eater. But one thing that I did notice, which is staying true is by the time the Dark Fairy in the story gets to the 7th task... they're transforming the blood of their victim the same way that we have seen in the Staples murder... They're using a Pagan / Gaelic ritual. As I said before, this book is about telling us exactly what they're going to do and why. It's our killer's own version of the 9 circles of hell."

James replied. "So all of this is a journey to be closer to God. They are the fallen Angel, trying to transform their soul in order to be closer to God, right?"

"Yes, that's what they believe."

"Okay, now that we've established that. How do we use this book to catch them?"

Well, here's the most shocking part... I don't know if any of you really caught on to it. Every one of the people that the Dark fairy is supposed to kill and rescue their soul, they're all connected. While the story doesn't specifically say what that is, there are many clues that point to these people being connected by something. That's why the task that the Dark Fairy has been charged with are so specific."

Maisie said. "You're saying that they're connected, but you don't know how, is it because the people the Dark Fairy is supposed to kill all know each other or maybe there's some kind of event that they were all a part of?"

Vanessa Shrugged. "I don't know, I think that's left up to interpretation. But there is a reference in the book regarding two different characters... It's almost the same line word for word. *He remembered his time at Sceleratis, the same as the others, and wished he could go back there now.*"

"Same as the others? You think he's referring to all of the other victims?"

"Yes, but also referring to a place that they had all been to, maybe a place they had all been to together, but a place they are at least familiar with. What's also strange, Sceleratis means unholy in Latin. I guess they are referring to a bad place."

Nobody said anything for a while. Each in their own way was pondering the theory that Vanessa proposed and the fact that the name of the place in the book meant unholy in Latin. James finally responded. "Maybe it's not about a place, maybe they're all connected by someone. The final task in the book is the hardest task that our killer will have to perform and as you mentioned earlier, that's where the Innocents will try and stop them. They're not killing just one person and saving their soul, they're going to have to kill many to complete the task, right?"

Vanessa curiously replied. "I suppose... That's one way of looking at it."

"Well, maybe it's the final person the Dark Fairy will have to kill, that's the one that connects everybody else and that's also why this person is last. Isn't the ninth circle of hell in The Divine Comedy treachery?"

"Yes."

"Suppose the final task is some kind of a great treachery, which usually affects multiple people!"

Maisie replied. "The final person that the Black Fairy kills has done something so treacherous that it is connected to all the other victims.... that's where you're going with this?"

"I don't know I'm just spitballing a theory."

Detective Morgan replied. Well, no offense, theories only get us so far and how does this help us catch the Killer."

Vanessa responded in a serious tone. "Understanding the symbolism of where they've been will show you where they're going." She looked around the room. "Or to put it more simply, if we're to believe that all of the victims are connected somehow, you find the one thing that connects them or the person that connects them., Do that then you'll know who The Black Fairy will target next and then you will catch them in the act."

Maisie asked. "Okay, then judging by this book, there's going to be a total of nine murders by the Black Fairy to complete their journey, how many murders have there been?"

James replied. "6... no, 7 victims. Either way, there's not that many left, and the clock is ticking!"

The dramatic warning made everybody in the room take pause. It was true; time was not on their side. However, everybody in the room felt at least a small sense of relief, knowing that they were getting closer. Understanding the book proved that. But finding that one singular connection among the victims would be their needle in a haystack. Personally, Jim gave his team 3 to 1 odds that they would find it, and that was him being confident.

39

Both Jim and Maisie stared at the huge pegboard that was put in the conference room. They had spent the day before laying out the profiles of the seven victims that they knew had been killed by the Black Fairy. He laid them out so they can have a clear picture of what they were dealing with and how to find one thing that tie them all together. Jim told them the day before that they were going to have to do deep background checks on all the victims... They were going to have to look for things that the police never did when trying to solve the murder. There was one thing that ties them together, he was sure of it. But truth be told, nobody knew where to start. It was as if they were starting from scratch with the investigation. Vanessa decided to stay an extra day and see if she could help in any way. After all, another pair of eyes and good insights couldn't hurt.

Vanessa was pouring herself another cup of coffee when she walked over we're Jim and Maisie were sitting and staring at the peg. Maisie looked at Jim and asked. "Where do we start?"

Jim replied. "We start at the beginning. We know what they all have in common. They're deviants and sexual predators. We know that Don Bennett and Jack Perry knew each other and are connected by an alleged rape party. But what about everybody else!"

Vanessa curiously responded. "Who is the first victim you have listed, is it Mike Sturdgess?"

Jim explained. "We've never actually talked about him. His name was given to me by the Feds when they made a deal with Aldo Martinez. Technically, I'm not supposed to have the file, but I asked a favor from a federal agent that I know and got a copy of it."

Maisie smiled. "Your sister?"

Jim winked at her. "It's good to have one who's an FBI agent."

They both laughed. Vanessa on the other hand was more curious about this first victim and ignored the humorous comment. Jim responded to her inquiry. "Mike Sturdgess was a high school English teacher in Albuquerque New Mexico. He was well-liked and popular, even won teacher of the year one time. But he was accused of raping two of his students. With the first, nothing happened at the school. They didn't find the girl credible and she never even went to the hospital to be examined. She was poor, considered a troublemaker, and basically not a credible witness. The second student who accused him of rape was another troubled girl, who lived in a trailer park with her prostitute mother, and had been busted for marijuana possession twice. Since the amounts were small, she didn't do any serious jail time except for 30 days at a juvenile detention center. It was the second accusation within a year so they did take it more seriously and suspended him. She even had a rape kit done, but it was inconclusive considering she was known to have a few male partners on a regular basis. Plus the guy wore a condom so nobody could be sure if he was the last person to have sex with her. What made the second situation worse was the fact that the student committed suicide when he wasn't charged and was able to get another teaching job at a different school. His former employer didn't want the controversy so they paid him for the rest of the year and didn't renew his contract."

Vanessa asked. "Did the suicide cause any kind of controversy?"

"In fact, it did, there was a big article written about the girl and the suggestion of a cover-up because he was a respected member of the community. And because nobody really cared about the troubled girl. The article did persuade the girl's family to bring a lawsuit against Mike Sturgess, but a jury quickly found that he wasn't liable. They did conclude that the police department was liable because they seriously prejudiced the investigation."

"Are you saying people took his word over the word of the two girls?"

"Yes, the officer who took the statement of the second girl, commented in his notes, they were nothing but trash and born liars. Anyway, his murder wasn't as elaborate as the others. He was found on the grave of the second girl who committed suicide. The body was positioned to where he was begging forgiveness, but he was pierced in the side and bled out like all the other victims. That's actually what killed him."

"Staged him like he was begging for forgiveness, uh, that's certainly original!"

Maisie commented. "So even with this being the first victim, the Black Fairy was still being symbolic... I wonder if this was part of the master plan or is the murder that started it?"

Nobody said anything for a moment, pondering the question that Maisie had posed. It was a philosophical question, and although sometimes they had their place in an investigation, it didn't give them certain facts that they were looking for. Jim replied to her. "I think that's an interesting question, but I don't think where the plan started really helps us find the one thing that connects all of these victims. However, I do think it's a question that should be answered and hopefully, we can at the end of all this.

"Fair enough, but besides the victims knowing each other, where do we start to find the connections?"

"To be honest, I think we have to look at their sexual proclivities... everything they were into... they were all into some dark shit. Maybe that's how they all knew each other."

Vanessa picked up on his idea and ran with it. She posed a question of her own. "The first victim, after he was found dead did they find anything on his computer... Videos or pictures of young girls since that was his thing or even maybe browser history. Like, where did he go online for stuff like that nowadays to find really depraved stuff like that you could go to the dark web, but back then people didn't hide their online search history all that well."

Jim grabbed this file and looked through it. Vanessa was onto something and he remembered seeing something in the notes to that effect. He said. "There is something here, about that. He paid money to a webcam service for young girls. They were supposedly teenage girls who would do anything you want on a webcam."

"I wonder what the name of the company is and if it's part of a larger company. Multiple porn sites are usually under one umbrella... Maybe it's one company that's making money off of stuff like that so what if everybody visited websites that were part of one bigger company? It would be something that connects all of the victims."

Jim and Maisie both nodded at Vanessa, acknowledging her valued insight. Jim even said. "That's good. I think we are on the right track so let's start with that idea." Jim went to a laptop and did a quick search based on the webcam site. It was part of a company called Erotic X Unlimited. With the resources that the detective agency had, it wouldn't be too hard to find everything the company did.

James had been listening to their conversation intently. He didn't disagree with any of their ideas, but he did have a different idea. He said to the group. "The Dark Fairy book talks about a certain place and it got me thinking... In fact, it reminded me of something from when I was a cop. Texas is known to have small Bunny Ranches all over the place...if there's a lot of religion in a place, then there will be a lot of prostitution. But there used to be places that cops could go and it would be safe for them. They were basically brothels they masqueraded as retreats or social clubs. These places were more high-end, places that rich businessmen could go. But they also cater to police officers in giving them sex for looking the other way. It was also a way to put police officers in a compromising position so they could look the other way on other criminal activities."

Curious, Jim asked. "How do you know about these places?"

"I used to be a cop and cops like to talk in their precincts as much as high school girls in the bathroom…something you've probably forgotten while working for State CID. If you're asking if I've experienced these places…no, but I know plenty of cops who have."

"Really, you've never experienced it even one time?"

James gave him a dirty look. No, I've always been an honest cop and I would never put myself in a compromising situation. Besides, I love my wife and she is sensational in bed, kinky as hell. Vanessa and Maisie both gave James a bit of a dirty look at the comment. But James continued. "I've never needed to stray from my bed. The best advice I can give for a long and happy marriage is to have a great sex life and you'll never need to stray from your bed. Anyway, these places prided themselves in fulfilling any sexual desire no matter how kinky. What if there is a particular place like this that connects all of the victims?"

"You mean they've all been to a place like this… not necessarily one particular place even though that's possible, but a place owned by the same people?"

"Yes, exactly."

"Do you know where these sexual hideaways are?"

"No, I've been out of the loop for too long, but I have contacts that would know. There's a chance that at least three of these victims would have visited a place like this because of their money, but maybe the other ones did as well. It's worth checking out."

Jim nodded in agreement. "Okay, follow it up." They group dispersed after that. They each had their own assignment. Mostly it would be doing deep background checks on each victim, especially their sexual desires and activities that were hidden from the public. But in the internet age, you can never truly keep those kinds of things hidden. And that's what the team was counting on. James called one of his buddies who might know where to find one of these so-called pleasure retreats. They would grab a drink in a couple of hours.

James found the small little dingy cop bar nestled in the tall buildings of downtown Austin. It was hidden and out of the way, made that way on purpose because it used to be a speakeasy. It had been servicing cops since the 1920s. Most people didn't know about it outside of law enforcement and that's the way the owners, who are former cops themselves, preferred it. James went there to meet his old pal, Tom Clayton. He was a former Vice Detective in Austin and Dallas who had been on the job for 30 years. For a small brief period, they even worked together in the early 80s. Tom had a private security firm that serviced high-end clients, his specialty. Tom was already sitting at the bar drinking an old-fashioned when James walked down the stairs into the small basement bar. And like some scene out of a Humphrey Bogart detective film, James walked up to the bar and said, "I'll have what he's having."

Tom laughed. He had used that line a few times himself, but this time he commented to his old friend. "Good choice, but that line really should be coming from a curvy dame what's great legs."

James smiled. "I'm sorry to disappoint you, old friend and have you ever considered that we might just be too old for that sort of thing."

"Speak for yourself, there's always one or two out there that have some daddy issues to where I can rescue them."

Both gentlemen laughed. James missed the camaraderie with other cops like he used have when he was on the job. That was the worst part about retirement. The bartender served an Old Fashioned to James and after taking a sip to make sure it was up to standard, Tom asked. "S, what can I do for you old friend?"

He took another sip of his old fashion. "I need some information."

"For you or for someone else?"

"Both."

"I was curious why you called me out of the blue."

"Do you remember those old pleasure houses that catered to businessmen, but also cops... they had one in every major city."

"Yes... are you looking to get laid!"

"No... nothing like that. Are they still around?"

"I guess it depends on who really wants to know... someone who wants an invitation or someone looking to make trouble."

James cracked a smile. "That's why I called you... even retired, you still have your finger on the pulse of the dark and seedy underbelly that lies within Texas."

"They say information is power and I hear a lot of things which works out well in my line of work."

"Some things haven't changed, but the answer your question, no one's looking for an invitation, and no one's looking to make trouble... Just trying to figure out if certain people have visited these places."

Tom gave him a disapproving look. "That can be a little tricky."

Don't worry; it's not one of your clients. The people I'm inquiring about are dead.

That shocked Tom a little bit. "Okay, in that case. What you're asking about doesn't really exist anymore. 12 years ago, it all changed. Everything got consolidated by one guy or at least that's what they say. Nobody knows who he really is. Pleasure houses turned into big corporate-like retreats with swimming pools and golf courses. No more of these little social clubs/brothels. All high-end and very exclusive."

"Let me guess, invitation-only."

"Yep."

"And you know this because some of your clients get an invite?"

"Correct? "Tom facetiously smiled. "With their kind of money, of course they do."

James softly laughed. "I don't suppose you know what the invite looks like?"

Tom got out his iPhone and click on the pictures app. "I have a copy of it here. It's only printed and hand-delivered, but I snapped a photo of it once. It's the same design, but the date and location change."

James looked at it intently. It looked familiar, he felt that he had seen it before. It was a very classy design that showed how truly upscale these were. Tom asked him. "The people you are inquiring about it, can you give me their names?"

James nodded yes and then pulled out a piece of paper. There were two groups. Three of the names were those who could definitely afford something like this, Hugo Blackmon, Jack Perry, and Don Bennett. The other three names were people who probably couldn't afford to go to one of these retreats. James wanted to see if Tom recognized any of the names and to see what he can find. After he got the list, Tom looked over the names. Immediately recognized three of them and commented. "Three of them would have definitely gotten an invite over the years. I know for sure Don Bennett had been to some of them. Is this have something to do with the Black Fairy Killer because the last time I checked he was serving a life sentence in federal prison."

"That's true, but there may be a copycat killer who's getting their instructions from Aldo Martinez. I'm working with State CID and the Austin Police department as a consultant to try and figure out how they may be targeted."

Tom gave him a strange look. "Word of advice, you're digging into some dark shit here. I can make some inquiries, but don't be surprised if you don't get the answers you're looking for. Anonymity is a prime asset when it comes to these places."

James tipped his glass at the advice. He knew what he was asking. He knew that these kinds of inquiries could get him killed. Sometimes the truth is worth the risk even if you don't like answers, but at the same time, the task force needed answers desperately.

The background checks were starting to get intense. Looking up one's pornographic and sexual history was a deep dark rabbit hole of misconception. Oscar Wilde once said that if you want a man to tell the truth then give him a mask. If you wanted to see how sick and depraved human beings really are, look at their pornographic and sexual history. Each one of them picked a victim and started doing research on them. Nobody wanted to touch William Staples, the Reverend who was addicted to snuff films. They would save him for last. Jim started looking into Mike Sturdgiss' background. He was the first victim, and he was the one they knew the littlest about. Jim was shocked at what he found. Having a fondness for young girls was putting it mildly.

While he had never been arrested for it, witnesses had come forth after his death, saying that he had been seen at some of the cheaper brothels looking for underage girls. One thing was for sure, Mike Sturdgiss had a pattern. As Jim was looking through what he could find, he got a phone call. It was Detective Lester, there had been another murder. It was the same pattern they had seen over and over. Jim knew it was coming and they were running out of time. But getting the phone call that it had actually happened was like the other shoe dropping.

The first question Jim asked was. "Have you identified the victim?"

Detective Lester replied. "Yes. And it wasn't too hard. You're not going to believe it. The victim he's a criminal court judge here in Austin."

Stunned at what he just heard; Jim didn't make a move for a few moments. "A judge, seriously?"

"I wouldn't lie about something like that. We now have a dead judge, and it fits the pattern of this copycat killer or whatever you want to call it. We are not going to be able to hide this with the press."

Detective Lester was definitely right about that. A Murdered judge was a whole new ballgame. Jim ask for the address and had Vanessa and Maisie come with him to the crime scene. Detective Lester told him that this scene was even stranger than the last one, which was hard to believe at this point.

The three of them arrived at a house. It was in a nice part of Austin, the Shady Hallow suburb to be exact. Police had the area surrounded when they arrived. There were always extra police when law enforcement or an elected official was found dead. I found Mike and he walked them to where the body was found. The judge was murdered in his study like some comic scenario out of the board game Clue. And then finally, the three of them saw the body. It was a dark and twisted scene, far different from the other murders and certainly symbolic.

The judge was sitting in his chair wearing his judge's robe with a gavel in his right hand and his left hand holding the scales of Justice. The most interesting part was what was on the scales. On one side tipping the scale was a pile of flesh and on the other side was what his penis was presumably. His right eye had been cut out and placed on the desk facing him, the same as in the Don Bennett murder. And just like in the William Staples murder they found the exact same vessel with the Gaelic Triskelion design. Through his robes, the judge had been pierced in the side like all the other victims and his blood drained out into the vessel. The scene was different, but very much the same and the first question that Jim asked is if they had found fairy wings anywhere. Detective Lester told him to look closely at the scales. On the desk was an outline of fairy wings and in the middle, the scales of justice.

Detective Lester commented. "It's the same MO, right?"

Jim replied. "There's only one way to know for sure. Yes, it looks the same, but with this killer it's all about the ritual. We'll have to get an autopsy done. He looked at Vanessa who knew exactly what he was thinking. Her snarky response was. "I guess it's a good thing I'm here."

Her reply made Jim smile. "For sure. because I wouldn't trust anybody else to do it."

Jim looked at Detective Lester. "I'm assuming you haven't found any physical evidence, especially fingerprints."

"No, we're not that lucky…same as the other crime scenes."

Jim started to think out loud. "Why a Judge? This just seems out of the ordinary for our killer. Mike, do you know if he was into anything? Was he accused of sexual harassment at some point? Or was there any kind of controversy of a sexual nature, surrounding him?"

Detective Morgan was standing nearby and answered the question. "None of the above Detective Summers. He was an upstanding citizen, well-liked, and respected by his peers. There were rumors of infidelity during his marriage which did end in divorce, but other than that, there's no reason to kill him like the others."

"There's always a reason to kill someone, Detective. You just got to find the motive. And I certainly don't believe he's completely innocent. The infidelity would suggest that."

"Probably so, but we don't know any reason why he would be murdered the same way as the other victims."

We'll have to do a deep background check on him, but in the meantime, what about his laptop!"

"Detective Lester and Detective Morgan gave him a strange look. Where was he going with this? She asked. "What about the laptop?"

"His porn history of course. let's see what the man was into. Maybe he's got some interesting videos on his computer."

The judge's laptop was on the desk near the body. Jim grabbed it and opened it. It was password protected. Jim asked them to look around the desk and see if the judge might have written down his password, but there was a crime scene computer technician there. Pulling out a flash drive, she walked over and said. "Don't bother looking for a password I have a tool that can get past that." She stuck the flash drive in. It took about thirty seconds for the tool to run and get into the computer. Jim and Maisie looked through the laptop...nothing. There was nothing out of the ordinary on the laptop. His browser history didn't have any porn sites in it.

Maisie said. "What if he has a different laptop for that sort of thing... a lot of people will keep a separate computer for their perversions or a separate hard drive."

Jim agreed. He told everybody in the room as they were searching the house to look for a separate hard drive or flash drive and to give it to his team. But he also thought that it might be somewhere in the study, so he started searching the desk. He didn't find a separate hard drive or flash drive, but he did find something else of interest. It was a card, the same size as a small postcard about 3 x 5 inches. It had a nice elegant black background with golden text. On one side, it said, "You are Invited to La Maison de Plaisir," and on the back, it had a location with a date and time. The event was in a few weeks. Jim didn't know what it was but somehow felt that it was important. He removed it from the desk and put it in his pocket. Technically it was removing evidence from the crime scene, but he had a hunch they needed it more than Austin PD.

Jim walked over to Vanessa, asking her. "Did you find something?"

"I don't know yet, but I did want to talk with you. I'm going to request that you stay on with the task force until we're done, however strong that may be. The killer clearly isn't done yet and we need all the help we can get."

Vanessa agreed. "I was going to request that as well. I need to see this through until the end. If nothing else for my own personal curiosity."

Jim nodded at her. "I don't need you to give me a reason, just say yes."

She smiled. "Yes, I'll definitely join your team."

"Good. And the first thing is to do an autopsy on the body. Let's see if he has unleavened bread in his system that was dipped in blood."

Detective Lester and Detective Morgan walked over to where Jim was standing with Vanessa. Maisie joined him. Detective Lassiter asked his friend. Do you have a theory?"

"You mean about why he was murdered?"

"Yeah."

Jim shrugged. He had to admit, he was at a loss with this one. "Honestly, I don't know. Everybody else has been a sexual predator who got away with it, but it doesn't appear that the judge fits that pattern."

Detective Morgan replied. "Appearances are almost always misleading... Perhaps we don't see it yet because we haven't dug that deep into his life. There's got to be some dirt there."

Jim was going to respond, but then he noticed Vanessa staring at something. He asked her what she was so focused on. She replied. "Look at the way he's positioned. He's a judge holding scales of Justice. Maybe it's not about his sexual past, but about how he ruled on the cases he presided over. On one scale, you have what appears to be a pound of flash, which outweighs the penis. Maybe one of his rulings exacted a pound of flesh from an innocent victim and the weight of that decision outweighs what he loves the most... his dick. Just throwing that out there."

The rest of the group stared at the way the body was positioned, especially holding the scales of Justice. All of them were trying to see what Vanessa saw and the symbolic nature of the crime scene. Everything else had been religious in nature, this was the only crime scene that really wasn't, but it had to do with Justice which is a very common theme in any religion. Detective Lester responded. "Wow, you see a hell of a lot more than I do. Maybe the Killer is just trying to be grotesque."

Jim looked at his friend and said. "I'm not saying you're wrong, it could be that simple. But I think we need to dive into all of Judge Craig Fitzgerald's rulings and we need to go back at least 15 years. I get the sense that this murder is personal. Nobody really disagreed. Even if it was just a simple, grotesque crime scene, they had to rule out every possibility. They needed to see if there was something in the judge's past that would get him murdered for it. As Detective Morgan said, appearances can be misleading, but there had to be something dark and disgusting in his past. However, there was one more thing that Jim was wondering about. He asked his friend, Detective Lester. "Who was the last person to see him alive?"

Detective Lester started looking through his little cop's notebook. He found the name. "The judge's last meeting of the day was with an insurance fraud investigator. Her name is Lori Kellerman."

That was a bit shocking. He knew her and it was obvious to everyone in the room from the look on his face. Detective Lester responded. "You know her, don't you?"

"Yes, I do. She's one of Gina's best friends and was just here the other day. I knew she had to meet with a Judge, but this is eerie. You don't suppose…" Jim didn't finish the sentence. It was a ridiculous thought, but regardless, they were going to have to question her because she was the last person to see the Judge alive and that is the very definition of suspicious.

Jim and Maisie arrived back at the detective agency. Vanessa followed the body back to the city morgue so she could do the autopsy. Jim's first priority was calling Lori. He didn't want her to feel like a suspect, but they needed a few questions answered. It was more or less routine in a situation like this. He didn't necessarily like making the call and certainly could have had Maisie do it. This was Gina's best friend and under the circumstances, she was a suspect for murder or at the very least, a person of interest. It's not like Gina would be happy about it and the last thing he needed was a little bit of friction between them before their big Thanksgiving dinner. he made the phone call and

Lori was a bit surprised to hear from him, but she at least understood the reason when she found out about the judge and she understood that because she was the last person to see him she may have some vital details that help them solve the murder. The questions were very simple. Did she see anybody harass him? Did he seem distraught or afraid of something? Was there anything out of the ordinary that might explain why he was murdered? It basically came down to what she saw or heard. Nothing! She didn't see anybody or anything that would cause concern. And she certainly didn't see him leave the building after she had already gone. It wasn't much help, but they still had to question her and Jim was glad that she was very understanding about everything.

But Jim couldn't ignore the coincidence. After all, it was a very big coincidence being that Lori hardly ever came to Austin and when she did, she was the last person to see a murder victim in a case that he was investigating. James was in his small office with the door shut when everybody came back. He was doing some research of his own. He was following up on a lead about the invitation. He had his own hunch about it. James was in his own little world when Jim knocked on his door to bring him up to speed about the murder and to ask a favor. James was the only one not surprised by the fact that a judge has been murdered and when Jim asked him why he wasn't surprised, he simply replied. "With all the strange circumstances that occurred in this investigation, why should we be surprised that a judge was one of the victims."

Jim thought about it for a moment. He actually made a good point. "Maybe you're right, I guess we really shouldn't be that surprised." But he did need to ask a favor. He told James about the last person the Judge saw and how she was a friend of Gina's.

James replied to that little coincidence. "Ouch, that can't be good for you."

Jim sarcastically laughed. "Yeah, our bed won't exactly be warm and friendly, which makes what I'm about to ask a little bit more difficult than usual."

James knew where he was going with this. So, he answered the question before Jim could ask it. "You want me to run a background check on her."

"Yes, but it needs to be a deep background...deeper than you usually go. I need her family and relationship history, plus extensive financial records. We need to be sure if she fits our profile so you're going to have to go all the way back to when she was a child."

"Okay, I have someone who can help with that. She's very good at digging up stuff on people. She's a grad student who works here part-time."

"I'll leave it up to you, but this has to be kept quiet and your researcher can't know the reason why we're looking at this person."

James nodded. "Understood."

Jim was about to walk out when he remembered the card he took from the crime scene. Oh, one more thing," He handed the card to James. "Have you ever seen something like this before, I'm hoping you have and know what it is?"

James confidently smiled and got out his smartphone. He showed the picture that his friend Tom had texted him. "In fact, I do know what that is, my buddy had a picture of it on his phone because some of his clients get an invitation."

Jim was beyond stunned. "Holy shit! Did he tell you what it is?"

"Yes...those old pleasure houses that I told you about. They're not really around anymore but have turned into something else. They're private events masquerading as corporate retreats where all of your fantasies can be fulfilled. They're for people who have lots of money and influence. And nobody knows who truly runs these events.

"Of course, because having plausible deniability is the key."

"It's the smart way to handle it. I am doing some more research on it...trying to see if I can find out more."

Jim nodded in an agreement, but he also pointed to the other side of the card he took from the crime scene. "Well, we know at least one thing we didn't know before... where they're going to be next."

James smiled. "Ah… I see a good old-fashioned sting operation on the horizon."

"Me tool and how much you want to bet, the final victims our killer is targeting will be there!"

James agreed with that assessment. Finding that card was a big break in their case, more than they realized. But the bigger surprises we're about to come. If Jim had learned anything after this point, nothing was truly out of the ordinary and should at all be that surprising with the Black Fairy murders. Tomorrow would be another day of research and would hopefully lead them closer to the final conclusion of this case.

41

Jim was driving home. It was late, but if he was lucky, he could still make it home in time for dinner. Ever since Jim and Gina and the kids moved to Austin, it has been important to do a family dinner. It wasn't necessarily for Jim and Gina, but it gave some sense of normalcy for Audra and Josh. Most of the time Jim was able to make it home on time for their family dinner, only when he had a big case did he miss it from time to time. This certainly qualified. He was stuck in traffic when he received a phone call from his boss. The tone in Robert's voice suggested that he wasn't very happy and rightly so... a story was about to break.

Jim answered the phone. "Robert, what can I do for you?"

"It's going to break tomorrow."

"What is?"

"The story about Judge Craig Fitzgerald's murder, it's going to break and they're reporting that it's a copycat killer."

"Well, we knew it would eventually. A murdered judge doesn't stay a secret in Texas."

"True, but I was hoping to have a couple more days before we had to explain what was going on to the press."

Jim softly laughed at the notion. "We knew this day was coming too. So why not just say we have a copycat murder and be done with it."

"That's what we're going to have to do, but I also have to tell the public about CID's involvement, which means your name is going to come up."

Jim wasn't exactly happy about that. He also knew he couldn't avoid it. He was the lead investigator on record for the Black Fairy case. He knew it would raise a lot of questions when dealing with a copycat murder. He replied. "I understand and I don't really care as long as it doesn't impede our current investigation. You're not going to want me to speak to the press, are you?"

"Absolutely not. This is still Austin PD's case and we're only consulting on it. They can handle the press conference, but I mainly wanted to let you know about the story breaking because I'm sure some reporters will try to seek you out."

The truth is Jim was already prepared for that. He knew one day he'd have to answer more questions about this case, which means the press could nitpick every part of his investigation and eventually assign him the blame for anything that went wrong. He said to Robert. "Maybe and I don't have anything to say to them. My team also knows that the only response we have is no comment."

"I figured you'd say that, but it's my job to remind you."

"Don't worry boss, we are on the same page."

Hearing that brought a slight smile to Robert's face. He never seemed to smile when having to deal with this particular case so it was refreshing to know that he could trust his lead investigator. But he also had to ask. "Do you have any information about why the judge was targeted?"

"Not much. Our working theory is, it's not so much about what he did as the cases he presided over and his rulings. We are requesting all of his cases from the county clerk's office and should have them tomorrow. We'll be going through those to see if we find any connections to our victims." Of course, there was more. He could tell them about the invitation he found. But for now, Jim wanted to keep that quiet until they knew exactly what they had. And while he did consider Robert a friend, he didn't know for sure if he could trust him with that information just yet. Too many powerful people went to these things and Robert in his own right is a powerful person in law enforcement. He may not have necessarily distrusted his boss, but he had to at least, entertain the possibility that Robert got invited to these events. For now, only he and James were the only ones that knew about it.

Robert did have one more thing to ask. "Jim, whatever you find…keep it quiet for now. Judge Fitzgerald was a respected judge and even if he was into something, we don't need to smear his name. The truth will come out eventually, but out of respect, any information we find, we keep to ourselves. "Jim understood. Robert wasn't necessarily wrong. In this job, tact was important. Just because you have the ability to spill all of someone's dirty little secrets doesn't mean you have to. The man was dead, and he couldn't do any harm to someone anymore. Jim finally made it home and as luck would have it, Gina and the kids were about to sit down for dinner.

The silence during dinner was annoying for Jim, everybody was in their own little world, but he also noticed that Gina was not exactly happy with him. He had a good guess why that was. When they did the dishes together, he did the only sensible thing that a partner or husband should do. He apologized. He said to her. I'm sorry that work has been so busy and I haven't been around as much. Sometimes, I forget the burden I put on you with cases like these."

She tried to smile, but Gina was still a little mad at him. She could hold onto a grudge like the best of them. "I know and I appreciate the apology. Sometimes I forget what it's like being with a cop who works long hours. If we didn't have Audra and Josh, I probably wouldn't be so annoyed. But there is something else bothering me and I need to talk to you about it."

"What is it?"

"Next week is Thanksgiving, are we still planning on doing dinner here or are you going to have to work?"

To be honest, Jim had forgotten that Thanksgiving was coming up and they were planning a big dinner with family and friends. This was the first time since living together that they were doing Thanksgiving at their house. It was a big deal. Lying a little bit, Jim replied. "I didn't forget and we're still doing dinner here."

"Okay, I'm going to hold you to that. And if for any reason whatever you're working on is going to get in the way, I need to know now so we can make other arrangements. Don't get me wrong, I'll be disappointed if something happens to where we can't do it, but I understand."

Jim sighed for a moment. He knew that tone. Gina might understand, but she would never forget the disappointment and her holding onto that grudge was something he could live without. Besides, he never liked disappointing her. He loved her too much and always felt guilty when he did. He said. "I think we can all take at least one day off so there's no reason to change our plans. Can't guarantee that Wednesday night won't be a late night for me, but we're not missing Thanksgiving

Gina admitted that she liked Jim's answer, but she also knew he was a cop and things were never a guarantee with him. She asked him. "Are you sure we can have that day and nothing is going to come up, we could also just do a small dinner for the four of u?. I'm just worried that something is going to happen with your case and you're going to have to work on Thanksgiving Day.

Jim understood her concern and she was right to have it. He didn't know what else he could say to make her feel confident that Thanksgiving would still happen, so he hugged her. He held her tight inside. I understand why you feel this way, believe me short of a murder happening on Thanksgiving Day, we're still going to have this dinner. I'm not going to let anything get in the way of it and I hope you can believe that." Being held made her feel more at ease. Jim had an uncanny ability to always make her feel at ease and take away her worries when he held her. It was one of the many things she loved about him. She simply replied. "Okay, then let's have a nice family Thanksgiving, but I also wish you didn't have to work this case. I may not know much about it, but I know that it's stressful and you don't need that."

"It is and you know that I can't tell you everything, but we are dealing with a copycat killer. Somebody who's mimicking the Black Fairy murders."

Gina was a bit surprised. "Why do you have to work that case, you've already worked it before."

"I know, but I was called in to consult because I have seen this before unlike anybody else at CID."

Gina didn't argue with that notion. After all, he was right, and she knew it. She didn't like it, but she knew that he was the only one in the state of Texas who had the best insights to that case. She gave him a soft smile and said. "That may be true, but you can't blame me for being selfish and not wanting you to be a part of that case. It's nice when you get home on time and aren't missing family events."

Jim agreed. "I believe this will all be over soon and then we can get back to normal. But I do have to see this through."

"Just as long as somebody else can investigate the next one." Her sarcastic sentiment made him laugh. He kissed her and said. "It's a deal."

There was one thing that Jim had forgotten to do over the past few days. He had been so busy that it completely slipped his mind. Jim found Audra in her room working on homework. Audra didn't hear him knocking because she had her headphones on blaring whatever the latest craze in music was for teenage girls. He tapped her on her shoulder, startling her a bit. It was a bit amusing for Jim, to deal with a teenager. It also made him happy. He had always wanted kids, but his ex-wife was never the motherly type. Sure, Audra and Josh weren't his and he really wasn't married to Gina, but this was still better than what he had before. He said as he handed back her copy of The Dark Fair book. "Thank you for letting me borrow this."

Audra smiled. "Did it help?"

"More than you know. I may not like the idea of you chatting online with strangers about serial killers, but this was a real find."

"So, it was written by the real killer?"

"You know I can't talk about that."

"I think you just told me because you have a lousy poker face."

Jim laughed at her comment. She was right though; he had never had a good poker face and therefore never really played the game. He was too much of a straight shooter to try and bluff someone. "I think you've always known the answer to that question. But I'm curious, what do you think the book really means, I'm assuming you've read it at least a couple of times."

"I think it's similar to Dante's The Divine Comedy, but instead of traveling through nine circles of hell to get closer to God, the protagonist basically has to kill 9 bad people and try to save their souls in the process."

"That's a very good analysis."

"So, I'm right?" Jim didn't answer, but he smiled at her. Audra continued. There's something else about the characters in the book, I think the 9 characters that the Dark Fairy has to kill are connected to each other... like either, they know each other, or they're connected by a place. What do you think?" He was impressed. It was virtually the same theory they had about the characters in the book and the victims.

"I think that is a very good theory. There is a lot of symbolism in that book and you're right about the Divine Comedy comparison."

"Well, if I'm right then the real Black Fairy isn't done."

"No, they're not. And judging by the timeline this could go on for years."

"Are you close to figuring it out?"

Jim didn't say anything for a moment. He didn't know how to answer the question without revealing too much about his investigation. But he also knew that Audra wouldn't be satisfied with the same old answer that he couldn't tell her anything. She was way too inquisitive, and he liked that about her. So, he responded with what police referred to as the *non-answer, answer.* "I wish it was as simple as a good old-fashioned mystery novel where with one turn of the page you get closer and closer, but it isn't that way. However, each day we investigate we find more of the missing pieces and put them together so we can see the bigger picture. You should be proud because you helped with that by showing me this book." That brought a smile to her face. She did actually feel a sense of pride, after all she was becoming quite the investigator herself a regular Nancy Drew that always seemed to outsmart everybody else. She replied. "I have a lot more questions."

"That I don't doubt. But you know…"

Audra interrupted. I know, I know…you can't tell me anything."

"Yep, however, I can listen to your theories. You might think of something we haven't. Plus, you get to help by being an unofficial consultant to State CID and the Austin Police Department. That excited Audra. Discussing the case was just something fun to do, but getting to be a consulting detective, was way better. It didn't feel like a hobby anymore. It felt like she was a part of something like she could make a difference. Sure, she had basketball, but it was just a game. Helping to catch a killer was something else… the kind of thing that makes a real difference in the world. And she knew, that's what she really wanted to do in life. Audra just didn't know how yet, but this was a good start.

42

Jim was a little late arriving at the office. He and Gina had stayed up later than usual because they hadn't been intimate in a while. It was a great night. Yes, there was a little bit more silence during dinner than usual, but after Jim and Gina had a chance to talk, things got back to normal and that included a night of making love. Jim also wanted to be nice since he knew they were going to have to be doing a lot of research today. He got breakfast for everyone from IHOP. Nothing like lots of eggs, bacon, and pancakes to make the day better. When he walked into the detective agency, it was hard to move around because of all the boxes from the county clerk's office. They had delivered copies of all the cases that Judge Fitzgerald had presided over. He'd been a judge for 20 years, so there was a lot to go through. Maisie was already starting to read through some of the cases. You would think that they were working at a law firm and just got discovery for some big class action lawsuit. It pretty much amounted to the same thing because they were looking for another needle in a haystack. They were looking for even the smallest thing that would connect the judge to the other victims. Jim wondered if they were going to have to be like third-year law students pulling an all-nighter. As he looked at all the boxes it was a good possibility.

    Jim looked over at Maisie as she was deep in thought reading through what seemed like her hundredth case file. She had two huge stacks of files sitting next to her. One stack was one that she had already read through, and the other stack was what she was about to go through. Unfortunately, that stack was a lot bigger. Jim asked her. "I don't suppose there's any kind of index that came with the case files to make it easier to find what we're looking for."

Maisie looked up from the file she was reading and the look on her face simply said, go to hell. She wasn't mad at Jim, but the dirty look certainly conveyed her frustration. She replied. "No, because why would the county clerk's office want to make it easy on us? You would think they've never heard of an Excel sheet. No, we have to go through these ones by one and cross-reference the names we're for looking for."

Jim winced as he felt sympathy for the task at hand. He was about to jump right in and start looking through the case files himself. He told her. "To make it simple, just look for the mention of any of our victim's names. We'll worry about the details of the case later if we actually find the names in a particular case."

"That's what I'm doing, but it's still taking a while. So far there hasn't been any case involving the State of Texas versus one of our victims so I'm having to look through everything and see if any of them were a witness or simply mentioned in a case. It's very tedious, so feel free to jump right in."

Jim sarcastically laughed. "I'll get started soon, but first I brought breakfast for everyone... might as well have some bacon, eggs, and pancakes while looking through all the boring details of the judge's cases."

Maisie smiled for the first time since Jim had gotten to work. "Pancakes would be good... I would never say no to pancakes or bacon. In fact, bacon is essential in life, it can make everything else great including chocolate."

Jim was curious about her last statement. "Shouldn't it be the other way around? He asked her. "How does bacon make chocolate good? I can see chocolate making bacon good…"

"You could look at it that way if you want, but don't kid yourself bacon makes everything better and the only reason chocolate bacon tastes good is because of the bacon. You can have bad chocolate, but you can never have bad bacon as my mother always used to say."

Jim had never thought about it before. He didn't disagree that bacon can make anything good or that might be one of life's essentials, but the fact that there was such a thing as bad chocolate and never bad bacon, well he definitely couldn't disagree with that. If there was such a thing as absolute truth, that would be it. Jim made himself a plate of bacon and eggs and pancakes, he was about to get started reading through case files when James called him into his small office. Jim told him to hold on a minute, but with a sarcastic tone, James told him that he could eat and listen at the same time because he was going to want to hear this. Jim entered the office and shut the door at James' request. He said. "We got some information back on Lori; you're never going to believe this. She changed her name a little over nine years ago."

"What...why did she change her name?"

"Well, that's the strange part... she didn't go through the legal process of changing her name, it was granted by a judge based on a case she was involved in.

That got Jim's attention, and even shocked him a little. "You usually don't change your name unless you need to. What are the basics of the case?"

"I don't know, because the records are sealed. Now we did a preliminary background check with the information you gave us... information on her education and where she's lived over the last nine years. We also found her marital status listed as a widow, based on a tax return that she filed eight years ago under what looks like a new social security number. So, it got me thinking, if she's a widow and there's a court case involving a legal name change granted by a judge, but the records are sealed then it can only mean one of two things."

Jim thought about it for a moment arriving at the answer before James could finish his sentence. "Her husband was murdered, and she witnessed it so to protect her from those who might want to kill her, the judge gives her a new identity without necessarily putting her in a witness protection program."

James nodded in agreement. "Yes, that's one possibility, the other is she killed her husband in self-defense, and to protect her from his family seeking revenge, she's given a new identity and a new life with sealed court records so they can't find her."

"Huh... that's a deliciously entertaining idea. Do you know where this occurred?

"Albuquerque New Mexico... she was there in 2007 at the time of the Mike Sturgess murder. The divorce doesn't occur until January 2008."

"No shit."

James smiled. "It gets better. The sealed court records prevent us from knowing what her other name is, but she was allowed to use the new name on her diplomas. Her new name was applied to her education history. I think what she did was take the court records and update every database where she has a diploma or educational record, and they just changed it to her new name without stating that she has any aliases. For example, she went to Rice University, they simply changed her name in their database on her school records and her diploma."

"How far back did you get with her education?"

James flipped through the folder and the documents about her education. "We got all the way back to Middle School. She was apparently living in Houston at the time. She went to a private Catholic School, from grades 6 through 12. St. John Paul Catholic School in Houston to be exact. I figure her father was probably in oil and that's how she could afford to be sent to that school. Her name was changed the same way as it was with the University. We have a record of a Lori Kellerman, but no record of an alias. It's like her old identity was simply erased."

Jim just shook his head. He couldn't believe it. That was a big coincidence. It certainly wasn't proof of anything except she changed her name, but it was a big coincidence that couldn't be ignored. "How do we get the court records?"

"The only way to get them is to petition the court and the only people who can do that or even have a chance of seeing those records are law enforcement. I can't do it, but maybe the State Attorney General can petition them. We won't be able to make copies, but we can look at them. If we get her other name, then it's worth a trip to New Mexico."

"Well, I guess I have a few phone calls to make. In the meantime, I'm going to see if I can get Dallas PD to put some tails on her. We need to at least keep an eye on her."

James nodded, it wasn't a bad plan, but he had an alternative. "I have a different suggestion. I have a bunch of old cop friends who are retired like me and just pick up extra work here and there to keep from being bored. I have a few in Dallas that would love to take shifts and tail someone. They could use the extra cash and it gets them out of the house. And besides, I can guarantee you, they're better than any Dallas police officer at following someone without being seen." Jim thought about it for a moment. "A bunch of old men following a young pretty girl, it's a little creepy don't you think?"

"Sure, and they definitely won't be mistaken for cops or tip her off that she's being followed by police so creepy old men is a step up."

Jim laughed. He was right, in this case, creepy old men were a better fit to do the job of following someone and that had to be a first when it came to a murder investigation.... or any kind of Investigation as a matter of fact. Jim told James to keep this quiet for a little while. He wanted to be absolutely sure before he included Lori as a possible suspect. And that was definitely not a conversation he wanted to have with Gina. Even if he was absolutely sure about Lori, it would still be an unpleasant conversation with the woman he loved, that thought kept lingering in the back of his mind.

Vanessa got back later in the day with the autopsy report. There was nothing out of the ordinary with it. She found exactly what she thought she'd find. There was unleavened or soda bread in his system that had been dipped in his own blood after it had been poured into the vessel with the Gaelic Triskelion. Except for some differences and how the crime scene was staged, it was exactly the same as it was with the last victim. There wasn't any doubt; this had been done by the Black Fairy killer. With the news being what they already thought it would be, Jim, Maisie, and

Vanessa went back to looking through Judge Fitzgerald's old case files. They were still searching for even the smallest connection that seemed to elude them. It was tedious work, but it had to be done.

About two hours later, they got a visitor. A woman walked into the office. Nobody recognized her except for Jim. It was his sister Hannah, the FBI agent. He was surprised to see her, especially since they hadn't talked in a while. Nobody else on the team had actually met her either, so it was a bit of a surprise to them as well. Hannah looked around the room and commented. "This is a neat little clubhouse of detectives, definitely suits you, big brother." He smiled at her sarcasm. Even when they didn't get along, she could still make him laugh. He replied. "Thank you, but what are you doing here?"

"I'm here to talk to you. I might just have the break in your case that you've been looking for." That got everybody's attention, but she wanted to speak to her brother alone. It was part of an FBI investigation so, therefore, sensitive information. They went to the bar next door and grabbed a drink. It was a dive bar, so cheap beer seemed appropriate, and they ordered a couple of cans of Texas' own, Lonestar Beer. Jim politely asked her what she had for his team.

Hannah took a sip of beer and smiled. "We found Amy Henderson."

Jim's eyes perked up. It was the winner for the most shocking news of the day. "Where did you find her? Did you guys arrest her?"

"No, nothing like that. She was spotted in Texas two weeks ago and we were able to trace her location because you remember that $140,000 that she had on a reloadable bank card, she finally used it."

"No shit... what did she use it for?"

Hannah pulled out a piece of paper from her pocket. It was a Google Earth image. "Apparently, she has started some kind of commune or shelter for battered women in Colorado. At least that's what it appears to be. The FBI has a warrant to search the premises or raid the place if necessary."

"What is she wanted for?"

Hannah took another sip of beer. "She's not wanted for anything per se, just a person of interest. But the warrant is so we can find any incriminating evidence that can be used to arrest her." Jim gave her a dirty look. "I think that's called entrapment."

Hannah sarcastically replied back. "For the FBI it's a gray area." She smiled at her brother and took another sip of beer. "All kidding aside, what we really need to do is talk with her about her involvement with one of the leaders of that Republic of Texas Patriots group. Apparently, she was involved with a Doug Houston years ago. Well, he was picked up six months ago for trying to blow up a government building. Also, the ATF wants him for smuggling illegal weapons. His brother David was with him when he tried to bomb the government building and he got away. We think Amy might know where he'd be hiding so that's the real reason we want to talk to her."

Jim was curious to say the least. He wanted to talk to her about the murder, but it sounded like she was involved with domestic terrorists. One thing was for sure, Amy Henderson was far from the person she used to be before she was raped by Don Bennett. Jim asked. "Was she involved in this bombing attempt?"

"No, we pretty much caught everybody except the brother who was involved. We figure he was the getaway driver. Plus, when we talked to Doug, he said that he hadn't spoken Amy in over five years. He seemed shocked that we were asking about her. But because of her involvement with him and the group, she would know where their safe houses that are off the grid were located."

Jim took another sip of beer. "I see... so she's not in Texas anymore?"

"No."

"Then why are you telling me? I don't have jurisdiction beyond the state line."

Hannah softly smiled. "I'm telling you because I'm about to do you a huge favor. Because she's a person of interest in the Black Fairy case, the FBI is going to let you question her."

"How can that be since the Black Fairy case is officially closed?"

Hannah shot him a sarcastic smile." Oh please, every Fed knows that the Aldo Martinez confession was bullshit. I know about the deal he made with the DEA. He's not the real killer and I also know that you're not investigating a copycat killer, you're investigating the same person you were four years ago. So, if you're telling me that Amy Henderson isn't a suspect anymore then we can forget this conversation."

Jim winced at her. "Okay, so apparently you know the whole story. Good for you. And yes, she's still a person of interest."

"That's what I thought. If you would like to hitch a ride with me and the agents who are going to Colorado, you will get a chance to talk with her. In fact, they want you to talk to her first because they're hoping you'll rule her out as a suspect to avoid the jurisdictional nightmare. If she turns out to be the real killer and we have to deal with the DEA and Customs over their deal with the wrong guy, well, let's just say it'll be a hell of a nightmare within the federal law enforcement community and I'm for one definitely don't need that headache."

Jim quietly laughed at her comment. "I'm not going to rule her out just to spare the Feds in this fucked up situation. It was a bad deal four years ago and still…the only thing that I really care about is finding the right person. If she is, then all of you just have to deal with it. She's coming back to Texas to stand trial."

Hannah shook her head and took another sip of beer." Can't you just play nice with the Feds?"

"Not when it screws up my case."

"Once a stubborn asshole... always a stubborn asshole!"

They both laughed as they tipped their bottles to one another. Harassing each other never got old. But in the end, Jim was grateful for the invitation from the FBI. This was a huge break and he wasn't going to miss it. It was happening fast, but he agreed to fly out with them in the morning. He was going to miss another one of Audra's basketball games and hopefully, she would understand. But Jim had been waiting four years for this break, there was no way in hell was he going to miss it. Too much was at stake.

43

Jim hated flying. He preferred transportation on the ground, and he hardly went outside of Texas. If it was too far to drive, then it wasn't worth going to in his opinion. So, we figured the plane ride to Colorado with the rest of the FBI team was going to be the worst part of the trip. Even more so than his sister giving him shit for it, it was just one more thing she could harass her brother about and of course, get some pleasure from it. In a perfect world, this would only be a day trip, but Jim planned to be gone at least a couple of days. When he told Gina about this trip, she wasn't exactly happy about it, but she was kind enough not to voice her disappointment. With less than a week away from Thanksgiving, the only thing she truly cared about was that he was going to be there and nothing was going to get in the way of their big family dinner. And that's why Jim prayed that there wouldn't be some kind of standoff with the FBI. But unfortunately, in this day and age, something like that was a real possibility.

It was a two-hour plane ride followed by an hour and a half car ride to the FBI camp that was just outside of Amy Henderson's commune. She wasn't too far outside of Colorado Springs, but far enough that people would pretty much leave her alone unless they wanted to be there, the way she preferred it. The FBI team also had a Tactical Team ready to storm the place if necessary. They were a little over-prepared, but that was the standard procedure by the FBI ever since their standoff in Waco Texas 24 years before. Jim followed his sister and didn't say anything. He was a guest at the courtesy of the FBI. However, when the FBI tactical leader started to lay out his plan, he didn't care about going in peacefully. He basically wanted to storm the place, so Jim spoke up and gave his two cents, much to the surprise of the agents who were there. He said. "Agent Hawkins, I'm sure you're good at your job, but this is a bad idea."

Annoyed that he was interrupted, agent Hawkins replied. "I'm sorry, who are you?"

"Detective Jim Summers."

He rolled his eyes at Jim and said. "Yeah, you're the detective from Texas here at the courtesy of the FBI. You're not a part of our investigation, you're only here because we're being nice and letting you question the suspect, but that takes a back seat to our objective. So don't fucking start with me or we'll just put you on a plane back to Texas."

"Sir, I'm not trying to get in the way of your investigation. But if you go in guns blazing and this ends up being a standoff, then I don't get to talk to Amy Henderson which means I can't rule her out in my investigation, and this turns into a jurisdictional nightmare."

"I honestly don't give a shit."

"That I believe, but violence isn't always going to get the answers you want, and even if you do arrest her, what makes you think she's going to talk and tell you anything you want to know? I'm saying that there's a better way to do this. If you don't treat her like a suspect and go in there just wanting her help, she might be more willing to cooperate. And the best way to do that is to let me talk to her first. After she feels like she's helping then it will be easier to get from her, the answers you're looking for."

Agent Hawkins was about to say something but then Jim's sister, Hannah responded. "Sir, he's right. We invited him here to talk to her; Detective Summers can probably help us out by softening her up and also gaining Intel on the layout of the commune once we are inside. Letting him go in first just makes it easier for us especially since we really don't know what we be walking into."

Agent Hawkins looked at her for a moment. He was skeptical of the idea. He thought showing force was a better idea. "You're his sister, right? "Hannah nodded yes. Agent Hawkins continued. "Are you saying all of this, just to stick up for your brother or do you really believe this is the right course of action?"

"I don't need to stick up for him. He's good enough at his job without me having to do that. I just think this is the best course of action."

Agent Hawkins thought about it for another moment. He didn't necessarily agree, but it would give them more time to get prepared in case they did have to storm the place. And he liked the idea of sending somebody that wasn't a part of this team to get the reconnaissance he wanted. Jim was granted permission to try and talk to Amy Henderson first. But they still needed to serve a search warrant, so an FBI agent had to go with them. Of course, his sister, Hannah volunteered. The base camp was about 300 yards from the front door. They were out of the way enough as not to be seen by anybody at the commune, but close enough to where they can quickly get to the front door and easily storm the place. Jim and Hannah drove up to the front door of the commune. It had high enough walls to where they couldn't see inside. It looked like a fortress more than a simple refuge for people who were trying to escape their circumstances. They didn't see any sentries and that was probably because there were two security cameras outside the front door. Amy Henderson wasn't taking any chances.

She wanted to ensure the safety has anybody who stayed there. And she certainly didn't trust strangers that showed up at the front door. Hannah was the one who knocked on the door and identified herself in front of the camera as an FBI agent. She said that she had a warrant to search the premises, but what they really needed to do was just talked to Amy Henderson. She didn't want to spook Amy by making her think she was a suspect so she borrowed the tactic from Jim's play and said that she was seeking Amy's help in her investigation. Jim and Hannah didn't have to wait long. A woman opened one of the big doors, letting them in, and then taking them to see Amy at her office. Jim was looking around and quietly remarked that the place looked peaceful. It didn't look like any kind of threat at all. Plus, all he saw were women. There was no trace of a man anywhere.

Finally, they arrived at Amy Henderson's office. It was technically the main office, but Amy Henderson spends most of her time there, it pretty much became her office. In a lot of ways, she was a one woman show and very hands-on. This was her project after all and when it came to building it up, she wanted to be a part of everything. The young woman who had let Jim and Hannah into the commune opened the door and they found Amy quietly sitting at her desk looking at expense reports. Knowing who they were, she skipped the pleasantries and said to them when they walked in. "Somehow, I knew I wouldn't have to wait long before the FBI showed up on my doorstep. Are you here to arrest me?"

Hannah, being the only actual FBI agent in the room, replied. "No ma'am. Although, we do have a warrant to search the area, you're not getting arrested today unless you provoke us. We do have some questions for you."

"I'm assuming there's an FBI team standing by waiting to raid this place?"

"Yes, if necessary. Will you talk with us a bit so it doesn't have to come to that?"

Amy was a little nervous and she had a right to be. She knew that she had been on a watch list for some years now because of her association with the Republic of Texas Patriots. But she also knew that she hadn't done anything wrong. Despite her involvement, she had never broken the law once. Despise her mistrust of government and the judicial system, she was still a cop at heart and still abided by the law. It was a tense situation, and one wrong word or move could turn this into a bigger ordeal, so she decided to trust the FBI agent at least for now. Amy replied. "I'll answer your questions to the best of my ability, but despite what you might think, everybody here is a law-abiding citizen. And before we go any further, you should know that we do have guns on the premises. They were bought legally, which means we have the right to own them, and we have all the paperwork, but we are not afraid to use them either. Can you live with that?"

As much as Amy was a cop, Hannah was very much an FBI agent at heart, and she didn't like to feel threatened. That felt like a little bit of a threat. She was about to say something snarky that could provoke Amy and Jim sensed it. His sister could have a bit of a temper, so he intervened and responded with the right answer for the situation. "Miss Henderson, we both understand. That's perfectly fine unless you plan on using them on us and as you can see we haven't drawn our weapons."

She nodded in agreement. "What are your names?"

"I'm Detective Jim Summers and this is Agent Hannah Walsh. I work for Texas State CID."

Amy was surprised. She just assumed he was an FBI agent as well. She wondered why a Texas Detective would be here asking questions. She said. "You're a long way from home... why do you want to talk to me?"

It's about former Senator Don Bennett who was murdered four years ago. I'm sorry to bring him up, but you've been a person of interest in his murder for a long time."

Amy shook her head. It was a little hard to believe they would still be questioning her all these years later, but she kind of understood why even if she didn't want to talk about it anymore. "I'm not a person of interest... I'm a prime suspect because he raped me and then I sued him."

"Yes."

"It was my understanding that somebody else confessed to his murder."

"They did, but they didn't really kill him. His murder is part of a larger investigation."

Amy got up from her chair and walked toward Jim. Normally she would have just dismissed this line of questioning since she wasn't the one who really killed him. But she was curious as to why a detective would still be questioning her about this murder when somebody else had already confessed to it. "Now, why would somebody confess to a murder they didn't commit?"

"The short end of the story is he confessed because he was going to be charged with killing some cops and he made a deal with some federal agents to become an informant since he's related to a couple of cartel bosses."

"So this has to do with the Black Fairy murders that happened 4 years ago."

"Yes, did you keep up with them in the news?"

Amy Softly smiled. "You don't think I just murdered someone...you think I'm a serial killer?"

"Are you? I mean you have a lot of motive not only to kill Don Bennett, but people who are associated with him and did the same things he did."

"Does anybody actually answer truthfully that kind of question?"

Jim laughed. "Not really, but there's always a first time."

"You're funny Detective, I'll give you that. I did hear about the murders. And to be honest, I didn't shed one tear when I heard Don Bennett had been brutally murdered. He deserved what he got."

"Really, that's a good reason to murder someone."

"Absolutely it is, but I didn't do it, detective. He was murdered sometime early in 2009 if I'm correct, I left Texas in 2008."

"We know you disappeared, we found that out from your sister and talked to the private detective she hired to find you. Just because you disappeared doesn't mean you actually left Texas. Can you prove it? Can anybody corroborate your story?"

Amy thought about it for a moment, trying to come up with a satisfying answer. "Probably not or at least not the kind of people that be willing to talk to you. But I'm sure there's already evidence to suggest that I left Texas. If the private investigator my sister hired was at least halfway decent at his job, he would have followed the money and figured it out, but I sold my old car out of state and got a new one in a different state."

That's true, but you also learned how to live off the grid, which means you could have come back to Texas without anybody knowing it."

With a sarcastic smile, Amy replied. "Prove it."

Jim ignored her last statement and continued to ask questions. "Do you know who Jack Perry is?"

"No, I never heard that name until it was mentioned in the Black Fairy case.

"What about Hugo Blackmon?"

"No? "

"Do you know a William Staples or a Judge Craig Fitzgerald?"

"No, should I know these people?"

"Maybe not." Jim paused for a moment thinking of his next question. It was clear that she wasn't going to answer yes to knowing any of the victims, so he tried a different approach. "How did you get involved with the Republic of Texas Patriots?"

Amy sighed. Back then it wasn't a good time in her life. And to be honest there were no simple answers to why she did the things she did back then. She replied. "That's a long story so I won't bore you with all the details. After I was raped by that pig and they wouldn't press charges, I was a wreck. I couldn't do the job anymore. Couldn't be what my family needed me to be. You see, this is one thing that you will never understand. When you're raped, you not only lose all sense of yourself and control over your own life... even control over your own choices. You lose the sense of power. You just don't have the strength to keep going because all of that was taken away from you. I wanted to get it back. Simple as that. So I started training with survivalist groups to get that back. I learned skills that will help me fight back and not feel powerless. I learned skills that would help me survive any attack. It was more therapeutic than talking to some psychologist."

Amy paused for a moment, trying to come up with an answer that justified why she did it. "Anyway, when you get involved with some of these survivalist groups it's not that much of a stretch to get involved with a group who simply wants to be free of anybody who seeks to control them, especially a government. Regaining the power over your own life goes hand-in-hand with just wanting to be free. And this guy, Doug Houston, just had a way with words when he talked about freedom. He was a different kind of Tony Robinson when it came to taking control of your own life and I fell for it. But eventually, I saw through that entire BS and realized that he was just one more right-wing Patriot who wanted to take down what he thought was an evil government."

Hannah interrupted and asked a question. "You were involved with him, correct?"

"Yes, for a little while. We finally ended things in the summer of 2008. He started to get dangerous. I remember Barack Obama running for president that year and he kept talking about how we were going to have to take back this country if that Muslim won. And he wanted to do something that would be an inspiration to other survivalist Patriot groups. I don't know exactly what he was planning, a bombing or an assassination, but it was something along those lines and I didn't want any part of it, so I got out. I only really got involved with these groups to learn how to survive and socialize with like-minded individuals who can accept me for me."

Jim responded with a question of his own. "When I talked to your sister four years ago, she said that you had a friend who was involved with you in that stuff and seemed dangerous, but she made it seem like you had a girlfriend. I think she said her name was Gwen."

Amy smiled when she heard the name. She hadn't thought about her in a long, long time. It seems strange to be asking about her. After all, Gwen wasn't even her real name. She answered Jim. "Her name wasn't Gwen, it was Sara. I think my sister was getting the name confused because her full name was Sara Gwendolyn Rogers. It's a unique name and we were talking about it one night at dinner with my family. Why do you want to know about her?"

"Like I said, your sister seemed to think that she was dangerous for you… that she was the one influencing you to do the stuff with survivalist groups."

Amy shook her head in disbelief at the notion. "My sister has a habit of blowing things out of proportion and can be a bit dramatic. It's true that we started doing these things together, but I was interested in that before I ever met Sara."

"How did you two meet?"

"We met in a support group sometime in the summer of 2006. I was just trying to find a support group that I felt would listen and none of the rape victim groups were that helpful so I found one that dealt more with general tragedy. We met, hit it off, and became friends."

"Just friends or more than friends?"

Amy gave Jim a snide look. "My sister told you we were lovers, right?"

"She eluded that you two were in a relationship."

"Yes and no. And my sister definitely didn't understand the kind of relationship that I had with Sara. It's true that we were close and even lived together for a short time. I loved her, but not the way you think. We didn't have some kind of loving lesbian relationship where we completely swore off men. I'm not even saying that we weren't intimate with one another, but it wasn't about sex and it wasn't about being in a monogamous relationship. It was about two people who came from tragedy and needed someone they could depend on and who were stable. That's what we were for each other until we had a falling out. But as a man, I don't expect you to understand that."

Jim slightly rolled his eyes. It was partially true; he didn't completely understand what she was talking about. It had nothing to do with being a man, it was because he was simple and how he viewed relationships. You were either friends or you had a relationship with someone that included sex, there wasn't an in-between He was going to make a comment to that effect, but remembered that small insults just got in the way of his true objective of getting as much information as he could that would get him one step closer to identifying the real black fairy. Jim asked her. "What did you two have a falling-out about?"

Suddenly, Amy felt sad. It was heartbreaking to have to remember her falling out with someone that she loved. She didn't know for sure if she had just forgotten or repressed the memory but having to remember brought on a wave of sadness that she could certainly do without. She said. "She got mad at my involvement with the Republic of Texas Patriots... I started to get more and more involved with them early in 2007. And that's when I met Doug Houston or should I say fell for him. He was the first man that I had wanted to be with since being raped. I can't tell you what he is now, but back then, he was kind and gentle, and inspiring. And unfortunately, I got involved with some of their illegal activities." Amy gave Hannah a harsh look when continued her statement. "I won't tell you what we did and you can't compel me to tell you. However, I will say that I got involved with some stuff that I shouldn't have and Sara tried to make me stop. Sometimes I don't know if it was because she was jealous of my relationship with Doug or she was just generally concerned about where my life was headed. I like to think it was the ladder because I could have very easily ended up being a domestic terrorist. Anyway, we fought and ended our friendship. I moved out the next day and shacked up with Doug and the rest of his group until I eventually left. But I have a question for you Detective."

Jim answered. "Okay."

"Why do you want to know about my friend Sara, what does this have to do with me being a suspect and your murder investigation?"

"To be honest, you fit a certain profile. You check all the boxes for the Black Fairy Killer, and you had the motive to kill at least one other victim. But I wonder if your reinvention or regaining power over your life was your decision or if you were influenced by someone else. Did you really choose to train with survivalist groups and live off the grid or did someone influence you to do those things?"

Amy gave him a dirty look. She didn't like where this was going. He was essentially insulting her by saying that she couldn't make her own choices and she was easily influenced. What woman wouldn't be insulted by that! She replied. "You think my friend Sara basically forced me to make those choices because I couldn't do it on my own, is that what you're getting at?"

"You tell me, how much did she influence you compared to you making those choices on your own?"

This line of questioning was starting to make Amy angry. It showed in her tone as she said. "Just because I regained power over my life doesn't mean that I lost my identity. You men think we're so fragile after a tragedy that we can't make our own decisions. You think we need somebody like you to come along and do it for us."

Jim interrupted. "That's not what I'm getting at. I just want to know how much of an influence she was on you or if it's possible that we're looking in the wrong direction when it comes to our profile. She seems to be just like you so I want to know more."

"Detective Summers, I've always made my own decisions. I may value the opinions of others, but my decisions have always been my own. Now whether my old friend Sara is who you're truly looking for, I don't have an answer for you. I personally don't think she's capable of murder. Even when she told me our first Christmas together that she wished she could take Don Bennett's life and ease my pain, I didn't think she was truly capable of killing him, it wasn't in her nature, but I guess you'll have to decide that for yourself."

"When was the last you spoke to her?"

"10 years ago. She used to be an actress and got an acting job in New Mexico for a little while. She came back to get some of the things that she left at my place. I couldn't find them at the time. But our conversation was cold and awkward. She went back to New Mexico and I never saw her again." Amy walked over to the little storage room in the office. She walked inside and grabbed a box. She told Jim. When I went back to Texas to see my sister, I also went back to get some of the things that I had left with her. I actually found a box of Sara's things. I think this is what she was looking for back then. I honestly don't want to hold on to them anymore so you can have them. And that's all I have to say about her." Jim didn't want to press the issue. There wasn't any need to, especially since Amy Henderson was willing to give up some of her old friend's things. Perhaps what was in that box could tell him more about Sara than Amy could. At the very least, she was worth looking into. Besides, the name Sara Rogers felt familiar to him, he could have sworn he had heard it before or seen it on some document. Either way, it was familiar.

Amy looked over at Hannah and asked. "Now what do you want to ask me? Jim stepped outside of the office while Hannah asked her questions. Surprisingly enough, Amy Henderson was very helpful about the Republic of Texas Patriots safe houses and where they might be able to find David Houston.

As Jim was standing outside, a young woman came up to him. She asked. "Are you here to arrest Amy?"

"No," he answered. "I don't think we need to. But can I ask why you're here?"

Hearing Jim's answer brought a smile to the young woman's face. Jim could tell that she saw Amy as a mother figure who would protect her. The young woman answered his question. "My husband used to beat me…almost every day. One day I just ran away and Amy found me in town. She gave me a place to live and when my husband came looking for me, Amy told him that if he ever came back she'd kill him. She told him that I was no longer his. She saved me and she's helping me file for divorce. Most of the women here are in the same situation. This place is a refuge and we all owe our lives to Amy Henderson"

    Jim honestly couldn't find fault in that. In fact, he couldn't find anything at fault or suspicious about this place. He always relied on his instincts when it came to potential suspects and after talking with her, he knew she wasn't the killer. All Amy Henderson really was, was a woman who survived a tragedy, rebuilt her life, and became a savior for women just like her. You don't arrest someone like that despite a few mistakes, you give them a medal or simply tell them thank you.

44

Maisie's eyes were we're starting to sting a little bit from reading dozens of case files. She had been at it practically all day and it was only a matter of time before her eyes started to hurt. But worst of all, she hadn't found anything yet. There was no connection between Judge Fitzgerald and any of the other victims. She finished with the file that she had been reading and then grabbed another one off the pile sitting in front of her. At this point, she was pretty much just skimming through the case files looking for certain names. She almost missed it, but then it popped up right in front at her. Finally, a breakthrough. Maisie cheered enthusiastically with a curse word. "Holy Shit!"

The words startled Vanessa who was sitting down at the other end of the conference table reading through files herself. Her yell surprised James as well, which led him to walk out of his office and see what was going on. Vanessa asked her. "What is it? Did you find something?"

Maisie looked up from the file, her eyes as big as a kid's eyes after walking into a candy store. Oh yeah, I just found something big. Vanessa and James both walked to where she was sitting and peered over her shoulder at the case File. She said. "In 2006 Hugo Blackmon was charged with making an erotic film with underage girls. The presiding judge was Craig Fitzgerald."

Shocked, Vanessa replied. "No shit, what happened with the case?"

"It was dismissed for lack of evidence." Maisie skimmed through the case file and found what she was looking for. "Here it is, the cameraman who helped shoot the film died of a drug overdose and then the film in question mysteriously disappeared so they had no choice but to dismiss it."

James replied. "But there was an actual film and a grand jury had to have seen it to indict, correct?"

"I suppose that's true."

Vanessa commented. "So, this not only provides a connection between the judge and another victim, but we have" evidence that Hugo Blackmon was into some dirty shit besides harassing women."

"That's what it looks like. It also suggests that he likes to make his own snuff films just like William Staples."

Vanessa thought for a moment. "Both victims were killed in Austin. They might have even known each other since they were into the same thing. "

Maisie replied to her. "It's a good possibility. But I'm also a bit surprised to hear that Hugo Blackmon was into snuff films. Wasn't the film director the head of a Texas Film Studio, that's the kind of thing that can get you shut down, right!"

James spoke up. "It's not really that far of a stretch to think he would do something like this, after all, early in his career he directed erotic films. And while that work wasn't really classified as XXX pornographic films, they were the kind of erotic stories that were supposed to have a story to them like 'skinamax' films."

"Really?"

"Yeah, I discovered that 4 years ago when I was doing a background check on him during our original investigation. And I do believe some of these films are listed under his imdb.com credits."

Vanessa asked. "If he directed pornographic films, directors tend to stay with the same company that produces them. Do you know the name of the company he made these films for?"

"No, but we can do a quick search." James went to his laptop and looked up the films and whom they were produced by. "There is a company that financed the erotic films, which he directed early in his career, it's called Erotic X Unlimited."

Hearing that name was shocking to Maisie and Vanessa, more so than the connection between the judge and Hugo Blackmon. They had heard that name before and Hugo Blackmon wasn't the only victim connected to that company. Maisie commented. "You got to be kidding; Hugo Blackmon directed films for the same company that provided the webcam services that the first victim Mike Sturgess liked to use. I think we're beginning to see a pattern and these victims are connected in more ways than one."

James softly smiled. "It's a small world among criminals. They may not necessarily know each other, but they're usually mixed up in the same kind of shit. Should we really be that surprised by the connections?"

Vanessa and did not disagree. This was getting better and better metaphorically speaking. They were finally beginning to see the light at the end of their proverbial tunnel.

It was time to go home. Jim and Hannah boarded the FBI plane, looking forward to heading back to Texas. It was a long trip just for a day. Sure, they could have stayed overnight, but Jim was also glad to be heading home. He'd already spent too much time away from Gina and the kids because of this case, spending the night in Colorado would do more harm than good, so it was worth taking a late-night flight back to Texas. As they were getting seated Jim asked his sister. "Did you get everything you needed from her?"

Hannah smiled. "Yes. She was very forthcoming. She had no problem helping us find David Houston. It's also very clear that she has no lost love for that piece of shit."

"So, the FBI won't be arresting her?"

"Not today."

"Good, she doesn't need to be arrested. She just needs to be left alone to do some good in this world."

"I agree. I have to admit, it's pretty impressive what she's done with her little commune. What about you? Did she satisfy your curiosity?"

Jim smiled. "Yes, she did and more."

"I take it she's not a suspect anymore?"

"Not by me."

"What about the friend that she told you about?"

"I don't know, I figure we'll at least look into her just to be on the safe side."

Hannah nodded in agreement. "It's interesting that she gave you a box of her friend's things, have you looked inside yet?"

Jim paused for a moment; he had almost forgotten about the box and even told his sister that. But he also said to her. "I'll take a look at everything when we get back to Texas."

Hannah nudged him like a little sister would when she wanted to bother her big brother. "You should open it now…I admit, I'm a little curious about what's in there."

Jim laughed at his sister's curiosity. She was always too curious for her own good, which in the end, made her a good FBI agent. Of course, being his little sister, he just considered her too nosey. But he gave in and opened up the box. It's not that Jim wasn't curious about the contents of the box; he was just going to open it with the rest of the team. As he looked inside, his sister asked, not being able to get a good look herself. "What did you find?"

Jim looked more closely. "Looks like there's an old laptop in the box, some books, and some old CDs." He started pulling the contents out. Hannah commented on the laptop. "Look at that thing; it's got to be like 11 or 12 years old. You know that's not worth anything." Jim laughed at her comment as he started pulling out the books. That's when Jim was finally stunned by the contents of the box. He looked at the titles and quickly got an eerie feeling. Some might call it déjà vu, considering what he and his team have been discussing regarding the profile of the Black Fairy. The only words that came to mind when he saw the titles of the book were, "fucking Christ."

His words startled Hannah. "What is it?"

"The books. Sara Rogers owned a copy of the Divine Comedy."

"What's so peculiar about that?" Jim and his team hadn't really talked to anybody outside of the task force regarding the fictional book, The Dark Fairy, and its similarity to Dante's The Divine Comedy. It was still pretty much just a theory at this point, and he wasn't quite sure if everybody believed the book was really written by the black fairy. Jim explained everything to her and how owning a copy of the book was important to their investigation. There was also a textbook on Christian Mythology and Symbols. And finally, the third book he pulled out was about Celtic Mythology, Symbols, and Folklore. While there were other books in the box, they were meaningless compared to the three that he pulled out. But as he started flipping through them, he saw that two of them were from the school library, a Catholic School library to be exact. Jim stared at a stamped portion on the title page. It read "property of St. John Paul Catholic School. It was the same school that Lori Kellerman had graduated from in Houston Texas. It was starting to make sense. One more piece of the puzzle and a coincidence that was turning out to be more than just a simple theory. It was still too early to tell if Lori might actually be the same person, but every part of Jim's Instinct was telling him that they had just found who they'd been looking for all these years. They had a name, not an alias, but a real name. While the initial shock was starting to wear off, Jim asked his sister if he had time to make a phone call. They still had a few minutes before takeoff.

He called James. He wasn't ready to tell the team everything until they knew more about this Sara Rogers but figured James could start on a background check. The phone rang twice, and James answered. He saw that it was Jim on his caller ID and said. "Hey, how is Colorado?"

Jim replied. "It's beautiful, would love to get some fishing in, but we're on our way back."

Curiously, James had to ask. "Is Amy Henderson still a suspect?"

"No, we can rule her out. But do you remember us talking about a friend she had, that she met in a support group and did all that survivalist stuff with?"

"Yeah, vaguely."

"Amy gave us her name and a box of some things that she still had from when they lived together. Inside the box, I found some books, The Divine Comedy, a book on Christian Mythology and symbols, and another book about Celtic Mythology and Folklore."

"Normally, I would say that's odd, but with this case, that's a huge coincidence."

"It gets better, the book on Christian Symbolism and Mythology along with the copy of the Divine Comedy we're taken from a Catholic School library...St. John Paul Catholic School in Houston Texas."

James was shocked as hell. Probably even more so than Jim had been when he saw where the books came from. Surprise filled his tone as he replied. "No shit. Can you tell when they were last checked out? Jim looked inside the copy of the Divine Comedy. It still had one of that old school library check-out history cards where you could see the last person who checked it out. "Last checked out by Sara Rogers in December of 1994."

James thought for a moment. "That's around the same time that Lori Kellerman attended the school, according to the school records we were able to get."

"I thought so... we have to find out her real name."

"What's going on with that?"

"CID is sending a lawyer to New Mexico tomorrow to petition the court."

So, I'm assuming Sara Rogers is the name since she was the last person to check that book out."

"Yes, but you need to look up her full name which is Sara Gwendolyn Rogers... it'll be easier to find that way. I need you to pull up where she has lived over the last 15 years. Let's see if we can put a timeline together."

James said he would do just that, but after thinking about it for a moment or two, he had to ask. "The name Sara Rogers, feels familiar. I feel like, I've read that name somewhere."

Jim laughs to himself. "You know I was thinking the same thing. I know I've heard that name somewhere or read it like in a case file. It feels very familiar."

James smiled. "I'm sure it will come to us eventually, but I'll get to work on the background check and have something for you when you get back to the office."

The flight attendants were motioning for Jim to shut off his phone because they were about to leave. He quickly got off the phone with James and then put everything back in the box. But as they were about to take off, there was a looming thought that Jim couldn't shake. He wondered what was on the laptop.

45

It was another day, another early morning when Jim arrived at the detective agency. He was tired and hoping the coffee would keep him awake. Yesterday had been a very long day with a trip to Colorado and even later getting back. But it was worth it; today was the day that they had what Jim would eventually call the perfect suspect. He wanted to get there before anybody else did, but he also knew that James would be the first one in the office. He knew that James would have a prepared preliminary report from his background check on Sara Rogers. Jim wanted to see it first. He didn't want any surprises before he presented what he had found to the rest of the team. As Jim walked into the office, he finished his Togo cup of coffee. James already had another cup waiting for him. Making him laugh, he commented. "Wow, thank you. You might just be better than a wife."

    Smiling, James replied. "I've just been doing this for a long time. And the first rule when investigating a hard case, always have plenty of legal stimulants to keep you going. In the 80s, we could just do cocaine, but now all we really have is nicotine and coffee."

    Jim took a sip and nodded as a way of saying thank you. He asked. "What did you find out?"

    James handed him a file folder. "Quite a bit, actually. I think we hit the jackpot with this suspect. Her history compared to the timeline of the murders is very interesting, putting it mildly."

Jim skimmed through the file. He looked up at James, stunned at what he just read. "Jesus, this is more than just a little coincidental."

Yeah. It's almost too true to believe, isn't it? I'm not saying that every little thing lines up, but there's an awful lot of interesting connections."

"I'll say. Did you ever figure out where you recognized her name? I still can't figure out where I've seen it."

James confidently smiled and then handed Jim a case file. "I did remember, and it was from a case... do you remember me handing you this case file to you 4 years ago because I thought it was interesting."

Jim looked at the title on the file. It was the dinner party murder. That was almost too shocking to believe as well. He replied. "I remember you handing me this, but how is she connected to the dinner party murder?"

"She was a person of interest because she was going to testify against the CEO of Lonestar Bottled Water after her brother-in-law mysteriously died." Jim looked confused so James went on to further explain. "Sara's sister, Christine was married to a man by the name of Michael Branson. He was a whistleblower for the bottled water company. He was a chemist and claimed that there were toxins in the water that were causing serious illness He was going to testify in a lawsuit. Anyway, the family mysteriously died, the autopsy report says they were poisoned because the water supply in their home was contaminated. Talk about the Irony!"

"Holy shit. I remember hearing something about that."

"Well, the lawyers that were bringing the lawsuit on behalf of the families were going to have Sara testify because supposedly her brother-in-law told her what he had found out. But without the primary whistleblower, everything was just hearsay and the case was dismissed. When the CEO and his dinner party mysteriously died. Sara was the police's main person of interest, but she had an alibi and they couldn't connect her to the murders."

Jim paused for a moment, pondering what he had just heard. The story was hardly forgettable and he understood why she would be a person of interest in the Dinner Party Murder. If he were investigating it, he would have looked at her too, because she was an awfully good suspect. As the two men continued to talk and make themselves another cup of coffee, both Vanessa and Maisie walked in. Detective Morgan and Detective Lester weren't far behind. A few minutes later everybody got settled in the conference room. Maisie was the first to ask. "So, Amy Henderson.... is she still a suspect?"

    Jim shook his head and replied. "No, I had a nice talk with her. She does have an alibi, but she did point us in the right direction. Remember the friend that her sister told us about when we talked to her 4 years ago." Maisie nodded yes. Jim continued. "We found out more about her and I think we have our prime suspect now. James did a preliminary background check, and we'll hand out copies. Her history, it's pretty interesting and we're going to go over everything. We're going to see how she connects to all of this. Also, another person of interest is Lori Kellerman since she was the last person to talk to Judge Fitzgerald before he was killed. We have a background check on her, and she and Sara Rogers may be the same person." The rest of the team by the looks on their face were surprised to hear that, but before Maisie could ask, Jim responded. "I know how shocking that might sound. I'll explain everything. I'm sorry that you're just now hearing about her, but James and I wanted to be sure before we presented anything." Nobody in the room put up an argument about their reasons for withholding information until now. It made sense. You could have dozens of theories in any investigation regarding a serial killer, but it was always better to narrow them down with actual facts so that you never get lost in the true narrative.

    Jim passed out copies of their preliminary background check. "Okay, this is what we have. Sara Rogers was born May 6th, 1977. Adopted in August of 1977 to Thomas and Martha Rogers. He was in the oil business, so she grew up in Houston. She had a sister named Christine who was born to Thomas and Martha in 1979. Father made really good money and sent both of his kids to a private Catholic School. Both of them went to St. John Paul Catholic School in Houston from grade 6 through 12. Sara graduated in 1995. She also got an undergraduate degree in computer science and programming from Rice University. She was actually a double major and her second degree is in modern drama. She did her Masters at Trinity University in English literature. And yes, in case you're wondering. She is Catholic and had a good Catholic education."

James took over since he had most of the information on Lori Kellerman. He said. "We don't have much information about Lori Kellerman especially since it was a name change after her divorce and her records were sealed, but because she was allowed to change her name in the databases of where she went to school. We know that she went to St. John Paul Catholic School in Houston and there is a record of her attending Rice University. While the records are incomplete because of the name change, we do know that she studied drama from the number of classes that are on her transcript."

Vanessa asked. "Are you saying she went to that school at the same time as Sara Rogers?"

"I'm sorry; I should have said that first. Yes, she was there at the same time. I have a graduation date of 1994. The birthday we have is September 14th, 1976. The birthdays and graduation dates are different. But that could be because of the name change and getting a new birthday with her new identity. It wouldn't be prudent to give her the exact same birthday. "

"So, you actually think that Lori Kellerman used to be Sara Rogers?"

Jim answered the question. "Yes. According to records, Sara Rogers has pretty much been off the grid since 2008. The last known record we have is her having an apartment in January of 2008. Lori Kellerman was granted a divorce in late December of 2001, her name change was certified in January 2008 and the divorce records were sealed. So, I think because the timeline correlates with one another... Lori Kellerman stopped being Sara Rogers in January of 2008 and started life under her new identity."

It made sense to a point, but there were still a lot of holes in their theory about Lori Kellerman and Sara Rodgers being the same person. Maisie had a lot of questions, but she started with just one. "Okay, so Lori Kellerman was married and then got a divorce. I'm assuming because the records are sealed we don't know the name of her husband?"

"No, but James was able to find that her marital status is listed as Widow, so we assume he's dead."

"Does Sara Rodgers have a marriage record?"

James looked at the report. He didn't know off the top of his head. "As a matter of fact, she does. She was married in 1999 to a man by the name of Roberto Costa. There was a petition for divorce in 2007, that's all we have."

"Well, maybe we can look at his records and cross-reference them to Sara Rogers and Lori Kellerman. Maybe we can look at their photos and confirm if they're the same person. Speaking of photos, have you done a comparison?"

James replied to her question. "We got Lori's photo off of her Facebook page. The only photos that I could find of Sara Rogers were production stills. She was an actress and had parts in some of the TV shows that were produced by Outlaw Studios, which by the way is the same Texas Studio that Hugo Blackmon was the head of. Anyway, there's no Facebook account for Sara Rogers and I even checked imdb.com. Her account was deleted, but she is still listed as part of the cast for some of the movies and TV shows produced by the studio on those individual pages. There are also production stills on the site and I was able to find her because she's listed in the photo credits."

Jim remarked. "Nice job. Way to really dig to find out what she looks like."

"Yeah, I actually had to work hard on that one. Sara Rogers is pretty much a ghost on the internet except for some records and a few of the films she was that you can find on amazon.com. But, I don't necessarily trust all that because she could be in makeup and a wig."

"True."

Maisie responded. "Well, are there similarities with the photos?"

James looked at her and said. Yes and no. "From what I can tell, Sara Rogers had long dark brown hair, almost black. She looks to be about 5'6" and Lori Kellerman looks to be about the same height as well. But Lori has lighter brown hair. I can't make out the eye color of either one of them from photos."

Maisie asked another question." Do you think Lori Kellerman's hair could have been dyed to look lighter brown?"

James shrugged. He had been a good detective, but he never noticed things like that. For him to notice the difference in hair, it would have to be a dramatic change like a complete changing of color and or going from really long to Audrey Hepburn short. He said. "Honestly, I don't know. I can't tell the difference, but I guess it's possible." He handed the photo to Maisie and said. "Take a look, you tell me." She did. She studied the photo for a couple of minutes. Maisie responded. "I agree, it's a possibility. It looks like it was probably dyed, but she could also be covering up gray hair or adding highlights. But I can't tell if her hair was naturally dark from the photo. They do look similar. But it's hard to tell from a production photo if Sara Rogers is in film makeup. I mean, I guess it could be the same person."

Detective Morgan finally chimed in. "Okay, besides two people who could be the same person, how do you connect her to all of these victims?"

Jim replied to her question. "We know she's connected to Don Bennett through Amy Henderson. When I was talking with Amy, she did say that when they were together, one time Sara mentioned that she wish she could kill Don Bennett and take Amy's pain away."

Detective Morgan nodded. "Okay, but that's one person. It's a simple association because of someone she was in a relationship with, hardly incriminating evidence." What about everybody else? Why and how is she targeting them?"

"Well, she was living in New Mexico in 2007 when the Mike Sturgess murder occurred. We have her in New Mexico from January of 2007 to January of 2008 and that's when the petition for divorce by Lori Kellerman happened."

"Okay, that particular timeline makes sense. But again, why target Mike Sturgess? I guess. What I'm getting at is, what makes Sara Rogers want to kill... is there a tragic event in her life that drives her to do this because I don't see her as someone being capable of killing another person."

That was the moment when James pulled out a copy of the Dinner Party Murder and the history of why it happened. At this point he and Jim were the only two people who really knew about it. He replied to Detective Morgan. "I think I can answer that question. I was telling Jim that I recognized the name Sara Rogers when he called me on his way back from Colorado. There was a murder that has always fascinated me and it was one of the files we were looking through four years ago. It's called the Dinner party murder. The CEO of the Lonestar bottled water company was murdered at a dinner party in 2006 along with his wife and all of his guests. His company had been accused of allowing toxins into the water that were causing people to be sick. They had a chemist on staff that became a whistleblower, but the case never went to trial because he died along with his family. They were poisoned from the water supply in their house. The Whistleblower is Sara Rogers' his brother-in-law. He was married to Sara Rogers' younger sister, Christine. Apparently, they all got really sick and died during a family dinner. The only reason Sara didn't die is she arrived late, and they were already convulsing when she got to the house. There was no direct evidence linking Lonestar water to that murder. But Sara also became the sole Witness in the lawsuit brought against the bottled water company because her brother-in-law had told her what was going on, but the lawsuit was dismissed when her brother-in-law died, and she was deemed an unreliable witness because it was all hearsay. Sara Rogers was the main person of interest in the Dinner Party Murder, but there was no evidence linking her to it and she had more than one alibi placing her somewhere else at the time. Nor was there any evidence of her being able to poison the wine that everybody was drinking at the dinner party that caused them to die. The murder is still unsolved."

Maisie replied. "You think she did it and this is what drove her to her killing spree?"

James softly smiled. "If you're looking for a tragic event that drives someone to want to kill people who get away with heinous crimes, don't you think this would qualify?"

"Sure, but it's still no proof she actually did anything and that's what we're really looking end of the day."

Detective Morgan spoke up again. "You're trying to match a timeline. We know that Sara Rogers lived in Albuquerque, New

Mexico at the time that William Sturgess was murdered. And if she became Lori Kellerman in 2008 where was she living at the time of the other murders. Was she living in Austin in 2009 when Hugo Blackmon was killed? Where was she living at the time of Don Bennett's murder and Jack Perry's murder or did she travel to where they were murdered? I mean it's not uncommon for a serial killer to travel outside of their area to kill people, so how does the timeline match?"

James replied." Lori Kellerman did live in the Austin area for about a year-and-a-half. She did move from New Mexico to Austin so she was there about the time that Hugo Blackmon was murdered in May of 2009. I believe she started renting an apartment in Dallas at the end of June 2009 and has pretty much been there ever since."

"So if we assume she really is the killer, then that means that she traveled to the Odessa area to kill Jack Perry and then has been traveling to Austin to kill the latest victims and of course, travel to Houston back in 2013 to kill Henry Frankston."

Jim replied. "That's our working theory, such as it is."

Vanessa hadn't really said anything at this point. She wanted to know more about the background information and going over every little detail. Something stood out and made her incredibly curious. "Well, it was more odd than anything else. She finally spoke up and said. "Sara Rogers was certified as a court reporter and Lori Kellerman is also certified as a court reporter. Sara Rogers was certified in 1997 when she was still in college and while we don't have an exact date for when Lori Kellerman was certified, we know that she was a court reporter and probably still certified."

Jim replied. "Yeah, so!"

"Why is she a court reporter at all? Sara Rogers was a double major and got a degree in computer science and drama and then a master's in English literature. She could get a high-paying computer programming job or be a college professor. I understand if she was doing court reporting when she was in college as a part-time gig. Why continue to do it when you're more qualified to do something else in your field of study?"

Maisie replied to our inquiry. "She was an actress for a number of years after college and even did production work. I can't imagine that pays very much at an independent studio in Texas, maybe she did court reporting as a way to make money and set her own schedule?"

"True, it is a possibility. But couldn't you get freelance programming gigs or tech support gigs that probably paid more? I see in her job history that she worked for a tech support company in New Mexico, but she still did court reporting too. I would think the tech job is more flexible and would pay more than court reporting. I just find it odd that she would keep doing it. Am I the only one that finds that odd?"

Ever since Vanessa mentioned court reporting, Jim had this eerie feeling when it came to Sara Rogers. Ever since he came back from Colorado he'd been trying to figure out where he had seen that name and then it finally dawned on him. He saw it in a court case file regarding one of the lawsuits against Don Bennett. It was a piece of paper that listed everybody involved with the case from the judge to the prosecutor to the defense attorney all the way down to the court reporter on file. Jim rushed out for a moment to go find the box that had court cases regarding Don Bennett. It took him a few minutes, but he found it. He had been sued multiple times for sexual harassment, but this particular case was brought on by two different defendants in the Austin area while he was a state senator. The court reporter on the case was Sara Rogers. Jim took the file back into the conference room and said to everybody. "I finally figured out where I had seen her name. She was the court reporter on record for one of the lawsuits brought against Don Bennett. This particular lawsuit happened in 2006." It was more than just a huge coincidence. It's what connected Sara Rogers to Don Bennett beyond being in a relationship with Amy Henderson. Everybody in the room was stunned, but more so when Jim posed the question that was on all of their minds... the what-if question. He said. "What if that's how Sara Rogers is targeting these victims, what if that's how she knows about them and how they got away with their crimes... who better to know their cases in and out other than the judge or the attorneys than the court reporter... the official record keeper. And isn't it possible that a court reporter could also double as a court clerk who would have access to old case files!"

Everybody in the room just paused as time was standing still by the sheer weight of his revelation. It was something nobody had considered and why would they? Nobody ever thinks about the court reporter. They keep the official record, know all the details of a case, but are never heard and rarely seen. For the most part, they are invisible in a court of law. Or as Jim put it, the least likely of suspects. He said to everybody in the room. "I know it may be a wild theory, but really think about it. Who would even notice? In my opinion, I think that's how she's targeting them and I think she might be connected to other cases regarding these victims because that's how she knows about their history. We've been looking at what connects all of these victims and trying to find what would connect her to them. They're not chosen at random. They're chosen for a reason and it's because she knows about them."

Maisie spoke up. "I have no argument against your theory, but while you were away we found a connection between Hugo Blackmon and Judge Fitzgerald. He was a presiding judge over a case where he was accused of making a film with underage girls. The case was dismissed, but now I wonder who the court reporter was because this case was also in 2006." Nobody in the room debated her logic. She went and found the case file, especially the document that listed everybody involved in the case. She found the name of the court reporter and it was shocking to say the least. She looked at everybody in the room. "The court reporter was Sara Rogers."

After all of these years, they had been wondering how the killer knew about these victims, and how they were targeted. Nobody had, had an answer to that question so it was assumed they were chosen at random and even with the Dark Fairy book explaining how all the victims were connected, nothing ever suggested how they were targeted. Finally, they had an answer. It was huge. Nobody could deny the simple logic of a court reporter targeting criminals who got away with it. Even Detective Morgan with all of her cynicism saw the possibility. And so here they were beyond any simple logic. Two court cases involving two of the victims and the one thing that connected all of it was Sara Rogers being the court reporter. Jim said. "We need to pull up every case where she's the court reporter on record and see if it matches any of our victims. We also need to find every court case where Lori Kellerman was the court reporter that involves any of our victims and cross-reference them."

Detective Morgan agreed with what they needed to do, but there was still something bothering her. It was her cynicism that wouldn't allow her to buy into one of their theories. She asked. "I get the theory about the killer having a Catholic Education. But I'm curious, couldn't any kind of religious education lead someone to do this? Why does it have to be a Catholic Education? And I get the use of the Divine Comedy as a metaphor regarding the supposed book she wrote, but it seems more conjecture when your theory is so specific. Are we absolutely sure that it's this Sara Rogers / Lori Kellerman. How do we prove any of it?"

Jim replied. "Amy gave us a box of Sara's old things that she still had. I guess they got mixed up with her stuff years ago, I didn't think anything of it until I pulled out the books that were in the box. I brought the box here." Jim laid out all the books on the conference table, but he showed Detective Morgan, the copy of the Divine Comedy and the textbook on Christian Symbolism and Mythology. He said. "If you look inside at the title page of both of those books, it'll say property of St. John Paul Catholic School. Those were her books she used for an elective course at the school about Christian Symbolism and Mythology. It doesn't get any more specific than that when it comes to the education level of our killer." Jim gave her a stern Look. "Do you still think this may not be our killer?"

The books were another shocking revelation. Nobody in the room could deny where the ideas and the symbolism behind her murders manifested. The ideas were rooted in her consciousness when she was an impressionable teenager. One could say that it was at this point it became ingrained in her own DNA. Up to this point, they'd always had more questions than answers... there were still plenty of questions, but they finally had more answers. They now had the biggest break to date in the Black Fairy case.

46

New Mexico Courts of Law have never been grand. They were simple and quiet. They had an intimate feel to them and judges never seemed superior even to the criminals who came before the courts. But that didn't mean that New Mexico judges weren't strict or stuck their noses up at any outsider trying to tell them how to interpret the law. The lawyer that Texas State CID had sent to petition for Lori Kellerman's divorce files was starting to get a sense of that as he stood before the judge. He didn't exactly receive a warm welcome when he went before Judge Newsome's Court, and they did everything they could to remind him that he was an outsider.

Judge Newsom carefully looked over the petition. He studied every point of law that the lawyer tried to make for his argument on why Lori Kellerman's files should be unsealed so they could see her real name. He thought to himself as he examined the judge's facial expressions while reading motion, he wasn't convinced. Finally, the judge spoke. "Mr. Renner. You've made a compelling argument here, but it isn't good enough. I fail to see any actual evidence linking this young woman to a bunch of murders in Texas. All your detective seems to have are a bunch of theories."

Mister Renner replied. "Your honor, we're not denying that there isn't actual physical evidence that ties her to these crimes. Yes, it's a lot of major coincidences, but when you're building a profile of a killer that's all you have in the beginning and that's what our investigators are working on in order to get the evidence you're asking for. One of the key pieces of information is to see what her real name was and to see if it matches to the name they have as their primary suspect.

The judge paused for a moment, taking in what the lawyer was saying. It was another compelling argument, but he wasn't being swayed. He asked the lawyer. "Can you 100% absolutely tell me that there isn't any other way to confirm their so-called theory about the identity of this woman? I ask because we sealed these records for a reason, it's to protect their anonymity even from what we consider unlawful searches and background checks."

"Your honor, I don't know if there's a 100% guarantee that this is the only way they can confirm her identity. I don't know if anybody can say that with certainty, but this is the only way we know how to do it. Now we're not asking to make copies of those files, if somebody can just show me what her real name was, that's it, and as a representative of the State of Texas, I can confirm that with the investigators.

The judge still gave him a dissatisfying look. "And what makes you so trustworthy to be given this information... am I to assume that out of the thousands of lawyers in the State of Texas, you're the one lawyer that can absolutely be trusted and isn't a crook? Because here in New Mexico, trust is a very important factor in determining whether you can be given such privileged information. We take a man's character into careful consideration."

"Your honor, I completely understand where you're coming from. But this is privileged information, and I am bound by the attorney-client privilege to keep this information secret... isn't that a form of trust."

"I haven't met a lawyer that hasn't broken the bond of privilege at some point or another in their career oh, it's just that not every lawyer gets caught."

The lawyer softly smiled. It was a snide lawyer joke and under the circumstances, it was a little humorous, but he understood where the judge was coming from especially since he clearly didn't like Texans all that much. But he did reply. "Your honor, my record in the state of Texas is exemplary; I've never had any complaints to the bar about my record or being able to maintain privilege with my clients."

The judge sarcastically smiled. That may be in Texas sir, can you say the same thing in New Mexico, which is a far superior state."

"No, your honor because it's the first time I've ever argued before a judge in the state of New Mexico. But I would hope that how I have acted in your court of law would prove that I could be trusted."

"It's too early to tell if that's true or not. But the simple truth is I'm not convinced that you need this young woman's real name for your investigation. If you had more sufficient evidence and not just a theory from a bunch of Texas investigators, that would do more to convince me. Surely there's another way to determine if she's your killer or not? When we seal records, we take the secrecy of those records very serious here in New Mexico because it's usually protecting an innocent person and the last thing that we want to see is a revenge killing by the family of someone who ended up dead from a spouse having to defend herself and protect her own life. I couldn't in good conscience reveal the contents of those files even if she's not living in New Mexico anymore."

The lawyer wasn't exactly happy with the answer, so he made one more argument to try and convince the judge before the final ruling. "Your honor, I completely understand and if she was still living in the state of New Mexico, I would probably side with your argument, but the fact that she's living in Texas should give us a little bit more leeway in seeing what her former name is. It's not like she is completely safe in Texas compared to the possibility of a revenge killing in New Mexico."

"Are you saying that she can only be safe in Texas compared to New Mexico, I hope you're not insinuating that we can't keep our citizens safe?"

"No your honor, I would never say that. I'm just merely pointing out the fact that living in another state shouldn't make the concern for her safety any higher than if she was still living here."

The judge sat back in his chair. He was attempting to be objective and see if the lawyer's last arguments could sway him. But unfortunately, he had already made up his mind. He wasn't supposed to be biased as a criminal court judge, but he simply didn't like Texans and their superior attitude. And that's all he saw in the lawyer from the moment he entered his courtroom. He said. "While your arguments are thoughtful and of Merit, it's not enough to convince me because of the lack of evidence tying Lori Kellerman to these murders in Texas. You just didn't give me enough evidence. Your petition is denied. Bring me new evidence to support your theory and you may petition my court again."

    Mr. Renner wanted to say one more thing in the hopes of convincing the judge, but the judge had already banged his gavel and that meant the proceedings were over. It was a finality that the lawyer couldn't argue against. For that's how a civilized court of law works... even in New Mexico just like in Texas. The lawyer simply said, "thank you, your honor," and rushed out of court. He grabbed the quickest flight, he could find in order to get back to Texas, where he figured he'd have an easier time convincing a judge to be objective and unbiased. It was something he couldn't say of a New Mexico Court as the whole experience left a bad taste in his mouth.

    It was the day before Thanksgiving and at most companies, employees would be trying to get out early to enjoy the holiday. However, the task force was working late. They would have Thanksgiving off, but there was a lot of research to do when it came to figuring out the timeline with Sara Rogers and the victims, and how they were all connected. Once Jim and the team figured out that she was a court reporter and that's how she was targeting victims, it was fairly easy to cross-reference all of the cases regarding the victims that she was the court reporter for. A shocking pattern emerged after they did that. Robert stopped by the Detective Agency in the afternoon before he left for the holiday. As he walked in, he noticed that the office resembled something like a newsroom. Everybody was bustling about in a frantic mode, trying to find the next piece of information to the rhythmic sounds of typing on computer keyboards. The whole case was one big puzzle, and they were each just trying to find one more piece to complete the big picture.

When Robert walked in, nobody noticed him at first, especially Jim, who had pretty much been staring at the big crime board for most of the day, trying to connect the dots between Sara Rogers and the victims. Robert walked into the conference room and immediately said. "Wow, you all have certainly made serious progress in this case."

Jim turned his serious expression into a soft smile. Progress was an understatement. Soon as they found a few key missing pieces everything started to connect more easily. He replied to Robert. "What brings you in, I figured you'd already be off, did you get my last report."

"I did get the report, thank you," he responded. "Just one more piece of business and then I'm gone. I still can't believe the court reporter connection. When was the last time that's been true in an investigation?"

"I think we're still having a hard time believing it ourselves. But we started cross-referencing her name with cases that she was a court reporter for, and we found quite a bit regarding the victims."

That piqued Robert's curiosity. He responded by asking. "Such as."

"Well, besides the criminal case against Hugo Blackmon that Judge Fitzgerald presided over, we found two different lawsuits against Don Bennett where she was the court reporter, one in 2004 and the other in 2006. Of course, the lawsuits were dismissed. We also found where she was the court reporter in a lawsuit brought against Mike Sturgess back in New Mexico in 2007. Both criminal cases were dropped due to the credibility of the witnesses. The parents of the second witness who committed suicide brought a lawsuit against him. The jury found that he wasn't liable. She was the court reporter on the case."

Robert was stunned at the information. So that's at least four cases where she was the court reporter regarding victims?"

"Yes. We're still looking for more, but that's what we got so far."

"That's still an amazing connection. Have you found how William Staples is connected to all of this?"

"Not exactly. The only thing we have to go on is the cameraman who accused him of making the snuff film that he was arrested for. He also worked as a cameraman for Outlaw Studios which was run by Hugo Blackmon. He was known to have made erotic films for a website owned by Erotic X Unlimited where you could upload any kind of erotic film, especially snuff films."

"You mentioned the name of that company before in your report."

"Yes, Mike Sturgess had a subscription to a webcam site owned by the company that featured underage girls."

"Do you think the connection is that they all used services with this company, especially the really, dark illegal stuff?"

Jim nodded. "It is the one thing that does connect them, but there are millions of users, so it begs the question, why these guys, specifically? I think there's a bigger connection that we just haven't found, but for now, this is what we have."

"And have you found a connection for Henry Frankston."

"Unfortunately, no. But I figure with her being a court reporter and part-time court clerk she had access to records and just somehow found out that he was a missing sex offender. Then she hunted him down and made him part of all this."

Robert softly smiled as he looked at the big crime board that resembled something more like some abstract puzzle with the various strings connecting each of the victims and the killer. He said. "Well, no matter what happens, you did an incredible job with all of this. I know a lot of people won't believe that a woman could have killed all these men, but the fact that you and your team found the connections is more than what anybody else could have done. You should be proud."

Jim replied. I'll be proud when we catch Sara Rogers." But Jim was also curious on why Robert even stopped by in the first place. This conversation could have easily been done over the phone. He asked Robert why he stopped by. Robert replied. "I wanted to tell you in person that the petition for Lori Kellerman's court records was denied."

"Why?"

"The judge didn't think you had enough evidence to unseal the records and get a look at Lori Kellerman's real name. Plus, according to our lawyer, he was a little biased when it came to Texans. He did leave open the possibility that we can petition the court again if we have more evidence, especially physical evidence. He made a point of saying that we didn't have enough during his ruling."

Jim wasn't satisfied with the answer which was obvious by the look on his face. "I don't know what to tell you about getting more evidence. I mean we've painted a pretty good picture of why Sara Rogers is our killer, but we don't have any concrete or physical evidence that ties her to any of this. It's like I've said before, we're probably going to have to catch her in the act. It'll be the only way we can connect her to a crime scene. So, I honestly don't know how else to find out Lori Kellerman's real name."

Robert had a confident look. It came with knowing more than the people under him as it should be with the boss. He replied. "I know it sucks about the court ruling, but I may have a different solution for you. Something that may be easier to obtain than petitioning a New Mexico Court."

"Okay, you have my attention."

"Your report said that Sara Rogers was adopted. I did some checking on my own. She was adopted in Ireland. She was adopted from a Catholic Convent. She was the child of an unwed young mother and of course back in those days under the law, you could just take a child and adopt them from a Catholic organization. It's not legal today, but back then one could get away with it, especially if they had lots of money."

Jim replied. Holy Shit…really? I wonder if she knew that."

"Maybe, but in order to bring an adopted child from a foreign country into the US, you have to fill out an I-600 immigration form. Now, Sara Rogers is a very American name, chances are they changed her name from the one given to her at birth."

"Okay, so her name was changed when she was adopted. I don't see how that exactly helps us."

Robert gave him a stern look. "That's what I'm getting at. On that form when you're filling out the information for the child, there are three boxes. One for the given name, one for the current name or the name that it was changed to, and one for any alias. That form would have her given name."

Jim was a bit surprised, but he saw a hole in Roberts's logic. "That's only useful if Sara went back to using that original name and knew where she was adopted from... I mean, it's a possibility, but not very likely."

"That may be true, but it is possible since no one in the states would know her real name...it would be easy to establish an identity from that record. Plus, Kellerman is an Irish name. Now, there's another reason why this document is important. All foreign adoptions have to be registered within Interpol's database. Because they keep track of given birth names that have been changed and any Alias that would go with that, Interpol would have that record. After 9/11 Interpol started adding more information to their databases when it came to names. Every record of a foreign adoption, including the new name they were given when they entered the U.S., But if their name changes for any legal reason during their lifetime, it would have to be updated in their system. Not just when their name changes if they get married, but if they change their name in a court of law. They do this to track potential criminals or terrorists who change their names to move in and out of foreign countries. It's their way of keeping track of what might be a false identity."

"You're saying that if Sara Rogers is Lori Kellerman the name change granted by the court would be recorded in their database?"

"Exactly. Plus, her immigration record would be updated with any aliases as well. You see, Federal and international agencies try to keep their database up to date and networked so it's easier to pull information on potential international criminals. We started doing a better job of that after 9/11 as well as Interpol. Instead of petitioning a New Mexico Court maybe we should have petitioned the immigration department or Interpol to see if there's any name that's been added to her file."

"That's brilliant. I didn't even know that about Interpol, but it does make sense."

"Honestly, I didn't until our lawyer presented that as a solution after the court denied our request. The problem is, only a federal agency can request documents pertaining to her immigration or Interpol."

"You mean a federal agency like the FBI!"

"Yes, but it's a good thing that you actually know an FBI agent that can help you out with that."

Jim gave him a dirty look. "You know how many favors I owe my sister, and this will be a big one."

Robert smiled. "True, but wouldn't it be worth it, if we actually found out Sara Rogers' real name, like for example…Lori Kellerman. I think you need to bite the bullet and ask her for help again…this investigation is too important."

Jim didn't say anything for a while. However, Robert was right. He told his boss that he would call her and get the ball rolling, but he also knew his sister would never let him forget that he had to ask for help again. That was almost worse than not being able to solve this case. In the meantime, Maisie walked into the conference room. She had some good news of her own. She said to Jim. "Hey, you know how you asked me a while back to check employment records with Highland security and see if the killer might have worked there?"

Jim curiously replied. "Yes, vaguely.

"Well, I think I got something."

"Great, what is it? Did Sara Rogers actually work there?"

"Not exactly. Her employment record had her working for a tech company part-time. Well, that company did service for Highland security, especially work on their server. I talked to a woman who has worked for them for like 20 years and she said there was a young girl who would always service that particular branch. She also said that she became really friendly with Aldo Martinez and believes that they even dated for a little while."

Stunned, Jim replied. "Really does she remember the name of this girl? I asked her if she recognized the name, Lori or Sara.

She said Lori doesn't sound familiar, but Sara does. However, she couldn't be 100% sure. I even emailed the photos we had and she said one of them with Sara Rogers looks familiar."

"Well, I guess that's something. It does Place her at Highland security and having known Aldo Martinez, which is something we suspected all along."

"Yes, it does, but there's more. According to the woman I talked to, the Service Company installed remote login software back in 2007 where they could easily get on somebody's computer or the server and take care of any problems that may occur. She also said that the software was only sold by that company as if it was a uniquely written piece of software sold by that particular tech company. Well, I dug a little deeper and with the use of that particular software, one could remote login to the server from anywhere in the world. They could see schedules and projects that we're going on. And Sara did have a background in computer programming. What if she was the one who wrote that software and installed it on their server so she could log in at any time and see everybody's schedules and the projects that were happening?"

Jim knew where she was going with this. So, you're thinking that she logged in, saw the schedules and figured it out when to kill her victims based on Aldo Martinez's travel schedule, essentially framing him if anybody figured out the pattern behind the murders."

Maisie smiled. "Now wouldn't that be something! It would be one more connection."

Jim confidently smiled. "Yes, it would. Good work Detective."

With each connection, they were getting closer to seeing the big picture. Jim couldn't remember the last time he was this satisfied with his work. Sure, they had had their fair share of ups-and-downs, and bad brakes, but they were starting to see the light at the end of this tunnel. The only question that really remained was how to find Sara Rogers. Of course, there was one piece of information still eluded them. What was the one thing that connected all of it? What was the final act of Sara Rogers's murder masterpiece? Jim could feel they were close to finding out. But he had to make a phone call. It was time to call his sister and ask for another favor. Hopefully, this one would lead to the true name of The Black Fairy.

47

Maisie and Jim pulled up outside of St. Thomas Aquinas Catholic Church. They had about 10 minutes before six o'clock Mass was over. It was the day before Thanksgiving and Jim had one final task to complete before he left for the holidays. His team had done a great job putting together a timeline based on the history of the victims compared to Sara Rogers' own history over the last thirteen years. But the biggest missing piece is what had happened since 2008 when her name changed. They had nothing to go on that put her anywhere close to the crime scenes or if she was the court reporter for any case regarding the victims. They really only had one lead and it was something that Jim had followed up on four years before, but had gotten nowhere. He figured he try one more time before he completely let the idea go. Maisie asked as they were sitting in the car waiting for Mass to be over. "Why are we here? Why did you want me to bring you to a church?"

Jim had asked to hitch a ride with Maisie back to Dallas since she was going home for Thanksgiving. He didn't really explain why, simply said that he was following up on a lead. He answered her question. "Four years ago, before I came back to Austin, I came to this church and ended up talking with a priest. I wanted to see if anybody had come to confession that might match our profile."

Maisie replied. "I wouldn't think he'd answer your question. I told you years ago that they're not going to reveal what's said in confession."

"You're right; he didn't give me anything even when I threatened to get a subpoena. But we had a nice conversation and he at least told me that there was somebody who came through the church that seemed to be troubled as he put it. This person didn't really give a confession as much as they just wanted to talk to someone. I think it was his way of saying there was somebody that matched our profile without actually violating the sanctity of confession. I want to show him the pictures that we have of Sara Rogers and Lori Kellerman and see if maybe by chance he recognizes them as someone who might have come to the church years ago. If he can at least tell us that, then we have a witness that can place Sara Rogers in Dallas at the time and it's another connection to our timeline"

Maisie's look on her face said she didn't believe it would work. But she was a smart enough detective to know that you had to try anything legal in order to get results. She said. "I don't think this is going to work, but what the hell, let's give it a shot."

Mass was finally over, and people were coming out of the church. Jim had already done his due diligence and found out that Father Kieran was still a priest there. He even found out his schedule and knew that he would be conducting Mass tonight. When the two detectives walked in, the priest acknowledged them, but he didn't actually recognize Jim. He gave them a welcoming look that he would anybody who came through the doors of his church. As Jim walked up to him, he was putting things away at the front of the church, he said. "Father Kieran, I don't know if you remember me. The father looked at him and sort of recognized him, he looked familiar, but he had forgotten his name. He said. "You're a police detective, right!"

"Yes, Father."

"I'm sorry; I've forgotten your name."

"I'm detective Jim Summers and this is Detective Maisie Green. They all shook hands and then Father Kieran replied. "Well, Detective, it's nice to see you again. If I remember correctly, you're not very religious so the fact that you're at my church is at least a small victory for God."

Jim had to laugh. It was funny that he should say that and he liked the priest for looking on the bright side of things, especially when it came to saving someone's soul. He hadn't forgotten their lengthy and philosophical conversation. He replied. "Thank you, Father Kieran, it's nice of you to say, but I'm not here for that."

"Well then, how can I help you?"

"I'm actually here about the same thing I was asking you about 4 years ago."

Father Kieran finally remembered why he came to his church and what he was really after. But he, too, also remembered their conversation and it always hope that it did some good in Jim's life, that maybe he inspired him to find a relationship with God even if it wasn't an ever-consuming influence in his life. He replied to Jim. "I'm sorry to tell you that my answer hasn't changed, nor my position on people coming in here for confession. I still can't tell you anything even if you threaten me with a subpoena."

Jim softly smiled. "I'm not here for that. I understand your position on that matter and I wouldn't dare ask you to try to violate your oath as a priest. But I think there is something you can help me with. I want you to take a look at a couple of pictures and just tell me if either one of these people has ever been inside your church... not whether they've been to confession, just if you've ever seen them in this church before. Maybe they were here for a service or just to pray. Just want to find out if you recognize them...that's all."

Father Kieran started to get annoyed. He felt like it was just a different way of asking the same question, which he still couldn't answer. "Look Detective, I told you before that we take the privacy of our parishioners very seriously, even when they just come through the doors to pray. I can't help you."

"Father, I understand that, but I'm not asking you about this person's confession and the law only protects you when it comes to the confessional booth. The entire church is not safe ground for a criminal."

"We are still protected throughout the entire church from having to reveal any information about our parishioners."

"Our lawyers say different and if you want to test that theory in court, we can do that. But all I want you to do is look at a photo and tell me if you've ever seen them here. Nothing else. We won't even ask you to testify in a court of law. All you're doing is confirming a theory of mine."

Still annoyed, Father Kieran asked. "And if I do recognize this person, which leads you to catch them, what then? You charge them with murder. They get sentenced and then they get the death penalty. I'm not going to help you condemn someone to death."

"It's true; this could help us catch them. But if it's the same person that we talked about 4 years ago, I doubt they'll ever see death row, more like a psychiatric hospital for the rest of their life because it's hard to argue that they're not insane. However, we need to get somebody like that off the streets so that they're not harming anybody else."

Father Kieran didn't say anything for a while. He was still trying to decide if he should help. But even if he agreed that a killer like this shouldn't be on the streets, at least in a psychiatric hospital, he could have a chance to try to save their soul. That's how he justified helping the detectives. He told Jim. "Okay, I won't tell you why this person was here, but I will look at the photos and tell you if I've seen them in this church before."

Smiling, Jim replied. "Thank you, that's all I ask. Jim showed him the picture of Lori Kellerman. The good father said. "No, she doesn't look familiar at all."

Then Jim showed him one of the production stills that they had of Sara Rogers. Father Kieran took longer looking at the photo. He looked at it up close and thoroughly examined it. "She does look familiar. I would say that I'm about 80% sure that she's been in this church. But the eyes are different. And the nose seems a little bit bigger. I remember the eyes because they were a piercing dark emerald green. They were hard to miss. And I don't see that in this photo, or at least I can't tell."

"When did you see her at the church?"

"Over 4 years ago, a few weeks before you and I talked to be exact." Jim smiled. He was happy to hear that answer because this essentially confirmed his theory. Sara Rogers was in Dallas four years ago under a different name and they now had at least one witness that could place her in Dallas at the time of the Don Bennett and Joe Teller murders. Plus, even better, it was a priest whose word was irrefutable that confirmed it. Jim and Maisie, both thanked him for his time and wished him a Happy Thanksgiving. But Jim said something else as they were leaving. "Father Kieran, four years ago you told me that my role with our killer is to craft their doom. That sentiment has never really left me, but I think there's something else you should consider. Most of the time when we catch a killer like this; it's also about rescuing them from themselves because some can't help what they do. They get a taste for it and can't stop. Some are driven to it because they're products of their environment or a tragedy leads to that place where murder is okay. It may not be my job to save their soul, but part of my job is getting them the help they need because the society I have sworn to protect can't always do that. That's why I really want to find this person because I think they need help and death row probably isn't the best place for that. I just wanted to give you something to consider."

    Father Kieran politely smiled. "Detective, if that is the case, I wish you Godspeed and pray that you can help this person. Perhaps that is the true will of God." Jim nodded as a way of saying thank you. Jim had to admit that the priest's words for comforting. He had gotten what he came for and now it's time to go home. Maisie drove him to the airport, and he caught a late flight back to Austin.

48

When Jim got home, it was late. There was a delay at the airport, and he didn't actually get back to Austin until right before midnight. Audra and Josh had already gone to bed, but Gina stayed up to pick him up from the Austin Airport. Jim was tired. He had been tired for weeks. The Black Fairy case always took a lot out of him, but there was always one constant that comforted him. It was Gina. When He got in the car, he noticed that she had cut her hair and dyed it. It took him by surprise but in a good way. He just stared at her for a moment, causing some concern with Gina that he didn't like it. Gina asked if he did so he replied "Absolutely, it looks great. Although I do have a confession, I've always liked redheads, especially darker redheads. I think that comes from my love of Gillian Anderson in The X-Files."

Gina smiled. "I'm glad you like it, I felt like a change and I've always wanted to do a darker, reddish color. I've had to wear wigs like this before in productions, but this time I decided to make it real."

"You get no complaints from me, I think you're gorgeous. The only problem I see is having to stop myself from taking advantage of you in the car." That made Gina laugh, it was a great compliment. Of course, he didn't, they just waited until they got home to ravage each other, and thus the perfect start to what would become a great Thanksgiving. This was a Thanksgiving that they would both remember for a long time, their first true family Thanksgiving.

Everything the next day was great, from the laughter to a superb feast to having one too many pieces of pie in Jim's case. He had always wanted a Thanksgiving like that and for the longest time, imagined what it would be like to be married with his own kids and a big family all there on Thanksgiving, eating too much and watching the Dallas Cowboys game. It never happened for him until now. He didn't have to be married to Gina, and Audra and Josh didn't have to be his biological children. They were his family and over the last four years, they had made a wonderful home. He treasured every moment of it, hoping that it would never end, even when the kids went off to college. He considered himself lucky, but luck has a way of running out. However, for now, on this one day, these small moments with the people he loved the most, he held onto it as if it was a permanent snapshot of what happiness could truly be.

As great as Thanksgiving had been, on Friday he was back at work. Everybody pretty much had the weekend off and wouldn't officially be back in the office until Monday. He and James were still going in and doing more research, today he'd be a little late. As Jim was gathering some of the files that he brought home with him just in case he had a chance to read through them, he had the news on in his small office at home. It was about 10:30 in the morning when breaking news came over the television. Most of the time he just ignored breaking news because as a police officer, he would have already known about it, but this piece of news didn't involve him or his investigation. It had happened so fast that news agencies were just barely getting all the information in order to put out a statement. He was half paying attention, but he recognized the name that the breaking news was about Sebastian Colón`s latest case had just been dismissed by a Travis County Criminal Court. Normally, Jim would have just ignored it if it didn't involve the case he was working, on but he remembered that four years ago when he began the Black Fairy investigation, the case against Sebastian Colón had been dismissed as well. It felt like a coincidence he couldn't dismiss. Spiritual people might call it a sign, he just felt like it was strange and remembered that this guy had been charged with operating a webcam company that featured underage girls. It was the kind of thing that some of the Black Fairy's victims were into so was it really just a coincidence or was there a connection between this guy and some of his victims.?

Jim called James to see if he had been watching the news. James hadn't made it into the office yet as well, but he answered his phone right away. He said. "Whatever you got I'll be in the office soon and we can chat then."

Jim replied. "Yeah, I'll be there later. I got to run Audra to school so she can get on the team bus for her away basketball game tonight. The reason I'm calling, have you heard anything about Sebastian Colón?"

"I've heard his name. He has a lot of business interests and donates a lot of money to different candidates. I know that he's been charged a few times and the case seems to always get dismissed or has been found not guilty. I think there have been a few lawsuits against him. But I'm not exactly sure what all of his business interests are, why?"

"I was just curious. Four years ago, when I started this investigation he was found not guilty of whatever he was being charged with at the time, I don't remember the details. This latest case, apparently, they had an emergency hearing this morning and the case was dismissed. He was charged with owning a website that featured underage girls on webcams. Doesn't that sound familiar?"

James had to admit, it was a little shocking. Even he didn't buy that this was a coincidence. "Okay, it does have a strange connection to what we've been investigating."

James had a confident smile on his face. "Call it a hunch, but I want to look into his background... I wonder if he has any connection to our victims."

"Okay, we can do that today."

"Maybe I'm just overly curious about this guy, but it seems like the law has gone after him quite a bit and they can't seem to make anything stick, I want to know why."

"Then let's find out."

Jim was on his way to the Detective Agency when is sister called. He answered the phone and she quickly dispense with the pleasantries. She said. "Just wanted you to know that I got your request pushed through for Sara Rogers' immigration records in connection with Interpol, but I won't have anything for you today."

Jim wasn't really surprised, and he replied. "Let me guess because it's Thanksgiving weekend."

"Yep, this kind of request is not really a priority during a holiday weekend. It will get sent through today, but they probably won't have an answer for you until Monday. And I would expect it to be late Monday. I hope you didn't need it right away."

"I do, but I understand, it can't be helped. Everybody's not really back until Monday anyway."

"Are you able to keep an eye on Lori Kellerman until then or do you need some help? We have some agents that wouldn't mind Moonlighting for few bucks in cash."

Jim thought about it for a moment. "No, that's okay. We got enough retired cops following her around to keep an eye on her for a few more days. Plus, we are tracking her phone. I think we'll be good until then."

Hannah smiled. "Okay. Text me the email address that you want this report sent to and a fax number. I'll have it sent both ways so you definitely get it."

Jim arrived at the agency and the only two people that were there were James and his intern or protégé if you want to be more accurate. Jim didn't really know what she was. For all he knew, she could have just been some college kid getting some internship credit. But she did really good work when it came to research. James told him as he walked in, that they had found some interesting things about Sebastian Colón. Then he introduced her to the young woman, her name was Charlie. He said in a surprised tone. "Mr. Summers, you have a bit of a spooky hunch when it comes to this guy...you're definitely on to something."

Jim confidently replied. "I'm right, he's connected to some of the victims.

"Yes, but not necessarily, directly connected. I think you stumbled upon the man behind the curtain who pulls all the strings so to speak."

"Oh really."

James and Charlie only had some initial info on the guy, but one of the first things they found was a picture of Sebastian Colón and Jack Perry. James continued I also found out that he donated money to Don Bennett's Senate campaigns... I realize that's not really a big connection because a lot of people donated to his campaigns."

Jim interrupted. "But for this case, it is a major connection, especially if he donated a large sum and met Don Bennett on multiple occasions. Have you found any record that they knew each other?"

"Not really, but we've only scratched the surface. Here's something that's interesting. His profile says he's an entrepreneur and has multiple business interests in Texas. He's listed as a CEO, but I can't find anything he actually owns. Yet he gets paid like a CEO and has a lavish lifestyle."

Jim thought that was strange. Is there any record of him owning anything at all?

"He was a silent partner in the Lone Star Bottled Water Company. But he sold his interest when the CEO was murdered."

"Okay, that's something. If he was in that company even a silent partner, then he's connected to Sara Rogers...maybe loosely, but it's still a connection."

"True, but how would she have known that he was a silent partner when the company was threatened with a lawsuit because of the toxicity claims? It wasn't revealed until after he sold his interest and consequently, that's when the company almost went bankrupt before it was bought by Trake Industries."

"It's still a connection. But how did he make his money...that's what I really want to know. Was he even born in Texas?"

Charlie finally spoke up and answered this question. She had a soft girlish voice that made her sound like she was still in high school, but she was very assertive and confident in her tone. "He was born in Colombia to a Colombian father and an American mother. Came here to the United States in 1996. It looks like he came from money. Don't know for sure, but probably drug money. He invested in Internet startups. Lost some of his money, but then started the right kind of company that can make money on the internet...porn. He was one of the first to start making money off webcam shows with different stuff from around the world. He was one first to invest in a company called Erotica Online... today; it's called Erotica X Unlimited."

Jim's curiosity really perked up when you heard that name. "Really... is he the majority holder or just an investor?"

"I think just an investor, but he also gets weekly deposits from them for marketing on top of his quarterly dividends."

"That's a little weird. What kind of marketing is he getting paid for?" This is the company that specializes in webcam stuff, right?"

"Yes, they pride themselves on being able to show your wildest of fantasies. They have dozens of websites and every one of them has a request form where you request your own private fantasy. You pay enough money and they'll put it together for you on a webcam. The company was sued back in 2007 for using underage girls. However, nothing could be proven so the case was dismissed."

Jim, looking at the huge crime board in the conference room, remembered some of the victims being customers. He said. "So that will connect Mike Sturgess and maybe William Staples. Doesn't this company own a website where you can upload private snuff films?"

Charlie looked through the list of websites that they had discovered. Yes, it's called snufftube.com. I guess it's basically YouTube for people's personal snuff films. He also invested in another company about 12 years ago called X-Factor Entertainment... it features entertainers for private parties or functions, mainly girls."

Jim had a sarcastic response. "It's an escort service."

"No, it just features girls for promotional purposes at functions and private parties."

James responded before Jim could say anything. "Charlie this is where your innocence is starting to show. No matter what you call it or what semantics you use; when an old rich dude is using girls for private parties or functions, it's just a mask for an escort service." Charlie blushed a little bit at the comment. She wasn't exactly a sheltered girl, but she was still innocent in a lot of ways.

Jim got even more curious about Sebastian Colón. "He's been arrested a few times and put on trial, right!"

James looked through a file folder. "Over the last 12 years, he was brought to trial three times. The first time, it was about operating an erotic or strip club without a liquor license. They tried to make it a federal case with the ATF because of the alcohol distribution, but his plea bargained it down to a fine and he got a new license. This was in 2005. In 2007 a complaint was made that he was using underage illegal immigrants. This one got dismissed because they couldn't find the underage girls... they disappeared. This case was presided over by Judge Craig Fitzgerald."

"I'm not really surprised that one of these cases would have been presided over by Judge Fitzgerald and that officially connects him to the Judge. How did the girls disappear, did they end up dead or just gone?"

"Not exactly sure, but in the ATF notes, they think the girls were deported back to where they came from and out of their jurisdiction to be used as witnesses. The case in 2013 is what was going on when the Black Fairy case started. It was a similar case to the one in 2007. He was operating a club in Dallas and there were complaints that underage girls were being used for sexual purposes. He was found not guilty because they were able to prove with birth certificates that the girls were of legal age and there was no actual evidence that they were anything but cocktail waitresses. The girls were Russian. The club was shut down after that and presumably, he opened it somewhere else. This latest case had to do with trafficking. A complaint was made that he trafficked illegal immigrants and made them sex slaves for corporate functions. As in 2005 and in 2007, the girls disappeared and there were no material witnesses."

Jim started shaking his head. Something else that was hard to believe. "They've been trying to get this guy on some kind of sex crime or trafficking for years but can never make the case stick.

He replied. "So basically, we have a pattern when it comes to Sebastian Colón. They have been trying to get him on some kind of sex charges and every time they come close, the case is dismissed. That doesn't make sense?"

"Sure, it does. He's tied to powerful people and if he's basically running an escort service for what they call corporate functions where they will fulfill any fantasy, these cases have to be dismissed or he has to be found "not guilty" so the truth doesn't come out about his clients. He knows too many power people and their secrets. For example, the reason the case was dismissed in 2007 by Judge Fitzgerald, the primary piece of evidence was a recording where they got Sebastian Colón talking about a new shipment of girls. Somebody recorded the conversation and turned it over to the authorities, but it was ruled inadmissible because they didn't have a warrant to legally record it, and the guy wasn't granted whistleblower status. Prosecutors couldn't find any other evidence or anybody to testify so the case had to be dismissed. The ruling about the recording was upheld during the appeal process as well. A jury never even got to hear it."

James had a point. The evidence was there, he was connected to very powerful people and it left Jim to wonder, was Sebastian Colón the true villain of the story, and was he the final act for the Black Fairy murders. He said. "You say that he's a CEO, but you can't find any company that he's truly in charge of, on paper he's only an investor, but he gets paid as a marketing manager, right, is that to keep him insulated from having any ties to the company other than an employee?"

"That's what it looks like."

"Have you ever seen something like this before?"

"It's what the mob used to do with a guy who ran a casino but couldn't get a license. You give him a different job title, but he's still the face of the casino."

Jim softly laughed. "I feel like that's what they did with Robert De Niro's character in the movie Casino."

"It's funny how accurate, they got that movie, isn't it. But I think the main reason he's not getting convicted of anything is even though he's not the one in charge on paper, it's because he's the face of the company so they go after him and can't make anything stick. I would have to look more closely, but it looks like X-Factor Entertainment and Erotic X Unlimited is owned by shell corporations, just enough degrees of separation from Sebastian Colón where he doesn't really own it, but still runs everything."

James sat back in his chair. He really pondered what James was saying. What he was doing wasn't unheard of, like James said; the mafia did it all the time back in Vegas. It was scary for Jim because he had never seen anything like this before. He had never encountered a guy who was so connected and could practically get away with anything. He looked at James and Charlie and said. There's a question we have to ask ourselves... the one question that has escaped us since the beginning... the final piece of this puzzle if you will. What if it's not a place that connects all of these people, but one person? What if the place is only relevant because of the one person that brings them all together and placates their deepest darkest desires?"

James replied. "It does make sense if you really look at everything…I mean really look at the evidence."

Jim tried to crack a smile. "Yes, it does and what if that one person is Sebastian Colón... the man who seems to get away with anything?"

James nodded in agreement. "We still have a lot more to go through. His history is just another dark rabbit hole that we will have to venture through, but from what I've seen so far, I have no argument against your theory."

"I feel, I should say it out load... Sebastian Colón is the final target of The Black Fairy."

#

They had worked through most of the weekend. Mostly just doing research. It was tedious work and Jim imagined that this is what law school felt like when it came to research. Jim, Charlie, and James dug up everything they could possibly find on Sebastian Colón and put together a detailed history over the last 20 years. They found a lot more than expected, but they all knew that it was probably not enough. He was into some dark and shady shit, but with each piece of information they found on him and how it connected to the Black Fairy's eight victims, Jim was more and more sure that he was the final target. By Sunday morning they had a pretty detailed history in a thick notebook, even the stuff they had to dig really deep on when it came to the Shell corporations that Sebastian Colón was attached to. It was time for Jim to make the call. It was time to start watching him closely.

    Jim and James were already at the Detective Agency by noon on Sunday. Jim slept in a little bit and even got to have a nice breakfast with the family, but it was back to the grindstone and Gina completely understood. Besides, she had some projects of her own that she needed to get to so Sunday turned into a workday for the both of them. Jim called his buddy Mike even though he knew he'd probably still be on vacation and didn't expect them back until Monday. It turned out that Mike was already back at work too. Jim carefully explained what they had found on Sebastian Colón and why he was a top priority, why they should put eyes on him immediately. Mike was stunned. The guy was also a topic of conversation at his own station. Mike explained. "It's funny that you're telling me all this, he's missing."

"What?"

"His girlfriend or were assuming his girlfriend, filed a missing person report early this morning. She said that he came home late Friday night after celebrating his case getting dismissed, slept in, then went to play golf on Saturday and she hasn't seen him since. It hasn't quite been 24 hours yet, so nobody is doing anything about it, but we're on alert because he's a high-profile businessman in Texas."

"You need to bump that up. This isn't a coincidence; he's missing for a reason."

"We can't officially do anything until it's been 24 hours and we still got 3 hours to go. Besides, it's not even my case; we're just supposed to be on the lookout for him."

"Mike, tell your captain that this is connected to your copycat case and get officers out there looking for him... you need to be questioning everybody. This is a priority, and he may already be dead."

"Okay, I'll see what I can do. But in the meantime, do you have a location for Lori Kellerman?"

Jim sighed a little bit. "Not at this exact moment, but we'll find out. She's supposed to still be at home in Dallas but will confirm that." As soon as they got off the phone. Jim told James what it happened. He asked about Lori's current location and if any of his guys had checked in. After a couple of phone calls, the update was still current, she was still at home. Her car hadn't left that house since Thursday. Being curious, Jim had to ask. "Are we sure she's actually there and didn't leave with someone else?"

James shrugged as if he didn't know for sure, but it was a good question. One of his old police friends did devise a plan to act like a delivery driver with Amazon and see if he could get her to sign for a package, therefore finding out if she was really home. As popular as Amazon was when it came to Prime delivery, it wasn't hard to fool the occupants of the house. The ruse worked, her boyfriend answered the door and confirmed that she had to fly to Austin. They had missed her and now she could be anywhere in

Austin. James told Jim and he only had two words for a response. "Fucking Hell."

The whole thing had become an emergency and it couldn't wait for everybody to be back on Monday. Jim called Vanessa and Maisie. He brought them up to speed and told them that they needed to get back to Austin as soon as possible. They had a lot of work to do. Later that night, both Maisie and Vanessa got back to Austin. Vanessa ended up taking a cheap flight after waiting on standby for a couple of hours. Maisie packed and within an hour after Jim's call was back on the road. Both women didn't even really get settled in their hotel before going to the Detective Agency. Detective Lester and Detective Morgan were both there. Still no word on Sebastian Colón. The last people to see him were from the men's club that he was at, which included a golf course. They concluded that he left there at about four in the afternoon. His car was still there, but after a quick test, it wouldn't start so the police just assumed he had gotten an Uber or Lift driver to take him home. There was no record of that, but somebody had driven him from The Men's Club and that's where the police figured he was kidnapped. There was still no word on Lori Kellerman's location. They were trying to find a record of a rental car that she might have gotten, but if she did, it wasn't at the airport. The task force was left with calling every rental car place in Austin, trying to find a record of her rental. It was made harder by the fact that they couldn't find a credit card charge for a rental car so at this point, it was like finding a needle in a haystack.

Jim started to bring everybody up to speed about what they had found on Sebastian Colón. He showed them every connection that they had made over the past few days on their huge crime board. At the very least, it was shocking. On paper when it came to all the shell companies that they had uncovered, he wasn't connected to any of them as the boss, yet he was connected to everything. He was the true face of these companies, the blow-harded boss who branded himself as a man who could get anybody anything, but yet, didn't run anything. He was like a Donald Trump, who cared more about his own image and what he could do for people than actually running a company and that's the way it needed to be to keep himself protected from the law.

When he had finished, there were no words from either Vanessa or Maisie. Even Detective Morgan couldn't muster her usual words of cynicism. It made sense. He was the man at the center of it all and for the first time they all looked at the final piece of the puzzle... the one thing that connected everybody.

While everybody was still trying to process the information they had just heard, Jim said. "We also found a couple of other connections that we haven't put on the board yet, one regarding Joe Teller and another regarding Henry Frankston. Joe Teller was a regular at the club that Sebastian Colón owned in Dallas. It was called the Silver Linings Club, where all of your fantasies could come true. For Joe Teller it was young schoolgirls, Russian mainly. Sometimes Hispanic. While we have no concrete proof on what he did there, we believe he had sex with them in the private rooms or he watched people have sex with him. But we did find financial records where he paid money to the clubs and emails requesting the schoolgirl package. We also believe that these were underage illegal immigrants forced into sexual slavery."

Maisie replied. "Fucking Christ." I guess that means he knew Sebastian Colón?"

"Probably, or at least, knew of him."

"And what about Henry Frankston?"

Jim nodded. "I think this one's the most disgusting of all. Before he was a convicted sex offender who failed to report and disappeared for two years, he was married. We found a record of him and his wife uploading videos to the snufftube.com website. It turns out, both were pedophiles, and they would upload videos of them playing house with children."

With a shocked tone, Vanessa had to ask. "When you say playing house, you mean..."

Jim interrupted. "Yes. Their videos where of playing dress-up and bath time if you know what I mean."

"Jesus, I've never understood how people could be so sick."

"I'm right there with you. His wife died of cancer, and he didn't upload any more videos after that. The last video they uploaded was in 2007, he got picked up while working as a school janitor for inappropriately touching kids and served three years. There's no evidence to suggest that he actually knew Sebastian

Colón, but he and his wife's videos were some of the highest rated and most viewed on that website. Plus, they were also some of the most shared videos. I believe that's exactly why he was targeted."

"No Doubt. I don't think anybody disagrees that he truly was an evil motherfucker."

Everybody in the room laughed because it was true and the best way to describe him. Jim said. "The key to finding our killer is finding him and the fact that nobody has found a body yet, means he may still be alive. I think we find him by finding Lori Kellerman. We know she came to Austin. But we don't know where she's staying so maybe by calling every rental car company and seeing if she paid cash helps us find her. If we can find that car, hopefully is has a tracking system on it like OnStar and that can lead us to the last victim, which will put her at the crime scene. This is our priority right now. And with that said, they went to work. Turned out there were over a hundred places where you can rent a car in Austin, Texas and with it being late on a Sunday night, it was going to be hard to find. They worked as much as they could, but most of it would have to be done Monday morning. They started very early on Monday and after about four hours with everybody calling rental car agencies, they finally found one where she rented a car with cash. It was a small operation that didn't rely on credit checks or ask a lot of questions. It was perfectly convenient and as luck would have it, the car did have a GPS tracking device. From there, it was easy to find the car and Lori Kellerman. She had been staying at a hotel in Round Rock. The room was registered under a different name, some guy named Sean Porter. Since this was still Austin PD's case, Jim told his buddy Mike just to put a team on her and follow her around. They couldn't arrest her yet, there still wasn't any evidence that she was The Black Fairy.

By late afternoon, Lori had not left the hotel. Her rental car has been sitting there since yesterday, according to the GPS record. Austin PD was getting antsy about what to do, but even now, they still couldn't move on her because they didn't have anything. It wasn't against the law to pay cash for a rental car and stay in a hotel under an assumed name. Suspicious, but not illegal. Finally, James told Jim that he had a break in their case. He had found the guy who made the vessels which carried the Gaelic symbols on them. He was a local pottery maker who had a little shop on the outskirts of Austin. It took a little while, but he had finally responded to a message from James and through their conversation he was able to confirm, he was paid for three large bowls with the Gaelic Triskelion on them. He said to Jim. "According to him, he was paid up front for all three bowls, but he would make one at a time and then drop it off at a delivery center of sorts for the customer to pick it up on their own time."

Jim replied. "So, he was paid up front for all three bowls...that's a little weird."

"Yes, I agree. He was paid through his PayPal account. I tracked the purchase, and it came from a business PayPal account under the name, Irish Crafts and Gifts."

"Is there a personal name under that account?"

"No, the debit card attached is one of those reloadable prepaid debit cards. No record of a name. And there's only a tax ID number attached to the PayPal account. We can look that number up and see who it's registered to but that may take a little while."

"Where did he drop off the last bowl?"

"It's one of those Pack and Mail places where you can leave packages to be picked up in person or they'll ship stuff out for you. I tried calling and seeing if it's been picked up, but they won't give me that information over the phone."

"Then we need to go by and flash a badge to see if we can change their mind." That's exactly what they did. Sometimes just the sight of a badge is enough to make someone talk when they're really not supposed to. That's what they were counting on. 30 minutes later they arrived at the Pack and Mail place and found a young college kid working behind the desk. He looked nervous when Jim showed him his badge as if he was about to be busted for the marijuana that he had in his pocket. It wasn't hard to break him. The kid quickly looked up the item to see if it was still there. They did on Saturday. Jim said. "Maybe she still has it on her. If the car hasn't moved from the hotel in a couple of days, maybe it's still in her trunk or her back seat. We need to get a warrant to search the car. If she has that bowl, then that places her at the crime scene, and we can pick her up. James agreed. Jim called Detective Lester and told him what they had found. It took a couple of hours to get an emergency warrant, but Austin PD now had cause to search the rental car. In the meantime, Jim and James went back to the agency.

Lori Kellerman had been shacked up in a hotel room with a guy for almost two days, so it was a huge surprise when the police knocked on her door and told her that they were searching for her rental car. Detective Lester and Detective Morgan led the search along with some uniformed police officers. Lori wasn't happy. She cursed the cops for the invasion of her privacy. Then she got even angrier when she figured that she was being linked to a copycat serial killer. She caused quite the scene outside the hotel parking lot and police had to detain her just to calm her down. After a thorough search, they didn't find any vessel with Gaelic symbols on it. The only thing that she had in her rental car were some bags from when she had done some shopping when she got to Austin. She looked as if she was on vacation.

Mike called Jim and told them what was going on. He asked. "There's nothing here, are we sure she's the right girl?"

Jim was surprised, but just because they didn't find the vessel doesn't mean that they could automatically rule her out. He replied. "Everything points to her right now and since we don't have any confirmation on what her old name was based on immigration records, this is all we have to go on. She could have picked it up and taken it to her next crime scene. You can still hold her for up to 48 hours without charging her, correct?"

"Yes, technically."

"Detain her... just tell her that you may have gotten some false information and you need to clear a few things up before you can let her go. We're still waiting on a fax or an email to confirm her immigration records. I say let's detain her until we can confirm her real name from those documents and then we can go from there."

"Okay, we won't put her in a cell, just yet. We'll just make her comfortable."

"Thank you." Jim looked at James for some advice. "What now, have any suggestions?"

"We can try looking into the internal GPS record of that Sean Porter's car, you know, the guy she was with, and see where it's been. We can also try cross-referencing Uber and Lyft pickups at the hotel over the last couple of days and see if they might have picked Lori or Sean up and then see where they went... the work might be a little tedious, but that's all I have."

Jim softly smiled. "It's worth a shot... I'll try anything at this point." Then he thought about something, an idea that the team had talked about a while back. Jim spoke up. "The locations where the victims were killed were always personal to the victim, most of the time it was their home or a place where they did their wretched acts. Why would it be any different for Sebastian Colón? He wasn't found at his home or any of the places he usually goes to?"

James answered the question. "Yes, that's correct."

"Then it has to be a place that we're not thinking of that's personal to him... what if he is the man who puts together these pleasure retreats?"

"I would buy that...I, mean it's not out of the realm of possibility."

"No, it's not, and isn't it strange that we found that invitation at the crime scene for Judge Fitzgerald? I mean, wouldn't the killer have gone through his desk to find any incriminating evidence against him. What if that invitation was left on purpose so we'd find it?"

James picked up where Jim was going with his thought process, so he responded. "We'd find it and look into it."

With a confident smile, Jim replied. "Exactly... the Black Fairy is steering us into the direction that we need to go, which means that might be the place where Sebastian Colón is going to be killed. It's not about the event itself, it's about the location and exposing what these events are really all about."

James responded. "Events where any fantasy is fulfilled no matter how illegal it may be."

Jim rushed to grab his coat and car keys. "I got a hunch; I'm going to check it out. Could be wrong, but anything is better than just sitting around and waiting."

James didn't argue, but he did have a suggestion. Don't you think you should take some back up?"

"No, let me run this down and if I need backup I'll call. Get started with tracking where Sean Porter's car has been or any Uber or Lyft that might have picked them up at the hotel. I just want to check this place out and then I'll be back."

As Jim was leaving, Maisie spoke up and asked. "Jim, where are you going?"

He was halfway out the door when he replied. "Gotta follow up on a lead."

"Well, let me go with you, you don't need to do it alone." Jim motioned for her to stop as she was walking toward the door. "Don't worry about it, I'll take care of this one on my own and I'll be back shortly. We're still waiting on that fax and email on Sara Rogers' immigration records. I need you to get that and confirm her real name so we can decide what to do with Lori Kellerman. Get that record and text me what you find, that's the best thing you can do for me right now." Maisie tried to argue with Jim about going alone, but he was already out the door starting to get into his car so he didn't hear a thing. She didn't necessarily like it, but she was a cop and she understood what it felt like when you have a hunch. Sometimes you just have to follow up on your own.

50

The drive was long and out of the way of anything. Even though it was only a half an hour outside of Austin, it almost felt like forever when Jim was driving to a place called Lakeway, Texas. There wasn't much there except a fancy retreat in what was commonly referred to as The Hills of Texas. It sat off the Colorado River, which gave plenty of nourishment to the surrounding areas and filled it with plush green hills and trees. It was perfect for a retreat that offered a pleasurable getaway. You couldn't see anything from the road; it was well hidden, which was on purpose. To a normal person passing by, it looked like one of many ranches throughout Texas. Jim had a hard time finding the actual entrance, but there in the darkness he found a small sign. It was a long dirt road, hidden from plain view that one would follow to a rich man's Shangri-La. The drive up to the big house was almost a full mile and you could easily see the small Golf Course that had been built around it. When Jim got to the big house, he saw all of the little condominium like buildings that surrounded it, which by his guess were only really used for one thing, private sex rooms for the rich and powerful where any fantasy could be fulfilled no matter how perverted or illegal it may be.

  The place was quiet, but Jim could see lights in the big house. He didn't know what to expect, but assumed that it was a maintenance crew, which he figured work around the clock to maintain the retreat. He couldn't see any cars; he thought that whoever was inside just lived on the premises in their own private servant's quarters. Jim automatically withdrew his service weapon and slowly marched towards the big front door. He also had a thought in the back of his mind that there might be some kind of booby trap or maybe he just got that idea from a movie where the cops slowly walk upon the killer in the middle of the crime. He was a little nervous walking into the big house, not knowing what he was going to find, but who wouldn't be in this situation.

Vanessa and James were deep within their research of trying to find where Sean Porter's car had been. Maisie tried to help but her mind was not on research, she was worried about Jim. She had some sickening feeling that he was walking into a trap and without any backup, only assumed the worst. But she was also preoccupied with looking out for a fax or an email with Sara Rogers' immigration records. She was pouring herself another cup of coffee when she heard the fax machine. It was a distinctive sound, and she wouldn't confuse it with any other sound in the office because it was rarely used. At the same time, she also got an email alert. The fax and the email came from the main FBI offices in Washington DC. It was the immigration records they had been looking for. The fax was taking too long to print out and it was quite a few pages too, so Maisie checked the email that had been forwarded to her. It was a simple PDF file and as she started scrolling through it, she found the page with the subjects given name or birth name, the name her parents had given her, and any aliases.

  Maisie stared at the given name on the application; she was shocked beyond belief and couldn't take her eyes off the form. It couldn't be. It had to be a mistake. It wasn't Lori Kellerman. She put the coffee down and grabbed her coat and rushed out of the office. Jim was in trouble, if the killer really was where he was going then he was definitely walking into a trap. She didn't really explain where she was going, all she said was that she was going to follow up on a lead and also see if she could get a hold of Jim at the same time. Maisie got into her car and sped out of the parking lot like a bat out of hell. Her only thought at this point was hoping that she could get to Jim on time.

The main house was huge and so it had a big outer hall that led to the main area of the house, which for the most part was a huge ballroom like area. It was built that way to host large events and to have plenty of room for lots of guests. The lights were dimmed in the outer hall, but Jim could see that there were more lights in the main area through the bottom crack of the big double doors that separated the two areas. He had a service weapon drawn, aimed, and ready to shoot. Not knowing what he was going to find, he took a deep breath and slowly pushed the two double doors open. He got one hell of a surprise when he walked into the main area. Suddenly realizing that he was too late, with each step he took he became more and more shocked at what he was seeing. Sebastian Colón was strung up; his feet were about eighteen inches off the ground. He was being held up by two thick ropes tied to each arm at a 45-degree angle therefore stretching his body out. It was similar to a crucifixion pose, but it was more of a pagan type of crucifixion. His eyes have been cut out. His penis had been cut off. His heart had been cut out from his chest. There was the typical piercing of his side where the blood could drain out of his body into a custom-made vessel that had the same Gaelic Triskelion symbols on it. The scene was very familiar, but also different for the final murder of The Black Fairy. There was a huge flat vessel that looked more like a pan that you would be put over a fire. The heart, the eyes, and his penis were laid on top of it, soaked in blood.

It was horrific to say the least, but not the most gruesome part of the scene. This was the second time that the killer had used extra bodies as part of the crime scene. There were two Hispanic men who appeared to be maintenance workers at the retreat. They were dead and in a kneeling position before Sebastian Colon's body. Their hands were positioned up as if they were worshipping the body that was tied up. It reminded Jim of early Renaissance paintings that showed Christ's followers kneeling before him on the cross and worshipping him or touching his body one last time. They also appeared to have blood tears. But since the victim's blood was a symbol in itself as a use of transformation, Jim had to wonder was it Sebastian Colon's blood that have been drained from his side or taken from the vessel that it had been drained into. There was no way to tell by just looking at the bodies, but he wouldn't be surprised if it was Sebastian Colon's own blood. Jim stared at the bodies for the longest time trying to examine every detail and learning what the killer was trying to say through the symbolism. Looking at the bodies was almost trance like, he couldn't look away. But then all the sudden he was startled by somebody coming through one of the back doors in the main area. The killer was still here, and they were just as surprised to see Jim there as well. He finally had a chance to catch the killer in the act. His Instinct had proven right and now stood before him, the real Black Fairy who was wearing all black and wearing a thin ski mask liner to cover their face.

    Jim pointed his service weapon at the Killer and said. "Freeze, put your hands behind your head and interlock your fingers."

    The killer didn't move, but they also didn't put their hands behind their head like Jim had asked them. She just stood there staring at the police officer who'd finally caught them. Jim started to repeat when he had previously said, but in a much harsher tone and that's when he heard the voice of the killer for the first time. He was cut off by some surprising words. "Jim, somehow I knew you'd figure out this place is where Sebastian Colón would die. I just didn't expect to still be here so this is an awkward surprise."

    Fear gripped within his stomach. He could feel the Goosebumps tingle on his arms. He knew that voice... that sweet, soothing, voice that had been with him every day the last four years letting him know that he had a reason to be happy, that he had a reason to love. The voice stopped him in his tracks. Hearing it felt more like a dream, so it took him a moment to process what he didn't believe to be real. Jim didn't want to say the name because once he did, it would definitely be real. But he knew he had to say her name, he couldn't avoid it. He responded with just one word that felt more like a question when he said it. "Gina!"

She took off the thin ski mask that hid her face. There was no going back now, she had to take her mask off and be completely honest with the man she loved. It was Gina. It had been her all along. She was the one he'd been chasing and the sad look on her face confirmed it. It wasn't a dream. He was wide awake. He saw her plain as the sun that rises in the east. Gina McCarthy was The Black Fairy. She offered a solemn reply. "Yes, and I'm sorry that you had to find out this way."

He struggled to find the right words. All Jim wanted to do was close his eyes and then open them back up as if to wake from some kind of bad dream. He asked her. "Why, I don't understand... why did you do all this?"

"You know why. You read my book more than once... the answers were all in there."

"No... I'm not talking about some bullshit metaphor you created so the public can debate your reasons why. Tell me the real reason you did... you owe me that much."

Tears began to well up in Gina's eyes. "Because you didn't have to watch your family die in front of you knowing that there wasn't anything you can do to save them. And you didn't have to watch the man who ordered their murder get away with it, all for the simple reason that they would lose money. That was more important to them than human lives."

"So all of this is about revenge?"

"No. What everybody calls the Dinner Party Murder was about revenge... pure cold-blooded sinful revenge...nothing more. The rest it was about showing the world that nobody escapes their sins. If the law can't bring them to justice, somebody has to step up and show the world their misdeeds to show them that nobody can get away with such vile acts. We will be punished for our transgressions ...we will be judged for the things we do."

Jim shook his head. He couldn't believe what he was hearing. Gina was sounding like some kind of religious zealot. "This little speech of yours, does that include you as well."

"Of course, it does. I may be fulfilling the will of God, if you want to believe that. I know what I am. I know where I'm supposed to go when I die. But even if it's God's will for the things that I've done, I will still be judged. And yet, I will still do these things without any regrets or apologies."

Jim got mad. "I guess you are an avenging angel, the likable vigilante, we're all supposed to get behind and accept because what you're doing is righteous."

Gina softly smiled. "People can believe what they want to believe. If you want to call me that, fine, but I have no illusions of what I'm doing…its murder, simple as that. But I believe it to be justifiable and if others want to believe that too, then who am I to stop them."

"This isn't a game, Gina; you murdered at least nine people that I know about."

She laughed, "I've killed more than that."

"Who?"

"The married man who tried to rape Lori, four years go. How about the asshole that got Audra and Josh's mother hooked on heroin and pimped her out because she didn't have any prospects after her divorce from their father. Then again…I've killed many more that you will never know about."

Jim shook his head, still not wanting to believe what she was saying. Somewhere deep down, he still expected to wake from a bad dream, but he responded. "Jesus fucking Christ, you know what you're doing is wrong, but yet, you still do it. I just don't get it, how can you justify murder."

"How can you not with the men I have killed? Do you really think anybody is going to miss these men... these disgusting, perverted souls who have done nothing but take advantage of innocent victims all for their own pleasure?"

"That's not the point. It's still murder and it's illegal no matter how you justify it."

"But that's not really for you or any other man to decide, that's up to God."

"Do you really think you can find forgiveness for what you've done and your soul is going to be transformed like in your metaphor?"

Gina paused for a moment, politely smiling, and collecting her thoughts so she could try and answer his philosophical question. Maybe he forgives me and maybe he doesn't. Maybe I belong in hell. Maybe nobody will fully understand what I've done, but I don't have any regrets. I have no intention of apologizing to you or anybody else for saving the world from these terrible men. Because of me, they won't be able to hurt anybody ever again."

Jim kept shaking his head at the constant disbelief of what he was hearing. However, he was curious about a couple of things. "Henry Frankston, you used a child as part of your scene, we know that he didn't die because of you, but what about his sister Heather... what happened to Heather Tyson? Is she dead, because if she is then for the love of god...tell me where she's buried."

Gina took a step closer towards "Jim. "She's not dead and no matter how evil you may think I am; I couldn't ever kill a child."

"I never thought you could, but what happened to the girl?"

"She's safe and living a good life now, but I just couldn't let anybody find her. If she ended up back in system, then she would have gone to the next closest relative. The next closest of kin is a pedophile, who's never been caught. I would never put that child through something like that. I won't tell you where she is, but trust me, she is happy and safe. She's felt more love in the last four years than she ever did in her entire life before."

"That's not good enough. We need to know where she is."

"Why, so you can do what you think is right, what the law says you're supposed to do. No, you don't need to know where she is, just that she's happy and loved by a man and woman who could never have children of their own but desired it more than anything. Trust me, there's no one in this life that will give her the love that she always deserved...nobody else that can give her the life that she always deserved."

Jim silently cursed. "You know that I can't just leave it at that."

"I know, but this is one time where you're going to have to let it go Jim... she will have a better life if you just let it go."

Jim had an angry reply, but he was still trying to process everything. How could Gina be The Black Fairy! How could he have missed it! But he had one more question to ask before he had to decide what to do with her. "Four years ago, when you bumped into me at that bookstore, was it by accident or were you trying to find out what I had on you?"

Gina didn't want to answer because the truth wasn't necessarily pleasant, but she owed him the truth. "It wasn't by accident, I did want to know what you had on me, I seduced you for that very reason, but the strangest thing happened, I started to like you. I saw that you were a good and caring man. You weren't hard to fall for. I didn't want to like you because I knew someday it would have to end and you would know my secret. But then I saw how you were with Audra and Josh, and you turned out to be somebody that I was always looking for. Somebody that I could love, somebody I could have a family with, somebody who made me laugh and love me no matter what. The man of my dreams! I've tried to hold on to it as long as I could, these last four years have been the best four years of my life. I love you Jim and no matter what happens next that isn't going to change. I'm sorry that you have to be the one to catch me."

Jim almost started to cry; he loved her too. That was the hardest part about all of this. He was still a cop at the end of the day, and he still had a job to do. "If the last four years have been so fantastic for you, why did you continue with the murders? You could have stopped, we could have gone on with our lives, and I probably would have never known."

Tears filled her eyes again. "I wanted to...believe me, I wanted to, but this was bigger than you and me. I had to complete this journey."

"Really, murder was bigger than you and me. That's horseshit."

"I wish it were that simple, but what these men did to society as a whole... the damage they caused to innocent people...

especially this last one, ridding the world of these men is bigger than you and me." She paused for a moment. "You should know I almost didn't complete this journey. I almost let it go because of you and the kids. You had that effect."

Jim tried to smile. "I guess we weren't good enough to make you stop. You just had to complete your own Divine Comedy, didn't you? We should be more important than that."

"Yes, you should, but we all have to go through our own circles of hell in order to complete our true journey. This was mine and resisting the happiness I could have with you for the rest of my life was the hardest part of my journey, but I had to complete it. Just like you will have to complete your journey, which includes making a choice what to do with me. This will be your greatest burden."

"Yeah, I guess that it is my burden because I do love you…completely and undeniably love. That's why this makes it incredibly hard…I have to arrest you."

Tears welled up in Gina's eyes. "I know you do, but I'm going to give you a choice." Jim had put his gun away and gotten out his handcuffs. He never saw that Gina actually had a gun on her. She surprised him by quickly drawing it. He was surprised and replied. "What are you doing? I don't believe you'll shoot me." She surprised him again and shot him, but it was only a small flesh wound as the bullet grazed his left arm. She wasn't mortally wounding him; she did just enough to get his attention, so that he would understand that she wasn't bluffing.

Shocked, Jim replied. "Holy fuck, I can't believe you just shot me."

Gina said to him." It got your attention, didn't it? I didn't want to shoot you and I certainly don't want to kill you. I know you think you have to arrest me…if I were in your shoes, that's how I would think too, but here's the choice I'm going to give you." She pulled out of her pocket, a flash drive and showed it to Jim. "You can take me in if that's really what you want to do, I won't put up a fight. Or you can take the information off of this flash drive and save two dozen girls who are going to come into Galveston tomorrow and be trafficked as sex slaves. There are some very young girls among this group; children will be used as nothing but a sex toy. Their innocence crushed by a bunch of perverts who don't give a damn. I have been doing research on Sebastian Colón for a long time and finally found out when and where he brings in the girls for his private parties. The next boat is coming in tomorrow night, and it will have the girls that they will be using for their next event right here in this place."

"What kind of choice is that?"

"An easy one, I hope. The flash drive is password protected so even if you try to arrest me and get it, you can't open it. You only get the password if you let me go. And your computer technicians won't crack my encryption on the drive."

Gina could say that it was easy to make that choice, but far from it. He looked at the bodies perfectly laid out in a gruesome, but symbolic crime scene. Then he looked back at Gina and asked her. "All of this, is it really about doing the work of God or are you just some murderous snake who can't stop?"

"It's easy to label me as that and maybe I am in some way. But despite your profile, I'm not a fallen angel or even an avenging angel. I might be a sin eater…who knows. But I know one thing for certain, I'm somebody who was willing to do what needed to be done and whether this is truly the work of God, none of us get to decide that… only he does. I'm sorry if that ruins your image of me, but I ask that you at least remember that I loved you and that we had something good. If you hold onto one memory of me, let it be that."

"You know what this is going to do to Audra?"

"I do and it can't be helped now, but I left her a letter explaining everything along with something that she needs to give you. Hopefully, one day, she'll understand. Hopefully, she will remember me as her friend, that I loved her, and took her in. I pray that, that's the memory she holds onto. For you Jim, what I have for you will be your saving grace in all of this. As you struggle with the truth about me and why this happened, my gift for you will set you free." She walked closer to Jim, pretty much face-to-face. Jim didn't do anything as she walked closer to him and then f she kissed him. It was the last kiss for the both of them, one last good memory. She said to him. "Time is running out. You have to make a choice." Jim paused for a moment, but then he took the flash drive from her hand and said. "Go before I change my mind."

Tears welled up in her eyes again as she started to walk out, but then she stopped and turned around. She looked at Jim one last time and smiled... killing somebody wasn't hard for her anymore, but the hardest thing for her was walking out on the people that she loved the most. She had one final thing to say. "The password is the names of the people I love the most, all one word so it shouldn't be too hard to figure out."

Gina walked out. Jim slowly followed her trying to make his last look of her linger as long as it could. He had no idea how she ended up at that place or where she parked her car, but he got a bit of a surprise when he saw another car pull up. It pulled up fast and almost out of control as if it were surprised to be there. The car pulled up next to Gina as she was walking out and the driver rolled down the window. It was Detective Maisie Green. Gina was shocked to see her, but because she knew who Maisie was, she just figured that she was coming to arrest her. Maybe she as Jim's back up, but that wasn't the case. She said to Gina. "Get in the car, you're not under arrest, but we need to get you out of here."

Gina was caught off guard. Was this some kind of trick? Was she walking into a trap all along? Maisie repeated. "Gina, it's okay, I'm not here to arrest you, I promise. Get in; it's time to make your getaway. She reluctantly got inside Maisie's small 4-door sedan and asked her. "Why are you doing this?"

Maisie smiled. "Because you don't belong in prison. You may be a killer, but you don't belong in prison."

"You know they're not going to let you get away with this. This is aiding and abetting, and they'll put you in jail for it."

"Maybe, but I'm not going to let them put you in jail. I just can't let them do that." And that was it; she sped out of the parking lot in front of the main building. Jim had already walked outside, curious to know about the car that had just pulled up. While he could not see inside, he recognized the car. He knew it was Maisie. He also knew that he should call it in, but whether it was out of his unspoken promise to Gina or his loyalty to someone who had basically become his partner in the investigation, he let it go. The only phone call he made was to his friend Mike, letting him know that he had found the last crime scene. When he was asked if he found Sara Rogers, he simply said. "I was too late. There's nobody here except the victims."

Charlie had come back into the agency to help with the research on Sean Porter's vehicle. But she also had another reason for coming back in. It was about the old laptop that had been found in Sara Rogers' things that Jim had gotten from Amy Henderson. She found James hunkered down in front of a computer screen and said. "Hey, you got a minute?"

"Yeah, kid, what's up?"

"Remember that old laptop that belongs to Sara Rogers and how we couldn't get it open because it was encrypted...a hacker friend of mine finally got it open. You're not going to believe what's on it."

Being a bit sarcastic, James replied. "I guess it's not really good classic porn, is it?"

Charlie laughed. "No... not even close. She turned it on and opened some of the files that she and her friend had found. There was a file marked Sebastian Colón. Charlie continued. "She's been doing research on some of these victims for some time and I think the first person she started with was Sebastian Colón."

"Holy shit." James took a moment to look through some of it. He could immediately tell that there was quite a lot of research on him. There was even more than they had found on Sebastian Colón, going back twelve to fifteen years. "This is unreal... she has, for the most part, all of his early history dating back to when he came to this country."

"Yes, I think it's safe to say that she has been targeting him for a long time. This is proof. But if you look through the drive, there's a hell of a lot more names in there besides the nine victims. She's kept tabs on a lot of people."

"We will definitely go through it, but that's for another day." Vanessa walked into James's office holding a piece of paper. She said, "Did you know you got a fax? I found it on the floor and according to the header, it's from the FBI."

James replied. "We were supposed to get a fax containing Sara Rogers' immigration records." Vanessa hadn't looked through it because she didn't want to be nosy, but now it made more sense why he would have received a fax late at night from the FBI. They both quickly looked through the pages and at the same time saw in the document, Sara Rogers' given name. As plain as day, it said "Regina McCarthy," and listed under aliases was the name "Gina. Everybody standing in the office was stunned. Charlie was the first one to comment by saying. "This can't be real, can it, I mean, isn't that Detective Summers' girlfriend?"

James replied. "Yes, it is. Vanessa, see if you can get a hold of Jim and tell him what we just found. I'm calling Detective Lester and Detective Morgan and telling them where they need to go. Jim's in danger and he needs backup."

Vanessa started to dial Jim and then she realized that Maisie had darted out of the office unexpectedly a little bit earlier. She commented, "Where did Maisie go... you don't think she already saw this and went to go find him."

James started to fear the worst. "Could be, but why wouldn't she tell us unless?"

Maisie and Gina had been driving for hours. The only thing Maisie knew for sure was she had to get Gina across state lines out of the jurisdiction of Austin PD and Texas State CID. She figured the easiest way to get her across state lines was to drive her to Louisiana. It took about three hours, but they made it. Her phone had been ringing and getting numerous text messages from James and Vanessa, and even Detective Lester and Detective Morgan.

They were letting her know that they had found the crime scene, but also trying to find out where she was. And they certainly had a few questions for her at this point.

Maisie pulled into a 24-hour gas station just across the Louisiana border and let Gina out. Instinctively she got some money out of her wallet, whatever cash she could find and gave it to Gina. She thanked Maisie and then also said. "You've been more than generous. But I've been prepared for this day for a long time." She reached down and pulled out what looked like a cell phone holder for runners, it had been attached to her ankle. Inside of it contained an ID, a credit card, and some cash. She had been prepared to go on the run for a very long time. She had always been ready to disappear and while Gina accepted the fact that her life was over and that it would be hard to just let go of the last four years with a family that she loved. They were the happiest days of her life and the only time that she could remember that she was finally at peace after having lived such a tragic life.

51

The aftermath hadn't fully set in yet. There was no doubt that Jim would be blamed for not knowing that Gina McCarthy was The Black Fairy, after all, how could you be sleeping with someone the last four years and not know they were a killer. He wasn't fully suspended, yet only because it was an ongoing investigation. Plus, the information that Gina had given him on the flash drive was valuable. She was right, the password wasn't hard to figure out, except for the order of the names, but they were Audra, Josh, and Jim... in that order. News Outlets had already found out that Sebastian Colón was found dead, but there wasn't any direct link to a copycat killer as of yet. Right now, all they were saying is that it might have been an accident. The police were trying to spin the story the best they could, especially since there hadn't been any official press conference by the police giving them the facts. It was only natural that rumors were circulating. However, they did have the name Sara Rogers as the copycat killer, but not the full story.

  During his initial report about finding the crime scene, Jim hadn't given up Maisie on her aiding in Gina's escape, but he didn't have to. It was clear that she had seen the immigration report before anybody else and because she had OnStar installed in her car, it was easily tracked to the crime scene and to the Louisiana border by GPS. She never returned back to the Detective Agency and ended up driving back to Dallas to see her family. She was smart enough to know what was going to happen next and so she was detained the next day for aiding and abetting a murder suspect.

It was definitely coming, Jim would be suspended, but it didn't happen the next day at the request of the FBI because of his assistance in tracking down a ship that was trafficking young girls. Gina's flash drive contained a report about a ship called *La Bella Vita*. It made regular monthly visits to the Houston Harbor and that's how they figured Sebastian Colón could traffic young girls for the purpose of being sex slaves to the rich and powerful. While it would normally take a few days to put together a Joint Task Force between US Customs and the FBI regarding trafficking, one was put together in less than 24 hours, mostly at Jim's sister's urging. Hannah investigated domestic terrorism and human trafficking with the FBI. She requested that Jim be a part of their Joint Task Force. 24 hours after Gina had been discovered, Jim along with a Joint Task Force between the FBI and US Customs we're in the middle of a sting operation waiting for the ship. It was on an unseasonably cold day in Texas, it was almost freezing, and it was made worse by the fact that they were near water. Jim was sipping coffee when his sister, Hannah asked him. "Are you sure that is the name of the ship?"

He gave her a dirty look. "For the hundredth time, yes. You saw what was on the flash drive; her research said La Belle Vita."

"Okay, just making sure. This is a big deal!"

"You don't have to tell me." He was going to make another snarky comment when a Coast Guard Captain radioed in saying that they had spotted the ship coming into the Harbor. They kept their distance and waved to the ship to keep up appearances... Law enforcement needed it to dock before they could do anything. Finally, about thirty minutes after it had been spotted, the cargo ship La Belle Vita, finally docked. Coast Guard boats swarmed around the ship to block it from moving and trying to escape. US Customs and the FBI quickly moved onto the ship and started searching. Every member of the crew was detained until a full search could be completed. It took a little while, but they finally found it. A cargo hold at the bottom of the ship that was hidden and made to look like anything other than a cargo hold. Unfortunately, for the captain and his crew of the ship, a porthole that seemed out of place gave it away. US Customs officials found hidden padlocked door and quickly cut the lock off only to discover the true cargo of the ship. They found twenty-three young girls and two young males accompanied by a young adult. None of them could speak English and every one of them was extremely scared, which was expected.

There they were the people that Sebastian Colón was sneaking into Texas. They had been promised a better life. Some of them had been promised to be reunited with their families who had immigrated to Texas. But that was far from the truth. Among them were Russians, El Salvadorans, Mexicans and even a couple from India. They had no idea what was about to happen to them. They were completely unaware that they were only meant to be some perverted plaything for some rich, powerful men. It was hard to watch knowing what was going to happen to them. Jim got a very sickening feeling in his stomach just looking at the kids and trying to get unwanted images of what was going to happen to them out of his head... They were clearly malnourished and in need of medical attention, which was even more sickening to watch.

Finally, when everything got sorted out Hannah said. "We have a total of 26, all of whom are underage except for the old girl who we assume is like their babysitter or something."

"What's the youngest age of the group?"

"9 years old and it's one of the two males."

Jim felt like throwing up right then and there. The sickening thought that some pedophile with money taking advantage of that kid made him nauseated. He commented. "At least they're safe now."

Hannah smiled. "Yes, they are. Today is a good day... I know yesterday was a shitty day for you... I know you're still mad as hell and probably sad at the same time, you have a right to be. But look around, we did something good today, we rescued 26 people who would have obviously disappeared and would never be heard from again after they were used and abused as sex toys by some really sick individuals. I hate what Gina did to you, but I will at least give her this. She did one heroic thing in getting this Intel."

Jim tried to smile. He didn't disagree with what Hannah was saying, but he still felt like this was a small consolation prize to how this investigation ended. He did make one interesting observation. "Hopefully, this will lead to a bigger network of trafficking and you guys can put a stop to it. Maybe, that's the only true victory we get out of all this."

Hannah put her hand on Jim's shoulder and said. "I hope this does lead to something bigger and that would just be one more victory. Again, take a look at those kids, rescuing them is a big victory and that's what you should take home with you tonight. In fact, you should remember that for a long time, despite what may happen to you. This is a good day."

Jim did smile at that last comment. She was right, it was a good day. And for a cop being able to save innocent victims from harm's way is the best day that you can have on the job. Jim needed reminding of that and taking one last lingering look at those young innocent victims was the perfect reminder.

Austin PD finally did an official press conference to quell some of the rumors that had been going on in the press. They were still sticking to the story that it was a copycat killer by the name of Sara Rogers. How many people actually believe that was a different story. There were plenty of people on the internet suggesting that Sara Rogers was the real Black Fairy including plenty of chatter in discussion groups about serial killers. The entire story had not been given to the press, only what they had found on the last three murders. Jim was listening to the press conference as he drove to Dallas. He was officially suspended pending a hearing at this point. He decided to drive to Dallas to see if he could visit Maisie who was still being detained by police. The name Gina McCarthy had not been given to the Press, so Audra and Josh were able to keep some anonymity. They didn't know all the details. Jim hadn't even sat down with Audra, yet, to go over everything because it was still a pending investigation, but Audra knew something was up and even suspected that Gina might be involved since she hadn't come home. Jim wouldn't elaborate on what happened to her, but for appearance's sake, he just told people that she was away and helping to settle the estate of a long-lost relative. The story was good enough for now. But Jim knew that he would have to sit down and talk with Audra eventually. After all, she was quite the inquisitive one and it wouldn't be too hard for her to put two and two together.

Jim made it to Dallas in good time. Despite being suspended, he was allowed a policeman's courtesy and got to visit Maisie at the Dallas County Jail. She hadn't been bonded out yet. They put him in a private visitor's room. Wearing an orange jumpsuit and handcuffs, the guards brought Maisie into the room. She smiled when she saw Jim but was also a little ashamed. He was happy to see her and truly felt bad for her situation. She was the first one to speak. "You didn't have to visit me, but I do appreciate it."

He tried to crack a joke to lighten the mood. "Somebody said you look good in orange, and I wanted to see if that was true."

She laughed. "I look good in pretty much anything, especially large jumpsuits, it's just this one is the wrong kind."

"I agree."

"Are you mad at me?"

"I should be, but I really can't blame you for anything. I let her go too."

"You did it to save some girls from sex trafficking, anybody with any inkling of morality would have easily made that choice. I helped her escape."

Jim softly laughed. "Yes, yours is definitely worse. I guess what I'm really curious about is..."

Maisie interrupted. "Why I did it."

"Yeah."

"Because I don't think she belongs in prison. I know that I violated my oath as a police officer and I definitely deserve to be punished for that, but I can't in good conscience, send someone who brought justice to sexual predators when the police and the courts failed to do it."

Jim had an angry look. "That's not our call. It never has been and that's what you signed up for. I thought you understood that and that's why this doesn't make sense to me."

Maisie paused for a moment, collecting her thoughts. She wanted to give Jim an answer that he could possibly understand, but there was only one thing she could say. "I don't expect you to understand. And I'm not necessarily saying what she did was right, but she did do what needed to be done. For that, she doesn't belong in jail."

"I don't think she belongs in jail either, but she doesn't deserve to be free at the same time. Maybe a psychiatric hospital is where she truly belongs. That I could personally live with and I'm the one who loves her."

"But can you see past your own oath as a cop and do something for the one you love even if it might break the law... I don't think you're even willing to do that and if you're not, then you can't fully understand what I did."

Jim shook his head. "You act like I have some kind of deformity if I think that way."

"No, I don't. I think you're a very honorable man and it's that kind of thinking that makes you honorable. Maybe you don't have as much humanity as you should because of what you believe as a cop, but it doesn't make you a bad man. Just different. Perhaps, I did what you wanted to do but weren't willing to do."

Jim sat back in his chair and gave her a funny look. She brought up an interesting point and he said as much. Perhaps you're right, maybe that's why I'm not judging what you did. Others may want to throw you to the wolves, but you don't belong in prison either. You're a good cop and one of the best partners I've ever worked with. I don't know if I ever told you that."

Maisie smiled. "No, but it's nice to hear."

Jim stood up and got a little closer to Maisie. I don't have the power to stop them from prosecuting you. In fact, you kind of deserve it. But on the other hand, if you're willing to take the bullet for me when it comes to Gina escaping, maybe I can do something nice for you. Actually, I already have. I and my boss at

State CID talked to the District Attorney. We're petitioning them just to give you time served, maybe probation. You will also lose your badge, but that's it."

Maisie almost had tears in her eyes. It was a nice gesture. She said. "Thank you. That means a lot."

"I can't condone what you did, but maybe I can help you out in some small way." Plus, they may take your badge, but they can't take the cop inside of you and you are a good one. You should know that, especially if we don't ever see each other again." They weren't allowed to touch, but Jim briefly grabbed her hand and held it with a compassionate touch to let her know that everything was going to be okay and that he was in her corner. It also let her know that despite what she did, they could always be friends and maybe someday work together again even if it wasn't as police officers.

A lot had happened over the last few days, but for Audra, it had been mostly about basketball. Jim had said they would talk soon, but that hadn't happened yet. Audra heard on the news that the copycat killer had been captured and that her name was Sara Rogers but didn't know any more than that. It was morbid to think this way, but she felt kind of inspired that the real killer was a woman. In some dark fashion it proved that a woman could do anything a man could; especially kill multiple people in the most gruesome way imaginable. And because she had been so busy, Audra didn't even notice the box that was sitting next to the desk in her room with a note on it that said, "For Audra, From Gina."

It was strange because it wasn't her birthday and Christmas was weeks away. Plus, if it was a gift, it wasn't wrapped. She opened it and found a laptop with a note on it that said, "Please give this to Jim, it will answer all his questions." She found that even stranger, but then she found a letter that was still in an envelope for her. The letter was from Gina. She sat down at her desk and started to read it.

Dear Audra,

I never thought that I would have to write this letter to you. I had hoped for the longest time that I wouldn't, but I know now, it was false hope. You're going to hear a lot of rumors about me and I know you're smart enough not to believe everything you hear, but I owe you the truth. You need to know the cold hard truth about me so you can make up your own mind. I am a killer. Yes, I'm technically a serial killer. And yes, I am The Black Fairy, although I've never liked that name. Jim has been looking for me for many years now and it's only a matter of time before he knows the truth. He's too smart for me to keep hiding the truth. He will know soon enough, but I wanted you to hear the truth from me and to tell you why.

I won't dare try and convince you that I'm a saint or some kind of avenging angel doing the work of God. Please make no mistake about it, I am a killer. I have committed one of the most egregious sins in that I have murdered multiple people. It's true that I don't think of it as murder, but on some level, if we go by society's standards, I should be punished for it. I remember a conversation you and I once had about The Duality of Man and that we have two sides to ourselves. Well, I very much believe that's true, and this is the darker side of myself. I'm not insane; I'm not crazy or even remotely psychotic even though that's what I have been called. I knew exactly what I was doing. And I know you probably think you have me figured out because you read my book. Sure, there's some truth to it. Symbolism is just another form of truth. I don't regret what I did, I absolutely believe that these men deserve to die for what they have done and how they have preyed on the innocent, but that doesn't mean that I think killing another human being is right. Certainly, don't think that what I have done is righteous, although I've read some comments that what I'm doing is righteous. I don't think that man has the right to judge me for what I've done. Only God can judge me and maybe when I die, he will look favorably upon what I did. And if not, I am prepared to have my soul damned.

My sister, her husband, and their kids were tragically murdered because he tried to do the right thing as a whistleblower for a company that was poisoning people. I had to watch them die knowing deep down that there wasn't anything I could do to save them. Perhaps this was the catalyst for my so-called masterpiece or killing spree; however, you want to look at it. Some will say that I committed murder out of revenge. It has nothing to do with revenge. It is my own warped sense of justice. I'm trying to save innocent victims from being preyed upon. I'm not justifying what I did, just trying to explain some of my reasons. Please don't look at me as some kind of hero. Murder is wrong. We shouldn't have to live in a society where we justify this. And we definitely shouldn't live in a world where bad men get away with disgusting and horrific Acts against the innocent. I wish that it had never come to this, but I do take full blame for my actions. I will not make excuses. I made a choice to kill every one of these men.

Despite what everybody may think of me because of these acts, there is one thing that I did great in my life. That was loving you and Josh. It was also loving Jim. I never meant for that to happen, but I was lucky enough to find a good man who loves me too. I don't have any regret about adopting you and Josh. It's the best thing that I've ever done with my life and these last four years with you two and Jim has been the best of my life. I'm just sad that I won't get to see you graduate high school and go off to college. I'm sad that I won't get to see you fall in love and maybe get married one day and start a family. But we both know that I can't stay. The police would never let that happen and they will always be looking for me. Plus, I can't do that to you or your brother. You deserve a better life than having to see your adoptive mother behind bars. Maybe it's not any better than not having me there. But take this to heart; I will always be with you. I will think of you every day. And I will never stop loving you. You are a beautiful and amazing young woman. It's true that I've had somewhat of a tragic life and psychologists will say that that's what drove me to murder, but befriending you and taking you in, saved me more than you'll know. So if you ever wonder why I fell in love with Jim and wanted all of us to be a family, it's because I knew that he would be a good father to both of you and could take care of you if I wasn't around. The only thing that I ask of you despite the sadness or anger you may have for me because I have to leave, remember me in a good way. Remember these last four years when we were a family, and we were truly happy. I will forever hold onto those memories when I think of you.

~ *Love Gina*

Audra had tears in her eyes when she finished the letter. It was shocking to hear that she was The Black Fairy. Audra like everybody else didn't see that coming. She didn't want to believe it, but she had to because she knew Gina had never lied to her. Audra knew that she should be horrified and angry at Gina's confession, but the truth was, she felt sadness more than anything else because she knew that she would probably never see Gina again. She was her true mother. She was the mother that she had always deserved. And she would never stop loving her despite being a killer because Gina had done the greatest act of kindness that anybody has ever done for her and her brother by adopting them. Gina was the one person who gave her a true family, the one thing that she had always wanted. She was happy that she at least got to have that within the past 4 years. Audra would never forget it.

Jim's meeting with his superiors and the State Attorney General didn't take too long. His report hadn't changed regarding the crime scene that he found. He never once said he saw the Killer's face. And he still wouldn't give Maisie up for helping Gina escape.

Also, Maisie when it came to her helping the killer escape. This meeting was to determine if criminal charges should be brought against Jim. Did he really not know that his partner of four years was a serial killer? Jim tried to remind them, how well do we really know anybody and that this could happen to any one of them. He didn't disagree that it looked bad, and he should probably be punished. But Jim loved being a cop. It's all he ever wanted to do since he started to get fascinated by police work while in college. He was definitely not an idealist and thought that he can make a difference as a policeman. He had by catching some pretty notorious killers in Texas. The State Attorney General heard all the facts. Because he worked for a state agency it was ultimately left up to the State Attorney General when it came to criminal charges.

Jim was essentially put on administrative leave with pay until they could decide what to do. When he left the room, his boss Robert followed him. He wasn't happy about everything and certainly didn't want to see one of his best police officers arrested. He said to Jim. "I'm sorry for how everything went down, but you should know that you did a hell of a job. I doubt the Behavioral Science Division at the FBI could have done any better."

Jim smiled. "It's nice of you to say, but I think we both know how this is going to end up. There's no way that they're going to let me be a cop again."

"Yeah, it does look pretty bad. You really can't be sleeping with a killer and not know that they are one when you're a police officer even though it could happen to anybody."

"Hey, I get that it looks bad, but I wasn't wrong when I came to our profile."

"Unfortunately, they're not going to see it that way because she did complete her final murder or so we think."

"Do you think I should go to jail?"

"No, and I don't think this has anything to do with your ability to be a good cop. If I had my way, maybe, a light suspension and then you get back to work and do what you do best."

Jim softly laughed. "In a perfect world that would be good. Unfortunately for me, we don't live in that kind of world so I have to accept the fact that this is the end of the road for me."

"Maybe, but I actually have a solution and I'm going to go and present it to them. Nobody can deny that this is a bad deal all around, but I looked up your file and in January you will have officially been a police officer in Texas for 20 years."

Jim was surprised. "Really, I've been so busy with this investigation; I didn't realize my 20th anniversary was coming up... time flies when you're trying to catch bad guys."

"Me, I think the perfect solution is to just suspend you until you can officially retire with your pension. In my book, ain't no sense of wiping away 20 years of good service because of one indiscretion that was out of control."

"You tell them for me, if they'll make that deal, I'll put in my papers immediately. As much as I don't want to, even I realize that I can't be a cop anymore after this." That's where Robert and Jim left it. It was a good solution, let the man retire with some honor and a little dignity. Robert didn't lie, it would be a hard sell, and there were certainly plenty of people who wanted his head on a platter so to speak. In the end, they were all left to wonder, what good it could possibly do to put the man in jail who found the most notorious female serial killer in Texas.

52

Jim and Audra had finally had a chance to talk. She showed him the letter that Gina had written her. Like her, he found it very moving. But also like her, it was still a shock to find out that Gina was the real killer. They consoled each other. Jim let her and Josh both know that he wasn't going to abandon them. They were family and he loved them as if they were his own. No matter what anybody might say about Gina, the only thing that they needed to know about her was what they knew about her these last four years. She loved them and was a good mother. That was their truth. Audra gave Jim the laptop. He had never seen it before and when he turned it on, of course, it was password protected with some pretty serious encryption. But he had a hunch that the same password used to open up the flash drive would open up the laptop if it was meant for him to see. Sure enough, the same password worked. He explored the files that were on there. All it had was a basic operating system and files upon files of research. Finding Gina was the serial killer he had been tracking was a shock, seeing the research that was on the laptop, was even more shocking. And the note that she had left behind about the laptop was true, what it had on it, were the answers he was looking for.

Jim called James and told him that he was stopping by the agency and that he had some new information. James told him that they had new information as well. When Jim got there, he was surprised to see that Vanessa hadn't gone back to Dallas yet. She had stayed; helping James do some research of their own. Jim being curious, asked her. "Why are you still here, I thought you would have headed back by now."

She softly smiled and replied. "I should be getting back, but I feel like what we know about Gina only scratches the surface. Call it morbid curiosity, but I want to know more so James and I have been trying to find more about her."

"Really, just her?"

James answered. "And other folks. You know that old laptop that was found with Gina's other things from Amy Henderson... well, one of Charlie's friends was able to get past the encryption and get it open... you're not going to believe what's on there."

Jim facetiously smiled. "Oh, I might." He got out the laptop that Gina had left for him and opened it up. "There's a ton of research on many powerful men throughout Texas. I think these are people that are connected to Sebastian Colón."

"That doesn't surprise me because we found what appears to be the beginning of her research, not only on Sebastian Colón, but the other man she killed. She studied her prey quite extensively."

"That's not surprising, but I think it's more than that. I think she has spent years gathering evidence on rich and powerful men who are just as depraved as her victims which leads me to question whether she was just going to stop at nine people or was targeting more."

Vanessa spoke up. "I don't think she was targeting anybody else. She had a plan and she fulfilled it, but she left that laptop for you on purpose. She left it for you before she killed Sebastian Colón, right?"

"I suppose, why?"

"To see what you would do with the information. I bet the information on there is just like the stuff that we found on her old laptop. The dirty little secrets of men who get away with everything. Do we give it to the police and let them investigate only to see them escape Justice like her other victims? Or maybe we tell the rest of the world about these men. Maybe we give this information to an honest and trustworthy journalist who's not afraid to investigate and tell the world."

Jim and James both stared at her for a moment. It made sense. Perhaps this was a test for them. Could they bring Justice to men who would always get away with it without having to kill them? Maybe just exposing their dirty little secrets was justice enough. Jim replied. "Perhaps that is our true role in this investigation; we continue exposing those who have gotten away with perverted and heinous crimes."

James commented. "There's a lot of information here and I think it's in our best interest to go through it. If nothing else to tell the complete story of The Black Fairy and why she did what she did before the media twists the narrative of her just being a murderer. Tell the whole truth and let the world decide what she is."

Jim nodded in agreement. He had the same opinion about the media. But he was curious about where James was going with all this. He asked. "Are you saying that we should paint a different picture of her other than being a killer because if you're telling me, you don't think she's a murderer..."

James interrupted. "I'm not condoning her crimes. She committed murder, there's no doubt about that and whether she belongs in prison or an insane asylum, that's not up for me to decide. All I'm saying is before anybody makes a judgment about her and I think they need to see the full picture. It would be a disservice on our part if we didn't show the complete and full picture. But I absolutely think we should expose some of these people who think they can get away with their crimes... we may not be able to arrest them anymore, but we can expose them."

Vanessa responded. "I don't necessarily condone what she did either, but the world is a better place without these men that she killed, I can't deny that. Sebastian Colón won't be trafficking young girls anymore. That was a hell of a thing that you guys did the other night."

Jim smiled at her. "I agree and that's why it's hard to look at her as just a straight-up serial killer."

James replied. "That goes for all of us, but maybe it's like she said; only God can really judge her soul. And for me, personally, I'm good with that. I don't even want to attempt to try to judge her for what she did, so I guess it's a good thing that I'll never be on the jury if she's ever tried for murder." His bit of sarcasm made everybody laugh. James went and got a file folder that contained the immigration records. Jim had yet to see them. He said. "Before we go any further and start looking more into her research, there's something you should know. I've been doing a little bit more digging on Sara Rogers also known as Gina McCarthy. I was able to get in contact with the convent where she was adopted from. It's in connection with a Catholic Church in the County of Cork called St. Mary's of the Immaculate. They don't have many records left over from 1977 and unlike sophisticated adoption agencies; they haven't put everything on the computer yet. Apparently, they had a roof cave in from a storm about 30 years ago and some of the old records got damaged by the rain. But I inquired about the name Gina McCarthy, and there was a very nice nun who helped me out. She told me that she couldn't find any record about a Gina McCarthy being adopted in the late 70s, although it was possible. But she did recognize the name."

Jim got extremely curious. "Recognized the name, how?"

James pulled out a picture. "She took this picture and emailed it to me." The picture was of a small, flat gravestone and it said Regina McCarthy. Born May 6, 1977 and died May 12, 1977. The nun recognized the name because she puts flowers on the gravestones in the cemetery next to the convent."

Jim was shocked and didn't say anything for a moment. "What, I don't understand. They're saying that Regina McCarthy died 6 days after being born?"

"Yes, and before you ask, no they didn't have any Regina McCarthy's be adopted out. Her explanation was simple. It could have easily been a mix-up in the records because everything was handwritten back then. Or they mixed up the names of two babies who were born prematurely and died days later. She did tell me that a lot of the children who were born at that time came from unwanted single women; most of them were drug addicts so their children weren't always the healthiest. They did have quite a few babies die days after they were born. It wasn't uncommon. So, the sisters made small gravestones and chiseled their names to remember all of God's children as she put it."

"What do you think happened?"

"I think it's possible to mix up records when everything is being handwritten, but I also did some more checking on Sara Rogers. She went to Europe when she was in college. And there was an update on that immigration record back in 1998. They updated the given name which means if there was a mix-up in the original records, you're allowed to petition the Department of Immigration and Interpol to update the correct name or the correct spelling."

"You think she visited the convent when she went to Europe, found out her real name, but then updated her immigration record with the name Regina McCarthy."

"I think it's possible. But I can't find out the old name that was on the record because it was updated, and it wasn't listed under aliases. Anyway, it's a theory, but I think you have to ask..."

Jim finished the answer to that statement. "What is her real name if it isn't Regina McCarthy?"

"Well, there might actually be a way to confirm that or at the very least a shot in the dark. You remember, Sara Rogers got married and then divorced around the same time as Lori Kellerman?"

"Yeah."

"It was an immigration marriage. Sara married a guy from Northern Ireland, by the name of Luke O'Brien. He came to school here in the states, trying to escape what at the time was a war-torn country because of the Irish Troubles. She married him so he could finish his education since his student visa had expired. He ended up going back to Northern Ireland in 2012. Has dual citizenship now. He might know something since they traveled to Europe together when they were in college. Chances are he was with her when she saw her birth records at the convent. He's married now with two kids, but I have his contact information and I think he's worth talking to."

"Definitely worth talking to. Good working on finding him."

"It's what I do."

"But even with all this new information, I can't help but wonder, who was I really with the last four years...it's a nagging thought that will always consume me. It would be easier to ignore if I didn't love her."

James shrugged, but he did have an answer or perhaps just another theory. He replied. "Personally, I think she was a chameleon. Look at her timeline and everything she did, she blended in. Lori Kellerman never remembered who she was from school because she was shy and not very noticeable. It was easy to assume that Amy Henderson was a serial killer because she had the most motive to kill Don Bennett and it turned out it was a woman that she was seeing. The same goes for Aldo Martinez, he dated her, she got to know him and found out about the paper he wrote in high school and worked for a tech company that service Highland Security, so she could know Aldo's inspection schedule. She befriended Lori when she moved to Dallas and virtually having the same background it wasn't too hard to look at Lori as a suspect without realizing that it was really her friend. I mean that can't be accidental. She is a chameleon that blends in with her prey and so we couldn't see who the real killer was, I actually think that's pretty brilliant."

Jim begrudgingly replied. "That may be true, and I see what you're getting at, but I still feel like I don't know who she really was now. And I can't tell Audra or Josh about this and leave them wondering who their second mother really was. I think the worst thing is for her to be viewed as some nameless face... no identity because if that's true, then the love that we thought that we got from her amounts to nothing."

Vanessa replied. "It doesn't amount to nothing. Maybe you don't know who she really is; maybe the name isn't really important. Who she really is was the person she was with you these last 4 years. She didn't adopt those kids and rescue them because she didn't care and she didn't playhouse and have a relationship with you for no reason, especially since you weren't investigating her case anymore. I think that was real and that's what you should hold on to."

Jim smiled. "You're right; I could go crazy debating this in my head. For me, Audra, and Josh, she has to be more than the timeline of her murders. Vanessa, you make a good point. Maybe that's all I really need to know about her."

"My mother always said, when you're in doubt, always hold on to what you know is real, especially loved ones, for that is the only truth that matters." Jim nodded, agreeing with that philosophy. It was a good saying, powerful and true. And that's what he decided to hold onto. James brought up another point. "You know I think it's interesting that she went back to using the given name on her immigration record as if nobody would ever find it. If she really did update that immigration record in 1998, I wonder if she started using her actual name, whatever that is."

Jim and Vanessa both nodded, agreeing with his assessment. Then he said something else that was interesting. "I'm also curious, now that she's on the run where would she go to lay low. I wonder if she's prepared for that."

Vanessa responded. "I know you both read the Dark Fairy book, but I thought there was a passage towards the end that was interesting and might be able to answer your question." She grabbed a copy of the book and found the passage inside. She read. *"When it is all done, when the final task has been completed, you will return to that sacred place where it all began. It was a place that will be your refuge. The place where the transformation of your soul will be complete, and you will see the face of God.* I think it's a clue to where she's going... a place that is familiar and where she's been before."

Jim sat back in his chair and thought about it for a moment. "I know where she would go... it would almost be the perfect refuge for her. But it's both a person and a place. A place where she could start over and find peace. And if I am right...we'll never see her again."

Amy was working late in her office, trying to figure out what supplies they were going to need at her commune next month. She only went into town about once a month, no more than twice if she could help it. There was a knock at her door. The young woman at the door told Amy that somebody was at the front gate asking for her. She said that she knew Amy from years ago. Amy was curious, so she stopped what she was doing and walked with the young woman to the front gate. Her hair was different, and she was wearing different color contacts, but she recognized the woman. She was definitely surprised to see her because the last time they spoke it was out of anger and deep down she thought she would never speak to her again. The young woman asked. "Do you know her?"

Amy replied. "I do know her. Her name is Sara Rogers. Let her in."

Two women opened the large front gate to let Sara into the commune. Sara and Amy just stared at each other for a moment, at first it was this cautious curiosity, but they both smiled about the same time. Amy walked over and hugged her. Then said. "It's good to see you despite the circumstances."

Sara smiled again. "I guess you heard."

"Yes…you made national news."

"If this is too much trouble for you, I can leave."

Amy smiled and hugged her again. "No, this is a refuge for broken women who need to escape their circumstances."

"Even a murderer?"

"I hate to break it to you, but you're not the only murderer here. There are a couple of women here who have killed their husbands, not as violently as you, of course, but you are in good company."

Tears came to her eyes. "I knew that I could count on you."

"You could always count on me. But I don't know what to call you, is it Sara or is it Gina because I've heard you used Gina McCarthy as an alias. Both are actually my names. It's a long story."

Well, you can stay here as long as you need to and that should give you plenty of time to tell me your story…the one you couldn't tell me years ago."

"You knew that I wasn't completely honest with you."

"Sure, but it didn't matter. I loved you...I figured you would tell me when you're ready. I'm just hoping that you're ready now because I'd like to hear it."

She smiled again. "For the first time, I think I'm ready to tell somebody my real story."

6 Months Later...

She sat in the waiting room eagerly waiting for her job interview. The magazines they had on the table weren't interesting enough for her to pick one up and start reading while she waited. She resorted to playing a game on her phone, which she always thought was unprofessional when waiting to be interviewed for a job. But this was taking a long time and she was bored. The office was busier than usual today; however, this was the only time she could interview for the job. There was a TV in the waiting area, it was tuned to CNN. Normally, she would ignore the news, but there was a little blurb about the Black Fairy killer. She was fascinated by the case and a lot more had come out about it over the last six months, including the alias the killer had used like Gina McCarthy. Texas State CID had tried to keep that a secret for as long as possible to protect Detective Jim Summers and the kids, but it was only a matter of time before it was going to come out.

Finally, the person she was interviewing with came to the waiting area to get her. The lady said. "Ms. Maguire." She stood up, still looking at the TV, and greeted the lady, but looked back at the TV to see what they were saying. "Hello, I'm Kathleen Maguire; it's nice to meet you."

"Nice to meet you. I'm Michelle Cooper. I'm sorry for the wait, it's just, we are shorthanded and have been doing a lot of interviews today."

Kathleen smiled. "It's no bother…gave me a chance to catch up on the news…apparently they have more information about the Black Fairy killer from Texas and about who she was targeting."

Michelle's curiosity piqued. "Oh, I know, I have been fascinated by that case too. Still can't believe Texas has its first true female serial killer and the way she killed her victims…gruesome and kind of cool, although I shouldn't say that."

Kathleen softly laughed. "I won't tell, besides, I think it's cool how she killed them as well."

"Then I have another confession if you're not telling. I kind of side with her considering who she killed…perverts and pedophiles. They deserve to die if you ask me, but I can't say that around here since we are supposed to remain objective."

"Me too… I think a lot of people feel that way."

"They say she's a killer, but maybe she's really a hero." Kathleen smiled at the comment.

They finally arrived back at Michelle's office. She did a quick once over of Kathleen's resume and then said. "Everything is in order here. You're certainly qualified and we are in desperate need of Parole Officers, but the only thing I have available is for sex offenders and we don't usually put women in those positions because of the nature of the crime."

Kathleen was curious. "Is it because you think women are too sensitive because of the crime or were just not tough enough?""

"Both…it's not my policy; though…the men in charge around here think we're too frail to handle such things."

Kathleen disapproved of the notion. Only a misogynistic prick would come up with a rule like that. The office must be filled with them she thought to herself. She replied to Michelle. "They can think all they want, but I'm a tough girl and I can handle it. I went to Catholic school and the nuns at my school can make a drill sergeant cry... if you can survive my old school then you can handle anything."

Michelle smiled. "That's definitely good to hear, but I can't promise you'll be able to succeed at this job."

"Give me a shot and let's find out. Besides, I can be a firm disciplinarian and I know how to punish bad men who break the law to where they won't do it again." Kathleen winked at Michelle and finished her statement. "I learned how to be a good disciplinarian in Catholic School."

Finally, Michelle laughed. She could tell that Kathleen was being a little sarcastic, but she also believed her. She replied. "Okay then. I'll try you out."

"Thank you, all I want is a chance. You won't be disappointed."

"That's good to hear. And if you don't mind, I wanted to say something off the subject."

"Sure."

"This has nothing to do with your interview, but I wanted to compliment you on your hair. I really love that dark reddish color. I'm assuming it's not your natural color?"

Kathleen smiled at the compliment and said. "Sadly, no. I saw this color on a woman who was cosplaying a dark fairy at a Renaissance Faire not too long ago... I loved her look and decided to have my hair colored the same way."

"It certainly suits you, especially with your deep green eyes that are like emeralds. And I can see you dressing up as a dark fairy. You definitely got the look."

"Thank you again for the compliment, it's always nice to hear."

Michelle laughed. "I just realized! It sounds like I'm flirting with you. I shouldn't be doing that after interviewing you for a job. Human Resources would have a field day."

Oh no, you're fine. I didn't take it that way and you're not offending me, so no harm done. You're just really good at giving compliments."

"I'm so glad to hear that. That makes me feel better."

Kathleen smiled while dispensing with some truth of her own. "I have a confession of my own, I definitely envision myself as a dark fairy, like for Halloween or something…you know, mischievous and mysterious, but with a strong sense of justice. Or at least, it's always been a fantasy of mine."

As Kathleen was leaving the office and trying to find her car, she noticed a symbol spray painted on the side of a building.

It was the symbol of The Black Fairy and underneath it was just one word. *Savior.* The symbols had been popping up, here and there, throughout the country. She heard a few were even found in Ireland where The Black Fairy had been born. Kathleen stared at the symbol for a moment and then smiled as she thought to herself. If the killer had truly gone through a transformation, the once fallen angel, might now have become a strange symbol of hope.

ACKNOWLEDGEMENTS

I would especially like to thank Playwright Blue McElroy for giving me the idea of The Black Fairy after an interesting discussion about serial killers. She's great at giving good ideas to writers. I would also like to thank Judge Peggy Hoffman for helping me with research about Texas Law. In addition, I would like to thank immigration attorney Eugene Flynn who can always lead you in the right direction on the law. I would like to thank my friend, Audra Farris, who loves to text me and yell at me about what I've done with my stories, but still remains a big fan and finally got a character named after her. And I would like to thank my mother Carolee who likes to keep me honest when it comes to sentence structure while proofreading because she gets to read the book early. I would also like to thank the wonderful staff at Trinity Hall Irish Pub in Dallas, Texas where I get a great deal of writing done because of the atmosphere and they have good whiskey.

www.ingramcontent.com/pod-product-compliance
Lightning Source LLC
Chambersburg PA
CBHW020136130526
44591CB00030B/63